Teaching Social Studies in Middle and Senior High Schools
Decisions! Decisions!

D1278335

WAYNE MAHOOD
State University of New York at Geneseo

LINDA BIEMER
State University of New York at Binghamton

WILLIAM T. LOWE
University of Rochester

Merrill, an imprint of
Macmillan Publishing Company
New York

Collier Macmillan Canada, Inc.
Toronto

Maxwell Macmillan International Publishing Group
New York   Oxford   Singapore   Sydney

To our students and colleagues

Administrative Editor: Sally Berridge MacGregor
Developmental Editor: Linda James Scharp
Production Editor: Linda Hillis Bayma
Art Coordinator: Lorraine Woost
Photo Editor: Gail Meese
Cover Designer: Russ Maselli

This book was set in Bookman.

Macmillan Publishing Company
866 Third Avenue, New York, NY 10022

Collier Macmillan Canada, Inc.

Photo Credits: All photos copyrighted by individuals or companies listed. Linda Biemer, p. 311; Steve Coffey, p. 318; Merrill Publishing, pp. 19, 52, 226, 300; Merrill Publishing, photographs by Andy Brunk, pp. 121, 253, 268; Jean Greenwald, pp. 81, 248, 363, 373; Bruce Johnson, p. 95; Lloyd Lemmerman, pp. 61, 157, 342; Doug Martin, p. 34; and Gail Meese, p. 241; Michael Siluk, pp. 5, 276; Stuart Spates, pp. 26, 170, 220; David Strickler, p. 130; Ulrike Welsch, p. 191.

Library of Congress Cataloging-in-Publication Data
Mahood, Wayne.
    Teaching social studies in middle and senior high schools: decisions! decisions! /Wayne Mahood, Linda Biemer, William T. Lowe.
        p. cm.
    Includes index.
    ISBN 0-675-21253-7
    1. Social sciences—Study and teaching (Secondary) I. Biemer, Linda Briggs. II. Lowe, William T. III. Title.
    H62.M2358   1991
    300'.71'273—dc20   90-43693
                                                    CIP

Printing: 2 3 4 5 6 7 8 9
Year: 4

Foreword

In the educational world, it is rare to find a book that combines content and process in a real-school setting and makes it a personal experience as well as required course reading. Often I have bemoaned the failure of methods texts to capture what really goes on in our schools. Nevertheless, the authors of *Teaching Social Studies in Middle and Senior High Schools: Decisions! Decisions!* have successfully related the standard methods text material to real school and classroom situations:

- The beginning teacher, faced with her first year, first course, first class: What shall I do?
- The social studies district coordinator, who must work with a mixed group of teachers to rethink the district's social studies curriculum: How can I get them to see, understand, and accept change?
- The veteran teacher, who, having found Nirvana early on, is reluctant to try "new-fangled" methods: Why should I try something new when what I've been doing has worked so well?
- The resident cynic: What, again? We did this in the 1960s, and it didn't work then.
- The college professor/realist, whose main concern is time and space in relation to creating the ideal environment for learning.

These are but a few of the people whom student users of this text will come to know. They and other residents of our school system are the people who really influence what goes on in our schools.

The authors of this text, themselves excellent teachers of teachers, rightly address the question: What are the questions, problems, answers, sources, debates, procedures, and techniques that social studies teachers—beginners and veterans—must consider in "a place called school?" It is no easy task to enter the teaching profession without knowing what to expect. Future teachers need more than techniques for conveying information and ideas. They need confidence builders that will reassure them that the experience they are about to face is not as dreadful as the Jeremiahs have led them to believe. It is the *ambience* of school—the climate of learning, the dedication to young people, the commitment to ongoing learning and changing—that is so difficult to convey between the covers of a book. One of the major contributions of this text is its emphasis on becoming a decision-making professional and maintaining that professionalism—an elusive goal in recent years. The authors propose that while the state may guide, the teacher must decide. If the professionalization of teachers indeed occurs, such empowerment will require these professionals to make sound and influential decisions. This text provides the base for creating that kind of reflective practitioner.

Another major feature of this text is its carefully integrated research base. At every step along the way, the authors have relied on and cited the research on which they have based their conclusions, recommendations, and activities. For example, they address writing in the social studies—a topic glossed over in most texts—in light of the latest developments in writing as a process but translate it into practical terms for the social studies teacher. They do the same with reading, concept learning, and development of basic rationales. The research is current, and the applications are direct and appropriate. Thus, the authors encourage the prospective teacher/decision maker: Use the research, and adapt it to your purpose.

Finally, the text confronts the issues that beset the field. There is little true agreement about what social studies is and what it should attempt to do in our schools. We are certainly a conglomerate subject, and the corporate model is permeated with great diffusion (some would say confusion) and fractured operations. Some might criticize this text for not presenting social studies in a stronger citizenship framework. But consider that the entire text is an exercise in civic responsibility: How do I, the beginning teacher, think about and make wise decisions about the learning that is best for my students while balancing the political interests of all the other people with whom I come in contact? How do we help teachers adjust to the problems of today's youth in an institution designed in the 19th century and an educational program devised for medieval scholars?

For instructors who seek a practical text for their methods course, for practitioners who want to update their professional knowledge base, and for others seeking a model approach to bottling old wine and introducing new spirits, Mahood, Biemer, and Lowe have achieved a breakthrough. While this is not a "teacher-proof" text, it demonstrates how a methods text can actually help an aspiring teacher. Thanks, folks, for helping me do a better, more professional job!

Donald H. Bragaw

Preface

Neil Postman and Charles Weingartner issued some challenges to new teachers, among which was to "require every teacher who thinks he knows his subject well to write a book on it" (*Teaching as a Subversive Activity* [New York: Delacorte, 1969], 138). That is, if you know so much, put it in writing.

We were prodded into accepting their challenge by several forces, including (1) the magnitude of harsh criticism being directed at schools, (2) the plethora of suggestions for reform which followed these critiques, and (3) our feelings that an updated text was needed. The biggest obstacle, however, was whether we three colleagues could summarize our very different views into a coherent whole and communicate these views clearly.

The reformers of the '80s disagree with each other on many matters, but two goals stand out: (1) the need to prepare responsible, reflective citizens and productive workers, and (2) the need for greatly improved academic or cognitively-oriented education for our youth. Despite some reservations about the nature of the critiques, we do support their basic thrust. There are marked problems with American education. Further, we are delighted with the attention being given to our schools, for too often in the past they have been neglected. Our hope is that readers of this book will be fully involved participants—true professionals—in the current and any future reform movements.

True professionals, it can be argued, are made, not born. We believe true professionals must:

- know the content of the subject they teach
- have a sustaining philosophy—know what they want to accomplish and why
- understand the diversity of their students; not only the amazing differences in development, but also aptitudes
- engage their students by guiding them using appropriate content, instructional techniques, and materials.

But this does not imply a "cookbook approach." This book aims to be a light and lively text, talking *to* not *at* students preparing to teach; reflecting current theory and practice in social studies; and filled with vignettes, "real-world" examples, and specific classroom activities. And it aims to avoid prescriptions, for we believe that good teaching demands decision making by individual instructors.

The immensity of this task became readily apparent when preparing the outline for the book. After much discussion, here are some ideas we hope to emphasize:

- teachers are, of necessity, decision makers
- as decision makers, teachers must know what curriculum is, what instruction is, what social studies is, how the field called social studies has evolved, and what the conflicting curricular alternatives are
- their decisions must also consider who the learner is and how learning may occur
- instruction, which follows, must be structured to adapt to these learners

Thus, the content of Part One (Chapters 1 to 4) of the text was determined. It deals with curriculum for secondary social studies and conflicting alternatives. Its undergirding themes are

1. Curriculum is basic. Instruction, including content, must flow therefrom.
2. Conflict over curriculum has always been present; it is inevitable and desirable.
3. Learners are diverse, yet share commonalities, including identifiable aptitudes, developmental stages, and learning styles.
4. Ultimately, the informed social studies teacher must decide how to structure instruction based on knowledge of curriculum and learners.

Part Two (Chapters 5 to 11) is an overview of instruction. It will assist you in

- planning units of instruction based on your knowledge of curriculum, learners, and learning

- creating environments which foster learning, including the wise use of schedules, resources, technology, and management
- encouraging speaking and listening skills in the classroom through lecture and recitation, grouping, discussion, and cooperative learning
- fostering reading and comprehension, recognizing the role of the textbook and varieties of print materials
- encouraging writing, which applies divergent and convergent thinking, and demands evaluating written work
- helping students to use special skills that are needed to read maps, graphs, cartoons, photos and to place events and artifacts in chronological perspective
- evaluating student learning

Part Three (Chapter 12) returns to our basic theme of the social studies teacher as a professional (i.e., a person who makes informed decisions based on considered beliefs, on research evidence, on learning and teaching, on productive collegiality with other educators including support personnel, on sound interaction with concerned members of the broader community, and on a commitment to continual growth and development).

We want to make explicit some basic definitions that guided us, relying principally on the 1976 National Institute of Education publication, *Current Issues, Problems, and Concerns in Curriculum Development.*

Curriculum is
"the intended outcomes of instruction (i.e., all knowledge, abilities, skills, attitudes, values, behaviors and other attributes intended for acquisition by learners)"; in other words, the deliberate, overt, planned goals.
Instruction is
"the process of providing opportunities to learn the curriculum (i.e., to acquire the intended outcomes)"; the *means* to achieve the curriculum.
And *learning* is
"the process of acquiring knowledge, abilities, etc., whether intended or unintended."
Finally, *instructional programs* are
"embodiments of the curriculum in the form of plans, (e.g., designs, goal statements, objectives, guides, descriptions, explanations, instructions) and materials (e.g., textbooks, films, filmstrips, videos, slides, maps, workbooks, ditto sheets, etc.) for use in instruction."

Above all, we want to remind the reader that the social studies is no more static than physics, biochemistry, or any other field of study. Research on curriculum, learning, and instruction no doubt will continue, new ways of viewing the familiar will occur, and the artistry that characterizes teaching certainly will endure. Simply, we have tried to capture the essence of what we believe and try to practice.

We sincerely hope we have communicated with you, the reader and prospective social studies teacher.

Wayne Mahood
Linda Biemer
William T. Lowe

ACKNOWLEDGMENTS

We would like to extend our appreciation to the following professors for their suggestions and comments: Catherine Cornbleth, State University of New York at Buffalo; Ernest B. Dorow, University of Pittsburgh; Walter E. McPhie, The University of Utah; John D. Napier, University of Georgia; Anne Ochoa, Indiana University; Stuart B. Palonsky, University of Missouri-Columbia; Jack Sheridan, University of Houston; Bruce Smith, University of Cincinnati; and William Wilen, Kent State University.

Our gratitude is also extended to the Merrill staff, especially Jeff Johnston, Sally MacGregor, Linda Scharp, Linda Bayma, and Lorraine Woost, and to free-lance editor Nancy Maybloom.

Contents

PART TWO
**The Instructional
Process**

5
Planning   **121**

6
**Environments for Teaching
and Learning**   **157**

PART ONE

The Foundations

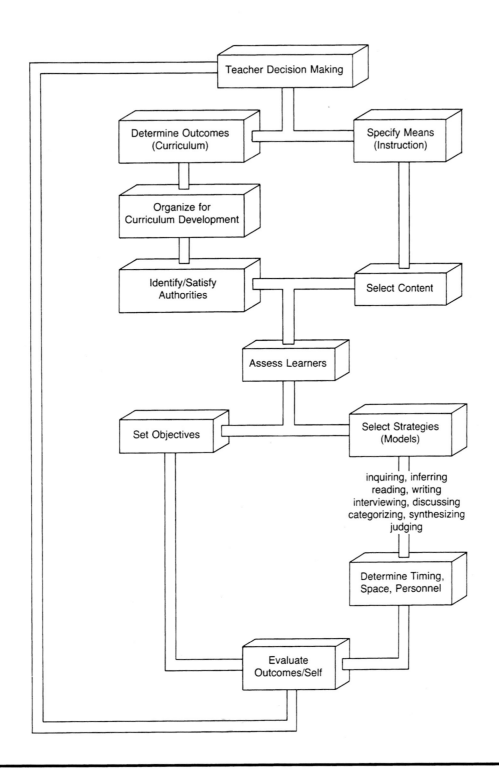

Chapter One

The Conflict over the Social Studies Curriculum and Content

There are numerous valid reasons for the continuing controversy over the curriculum, or goals, and the content for the secondary social studies program. To be a successful teacher, one must analyze this conflict and come to a personally satisfying and socially responsible position.

There were only three weeks remaining in the school year when the letter arrived from Mary Ellen R., the new district coordinator of the social studies. It created little interest among the social studies department heads of the 12 middle and high schools, who had other things on their minds: plans for review and examinations, anxiety about the pupils who were failing, finding the time to respond to student papers/projects, writing letters of recommendation, making summer plans for themselves, and on and on.

To be sure, they expected they would have to revise, or at least reconsider, the social studies program. There had been discussions about the "new" state program, and they were aware that the coordinator, as well as one teacher from the district, had been members of the state curriculum writing team. Some of them had even skimmed the material emanating from "state ed." But despite all the political heat the syllabi had generated elsewhere, most of these social studies chairpersons weren't too excited. The recommended changes seemed somewhat insignificant, and the teachers knew that the state authorities encouraged districts to develop local alternatives. Some tended to think, "We'll just keep on doing what we have been doing." But the most common reaction to the letter was a feeling of too little time and too much preoccupation to think about revision—at least for now.

Coordinator Mary Ellen R. had expected this response. She knew that most teachers had to be motivated to commit the time and energy required for serious curriculum development work. She understood further that most people resist change and, in the area of curriculum and instruction, with good reason; one cannot and should not indiscriminately jump on every passing bandwagon. But she also believed that the program had serious problems. In fact, she had been brought into the district, in part, to "stir these teachers up."

Mary Ellen had been through revision activities many times over the 20-plus years she had taught social studies in various districts. She had a solid background in political science and social psychology and recently had completed her doctorate in curriculum and instruction from the local university. Her colleagues generally respected her, although some believed she had been unwisely selected for the job over some "well-qualified" teachers from within the district. She was ready for the assignment.

Key paragraphs from Mary Ellen's letter follow:

Dear Colleagues:

As you know, we have been charged with analyzing the 6–12 social studies program of the district. If we are successful, our efforts should result in improved teaching. . . .

I earnestly believe that this is a fine and long overdue opportunity. After all, it has been nearly 10 years since this district completed such a formal study. Of course, I fully realize that you have been making adaptations over the years, and there are marked differences among the programs in our various schools. But clearly a host of dramatic social changes have occurred during this period, and there has been a great deal of valuable research and development activity in social studies education. Surely these changes should be systematically reflected in our curriculum (goals) and instruction (means). Obviously our current programs have strengths, but there is plenty of room for improvement. . . .

As anticipated, the associate superintendent for curriculum and instruction has authorized me to offer each of you up to five days of compensation for our summer curriculum development work. We also have a modest but reasonable amount of money for consultants and other resources. Furthermore, our Teacher Center has agreed to support this activity in a variety of ways, including providing some release time for us and our colleagues during the coming academic year. Given our tight fiscal situation, I believe this represents an impressive, tangible commitment to the task.

I hope that during the summer we will, among other accomplishments, develop a realistic "plan of action" so that we can complete our assignment during the next school year. By this time next spring, we need a sound, scholarly, well-crafted, but thoroughly practical and widely supported document that will help us and our colleagues be more effective teachers. Its format is uncertain at this point.

Our first meeting will be at 8:30 A.M. on July 1 here at the central office in the conference room on the third floor.

Please carefully review the enclosed state guides before that date. Also, reexamine the materials for this district. By all means, bring along any other curriculum documents or critiques you may want to share with us. . . . But your most important "homework" is to come up with a list of criticisms of the status quo, not only your beliefs but any critical comments you have picked up from students, other teachers, parents, other community members, and published sources.

I truly look forward to our important cooperative efforts.

Best wishes for your end-of-the-year activities.

Sincerely,
Mary Ellen R.
Coordinator of Social Studies

July 1 arrived, and so did the coordinator and the 12 department heads. Over coffee, tea, and Danish, there was friendly talk, which Mary Ellen R. encouraged for some time. She recognized that although many members of the group had been in the district for years, they didn't know one another very well. Spending time getting reacquainted could pay off.

Then Mary Ellen became quite task oriented. She asked for and received permission to tape the discussion with the promise that only the 13 team members would have access to the recordings. She went to an easel covered with newsprint and, while reviewing the goals and the timing of the team's assignment, wrote "What's wrong?" She noted that their work would not— and could not—solve all the problems involved in teaching and learning social studies in the district, let alone the broader problems of society or even of the local community. However, she said, "Let's see what we think the problems are. Surely we can't hope to make any progress unless we know what *might* be wrong with the status quo."

For awhile it was slow going. But then the comments began to flow so quickly that Mary Ellen could barely keep up. In hindsight, she wished she had asked someone else to serve as recorder, but she knew she had the tapes to rely on. Moreover, the group members were quick to clarify points when they thought she hadn't captured the gist.

Voices became louder and more strident. Debates and disagreements were rampant, often two or more going on at once. But while Mary Ellen urged the group to get all the purported problems on the table first, she didn't "clamp down" too tightly; she believed that a fairly unstructured discussion would effectively serve her goals. Also, her colleagues apparently were thoroughly enjoying themselves during the virtually uninterrupted four hours of listing and debating "problems." Every member of the group was now convinced that a careful rethinking of the social studies program was a worthwhile effort.

After lunch, Conrad C., an unsuccessful internal candidate for Mary Ellen's position, volunteered to prepare a written summary of the issues identified in the morning session. Mary Ellen was delighted by this turn of events and returned to the task: "Now we have to understand the goals before we can begin to consider improvements in instruction. Every aspect of what we do must or should be tied to our purposes." To this, not surprisingly, came the remark "Please, let's not reinvent the wheel yet again." After Mary Ellen reassured them that this would not be the case, the group agreed to examine the work of other contemporary curriculum developers.

Finally, a consensus about the following major tasks emerged:

1. *To identify the range of significant views concerning the nature of the social studies.* To accomplish this, we need to study a variety of expert definitions for the field and get a stronger sense of its history.
2. *To try to settle to our own satisfaction the authority issue, that is, to reach agreement about who* does *and who* should *decide on the goals of the social studies program.* If at all possible, we need a statement we can all accept on the appropriate authority/authorities.
3. *To reach agreement on the reasons for the continuing conflict and controversy over curriculum in the social studies and to ascertain the impact of these disagreements.*
4. *To debate the various positions on the social studies curriculum.* Perhaps we will reach agreement, but probably we won't.

Everyone left the meetings tired but with a warm feeling of accomplishment.

ASIDE TO THE READER: The foregoing tasks are the goals of the first two chapters of this book, and they will profoundly influence the remainder of the text.

DEFINITIONS OF THE SOCIAL STUDIES

Later that summer, the group reconvened. Everyone seemed refreshed and highly motivated. During the break, however, Mary Ellen had done some homework.

First, she had gotten Conrad C. to agree to put his summary of the problems previously identified "on the back burner" so the group could concentrate on the definitions of the social studies field and subsequently on its history.

Second, she had spent a good bit of time collecting a roomful of materials for the use of the social studies chairs. Most of these came from the district's Professional Resource Center (PRC). Mary Ellen was proud of her district for supporting the center, which was jointly sponsored by two colleges, the regional university, four school districts, and the Roman Catholic diocese. The impressive collection of instructional materials included textbooks, curriculum guides, professional journals, books and monographs, software packages, audiovisuals, research reports, reference works, and so on. Also, there were computer links to the university library, and interlibrary loans were easily obtainable.

Third, Mary Ellen had invited her doctoral advisor to discuss the history of the secondary social studies curriculum with the group, and a date was set.

The group spent the morning of their second day in extensive reading and unstructured browsing to locate appropriate sources. The afternoon session was devoted to sharing ideas and was rich in point and counterpoint. The following conclusions emerged:

1. There is no consensus among us over the meaning of the field.
2. This lack of consensus is not only a reality; it may be inevitable—even desirable—in our political system. (Mary Ellen made a note to return to this point.)
3. However, every social studies teacher should have an operational and personally satisfying definition of the field to guide his or her practice. It must be socially and professionally responsible, but each teacher must have a personal sense of ownership.
4. Robert Barr et al. have provided some valuable scholarship in terms of definitions for the field [Barr, Barth, & Shermis, 1977]. The following information was particularly helpful:

The most enduring definition was developed by Edgar Wesley some forty years ago. "The Social Studies," said Wesley, "are the social sciences simplified for pedagogical purposes." This early definition has held on with an enduring tenacity and, even though few have ever been completely satisfied with it [including, in recent years, Edgar Wesley], most recent definitions reflect its origin. The *Thesaurus of ERIC Descriptors* states that the "social studies consist of adaptations of knowledge from the social sciences for teaching purposes at the elementary and secondary levels of education." This parallels closely the definition found in the United States Office of Education's *Standard Terminology for Curriculum and Instruction*, which states, "The social studies are comprised of those aspects of history, economics, political science, sociology, anthropology, psychology, geography, and philosophy which in practice are selected for instructional purposes in schools and colleges." These definitions are strikingly similar to the one found in the National Council for the Social Studies Charter. "The term *social studies*," the charter reads, "is used to include history, economics, sociology, civics, geography, and all modifications of subjects whose content as well as aim is social." In all these content definitions, the social studies is conceived as the subject matter of the academic disciplines somehow "simplified," "adapted," "modified," or selected for school instruction.*

5. Barr and his colleagues probably speak for the majority of the writers in the field of social studies education when they say, "The social studies is an integration of experience and knowledge concerning human relations for the purpose of citizen education" [Barr, Barth, & Shermis, 1977, p. 69].

6. Using the above sentence as a springboard, the Connecticut State Board of Education [1982] adds,

> Citizenship education implies membership in the American and human community [sic] and the commitment to work effectively with diverse peoples and to accept differences in cultures, in values, and in responses to societal issues. . . . Because the social studies deals with the interrelationships and interactions of individuals in all aspects of society, past and present, it can provide youth with the knowledge, values and skills necessary for survival in the future.

HISTORY OF THE SOCIAL STUDIES

Earlier Mary Ellen's doctoral advisor had agreed to make the presentation on the history of the field under the condition that the participants first read carefully Hazel Hertzberg's work *Social Studies Reform, 1880–1980* (Hertzberg, 1981). From this the advisor extracted several milestones in the history of social studies (see Figure 1.1) and presented them to the group on an overhead.

*From *Defining the Social Studies* (pp. 1–2) by R. D. Barr, J. L. Barth, and S. S. Shermis, 1977, Washington, DC: National Council for the Social Studies. Reprinted by permission.

FIGURE 1.1
Some Milestones in the Development of Social Studies

Early period	First American history text, 1787
	First American civics text, 1797
Nationalism period (19th century)	Chauvinistic focus on American history, civics, and physical geography

Era of national committees
1890s–1940s

Committee of 10 (NEA), 1893
    K–6—biography and mythology
    7—American history and government
    8—Greek and Roman history
    9—French history
    10—English history
    11—American history
    12—optional studies in depth
Committee of 7 (AHA), 1899
    K–6—chronological study of history
    9—ancient history (Western world)
    10—medieval and modern history
    11—English history
    12—American history and government
Commission on Reorganization of Secondary Education (NEA), 1916 (used the terms *social studies, citizenship, and problems of democracy*)
    7—local and/or national history
    8—U.S. history
    9—civics and consumer economics
    10—European history
    11—U.S. history
    12—problems of democracy
Commission on Social Studies in the Schools (AHA), 1926 (sanctioned the 1916 report)

Era of national projects (late 1950s–early 1960s	The "new social studies" resulted from a series of projects in the disciplines, e.g., "The High School Geography Project" and "Sociological Resources for Secondary schools." Focused on cognition and inquiry. Downplayed history in favor of "cultural" studies.
Humanistic era (late 1960s–early 1970s)	Values and moral education, e.g., "Values Clarification" and "Moral Development"
Problems era (late 1970s–early 1980s)	Multidisciplinary studies (peace, ethnic, women, law, future, environmental, global, etc.)
Accountability era (1983–present)	Single disciplines emphasized, testing, skills, state mandates, "rigor"

The presentation was well received. While many of the examples in the outline were discussed, the department heads showed particular interest in the last four periods identified in Figure 1.1. This led to a number of generalizations and/or conclusions about the history of the field. Five of the most important of these were:

1. *Lack of consensus.* The history of the social studies is loaded with conflict and controversy.
2. *Shifting foci.* The disagreements of the past continue. So far there has been no steady, consistent progression in any one direction; rather, the development has been pendulumlike, shifting from one focus to another and returning to earlier positions.
3. *Accretion.* Content is continually being added, with little dropped; more and more ground is supposed to be "covered."
4. *Expanded horizons.* There has been a tendency to operate on an "expanded-horizons" or "concentric-circles" approach; that is, we have tended to believe that children should first be exposed to the familiar and then move outward—start with the self, then the family, then the neighborhood, and so on, ending with the interdependent world. (Even this view has been sharply criticized, but it has influenced our history.)
5. *Sense of permanence.* Despite the conflict, the 1916 report has been seminally important. For over 60 years, the social studies have followed the pattern set in this document.

It would be very valuable for you to do some independent research on the history of the field, particularly from the late 1950s on. In addition to Hertzberg, we suggest starting with Bulletin 78 of the National Council for the Social Studies, Social Studies and Social Sciences: A Fifty-Year Perspective *(Wronski & Bragaw, 1986). It would also be very worthwhile to discuss these developments with your classmates.*

THE AUTHORITY ISSUE

Tom S., a participant in the meeting, could not accept the majority view concerning the inevitability and desirability of a lack of consensus over the basic definition of the field. He insisted that social studies instruction was in a sorry state precisely because teachers couldn't agree: "While we will never get universal agreement among scholars, students, parents, and others over the nature of the field, we social studies teachers must reach general agreement; otherwise we will continue to flounder. Don't you want to be in control of your professional destiny? If so, we teachers and other leaders of social studies must collectively decide what our field is about."

Mary Ellen quickly asserted that Tom was really questioning where the authority of the field should reside. She reminded the group that they already had decided that they must examine this issue. She said, "I am prepared to lead our thinking on the subject. Please hear me through, and then we can spend as much time as you wish in discussion."

Here is the gist of her remarks:

Who *should*, and who actually *does*, determine the curriculum? The need to address this highly controversial issue is underscored by the National Institute of Education, the research arm of the U.S. Department of Education. NIE says the authority question is the most important curriculum issue that we as a society currently face.

Recall from your study of the history and governance of schooling in American society that the framers of our Constitution did not include one word about public schools. Thus, the authority for schooling by virtue of the Tenth Amendment is "reserved to the States respectively, or to the people." Many of us have long prided ourselves on this rare decentralized model of school governance.

In practice, the states, to sharply varying degrees, have delegated decision making for schools to locally elected or appointed citizens called "school boards," "school trustees," or other such titles. These citizen groups have responsibility under state guidelines for making most policy decisions, including the authority to determine the curriculum. Again, to widely varying degrees among jurisdictions, these boards have normally called upon educators to be responsible for recommending the specific programs of the local school system.

But in fact, the real power for determining the curriculum of social studies— and for all other subjects—has continually shifted from one authority or coalition of authorities to another. Currently there is widespread dissatisfaction with giving local school boards this vital responsibility. The discontent comes from many sources.

In a moment I want you to examine my transparency [see Figure 1.2], which attempts to identify the major contenders for the ultimate authority for the curriculum. Before doing so, however, let me quickly add two further comments on this struggle for power.

First, the period of the 1980s to date has seen dramatic growth in the direct influence on the curriculum exercised by state bodies. There has been a remarkable increase in the number of state-mandated courses, statewide testing programs, state-generated goals statements, and so on. Further—and this frequently has not been the case in the past—these requirements often are being strictly enforced. State aid often is the means of enforcement, but published test results and even the removal of accreditation or registration, as well as other means, are being used.

I do not approve of this development, but I am trying to be objective. The increase in direct state power often has resulted from the good intentions of state legislators and governors who were convinced that schools must be accountable and that they were failing to adequately serve large numbers of youngsters. Their commitment has been demonstrated by increasing state financial support, though we know that with money comes greater state control. I recommend *Time for Results: The Governors' 1991 Report on Education* as an excellent source on this movement [National Governors' Association, 1986].

**FIGURE 1.2
The Authority Issue:
Who Should Determine
the Curriculum?**

1. Students:
individually or
collectively.

2. Local educators:
individual teacher,
groups of teachers,
principals,
supervisors, etc.

7. National bodies:
federal government, national
societies, commissions,
large private
foundations,
economic elites,
academic elites,
etc.

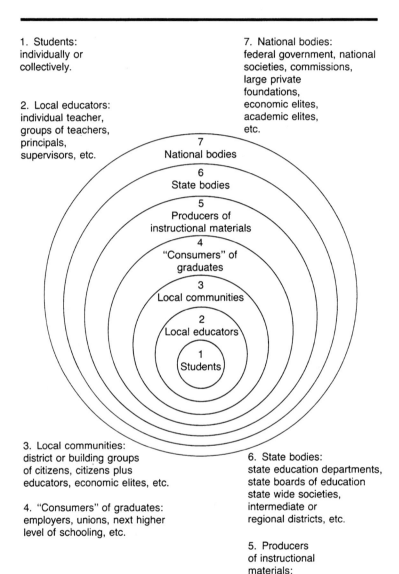

3. Local communities:
district or building groups
of citizens, citizens plus
educators, economic elites, etc.

4. "Consumers" of graduates:
employers, unions, next higher
level of schooling, etc.

6. State bodies:
state education departments,
state boards of education
state wide societies,
intermediate or
regional districts, etc.

5. Producers
of instructional
materials:
textbook publishers,
test creators, etc.

The other point I want to make in the interest of fairness is my own "radical" conviction on the authority matter. I firmly believe that individual teachers, after making an honest attempt to study the views of all concerned individuals and groups, must have the ultimate authority to determine the why, the what, and the how of their teaching. I am convinced that anyone worthy of the title of teacher, an exalted role from my perception, must control curriculum and instruction in his or her classroom. Yes, teachers can and should get help as well as be open to others' ideas, but ultimately *they* must be in charge.

You can imagine the reaction to Mary Ellen's remarks and her repeated query "Who should have ultimate control over the curriculum?" One department head argued vigorously that kids should be "in charge." Another defended strong state control, stressing that "beginning teachers are incompetent to make sound decisions about the curriculum."

But the majority view was Mary Ellen's: Individual teachers ought to have, and exercise, a great deal of authority over the curriculum in their social studies classrooms.

Tom was not convinced.

PROBLEMS AND DISAGREEMENTS CONCERNING THE SOCIAL STUDIES CURRICULUM

Mary Ellen decided it was now time for Conrad to share his summary of the "problems" the group had identified at the first meeting. Conrad loved history and teaching and also loved to play with words. But his strongest love was his students, and this relationship had been reciprocal for many years. Reputedly the senior teacher in the district, Conrad refused to even think about retirement. In somber suits and ties and immaculately groomed, Conrad had an endearing, if quaint, sense of humor. Many in the district thought of him affectionately as the "senior statesman" of the social studies. However, he was also considered a bit of a pedant. Following is Conrad's presentation.

The following list at least partially reviews issues mentioned in earlier sections of the chapter and at the same time introduces topics that we will address more fully at later points.

CURRICULUM (as well as) CONTENT and CLIENT CONCERNS:
*Corresponding on Our Challenging Confabulation of Caring
but Conflicted and Confused Chairpersons
Called by our Coordinator on 7/1 by Your Colleague,
Conrad C.*

On Goals and Content
- Chronology (history) should provide the organizing construct for the social studies program, *and* history should dominate.

- Culture (anthropology) should be emphasized.
- Place (geography) should be paramount.
- Interaction in groups (sociology) is the key.
- Coping with scarcity (economics) lies at the heart.
- Et cetera for each of the social disciplines.
- We need to be more "humanistic," *or* we need to be more "scientific," *or* we must reject this "two-cultures" view and be "scientifically humanistic."
- Greater breadth *versus* greater depth is needed.
- Our roots must be emphasized—patriotism is a valid goal—*versus* the program is chauvinistic, placing far too much emphasis on the United States and Western Europe. We must have much more "non-West."
- Pluralism (separatism), not assimilation (common culture), is the answer, *or* vice versa. The current program (and the instructional materials) is racist, sexist, and ethnocentric.
- We need to stay abreast of current issues and trends and spend far more time on the contemporary *versus* we are already too trendy and faddish.
- The organization of the program should be based on separate, distinct social disciplines *as opposed to* integrating the disciplines based on social problems, themes, and other such criteria.
- Censorship and fear of censorship create impossible pressures—thus, we must stay in the mainstream of popular opinion—*versus* we must emphasize controversy and highlight the range of views. Differing values are at the very core of our field.
- Teachers must avoid taking stands on controversial issues *as opposed to* the view that teachers must be opinion makers.
- We need more study of organized religion *versus* we must avoid organized religion in the public schools.
- Content is redundant and desperately needs articulation *versus* we should concentrate on the same basics at all levels.
- We must have more a more coherent, generally recognized structure *versus* flexibility and adaptability are the keys.
- We need to be far more concerned with vocational skills and career education *versus* we need more academic requirements.
- We need to pay more attention to family and other primary groups *versus* "no way."
- We need to focus on adolescents' problems, needs, and interests—social, psychological, and developmental—*versus* the view that we are *not* counselors.
- There are too many facts and too few concepts and generalizations *versus* students don't know but should know the state capitals.
- There is too much emphasis on the cognitive and too little on the affective.
- We lack a developmental, sequential hierarchy of content and skills *versus* no such organization has general acceptance.

- We need to focus far more attention on the virtually neglected areas of law, philosophy, the arts, literature, and so on *versus* we are spread too thin now.
- We need more central (state/national) direction *versus* local. Individual teachers in particular have too little freedom.
- *In sum,* either our disciplinary base is too broad and conflicting, *or* the strength of the social studies is its breadth.

On Instruction

- We need more individualization—student choice based on interests and needs.
- We wrongly emphasize competition over cooperation.
- We must give students far more responsibility to teach one another.
- Social studies, more than any other field, has ignored helpful advances in technology.
- Most films, videos, and especially computer programs are terrible, and they are grossly overused.
- Social studies texts are awful from every perspective. They must be improved.
- Improving texts is not an answer, let alone *the* answer. Instead, we need to use a variety of the rich sources already available.
- Kids can't write, speak, listen, or—especially serious—read. We need to concentrate on communication skills.
- We should emphasize skills having special importance for social studies, such as reading and interpreting maps.
- The real problem is that kids are lazy and apathetic.
- Worse, kids are violent and antisocial.
- Students come from one culture, teachers from another.
- The program is unpopular with students; they are unmotivated. We need to be relevant.
- Achievement on national tests is shockingly low. We must emphasize getting kids ready to take these tests.
- Standardized tests are vastly overemphasized. They are counterproductive, or at best irrelevant, to good program development, and they are necessarily biased.
- Both curriculum and instruction are too teacher centered and teacher dominated.
- Teachers need to reassert their leadership.
- Teachers are the problem—they are dim, lazy, timid, and unmotivated. Good teachers (and good teaching) will solve all the problems. Get good people who use what we know about teaching and learning, and there will few, if any, significant problems.
- Professional societies are unresponsive to our needs; thus, we don't join them.
- Our colleagues from other subjects don't understand or appreciate us.

- Sound research and scholarship from our disciplines and about teaching and learning are in short supply, but what is available tends to be ignored.

Smiles and a few groans greeted the alliteration in the heading to Conrad's list, but other reactions were muted. The majority view seemed to be "OK, we do have significant conflict, but let's get on with our task."

While, as noted, we will revisit these problems later in the book, we urge you to ask questions about the meaning of items that are unclear. We also encourage you to amend this list: reorganize it, rank order it, rewrite unclear items, add or delete ideas, and identify those with which you agree and disagree.

NATURE OF THE CONFLICT

Mary Ellen praised Conrad and suggested that the group analyze his list with respect to three broad questions:

1. Is this conflict generic or endemic to the social studies?
2. Is it avoidable?
3. Is it destructive?

General Issues

The first point generated a lively discussion of the problems with America's secondary schools. Clearly the 1980s was a period characterized by heated criticism of secondary schools; dozens of critical reports had been written and widely distributed. The group touched on many of the writings of that period and discussed Goodlad's, Boyer's, and Sizer's work in some detail.

We won't take the time to summarize this discussion here, but we strongly recommend that you read the works cited. Goodlad (1984), Boyer (1983), and Sizer (1984) emphasize many of the same issues found in Conrad's list and indicate that these problems cut across most subject areas.

Specific Issues

The group members agreed that certain specific factors tended to make curriculum decision making in the social studies field particularly difficult and controversial. Following are the most important of these concerns.

Curriculum decisions in social studies are often controversial.

Breadth and Diversity of the Disciplinary Base. While reviewing the established definitions of the social studies, the group noted that there was wide disagreement among writers about which fields to include in the disciplinary base. (There was also disagreement regarding the relative importance of specific disciplines, or the disciplines in concert, in shaping both the curriculum and the content of the field.) Almost all writers in the area, however, included history, geography, economics, political science/government, anthropology, and sociology. Many others added psychology. Some included such areas as law and philosophy; a few incorporated virtually all subjects with significant social content, such as literature, the visual and performing arts, biology, and so on. Figure 1.3 summarizes the disputed disciplinary base of the social studies.

The group concurred that even if the disciplinary base were narrowed down to the six fundamental areas listed in Figure 1.3, some particularly difficult problems for the social studies teacher would remain:

1. There is an almost "bottomless pit" of content possibilities to consider in selecting what should be taught.
2. The six basic disciplines differ fundamentally from one another. The methods of inquiry, the working vocabulary or building-block concepts,

FIGURE 1.3
Disciplinary Base of the Social Studies

Fundamental Base	Expanded Base
History	History
Geography	Geography
Economics	Economics
Political science/government	Political science/government
Anthropology	Anthropology
Sociology	Sociology
	Psychology
	Law
	Philosophy
	Literature (social content)
	Visual and performing arts (social content)
	Biology (social content)
	Others?

the perceptions of the nature of scholarship, and even the "views of the world" are distinct and, in several important ways, conflicting. Teaching professionals in some fields contend they are part of the humanities; some wish to be considered scientific; others, such as geography teachers, can't decide where their fields fit in.

3. Staying abreast of the scholarly developments in any one of these fields is impossible for the busy teacher; trying to be reasonably informed in all of them is a hopeless task.

4. Each field is characterized by deep internal tensions. Each has "identity" problems that are fascinating but make it extremely difficult for the teacher who is trying to introduce the field to young students.

5. The breadth and diversity of the disciplines included in the social studies may be major contributors to a potentially serious political problem for social studies educators.

As noted, many leaders in the field argued that citizenship education is justifiably the central goal of secondary social studies. Other interdisciplinary approaches were touted. Simultaneously, "curricularists" in other subject areas tended to argue for in-depth study in the traditional disciplines. But the group agreed that regardless of the merits of each case, the fact that social studies was "out of sync" with its sister fields was fraught with danger. While clearly it could be argued that citizenship education was social studies' only claim to distinction, it seemed obvious that if the field remained outside the mainstream of curriculum thought, it would have difficulty attracting popular support and resulting financial resources.

The group recognized that divisions existed in all of the broad fields of knowledge taught in the secondary schools. The languages, the arts, the natural sciences, mathematics—all had internal and organizational problems, but they also enjoyed a degree of unity and coherence that social studies lacked. Perhaps the most fundamental issue was: *Does attempting to treat social studies as a distinct, identifiable arena of knowledge make sense?*

To more sharply define this issue, the group considered teacher preparation and certification. Should teachers be certified in history or one of the other social disciplines, or should they continue to receive certification in something called "social studies?"

Controversy and Censorship.   It was evident that controversy existed in all of the fields taught in the secondary school, including, much to the surprise of outsiders to the field, mathematics. However, social studies seemed to be "special" in this regard. Every topic was potentially controversial. Propaganda, indoctrination, and manipulation were ever present possibilities for divisiveness. As a result, persons from every shade of political orientation who carried strong convictions about almost every subject occasionally had tried to influence or even censor social studies teachers and their instructional materials. Censorship had always been with us and probably was inevitable. But it was evident that in the 1980s, as in few other periods in our educational history, the forces of censorship were particularly active and effective.

To be sure, the conflict in the social studies field was not necessarily a negative factor; indeed, it may have been a measure of its vitality and significance. But the social studies teacher needed to be constantly "on guard" about this matter. At the very least, clear and widely accepted procedures for dealing with censorship had to be in place before challenges were made.

Status Problem.   The social studies program faced an array of serious status problems. It tended to be more unpopular with students than most other fields. Teachers of other subjects and building and district administrators seemed relatively more dissatisfied with and confused about the social studies curriculum. Even scholars from the associated disciplines tended to be highly skeptical of the worth of the high school offerings. These negative images of the field were reported again and again in the literature.

Of course, it seemed to the group that the study of the social phenomenon should fascinate everyone. But what could and should they do to convince others? Clearly they had an unavoidable "public relations" responsibility.

Recency.   The department heads realized that change is constant in all fields of knowledge. When knowledge was unchanging, it probably should be put in reference books instead of being taught. However, the social studies appeared to have a special problem. All of the supporting disciplines were rapidly changing. Last year's accurate data were incorrect this year. Political geography, economics, demographics, and so on were in constant flux. Perhaps history could be considered more durable, but revisionists were actively at work in every subdivision of the field.

Other implications of the state of constant and rapid change were evident. As one important example, social studies educators had to cope directly with the issue of how to organize the teaching of current events. Should contemporary affairs be the core of the social studies program, using "flashbacks" when appropriate? Or should today's happenings be ignored on the grounds that solid analysis was not yet available? Should lessons on current events be relegated to certain days (Fridays seemed to be especially popular for those who elected this approach)? Should current events continually be applied to the regular content? Closely related, what instructional materials should be used for current events lessons? All of these were important and truly perplexing questions.

What do you make of these subject-specific issues? Do they trouble you? Do you have any solutions?

Impact of the Conflict

On the inevitability and desirability of the conflict, especially in the social studies, the group remained divided. The careful reader will remember that Tom S. in particular insisted that a consensus among the teachers of the field was essential. However, Nancy S., another chairperson, spoke for the majority:

> I recognize, of course, that there is little consensus over the curriculum of the social studies, but at the risk of redundancy, I think this lack of agreement is both inevitable and highly desirable. I would be deeply concerned if there were a uniform view. With the decentralized governance model in American education previously identified by Mary Ellen (which I cherish), and in a field that is loaded with controversy—where value issues lurk behind nearly every topic—I hope that this conflict will always be with us. From my perspective, lack of consensus over the social studies curriculum becomes a problem *only* if one or both of the following conditions occur.
>
> First, the conflict is dangerous if it becomes so intense that the various parties who have a vested interest stop listening to one another and close their minds. Such situations do occur, and when this happens positive change stops. Not only is there no effort to accommodate the views of others, but the participants refuse to perceive realities; they ignore new evidence.
>
> Second, conflict can also lead to bland, grey, apathetic mindlessness. People can reach the conclusion, either consciously or—more likely—by default, that there is so much disagreement that it makes no difference what the curriculum is. Whatever the curriculum, there will be criticism. Given the all too common view that conflict is a bad thing—and clearly it is not—the object becomes to accommodate as many as possible or to avoid "making waves."

Of the two, the latter is far more common and far more pernicious. Indeed, it might be argued quite convincingly that most potential participants in the curriculum decision-making process are passive. They are only too happy to shift the responsibility to someone else—the textbook author, the curriculum committee, the testmaker, censors, and so on. However, it should be clear by now that *I am firmly convinced that an individual teacher who "opts out" of the process cannot be a successful teacher.* My fondest hope for this curriculum revision process is that our teachers will permanently become informed activists on curriculum matters.

FINAL STAGES IN THE CURRICULUM DEVELOPMENT PROCESS

The five days of curriculum development work had flown by. Mary Ellen felt that much had been accomplished, but she knew that the heart of the task remained: The group still needed to analyze the possible positions in the social studies and then discover ways to help each teacher in the district find a personally satisfying curriculum to which she or he would commit.

Toward that end, Mary Ellen suggested a framework for accomplishing these goals. Noting that the first step was to bring the teachers up to date on the work that had been completed this summer, she volunteered to provide a written summary of this activity that could be used as a springboard for discussions to be held in each of the 12 schools during the early fall. She would also provide each teacher with the broad outline of goals and content that the state had provided. (She thought this outline was so general in character that it would permit, and even encourage, each teacher to make personal curricular and instructional decisions after discussions at building-level meetings.)

Next, meetings would be held in each school with five of the social studies department heads, acting as outspoken advocates, each presenting one of the five major and enduring positions in the social studies.

Eventually a written guide would be prepared emphasizing the issues a teacher had to consider before making sound program decisions. Some general recommendations would be made and alternative options outlined. This guide would also include some recommendations for improving teaching regardless of the specific curricular position elected by a particular teacher.

The chairpersons found Mary Ellen's suggestions appealing but wanted a typology of the major positions. Understanding their concern, Mary Ellen indicated that she was particularly attracted to a system that had been used by her doctoral advisor, who had spoken to them previously. Here is her typology (of course, other scholars use different schema):

1. *Cognitive/disciplinary.* Facilitating the study of history, geography, and the social and behavioral sciences
2. *Socialization.* Helping students find appropriate roles in the groups to which they currently belong and might belong in the future

3. *Individualization.* Helping students understand and appreciate themselves

4. *Process.* Focusing on skills and procedures for knowing, believing, communicating, and so on

5. *Eclectic.* All of the above

After briefly clarifying the typology, Mary Ellen asked for and readily received volunteers to explain and defend each of the five positions during the coming school year.

As she left the meeting, Mary Ellen emitted a sigh of relief. Though tired, she was also exhilarated—more than satisfied that the job would be well done.

In reality, this would be far from the end. A district social studies coordinator or school department head no doubt would encounter more, sometimes unexpected problems. Not all would be as politically savvy as Mary Ellen, nor would they have the necessary district support, including materials, money, teacher center, and capable and enthusiastic participants to do the job right.

Summary

Our goal in this chapter was to convince you of the importance of developing your *curriculum.* We hoped to get you to think about your purposes for teaching social studies by presenting a hypothetical illustration of a curriculum development process in a "typical" school district. Although the specific people and events were fictitious, they were created from real experiences.

We explored four substantive topics: (1) definitions of the social studies; (2) the history of the field; (3) the ultimate authority for determining the curriculum; and (4) the nature of the conflict in the social studies.

We dodged responsibility for *defining the social studies.* Instead we provided some standard reference book definitions, which admittedly tend to be unsatisfactory to most practitioners in the field. We documented one definition that has a citizenship focus and currently is the mainstream view. We believe that *you* should define the field in a personally useful way. It is essential to develop an operational definition.

On the *history of the social studies,* we provided a skeletal outline depicting the swings of the pendulum. We urged you to become knowledgeable about the history of our field of study and gave you several good sources to get you started.

On the *authority* issue, we were quite explicit. While many groups and individuals wish to be involved in determining the curriculum, we expressed our firm and somewhat "radical" conviction that individual teachers must control the process. Also, we provided a list of other contenders for the role of ultimate authority and briefly noted the sharply increased power of state authorities in contemporary times.

In examining the *nature of the conflict,* we outlined some general and specific issues that are particularly troublesome for the potential curriculum decision maker in the social studies. Among these are the breadth and diversity of the disciplinary roots; the controversy in the field and the resulting attempts to censor its practitioners; the low status of social studies in the secondary school; and the rapidity of change in the knowledge base.

No doubt we have generated more questions than answers, but hopefully this will not discourage you. Teaching social studies is a noble calling. Indeed, from our perspective there is no more rewarding, albeit challenging career.

Decisions! Decisions!

1. How do you react to the claim that the social studies is a field fraught with conflict? Is this really true? If so, is this a healthy or unhealthy state? Are you encouraged, discouraged, or indifferent to the claim? Why?

2. Imagine that you are asked to describe and defend the social studies program to the parents of your first class. Could you do it? Which issue(s) would pose the greatest difficulty for you? Why? Would you want some assistance from your method instructor or your peers to prepare for this assignment?

References

Barr, R. D., Barth, J. L., & Shermis, S. S. (1977). *Defining the social studies* (Bulletin No. 51). Washington, DC: National Council for the Social Studies.

Boyer, E. (1983). *High school: A report on secondary education in America.* New York: Harper & Row.

Brubaker, D. L. (1967). *Alternative directions for the social studies.* Scranton, PA.: International Textbook.

Connecticut State Board of Education. (1982). *A guide to curriculum development in social studies.* Hartford, CT: Author.

Goodlad, J. (1984). *A place called school: Prospects for the future.* New York: McGraw-Hill.

Hertzberg, H. W. (1981). *Social studies reform, 1880–1980.* Boulder, CO: Social Science Education Consortium, Inc.

National Council for the Social Studies. (1987). *Survey of opinions of NCSS members.* Washington, DC: Author.

National Governors' Association. (1986). *Time for results: The governors' 1991 report on education.* Washington, DC: Author.

National Institute of Education. (1976). *Current issues, problems, and concerns in curriculum development.* Washington, DC: Author.

Sizer, T. R. (1984). *Horace's compromise: The dilemma of the American high school.* Boston: Houghton Mifflin.

Wronski, S. P., & Bragaw, D. H. (Eds.). (1986). *Social studies and social sciences: A fifty-year perspective* (Bulletin No. 78). Washington, DC: National Council for the Social Studies.

Chapter Two

Cognitive/Disciplinary Position
Socialization Position
Individualization Position
Process Position
Eclectic Position

Alternative Positions in the Social Studies

A range of time-tested curricular positions for teaching the social studies has emerged from the enduring conflict in the field. Once they understand the valid interests of others, effective teachers must discover their own directions.

The meetings held to review the early work of the social studies department heads at the district's 12 secondary schools had gone reasonably well. However, there was little discussion; in fact, many of the participants seemed a bit apathetic. But coordinator Mary Ellen R. was not overly concerned, because she was counting on real engagement once the positions were described and debated.

General sessions were scheduled on a fortnightly basis to discuss the five positions identified in Chapter 1. All secondary social studies teachers in the district were encouraged to attend. Key elementary school teachers, coordinators of other departments, and representative parents also were invited. All invitees received a solemn promise that no session would last more than two-and-a-half hours. The invitations noted that the order of the presentations was not significant, but participants were "strongly encouraged" to attend the entire series.

COGNITIVE/DISCIPLINARY POSITION

Ray J. volunteered to describe and defend the *cognitive/disciplinary position*. Ray had entered teaching rather late in life. He had a doctorate in history and had been an historian for the county because he liked working in the archives. But he wanted more direct contact with people. Therefore, with a very modest amount of professional training, he became certified and was assigned to the academically elite high school in the district. Ray was a successful teacher in a variety of settings, but his "pride and joy" were his two sections of Advanced Placement American history.

Ray began his presentation:

> I firmly believe that the primary function of the social studies is to develop the rational powers of each student through a systematic encounter with history, geography, or one of the social and behavioral sciences. Together teachers and students can engage in a search for truth and understanding about the social, cultural, legal/political, economic, and psychological factors that make us human. That is, they can study the "big" ideas—the generalizations, concepts, principles, and methods of knowing from the social disciplines of knowledge.

ASIDE TO THE READER: Ray's opening statement is packed with important ideas. Read it again, and think about it carefully. What is history? What is geography? What are the social and behavioral sciences? How do these domains of knowledge differ? Having been introduced to this issue in Chapter 1, have you thought about the significance of these differences? What does Ray mean by students and teachers embarking together on a search for truth and understanding? What are generalizations? Concepts? Principles? Methods of inquiry? Obviously these are weighty and difficult questions. Many scholars spend their entire lives studying them, and when they report their beliefs on these matters, they fully expect other scholars to disagree with them. Despite the disagreement and the complexity of these issues, however, these considerations are vitally important, and a teacher of the social studies should develop a reasoned view about them.

FIGURE 2.1
Adler's Essentials of Basic Schooling

The Same Course of Study for All

	Column One	Column Two	Column Three
Goals	Acquisition of Organized Knowledge	Development of Intellectual Skills —Skills of Learning	Enlarged Understanding of Ideas and Values
	by means of	by means of	by means of
Means	Didactic Instruction Lectures and Responses Textbooks and Other Aids	Coaching, Exercises, and Supervised Practice	Maieutic or Socratic Questioning and Active Participation
	in three areas of subject-matter	in the operations of	in the
Areas Operations and Activities	Language, Literature, and The Fine Arts	Reading, Writing, Speaking, Listening	Discussion of Books (not Textbooks) and Other Works of Art and Involvement in Artistic Activities e.g., Music, Drama, Visual Arts
	Mathematics and Natural Science	Calculating, Problem-Solving, Observing, Measuring, Estimating	
	History, Geography, and Social Studies	Exercising Critical Judgment	

The three columns do not correspond to separate courses, nor is one kind of teaching and learning necessarily confined to any one class.
Source: Reprinted with permission of Macmillan Publishing Company from THE PAIDEA PROPOSAL: AN EDUCATIONAL MANIFESTO by Mortimer Adler. Copyright © 1982 by Institute for Philosophical Research.

Ray correctly assumed that his audience had considered these issues previously, so he hurried on. In defense of the cognitive/disciplinary position, he recommended that his colleagues read a powerful paperback by Mortimer J. Adler, *The Paideia Proposal: An Educational Manifesto* (Adler, 1982). Ray noted that this text was general (it examines the total K–12 curriculum, including the social studies) but nevertheless was concise, clear, and convincing. In particular, he referred the group to Adler's summary of the essentials of basic schooling (see Figure 2.1), adding that it contained all they needed to know about curriculum and instruction in the schools.

Ray spent a few moments in "Socratic questioning" to ensure that his audience understood Adler. It was reasonably clear that they did. Next, he provided three examples of books that discuss the cognitive/disciplinary position in the social studies:

Social Studies and the Social Sciences (American Council of Learned Societies and National Council of the Social Studies, 1962)

Structure and the Social Studies (Lowe, 1969)

Social Studies and Social Sciences: A Fifty-Year Perspective (Wronski & Bragaw, 1986)

Challenge shone clearly on the faces of his audience, but Ray wanted to make one other point: Most of the secondary school "reformers" of the 1980s (except, interestingly, many leaders in the social studies) were promoting some form of the cognitive/disciplinary approach. He noted that the department heads had spent a good deal of time reviewing some of the more "moderate" of these critics. However, Ray recommended that they read some of the "conservatives," particularly Chester Finn, Diane Ravitch, Eric Hirsch, and William J. Bennett (Finn, Ravitch, & Fancher, 1984; Hirsch, 1987; Bennett, 1987; Ravitch, 1985; Ravitch & Finn, 1987).

Using an overhead, Ray projected the outline of the social studies content for the senior high school recommended by former education secretary Bennett (see Figure 2.2), adding, "This is exactly the program I want to implement in my classroom." Unlike Bennett, however, who urged the same program for all, Ray conceded that it was quite inevitable and reasonable that others would disagree and that these individuals should be permitted to make their own well-informed decisions.

At this point, a lengthy discussion ensued. Here are some of the major issues:

Q: This position may be OK for the intellectually elite, but most students (and some teachers, for that matter) just aren't interested in becoming practicing scholars. Studying the "big ideas" of the disciplines is very hard work, and it requires a lot of motivation. Isn't this position hopelessly idealistic and, at the same time, elitist?

FIGURE 2.2
Cognitive/Disciplinary Conception of Grades 9–12 Social Studies

Western Civilization (9th Grade)

A general survey history of Western civilization from its beginnings through the early 20th century. Includes a brief review of classical Greece and Rome; the development of Judaism and Christianity; Medieval Europe; the rise of Islam; the Renaissance; the Reformation; the age of commerce, colonies, and discovery; the Enlightenment; the American and French Revolutions; the industrial revolution in England; nationalist and unification movements in 19th century Europe; Western imperialism; and great power conflicts before World War I. Knowledge of geography should be emphasized. Writing assignments are made throughout. Where possible, students also discuss literary and artistic developments. *One year, required.*

American History (10th Grade)

A general survey history of the United States from European discovery through the present. Includes attention to colonial America; the American Revolution and the rise of American political thought; the Federalist and Republican eras; westward expansion; Jacksonian democracy; manifest destiny; slavery; the Civil War; Reconstruction; the Gilded Age; immigration; America as a world power; the Progressive era; American participation in World War I; the 1920s; the Depression; the New Deal; the United States in World War II; and domestic issues since 1945. Knowledge of geography should be emphasized. Writing assignments are made throughout. *One year, required.*

Principles of American Democracy (11th Grade, 1st Semester)

Fundamentals of American government and political philosophy. Includes attention to the structural development of the modern federal and state governments; the idea of federalism; the rise of the party system; electoral, legislative, and judicial processes; the presidency; and the history of major constitutional questions, especially as treated by the Supreme Court. Includes detailed study of the intellectual roots of the American Revolution and Declaration of Independence, the Philadelphia Convention and the Constitution, and readings from *The Federalist,* the Gettysburg Address, Martin Luther King, Jr.'s "Letter from Birmingham Jail," and other speeches and essays by American statesmen. Writing assignments are made throughout, and a research paper is required. *One semester, required.*

American Democracy and the World (11th Grade, 2nd Semester)

American democracy and its rivals in the 20th century. Topics covered may include World War I; revolution in Russia; the rise of totalitarianism; World War II; the postwar reconstruction of Europe; the Soviet Union as a world power; the United Nations; Israel in the Middle East; NATO, the cold war, the Truman Doctrine, and containment of communism; the Warsaw Pact and the partition of Europe; the Korean War; the Sino-Soviet rift; the Berlin blockade and airlift; the Cuban missile crisis; Vietnam; detente and arms control; the United States and the Soviet Union in the Third World; democracy as a goal of American security, trade, and foreign aid policy; and political conditions today in Europe, the Middle East, Africa, Latin America, Asia, and the Soviet Union. Writing assignments are made throughout, including a research paper. Students should become familiar with the contemporary world map and changing political boundaries since 1945. *One semester, required.*

Source: From *James Madison High School: A Curriculum for American Students* by W. J. Bennett, 1987, Washington, DC: U.S. Department of Education. Reprinted by permission.

RAY: No! Every learner is worthy of an encounter with these disciplines, and nearly every learner is intellectually curious. Only a tiny percentage of severely or profoundly handicapped youngsters are incapable of or uninterested in serious intellectual activity. If a given child seems "turned off" by the world of ideas as drawn from the social disciplines, all he or she needs is a good teacher. If you really want to talk about elitism, I'll tell you what it is: Elitism is deciding in advance that *some* kids are rational, others are not; that only *some* learners are capable and motivated. Now *that's* elitism.

Q: But wait—intellectual activity is not the only important aspect of life. It's not even the most important. Physical fitness, emotional well-being, aesthetic appreciation and judgment, personal integrity or active moral standards, ability to get and hold a job, social commitment, and so on are just as important—and probably more so. These things constitute the social studies. Isn't this cognitive/disciplinary stuff one-sided? Aren't the social problems that engulf us, such as crime and violence, the result of deficits that have little to do with cognition or the intellect?

RAY: Quite so. But you are making two fundamental errors in your reasoning. First, the school is not the only educational agency or institution in our society—in fact, it isn't even the most important. For example, for most of us families are far more significant. Joining the family are a host of individual and social activities and organizations that help to educate: churches, peer groups, the workplace, media, sports, travel, recreational reading, and so on. One of the major problems of schools, especially the social studies, is that we teachers are willing to take on the functions that legitimately belong to others in the educational process. To be sure, some of these added functions are forced on us. But regardless, we have much too much to do and, as a result, don't do anything well. Further, we raise false expectations that set us up for failure. The social studies curriculum ought to concentrate on what it can do effectively, on what other educational institutions are willing to have it emphasize—intellectual development.

The second, and closely related, fault in your logic is that many social studies teachers try to plug gaps unfilled not only by other parts of society but by other parts of the school. Let me illustrate. Undoubtedly we have a serious substance abuse problem in our society and in our schools. But *if* the schools try to resolve this issue at all, then the health curriculum and maybe the science, physical education, and home economics curricula, plus the extra-class activities program, should deal with the problem, *not* the social studies curriculum. However, social studies educators seem to be clamoring to add drug abuse education to their curriculum. We are well intentioned, but in the process we neglect our essential function, which no other department or activity is equipped to do: to systematically study history, geography, and the social sciences. I hate to say it, but we social studies types are trendy, faddish, all-encompassing, and thereby inefficient and ineffective.

Q: Look, even if I could buy your argument that intellectual development is or ought to be the prime function of the social studies, I would reject the notion that studying the social disciplines is the way to develop thinkers. I'll tell you why. Studying the disciplines leads to rote memorization of facts and isolated details that are promptly forgotten by even the best students as soon as the exam is over. In this position the teacher, the book, or whatever tells the student what to know. Then the student regurgitates this stuff to the teacher in order to pass the test and get on to more important things. Besides, the disciplines are, by definition, conservative—slow to move. Our world is on fire; we can't afford to have our young people sit around contemplating their navels. We need action-oriented problem solvers. Studying the disciplines leads to supporting the status quo at a time when great changes are needed. Besides, we have tried this cognitive/disciplinary approach for many years, and it just doesn't work for most people. If you want to develop thinkers, teach problem solving directly. Give students the opportunity to solve *real* problems, ones that cut across the musty disciplines of knowledge.

Let me add a postscript to this issue. As we all know, even the scholars in the disciplines are hopelessly divided. They sharply disagree about which disciplines to teach and, even within the same discipline, they dispute the matter of which content or which ideas to emphasize. Historians battle with political scientists, anthropologists fight with economists, and no two historians agree on the fundamental purposes of the field or about which historical content is the most worthy. So, even if I accepted your idea about the role of the social science disciplines in developing the rationality of students (which I do not), we still would be left with tough decisions. If scholars can't agree on the curricula of their fields, how can teachers, school boards, or anyone else make sound decisions?

RAY: You've crowded many issues into your question/speech, but no, I don't agree at all. And, at the risk of offending you, I must say that you just don't understand what disciplinary study is all about. Evidently—and unfortunately—you've never had the opportunity to engage in scholarly activity. Studying history, or any of the other disciplines included in the social studies, is by its very nature exciting and even radical activity. Nothing is taboo except indoctrination. Nothing is taken for granted. Every source, every authority, every idea, every hypothesis, every "fact" is assessed and evaluated. There is no inculcation, no filling of heads with details, no authoritarianism in a respectable disciplinary classroom or learning laboratory.

Further, yes, I would argue that it is desirable, and often necessary, to draw on scholarship outside the field being studied. But the traditional—and ever-changing—disciplines of knowledge provide the best framework we have for developing our rational powers. Each discipline has a unique set of concepts, generalizations, principles, and methods of inquiry that need to be critically examined. The world of scholarship is organized around these domains. Think about it. One cannot fully use a library unless one understands the nature of these disciplines, because library collections are organized around them. That is why I'm particularly fond of introductory secondary school courses that help students discover for themselves the unique characteristics of the disciplines included in the social studies.

Sure, there are disagreements within and among the social disciplines. This is the way it ought to be. In value-laden areas, this is inevitable. But the scholars aren't going to be the curriculum decision makers for the schools. As our social studies coordinator said this summer, individual teachers must make these decisions. I am, however, pleased that you made this point. It demonstrates the rich intellectual ferment that is a necessary feature in the study of the disciplines.

This list of questions could be expanded almost indefinitely. We hope the discussion has given you a sense of the conflict generated by the cognitive/disciplinary position and urge you to raise your own concerns and try to respond to them as an advocate of the position might. We think these "questions and answers" will provide you with the foundation for highly valuable interaction with your colleagues.

SOCIALIZATION POSITION

Helen C. volunteered to lead the discussion of the *socialization position.* She had been an effective middle school teacher of social studies for 25 years and chaired a department for the last 5. Although she majored in sociology in college, she had a rich preparation in many of the social disciplines. She read widely in many sources, especially those emphasizing contemporary events. Proudly considering herself a "real professional teacher," she spent an almost equal amount of her energy on community affairs and had been elected to numerous leadership roles in her region.

Helen began the session by explaining that socialization is a useful but tricky and complicated concept used heavily in sociology. It basically means the process by which one learns the knowledge, behavior, and attitudes or values needed to function effectively in society. Helen continued,

We all belong to a variety of groups—social, political, economic, and so on. We are parts of families, clubs, associations, government units, institutions, occupations or professions, racial groups, ethnic groups, age groups, gender orientation groups, and on and on. Some are formal, some informal; some are primary, some secondary; some are vitally important to us on a daily basis, some are not. Our happiness, productivity, security—indeed, our fundamental worth as individuals—are profoundly influenced, if not determined, by the groups to which we belong and by our effectiveness in playing our various roles within these groups. Thus, from my perspective, the primary focus of the social studies—in fact, of the entire school—should be to help students play the roles they must or ought to play now and in the future.

This is the major rationale for career education, future studies, ethnic studies, women's studies, many forms of global studies, values education, parenting education, family studies, environmental studies, law-related education, and dozens of other movements that have played a major role in the development of social studies education. However, the most common label for socialization in the social studies has for many years been, "citizenship education."

In fact, social studies education was actually called "citizenship education" in New York State for a number of years. Moreover, as previously noted, most curriculum theorists in social studies education assert that citizenship education is the *raison d'être* of the field. It has been called the "primary overriding purpose," the "centering concept," and the "ultimate justification" [Superka & Hawke, 1980, p. 579].

Given the popularity of the idea, at least among the leaders in the field, it is not surprising that there have been a large number of content guides and curriculum statements reflecting this position. The proponents, coming from all shades of political thought, vary enormously, but all agree that socialization ought to be the primary goal.

Identification with social groups has an influence on all social roles.

Helen proceeded to illustrate the socialization position by reading a passage from the curriculum efforts of Project SPAN (Superka & Hawke, 1980):

> We believe that if social studies is to contribute more fully to the development of effective participants in our society, it must be refocused on how most people participate in that society—how they spend their time and where they put their energy. Most people's social lives revolve around seven major roles: citizen, worker, consumer, family member, friend, member of various social groups, and self. . . .
>
> Each of the seven roles defines an important area of social life in which nearly all persons participate. As citizens, we participate in various ways and at several levels in the political (governmental and public policy) aspects of society. The roles of consumer and worker define our essential relationships in the marketplace and workplace, respectively. The two major areas of close interpersonal relationships are defined in our roles as family members and friends. We are also members of various social groups, among them racial groups, ethnic groups, gender (male-female) groups, age (child, adolescent, adult) groups, religious groups, and socioeconomic classes. Our identifications and relationships with the latter groups can have a significant influence on the previous five roles and on the last role: self. . . . This role is at the core of all the other social roles, but it also involves something beyond these roles.
>
> While each role defines a distinct set of relationships and activities, all seven roles are interrelated. . . . Social studies programs can highlight both the distinctiveness of and the interrelationships among the seven social roles. . . .
>
> We believe that these social roles can serve as a useful framework for determining what to teach in social studies and why to teach it. We also believe that social roles, in combination with knowledge about student development, can provide a concrete oasis for organizing curriculum content and learning activities in social studies.*

Helen then recommended a book by R. Freeman Butts, *The Revival of Civic Learning: Rationale for Citizenship Education in American Schools,* for a lengthier and more complete justification for the citizenship/socialization approach in general terms (Butts, 1980) and Fred Newmann's action-oriented work *Education for Citizen Action: Challenge for the Secondary Curriculum* (Newmann, 1975). Then she continued,

> Unfortunately, we don't have time to go into any of the details concerning the specific forms of socialization the curricula have taken in secondary social studies. [Actually, many of these forms have appeared in other subjects and levels as well.] But before I sit down, I want to provide you with a written list of sources of information and some comments on a few of these forms that particularly interest me [see Figure 2.3]. I will be happy to answer questions or accept comments if you like.

Helen's list of socialization criteria and recommended sources generated a great deal of stimulating discussion. One colleague vigorously defended

*From "Social Roles: A Focus for Social Studies in the 1980s" by D. P. Superka and S. Hawke, November/December 1980, *Social Education*, pp. 577–585. Reprinted with permission.

FIGURE 2.3
Selected Socialization Curricula

___

Global Education

There are numerous organizations and groups that aim to influence or educate teachers about international education in the curricula of schools and colleges. The American Forum is especially noteworthy. This group is a recent merger of Global Perspectives in Education , Inc., and the National Council on Foreign Language and International Studies. It is a private, nonprofit organization "committed to increasing American competence in world affairs."

The Forum recently produced a brief but very valuable list of resources to help educators prepare for the "challenges of national citizenship in a global age" (*Publications Catalog*). You can write to the American Forum, 45 John St., Suite 1200, New York, NY 10038 for assistance.

Law-Related (Civics) Education

As the heading suggests, this curriculum movement recently has been broadened from its original focus on just legal issues to a wider political socialization emphasis. Again, there are a great many groups, projects, individuals, and agencies anxious to inform and otherwise assist educators in this area. However, many people speak of the "big six": the Children's Legal Rights Information and Training Project; the Constitutional Rights Foundation; Law in a Free Society; the National Street Law Institute; Phi Alpha Delta Law Fraternity International; and the Special Committee on Youth Education for Citizenship, American Bar Association.

To select one "best" source is difficult, but I am willing, in the spirit of helping busy teachers, to provide a "jumping- off" place for the serious student of this movement by recommending the American Bar Association effort (1155 East 60th St., Chicago, IL 60637). This organization offers many valuable publications, including *A Directory of Law-Related Education Projects* and *Update,* an award-winning journal published three times a year. The ABA project maintains direct ties with most of the national, state, and local efforts. At the very least, get on the ABA's mailing list.

___

environmental studies as a major focus of the social studies, arguing that this topic provided an ideal context for integrating the science and social studies programs of the middle school. Another spoke forcefully about the importance of concentrating on values education.

The following questions were raised:

1. Isn't this issue really moot? That is, isn't socialization unavoidable and inevitable? The "people," the real ultimate curriculum authority, demand that we try to produce good Americans, good workers, and so on.
2. Isn't socialization in the social studies really indoctrination? If not, how can the two be separated? One teacher immediately hollered out with great conviction, "Political socialization of the proper and only acceptable kind in our society is *not* indoctrination. It's just the opposite: It is the preparation—socialization, if you wish—to be an outspoken, thoughtful critic of government and other institutions at all levels and at all times." Another teacher asked, "What's wrong with indoctrination? I think it is necessary

Multicultural Studies

Even when the area of international education or global studies is largely excluded from this category, as I have done above, it is so diverse that even the name is controversial. *Black studies, ethnic studies, multiethnic studies, urban studies, intergroup relations, human relations, religious studies,* and many other titles are used. Nevertheless, I recommend three especially valuable sources: Pamela and Iris Tiedt, *Multicultural Teaching: A Handbook of Activities, Information and Resources* (Tiedt & Tiedt, 1986); James Banks, *Multiethnic Education: Theory and Practice* (Banks, 1987); and the regularly distributed catalogs from the Anti-Defamation League of B'nai B'rith, 823 United Nations Plaza, New York, NY 10017 (*Human Relations Materials*). These three sources suggest literally countless ideas for teachers.

Women's Studies or Gender Studies

One of my personal disappointments as a "socializationist" in curriculum is that women's studies have not really caught on in the secondary schools. In the 1970s the movement appeared to be healthy and growing, but I would reluctantly characterize the movement as being in a state of decline at this time. One reason for this state of affairs is that a good many people have the mistaken impression that prejudice and discrimination based on gender is a problem that American society has already solved. To convince any fair-minded reader that this is not true, I strongly recommend *Modern Sexism: Blatant, Subtle and Covert Discrimination* by Nijole V. Benokraitis and Joe R. Feagan (Benokraitis & Feagan, 1986).

Further, I suggest two valuable recent sources on women's studies in higher education, where the movement is very much alive and well: *Women's Studies in the United States* by Catharine R. Stimpson with Nina Kressner Cobb (Stimpson & Cobb, 1986) and *Gendered Subjects: The Dynamics of Feminist Teaching,* edited by Margo Culley with Catherine Portuges (Culley & Portuges, 1985).

I hope these three books will stimulate you to consider adding more gender issues to your teaching. I can personally testify that such activity is extremely worthwhile and highly satisfying.

---

and desirable, though there are acceptable and unacceptable degrees of it. Think of a continuum with 'gentle' indoctrination on one end and 'authoritarian' indoctrination on the other."

3. Private schools in our society were created in part because their founders wanted to socialize their young people in certain ways. Our government at all levels has supported this practice. But should it? Is socialization acceptable in private schools but not in public or government-operated schools? If so, why?

4. Is socialization in the social studies appropriate *if, and only if,* the socializers

Represent widely accepted, mainstream views?

Are controlled by a truly democratic process?

Are representative of and fair to the "full range of acceptable views?"

Agree with me?

5. Is socialization acceptable in some parts of the school but not in others, that is, in vocational education but not in social studies? In extracurricular clubs, athletics, and so on but not in "academic" subjects, including the social studies?

6. Is socialization appropriate in some aspects of the social studies but not in others? For example, is occupational socialization all right but not political socialization?

7. Even if socialization is desirable or inevitable, we cannot socialize for all of the roles people play. How does one determine the appropriate roles? For example, is it desirable to socialize for parenthood but not for membership in a particular political party? How does one choose from among the wide range of alternatives?

8. Is socialization really in conflict with the cognitive/disciplinary position? That is, can't one accept parts or all of both positions?

Ray J. jumped in at this point and declared that the two positions were flatly contradictory: "You can't be engaged in a search for truth and assist people in finding appropriate roles and statuses at the same time."

At this point, it should be obvious that socialization is a time-honored, enduring, and popular position in the social studies. Is it yours? Why or why not?

INDIVIDUALIZATION POSITION

Terry S. spoke for the *individualization position*. A student during the 1960s, he served in both the Peace Corps and the domestic VISTA programs. He had undergraduate and graduate concentrations in sociology and psychology. Terry was an extremely popular teacher/counselor in his middle school.

Terry began his presentation by noting that the individualization position also has been around for a long time and has its advocates today as it has throughout the history of the social studies. But he also suggested that the position probably does not have, and never has had, the number of proponents that the other four positions enjoy. Terry noted further that even many of the position's supporters admit that the approach really can't work in compulsory schools. These advocates suggest that a wide variety of alternative schools and nonschool types of educational experiences would have to be available, and such opportunities would have to be voluntary for the idea to become truly functional.

Terry continued:

The position has diverse roots: existential philosophy, some forms of organized religion, especially Eastern religions, the arts, "radical" social sciences, humanistic psychology, even the drug culture. As you would expect, coming from all of these "ideologies," there are sharp differences within the broad category.

Terry was warming to his subject and spoke with obvious conviction:

> What is the essence of the individualization position? Simply put, the heart of the matter is that each individual student must determine his or her own curriculum. There cannot be a single set of intentions or, for that matter, a single body of content or group of instructional procedures that will serve all students. Kids are different. Their schooling must be different. They, and only they, can know what they want and need.
>
> Who are schools for? Students, that's who! We constantly forget this fundamental truth. This curriculum development project is a waste if the object of schooling is to cram something down the throats of our students.
>
> I flatly reject the first two positions so eloquently argued. I don't want this taken personally, but I especially object to the socializationists. Schools must protect the child from socialization. I desire—no, *demand*—that schools nurture uniqueness, build self-esteem, and facilitate the unfolding of the individual.

Terry continued emotionally,

> Schools are actually propaganda machines. In the process, they are oppressive and repressive. Conformity is our overriding goal. Of course, we try to hide our intentions. We try to trick our students by saying, for example, "Let's discuss" when we mean "Answer my question in the prescribed way." "Think about it" means "You had better agree with me." "This is really a significant point" equals "It's on the test." The translation for "I'll wait for you" is "Shut up, or else."
>
> Our students fully understand that we are playing games with them. If they are generous, they just write this off as teacher doublespeak. But it is dishonest, and it encourages our students to engage in similarly deceitful conduct. It is wrong! It is immoral! It must be stopped!

The group was dismayed by the intensity of Terry's remarks. Terry was aware of the stir he was creating, and he delighted in it. However, he continued, more calmly:

> I can't recommend a particular social studies educator for this position, but I do encourage you to read a couple of "generalists," beginning with the "radical" perspective of the classic *Deschooling Society* by Ivan Illich [Illich, 1970], which states that we must deschool, or deinstitutionalize, learning. Indeed, Illich argues that not only must education be controlled by students if durable learning is to occur; the only way to ensure that this happens is to give the learner complete power over the *when, how,* and *where* of his or her learning.
>
> From a legal or constitutional perspective is the provocative *Compelling Belief: The Culture of American Schooling* by Stephen Arons [Arons, 1983]. Arons insists that state-operated schools have become monopolistic and authoritarian despite the intent of the framers of the U.S. Constitution and that students and their families need to exercise their right to participate in curriculum decision making. Interestingly, Arons specifically attacks deschooling.

Both of these works are great books, but don't expect them to provide you with a blueprint for the curriculum. For obvious reasons, none of the individualists will do that. We can see from just these two examples that we individualists are very diverse. However, we think there are some ideas common to all of us. Here are three such foundational beliefs.

First, all individuals are inherently curious; they want to know. They have a basic need to understand, to learn, and, unless our institutions rob them of this curiosity, they realize this fact about themselves.

Second, people learn and retain only what interests them. We can't force people to learn what serves no need for them. Internal, intrinsic motivation is vital.

Third, institutions, to the extent that they restrict individual freedom, are antithetical to learning. Schools—nearly all of them almost all of the time—try to limit freedom. Thus, they block learning.

It's true that we disagree about whether or not compulsory schools can ever be reformed to the point where they promote learning for most, if not all, students. I continue to believe that they can.

For over an hour, people argued with Terry. At first he seemed to be alone in his views, but he more than held his own. Indeed, some group members began to soften their opposition. One teacher admitted that she would like to be the kind of teacher Terry was, but the "system" wouldn't let her.

At this point, Terry showed some hint of compromise as his fundamental optimism came through:

Wait, you don't have to be the flaming radical I am to be influenced by this position. Many significant ideas in secondary schooling are based, at least in part, on this curriculum ideology [see Figure 2.4].

If you want kids to learn, find ways to give them as much control over their learning as the system will permit. It is equally true that really successful teachers—those who are continually growing and developing—also need to be in control of their education. While very unhappy with numerous aspects of the so-called

FIGURE 2.4
Means for Achieving the Individualist Ideology

- Alternative schools
- Apprenticeships
- Coaching (as a teaching technique) (Adler, 1982; Sizer, 1984)
- Cooperative learning
- Cross-age or peer tutoring
- Electives
- Home schooling
- Independent study
- Magnet schools
- Minicourses

- Optional public or community service for students
- Parkway-type schools
- Seminars
- Student membership on policymaking bodies
- Travel experiences
- True individualization (versus self-pacing or "mastery learning")
- Vouchers and tax credits

reform movement of the 1980s, I am encouraged about the progress toward improving the status of teachers. A few of these developments are:

- Teacher centers in which staff development is planned, operated, and controlled by teachers.
- Differentiated staffing plans in which staff members decide on the rank and corresponding duties for which they apply.
- School-based planning in which teachers truly share in decision making in schools.
- Professional development sites at which new and seasoned teachers work together to become more effective professionals.

Do you understand the ideas contained in Figure 2.4 and in the above list? What would you add to these lists, that is, what student-centered activities have you experienced that seem to work?

It was time to leave, but Terry said he wanted to give more advice, for which he credited two of his heroes, Jonathan Kozol (1981) and Doris Lessing (1962). These authors recognize that it is extremely difficult to achieve individualization when faced with so much pressure to conform. Lessing suggests leveling with one's students as follows:

> You are in the process of being indoctrinated. We have not yet evolved a system of schooling that is not a system of indoctrination. We are sorry, but it is the best we can do. What you are being taught here is an amalgam of current prejudice and the choices of this particular culture. The slightest look at history will show how impermanent these must be. You are being taught by people who have been able to accommodate themselves to a regime of thought laid down by their predecessors. It is a self-perpetuating system. Those of you who are more robust and individual than others will be encouraged to leave and find ways of educating yourself—educating your own judgment. Those who stay must remember, always and all the time, that they are being molded and patterned to fit into the narrow and particular needs of this particular society.*

Do you know any teachers like Terry? Twenty years ago, there were a lot more of them than there are today. Such teachers can have a profound impact on the schools in which they teach. Do you want to be this kind of teacher? If so, what makes this position more appealing than the others? Do you want to have teachers like Terry in your department? We encourage you to think seriously about this enduring position.

---

*From *The Golden Notebook* by Doris Lessing, 1962, New York: Simon & Schuster. Copyright © 1962 by Doris Lessing. Reprinted by permission of Simon & Schuster, Inc.

PROCESS POSITION

Gene D. presented the *process position*. Gene had successfully taught ninth-grade social studies for 15 years and commanded respect throughout the district. He also taught "Introduction to the Social Sciences" at the local community college. This opportunity provided him with needed extra income and gave him an added perspective that he claimed was very valuable in teaching his high school students.

Gene began his presentation by distributing copies of the following passage from Louise Berman's *New Priorities in the Curriculum* (Berman, 1968), which had profoundly changed his view of curriculum:

Any carefully designed conception of curriculum must be based upon some basic assumptions about man. The search by this author for a view of man led to a description of him as a process- oriented being. Process orientation, as used in this book, means that a person has within his personality elements of dynamism, motion, and responsibility which enable him to live as an adequate and a contributing member of the world of which he is part.

It is our assumption that all persons are process-oriented to some degree and can become more so through planned experiences. Furthermore, it is our assumption that it is "good" for persons to have some degree of process orientation. What are some of the characteristics of such persons?

These persons are ongoing, growing, developing beings. They may achieve stability under certain circumstances, but inertness, staticism, unthinking behavior, or rigidity seldom characterize them. . . . Highly process-oriented persons do not stagnate under the debris of nonessential or nonmeaningful aspects of life. They see purposes to the degree of change and movement they plan for themselves.

Process-oriented persons have broad rather than narrow or restricted fields of vision. They utilize a wide range of intellectual skills such as comparing, analyzing, elaborating, and evaluating in solving problems.

They can be compared to generators as opposed to parasites, to reconcilers of conflict rather than avoiders of conflict. Process-oriented persons are interested in the possible rather than the probable. They are often spontaneous as opposed to deliberate. When challenged to carry out worthwhile tasks, they are zealous, extravagant, and fervent at times as opposed to being continuously moderate.

They tend toward internal integrity rather than outward conformity, toward friendliness to difference and newness as opposed to hostility to the unknown. They pace their activity in a variety of ways rather than in one way.

Their mistakes arise from the premature rather than the after-the-fact sharing of ideas, from errors of commission rather than omission, from overestimation rather than underestimation. When a mistake has been made, persons with a high degree of process-orientation tend toward bravery rather than cowardice. They are more likely to anticipate rather than regret: they possess more foresight than hindsight and live in terms of prospect rather than retrospect.

Process-oriented persons are concerned with the moral and ethical. They are interested in the past as it relates to the present and future. Their energies are not dissipated into a variety of areas; rather they are channeled to promoting causes which are identified as worthwhile or to bring about constructive changes within fields of knowledge, institutions, or persons. In the attempt to be change agents, such persons have acquired judgmental skills and the capacity to resolve conflict both within themselves and the situations of which they are part.

In summary, process-orientation characterizes persons who are able to handle themselves and the situations of which they are a part with adequacy and ease. Such persons are the contributors to, as well as the recipients of, society's resources.

All educational institutions, particularly the school, should give high priority to fostering process-concepts in today's children and youth, if personal adequacy and individual responsibility are among the major goals of school programs.*

Following the reading, Gene pointed out to the group that Berman identifies and describes eight essential processes that should form the core of the curriculum in all subjects, including the social studies:

- Perceiving
- Communicating
- Loving
- Decision making
- Knowing
- Patterning
- Creating
- Valuing

Gene readily admitted that not all "processors" agree with Berman's list of skills. Some emphasize the cognitive and others the affective. Further, he said that many critics of the process position deny that the position is distinct; rather, they claim that it is a form of eclecticism because it contains parts of each of the three positions we have examined so far. But Gene contended,

I believe the process position has a unique focus because knowing *how* is the essence as opposed to knowing *what*. I reject socializing or individualizing kids, or filling their heads with particular content, as legitimate ends. Instead, I want my students to learn and practice the skills and competencies they will need in life. If I had to use one phrase to describe my curriculum, it would be *critical and creative thinking*.

We advocates of the process position may disagree with one another on the details, but we agree on at least two propositions. First, no specific body of content is crucial or essential. Yes, the teacher will need to teach some content to give the processes a vehicle or context, but one choice is probably no better than another. What interests the teacher or interests the learner(s) are good criteria for determining the selection of the content. Another criterion, which has been promoted by Lawrence Metcalf, is to select the most controversial content possible. Metcalf recommends those areas that are frequently taboo— what he calls the "closed areas"—both because they are significant and be-

*From *New Priorities in the Curriculum* by L. M. Berman, 1968, Columbus, OH: Merrill. Reprinted by permission of Louise M. Berman.

cause they are inherently motivating [Hunt & Metcalf, 1955]. Besides, we processors believe that learning any particular body of content is inefficient because it is quickly forgotten, readily outdated, and usually nontransferable to the real world of daily living.

On the other hand, we firmly believe that direct study of the "how-to's" is vitally important. Learning the processes doesn't just happen as an automatic outgrowth of studying even in very interesting classrooms. For example, simply conducting classroom discussions will not necessarily lead to improved discussion skills. The same is true for using maps or the library, conducting interviews, and so on. We teachers must give sustained, systematic attention to skills with ample opportunities for practice if they are to be learned and retained.

What specific processes am I talking about? There are many valuable sources that describe and illustrate the teaching of processes in the social studies. My bibliography includes Hunt and Metcalf [1955], Beyer [1979], Chapin and Gross [1973], Lee, Ellenwood, and Little [1973], Kurfman [1977], and Carpenter [1963].

Before I close, I would like to share a graphic with you that I consider extremely valuable [see Figure 2.5]. It is the work of Professor Barry Beyer [Beyer, 1979, p. 29]. While I think this one diagram eloquently speaks for itself, permit me to direct your attention to a couple of major points.

First, what I call *process* Beyer calls *inquiry*. Beyer thinks inquiry has three major components: a knowledge base; an affective base, including feelings, attitudes, and values; and a process base, which is the steps or procedures involved in inquiring.

Second, Beyer emphasizes that thinking/ inquiring is very complex. Scholars have conceptualized it in many different ways. Further, while the three components are identified separately, they are not distinct. The thinking act molds the three bases into an almost indistinguishable whole; no one part operates with complete independence from the others.

When you consult Gene's references at the end of the chapter, you will find that some of the authors are not "pure processors." In our judgment, however, they all have this orientation. Also, see Chapter 5 for a valuable hierarchical list of cognitive and affective skills.

His presentation concluded, Gene put aside his notes, satisfied that he too had generated intense discussion.

To summarize, the major issues raised in the discussion were as follows:

1. Should processes be *the* priority? Will they be better understood in other contexts?
2. Can processes really be taught effectively? (There was particularly intense discussion over whether one can teach creativity.)
3. Is process-oriented education appropriate for some courses or parts of courses at certain levels but not for others?
4. How would one go about organizing and planning a coherent process-oriented curriculum?

FIGURE 2.5
The Process of Inquiry

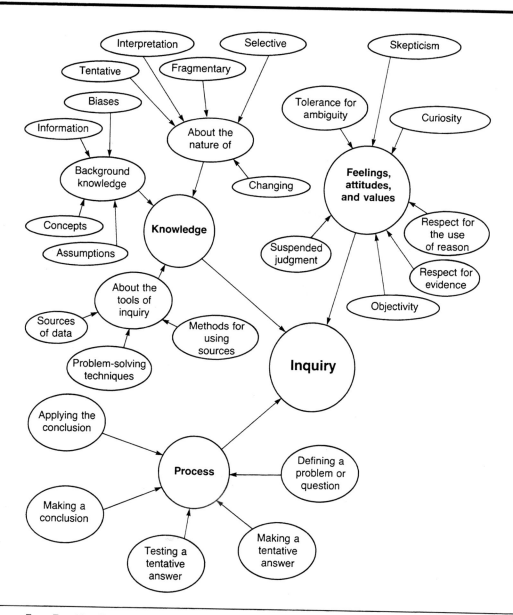

45

5. Shouldn't processes simply be a part of other positions? (Gene vehemently said no, because when this is attempted, the processes get short shrift.)

Think about these matters. Talk about them. Try your hand at planning and, if possible, teaching a lesson with a process or inquiry approach. If the lesson is successful, how about trying a unit? A course? The entire program? A process—or critical-thinking or problem-solving focus—is a very popular idea in fields such as mathematics and writing. How would it be valuable in social studies?

ECLECTIC POSITION

Nancy S. rose to address the group on the *eclectic position.* An avowed "eclectic" herself, Nancy had been a fine teacher for many years as well as a widely recognized leader in the social studies education profession. She had been elected and appointed to numerous important positions on the local, state, and national councils for the social studies.

Nancy opened her presentation:

You should realize that I am proud to be an eclectic—that is, I unabashedly accept much of what has been said by *all* of our colleagues in these meetings. If all, rather than just one, of the four broad positions previously described appeal to you, and you want to include all or some of them, you too are probably an eclectic. If this is the case, you and I have, at the same time, selected the most common position among social studies teachers—and the most difficult one.

Since most of us do not consciously select the most problematic and troublesome philosophy to guide ourselves, I would submit that most eclectics are, unfortunately, members of this group by default. (This excludes you and me, of course.) They haven't really thought about the matter carefully. Instead, they follow the path of least resistance. When someone, anyone, makes an appealing case that they should attempt this or that in their classrooms, these unthinking eclectics try to do it without carefully considering the consequences.

This is a particularly important point. Permit me to elaborate. As should be obvious by now, proponents of each of the four positions we explored earlier sharply disagree about many things, but they are united in their contempt for the eclectic. They argue that being, or trying to be, all things to all people has gotten the social studies in big trouble. Eclectics, they say, raise false expectations for the results of social studies instruction. Moreover, they insist that these four positions are mutually exclusive; that is, they believe that it is flatly illogical, for example, to try to be a cognitive disciplinarian and a socializationist at the same time. In the first case, students are searching for truth and beauty without predetermined results. In the second, the teacher is guiding the students to accept certain "truths," behaviors, and attitudes. Similar conflicts exist, they assert, between any two of the positions.

Although I reject these arguments, I do find them seductive. In fact, for years I insisted that it's impossible to be a thoughtful generalist. But gradually I have changed my mind. Still, I recognize that it is extremely difficult to be an eclectic and maintain equilibrium. I admit that students and teachers in eclectic class-rooms are in grave danger of being confused and conflicted or of drifting aimlessly. No one ever said curriculum development was easy!

However, to return to the crucial element of my argument, I insist that aspects of all four of the previously described positions are necessary. None of the four is sufficient by itself; they are intrinsically related. To accomplish one, you must attend to the others. Balance is desirable—no, essential—if maximal growth and development are to occur. An effectively socialized individual necessarily has strong feelings of self-worth; hence teachers must try to socialize and individualize simultaneously. While attempting to achieve that delicate equilibrium, we must encourage the study of the traditional domains of knowledge and get students engaged in their independent (but controlled!) search for truth.

At the same time, we must attend to the development of cognitive, affective, and psychomotor skills and processes. You just can't have one without the other. Flexibility—shifting foci based on the teacher's judgment regarding the greatest need at a given moment both for the group and for the individuals within it—that's what teaching is all about. Furthermore, that's what the community—those who pay our salaries—demands.

Countless lists of eclectic goals in the social studies exist. State and national bodies as well as local groups have produced such enumerations. My handout provides just one example from the revision of the social studies program in New York State [see Figure 2.6]. Obviously New York has provided more specific objec-tives for the various courses included in the program, but they are all keyed to these 19 broad goals, which I urge you to study carefully. Note that there are examples of goals from each of the four positions we have discussed.

Now, as many of you know, I don't think states should provide details on curriculum or instruction, because I believe these decisions should be made at the classroom level. But I do think it is legitimate for states to provide broad purposes as guidelines. I think the ones provided by New York make sense. How could a teacher omit any of these broad goals and still do an adequate job? I don't think this would be possible.

Before I close, let me recommend some reading. First, there is a highly persuasive statement on the eclectic approach to the curriculum of the entire secondary school in *Horace's Compromise: The Dilemma of the American High School* by Theodore Sizer [Sizer, 1984]. Another valuable source, which will provide a useful demonstration of how difficult it is to resist being an eclectic, is John Goodlad's *A Place Called School: Prospects for the Future* [Goodlad, 1984]. Goodlad spends a good part of the book rigorously attacking the all-purpose secondary school—and then he endorses exactly that! It appears that his justifi-cation for this "inconsistency" is that one, "the people" should control the curric-ulum, and two, they "want it all." As you know, I think individual teachers should control the curriculum in their classrooms, but Goodlad is worthwhile reading. Finally, there is a fine short piece in our field, published by the AFT, called *Education for Democracy: A Statement of Principles* [American Federation of Teachers, 1987]. If you read only one statement on the eclectic position in the social studies, let it be that article.

FIGURE 2.6
Goals of the 7–12 Social Studies Program in New York State

Upon completion of the social studies program, the student will be a person who can demonstrate the ability to make rational and informed decisions about economic, social, and political questions confronting himself or herself, the society, and the interdependent world. Such decisions will draw upon the lessons of history and the social sciences.

Specifically at the end of the 7–12 social studies program, students will be able to:

1. Describe and analyze major historical factors in the development of the United States
2. Explain the historical, economic, social, and political roots of major cultures of the world
3. Participate as informed citizens in the political and economic system of the United States
4. Demonstrate knowledge of the increasing international connections of nations and cultures that make them interdependent within the various global systems
5. Explain the fundamental similar ties and differences among major economic, social, and political systems and how these systems operate in an interdependent world
6. Explain how societies teach individuals to live within specific value systems
7. Discuss the nature and effects of change on societies and individuals
8. Analyze the effect of geography on the development of cultures
9. Empathize with the values that guide the behavior of people from different cultures
10. Value the principles and ideals of a democratic system based on the premises of human dignity, liberty, justice, and equality
11. Compare the rights and responsibilities of citizens of the United States with the rights and responsibilities of citizens of other societies
12. Gather information by listening, reading, and observing with accuracy and comprehension
13. Organize, analyze, and interpret information in all forms
14. Communicate information clearly and effectively in both oral and written form
15. Demonstrate the skills that enable people to participate reasonably in a democratic society
16. Use the vocabulary of social studies in appropriate contexts
17. Identify important social studies ideas and methodologies and apply them to new information and experiences
18. Explain the relationship between social studies learning and learning that takes place in other disciplines and other institutions
19. Demonstrate an enhanced perspective of self as one who benefits from the human experience and who participates in and contributes to that experience

Source: From *Leaders Guide: N.Y.S. Social Studies Program, K–12,* 1987, Albany, NY: Bureau of Social Studies Education, New York State Education Department. Reprinted by permission.

Nancy's talk had excited all of the "purists" in the room. The antieclectics insisted that:

1. A teacher must have priorities. We cannot do it all.
2. If you accept two or more of the positions we have explored, you have no basis for determining your priorities.
3. Guidelines such as the broad list of goals from New York (Figure 2.6) create confusion for students, teachers, and their communities.

Nancy sat down, clearly delighted with the thoughtful and provocative discussion that permeated the room.

Summary

In this chapter, we explored five broad and pervasive positions on developing the social studies curriculum. (See the "Decisions! Decisions!" section that follows for a brief summation of the five positions.) We hope we tempted you to "buy" the one that offers the most attractive balance of idealism and realism from your perspective. We think the disagreement over the positions is one of the most exciting aspects of being a social studies teacher. At the same time, we also recognize that the conflict can be intimidating, especially for the beginning teacher.

Decisions! Decisions!

Are you a *cognitive/disciplinarian*? Are you interested primarily in the development of your students' rational powers through systematic encounters with the social disciplines of knowledge?

Are you a *socializationist*? Will you center on helping your pupils identify and successfully perform in the various roles they must or should play?

Are you an *individualizationist*? Is your main direction toward helping each student feel appropriately good about himself or herself?

Are you a *processor*? Is your most important job to teach your students how to think, value, and act accordingly?

Are you a deliberate, purposeful *eclectic*? Do you believe you must try to answer all of the above questions positively?

How certain are you? How do you know your choice was the right one? What would cause you to change your mind? (Changing one's mind certainly is legitimate!)

References

Adler, M. J. (1982). *The paideia proposal: An educational manifesto* (p. 23). New York: Macmillan.

American Bar Association. (1986). *Directory of law-related education projects.* Chicago: Author.

American Council of Learned Societies and National Council of the Social Studies. (1962). *The social studies and the social sciences.* New York: Harcourt, Brace & World.

American Federation of Teachers. (1987). *Education for democracy: A statement of principles.* Washington, DC: Author.

Anti-Defamation League of B'nai B'rith. (1987). *Human relations materials for the school, church and community.* New York: Author.

Arons, S. (1983). *Compelling belief: The culture of American schooling.* New York: McGraw-Hill.

Banks, J. A. (1987). *Multiethnic education: Theory and practice* (2nd ed.). Boston: Allyn & Bacon.

Bennett, W. J. (1987). *James Madison High School: A curriculum for American students.* Washington, DC: U.S. Department of Education.

Benokraitis, N. V., & Feagan, J. R. (1986). *Modern sexism: Blatant, subtle and covert discrimination.* Englewood Cliffs, NJ: Prentice-Hall.

Berman, L. M. (1968). *New priorities in the curriculum.* Columbus, OH: Merrill.

Beyer, B. K. (1979). *Teaching thinking in social studies.* Columbus, OH: Merrill.

Bureau of Social Studies Education. (1987). *Leaders guide: N.Y.S. social studies program, K–12.* Albany, NY: New York State Education Department.

Butts, R. F. (1980). *The revival of civic learning: Rationale for citizenship education in American schools.* Bloomington, IN: Phi Delta Kappa Educational Foundation.

Carpenter, H. M. (Ed.). (1963). *Skill development in the social studies* (33rd Yearbook). Washington, DC: National Council for the Social Studies.

Chapin, J. R., & Gross, R. E. (1973). *Teaching social studies skills.* Boston: Little, Brown.

Culley, M., & Portuges, C. (1985). *Gendered subjects: The dynamics of feminist teaching.* Boston: Routledge & Kegan Paul.

Finn, C. E., Ravitch, D., & Fancher, R. T. (1984). *Against mediocrity: The humanities in American high schools.* New York: Holmes & Meier.

Goodlad, J. (1984). *A place called school: Prospects for the future.* New York: Mc-Graw-Hill.

Hirsch, E. D. (1987). *Cultural literacy: What every American needs to know.* Boston: Houghton Mifflin.

Hunt, M. P., & Metcalf, L. E. (1955). *Teaching high school social studies:*

Problems in reflective thinking and social understanding. New York: Harper & Row.

Illich, I. (1970). *Deschooling society.* New York: Harper & Row.

Kozol, J. (1981). *On being a teacher.* New York: Continuum.

Kurfman, D. G. (Ed.). (1977). *Developing decision-making skills* (47th Yearbook). Washington, DC: National Council for the Social Studies.

Lee, J. R., Ellenwood, S. E., & Little, T. H. (1973). *Teaching social studies in the secondary school.* New York: Free Press.

Lessing, D. (1962). *The golden notebook.* New York: Simon & Schuster.

Lowe, W. T. (1969). *Structure and the social studies.* Ithaca, NY: Cornell University Press.

Newmann, F. (1975). *Education for citizen action: Challenge for the secondary curriculum.* Berkeley, CA: McCutchen.

Publications Catalog. (1987). New York: American Forum.// Ravitch, D. (1985). *The schools we deserve: Reflections on the educational crises of our times.* New York: Basic Books.

Ravitch, D., & Finn, C. (1987). *What do our 17-year-olds know? A report on the first national assessment.* New York: Harper & Row.

Sizer, T. R. (1984). *Horace's compromise: The dilemma of the American high school.* Boston: Houghton Mifflin.

Stimson, C., & Cobb., N. K. (1986). *Women's studies in the United States.* New York: Ford Foundation.

Superka, D. P., & Hawke, S. (1980, November/December). Social roles: A focus for social studies in the 1980s. *Social Education,* 577–585.

Tiedt, P. L., & Tiedt, I. M. (1986). *Multicultural teaching: A handbook of ac-*

tivities, information and resources (2nd ed.). Boston: Allyn & Bacon.

Wronski, S. P., & Bragaw, D. H. (Eds.). (1986). *Social studies and social sciences: A fifty-year perspective* (Bulletin No. 78). Washington, DC: National Council for the Social Studies.

Chapter Three

Learners and Learning

The curriculum—content and instruction—is aimed at learners who are diverse yet share many characteristics, including identifiable aptitudes, developmental stages, and learning styles.

WHO ARE THE LEARNERS? PROFILES OF THE ADOLESCENT

It did not take Barbara, a first-year teacher, long to determine that Jim was not the brightest student in the sixth-period social studies class. However, her worst fears were not realized until she checked Jim's cumulative record and talked to a guidance counselor. Jim, a high school senior approaching his 20th birthday, was attending school partly to satisfy his probation requirements. He was an ex-convict and, consistent with research, a poor reader. How was Barbara to work with Jim?

At the time, her fledgling teaching philosophy resembled Charlie Brown's assessment of his teacher's approach: "Teaching is a lot like bowling. You just roll the ball down the middle and hope you hit most of the pins." Unfortunately, many students, like lonely seven-pins, miss the teacher's message.

One day, while mulling over how she would work with Jim, Barbara decided to visit the school's vice-principal. The vice-principal was engaged in a lengthy discussion with a student. This usually meant a problem, for he was not one to mince words. Eventually the student emerged from the office, and the teacher was astonished to see that it was Mike—senior class valedictorian, football captain, and class president.

When Mike was out of earshot, Barbara was about to ask the vice-principal of what transgression Mike could possibly be guilty. Anticipating her question, he replied, "No problem. Mike simply wanted permission to make a college visit. It's a pleasant change to talk to a student who is not in trouble." Barbara understood his enthusiasm. Having Mike in class certainly was a pleasure. But it was also a mixed blessing. Mike often asked questions to which she had no answer. Every time Mike began squinting, she felt her insides start to quiver despite her bachelor's degree from a creditable college and her sincere desire to teach history. How was she to teach both Jim, her "turtle," who had learned about citizenship by serving time in a state penitentiary, and Mike, the "bluebird," who would get his citizenship education by "learning and doing"—not to mention the other 150 students who made up her social studies classes?

Barbara decided to take her problem to one of her colleagues, a seasoned teacher who had taken her under his wing. (The term *mentor* has been used to describe such a person.) His response was simple: "Welcome to the real world!"

While our descriptions of Jim and Mike may sound stereotypical, these students represent real people in real classrooms. Yet, like all students, Jim and Mike are special. Sizer rather simplistically labels this characteristic "diversity" (Sizer, 1984, p. 35). Barbara's job, like all teachers', is to develop a teaching philosophy adaptable to individual differences among learners, an admonition that goes back at least six centuries (Corno & Snow, 1986, p. 605). However, this is a monumental task considering the following demographic data:

* The divorce rate doubled between 1973 and 1983.
* Approximately two in every five children born between 1973 and 1983 will spend at least part of their youth in single-parent homes.
* More than half of all mothers with school-age children and over a third of those with children under age 3 now work outside the home.
* One out of three schoolchildren lives in a home headed by only one parent or relative.
* The average number of children per family dropped from a high of 3.8 in 1957 to 2.04 in 1984, not only further constricting the natural nuclear family but expanding legal kinships through divorce and remarriage (*Education Week*, 1984, pp. 18, 19).

Like Jim and Mike, students differ in several ways: academic ability, physical size, race, socioeconomic class, maturity, and so on. But as Sizer points out, they do have a "commonality"—they are adolescents, caught between what Erik Erickson labeled "childhood" and "adulthood." Identity is a big concern for them ("who [or what] am I?"). Even the athletically inept student—the last one chosen for pickup games in elementary and junior high school—may imagine himself making a two-handed, over-the-head slam dunk in the NBA championship game. Or the quiet, dreamy girl may fantasize about liftoff as backup pilot for a space shot. Working through these fantasies helps sustain these youngsters as they emerge from their cocoons into butterflies.

The onset of adolescence creates severe role confusion for most individuals. For example, few of us were "destined" to be teachers, though we may have played school on the porch steps with younger siblings or heard from others that we were "born teachers." We try out roles just as we try on a new pair of jeans or tennis shoes. At first the new roles may feel uncomfortable, like the new jeans or shoes. We have to scuff up the shoes and wash the jeans before they feel "right" to us. Similarly, we must adapt to roles as we try to find a "fit." If "class leader" does not fit us, maybe "class clown" will. If "beauty queen" seems unattainable, perhaps "most outgoing" will suffice for now. Thus, we should be neither surprised nor exasperated when we find students acting differently from day to day.

A dated but poignant film called *Brian at 17* follows a 17-year-old in his daily activities. Brian is self-centered, "cool," wants to be above the rules, is disenchanted with and disconnected from school, feels isolated (age segregated), and lacks self-discipline. The classic line in the film is Brian's explanation of why he did not inform his mother that he was going to stay out all night: "I knew I was OK." To Brian, this logic is foolproof—if things had gone wrong, his mother would have been notified.

Abraham Maslow (1962) depicted the need most pressing at this stage of one's life as a psychological—the need for *love*.

Maslow's Needs Hierarchy

Self-actualization
Esteem
LOVE
Safety
Physiological

As in Brian's case, peer pressure plays a highly significant role during this stage. Growing autonomy, including autonomy from one's parent(s) or guardian(s), is necessary but scary. Peers represent what sociologists refer to as *significant others* or *referents*—those with whom we identify and compare ourselves. Love of others is highly valued.

From a review of six studies of adolescents, David deRosenroll (1987) concluded that there is a "correlation between the age of the adolescent and the degree of self consciousness" (p. 800). While this is not a particularly startling conclusion (most teachers learn this early on), the implications are worth noting. Consciousness of oneself appears to increase dramatically between childhood and early adolescence (middle or junior high school age) and decline after that.

Accompanying this "self consciousness" is a developing "other consciousness," which leads early adolescents to become more aware of others' "normal" and "nonnormal" behaviors. Concerns include physical appearance (e.g., fuzz on the upper lips for young males; figure development for females), dress codes, TV, and so on. Moreover, adolescents at this stage tend to be extremely critical of others. Many a parent or guardian has wrung his or her hands when a teenager headed for school in an outfit better suited to a rock concert or picnic. Wearing a sweatshirt with a colorful logo on an 85-degree day may seem terribly out of place to the parent or guardian, but it's just right to the adolescent.

The point is that these adolescents, with their myriad changes in physical appearance, mood, and clothing, are the social studies teacher's responsibility. What makes them ready to learn?

READINESS TO LEARN SOCIAL STUDIES

Readiness to learn is based partly on adolescents' developing consciousness. Several factors are believed to influence development of consciousness:

- Change in thought processes from concrete to early formal operations (see Figure 3.1)

FIGURE 3.1
Piaget's Stages of Mental Development

Stage	Onset	Typical Activities
Sensorimotor	Birth	Perception, recognition, means-end coordination, lack of objective reality
Preoperational	1–2	Egocentric thought
Preconceptual	2–3	Perceptual dominance
Intuitive	4–5	Comprehension of functional relations, symbolic play
Concrete operational	6–7	Invariant structures of classes, relations, numbers, reversibility in thought
Formal operations	11–12	Generality of thought
	14–15	Propositional and hypothetical thinking

Source: From PIAGET'S THEORY OF COGNITIVE AND AFFECTIVE DEVELOPMENT, Third Edition, by Barry J. Wadsworth. Copyright © 1984 by Longman Inc. Reprinted with permission.

- Physical and emotional changes related to puberty
- Changes in social relations, especially with peers
- Degree of parental affection and support (deRosenroll, 1987, p. 801)

The first factor—change in thought processes from primarily "concrete" to "formal" operations—is described in the work of Jean Piaget (1964). Based on Piaget's research, it can be argued that most secondary school students, and an increasing percentage of middle or junior high school students, should be functioning at the formal operational level; that is, most middle and secondary school students should be able to perform certain higher-level intellectual tasks, or "operations" (Piaget, 1964, p. 176), including classification of similar objects, events, or data. They should be able to reason *inductively:* identify relationships between their actions, or others' actions, and events. For example, *given help* they might be able to represent a relationship between the spending habits of American consumers, government, and businesses and the resulting trade imbalances and debilitating deficit. In other words, they should be thinking critically.

Middle and secondary school students also should be able to reason *deductively,* that is, state and examine a syllogism such as the following:

If all persons carried guns (a Fourth Amendment right), our houses and persons would be safe.

John Smith carries a gun.

Therefore, John Smith and his house are safe.

In other words, adolescents' ability to think critically is related to the degree of *ego identity* (consciousness of self) they have attained. According to

Wagner (1987), the transition to formal operations occurs in middle adolescence (ages 13–15). For example, in middle adolescence students can determine combinations of elements, but the ability to perform operations that require proportionality (e.g., to analyze consumer spending, saving, and public debt) does not emerge until late adolescence.

The four factors involved in mental development that Piaget identified from his observations are: (1) maturation, (2) experience, (3) social transmission, and (4) equilibration (Piaget, 1964, 178). The first factor presupposes that our students—Jim, our "turtle," and Mike, our "bluebird"—will be mature enough (i.e., have a sufficiently developed nervous system) to learn the content we are to teach them. The second element assumes that our students will have both physical experience (to be able to represent ideas concretely) and logical-mathematical experience (to recognize what happens to objects on which certain actions have been directed). Third, students are assumed to have learned how to structure experiences logically. Finally, it is assumed that the three preceding factors have been brought into some equilibrium—a balance between discomforting information and prior experience.

Particularly important to Piaget's theories about development and learning is the notion that learning is possible only when there is "active assimilation"; an interaction between the student and the content; and the integration of "any sort of reality into a structure" (Piaget, 1964, p. 185). In other words, learning is dependent on the student's recognition of some structure in newly perceived information and reconciling that structure with structures already existing in his or her mind. This notion is reinforced in a study by Carnine (1990), based on Nobel laureate Gerald Edelman's research, which found that categorization and recategorization by the brain help learners make connections—find sameness between incoming stimuli and their environment. Thus, it is vital that teachers find ways to help students encounter new experiences, make some sense out of them, and then adjust the new experiences to past ones—no easy matter when we consider the content of the social studies! How, for example, can we help students to think critically, to "experience" and assimilate notions such as the electoral college, the multiplier effect, the Renaissance, rights (civil and procedural), and causation?

Aptitudes

Just as adolescents differ in terms of mental development (and, consequently, readiness to learn), they vary in aptitudes broadly categorized as (1) cognitive, or intellectual abilities; (2) affective, or personality characteristics; and (3) conative, or cognitive and learning styles (Corno & Snow, 1986, p. 606). Although these categories appear distinct, it is the combination of the three that influences educational performance and that must be viewed as developmental rather than static (see Figure 3.2).

It is also important to recognize that goals for schooling differ as well. Students (and their parents or guardians) have their individual goals or personal preferences about what is to be learned, just as society, through its

**FIGURE 3.2
A Schematic
Conception of Aptitude
for Learning in
Relation to Educational
Performance**

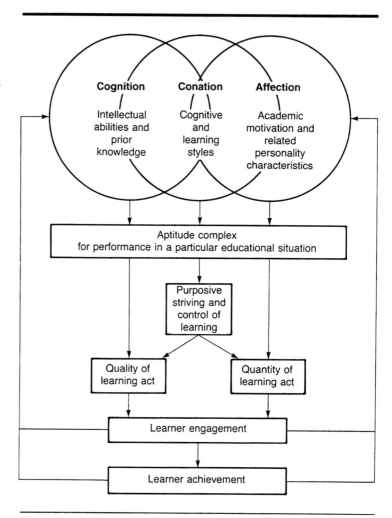

Source: From "Adapting Teaching to Individual Differences Among Learners"
by Lyn Corno & Richard E. Snow, in *Handbook of Research on Teaching,* 3rd
ed., edited by Merlin C. Wittrock. Copyright © 1986 by the American Educational
Research Association. Used by permission of Macmillan Publishing Company.

schools, sets goals for individual learners. Because the two sets of goals may
be quite distinct, further adaptation of the classroom learning environment
is needed; that is, the teacher must make the environment for learning
"nurtural" rather than merely "natural," a task that requires "moment-to-mo-
ment and month-to-month" decisions (Corno & Snow, 1986, p. 607). To do
so, the teacher must focus on students' aptitudes.

Cognitive (Intellectual) Ability. *Cognitive* or *intellectual* abilities (those
that determine the quality of learning) are the raw material of educational
performance. However, they build up over time as the learner encounters

different experiences; that is, although it sure helps to be "smart," experience helps us perform well intellectually. But intellectual abilities can be differentiated further, into verbal-educational, analytical, and spatial abilities. *Verbal* ability appears to develop during the schooling process, while *analytical* (or problem-solving) ability tends to prevail earlier, especially in informal learning situations (Corno & Snow, 1986, p. 616). *Spatial* ability appears to enable individuals to comprehend and manipulate two- and three-dimensional relationships that are particularly applicable to success in geometry, architecture, and mechanics.

While we teachers cannot directly transform all of our students into "bluebirds," we can adapt our classrooms to make them more "nurtural"; that is, we can help our students build on their prior experiences to achieve academic performances more consonant with their intellectual abilities. We can create classrooms in which students are academically engaged.

Student-Engaged Time. One person we know who has been out of high school close to 30 years remembers her sophomore social studies teacher beginning the first class of the semester with the question "Why might you be skeptical about an archeologist who presents you with an artifact dated 357 B.C.?" Most of us too probably can remember a class in which we found ourselves so engaged in an activity that we forgot to pack up our notebooks 10 minutes early preparatory to tearing out the door. This involvement by students has been labeled *student-engaged time:* "the amount of time that an average student is actively engaged in or attending to academic instruction or tasks" (Good & Brophy, 1987, p. 35). In other words, if during a 45-minute class students are actively engaged in learning the material being presented for 75% of the time, it can be said that the average student-engaged time is 33 minutes. The point is that if the teacher actively engages the intellectual abilities of his or her students, academic performance should follow naturally.

However, secondary school teachers may run into a student like Brian, the 17-year-old who stayed out all night to express his developing autonomy ("I knew I was OK") and need for love. Brian clearly was uninvolved in school. Typically he found a way to avoid school—staying home with friends and smoking pot while his mother, a single parent, was working. Another day it was flying kites, and still another day Brian was going around with his camera experimenting with techniques he was learning in a photography class.

Brian may represent a phenomenon familiar to experienced teachers, namely that older adolescent boys (grades 10–12) are "especially susceptible to anti-intellectual influences from peers" (Schneider & Coutts, 1985, p. 47); that is, students may work toward and accept poor grades to avoid critical comments by their peers. Despite the suggestion by a television show that aired in the late 1980s and early 1990s that intelligence and academic performance are not a handicap to peer relations (i.e., that "nerds" are all right), male students in particular are not expected to shine academically. This presents another obstacle for teachers. Note that Brian was not only intellectually but also *physically* uninvolved in school.

However, more often students are physically in school but mentally elsewhere. A hamburger ad some time ago depicted a student in math class daydreaming about hamburgers represented by math symbols. Without involvement, students are not very likely to learn what we want them to learn. (Nevertheless, they will learn *something*, though it may not correspond to our goals.)

Affective Ability.   A second category of aptitudes is *affective* ability (motivation and personality), which is linked to intellectual ability. Academic motivation and self-concept clearly influence academic performance. Even the greenest teacher can quickly identify the student who seems interested in learning. For example, the teacher might recall the junior high school student who, in his eagerness to be involved in a class discussion, somehow wriggled his legs through the slot in his chair between the back and the seat until his legs were supporting him and the chair was suspended in the air by his rear. Imagine his classmates' laughter when he tried to free himself to sit again! But he laughingly extricated himself with no loss of esteem, for his self-concept was as strong as his motivation.

Motivation.   When we stop to think about it, we know that we do not remember everything we have heard, seen, or read. Sometimes the content does not make sense to us. Possibly too we did not pay attention or were distracted.

Motivation suggests *involvement.* Many of us can remember wanting to learn word processing and diligently watching someone else hacking away at a computer only to forget everything we learned when we later tried it ourselves. Or, the first time we voted, we found that we didn't even know how to close the curtain in the polling booth despite the thorough description of the voting process our parents had given us. Many of us listened carefully and read everything available on the 1986 tax code, but not until we actually started to complete the new 1040A form did we realize how little we knew. In all of these cases, we were *motivated* but were not actively *involved.* This is the *affective*, or emotional, aspect of schooling.

Students' (and teachers') attitudes toward school (and toward one another) significantly affect learning. Probably we can recall someone who tried everything to avoid going to school: illnesses, injuries, missing the school bus. One of the authors vividly remembers his own child in third grade. The child could state how many years, months, and days remained until he was 16 and could legally drop out of school! School was that unpalatable. Fortunately, his fourth-grade teacher, aware of the affective side of schooling, involved him in school again. Later other things were equally influential, including "side payments"—the opportunity to play sports—which he would sacrifice if he were absent from school. Then not even a real illness would keep him out of school.

Equally important, we teachers need to help students become oriented toward learning rather than just toward performance; that is, we must help students perceive effort as a means to achievement, "to explore, initiate, and pursue tasks that promote intellectual growth" (Dweck, 1986, p. 1042). Students who tend to think in terms of long-range learning goals rather than short-run performance goals frequently are more malleable and adaptive. They will stay at tasks longer, for they are *intrinsically* motivated.

In contrast, students who are motivated to gain praise or avoid criticism are more prone to act on the basis of their perceived abilities. They will choose or stay with challenging tasks only so long as their confidence remains high (Dweck, 1986, p. 1043); therefore, they may need regular praise or encouragement from the teacher. Their learning thus tends to be *extrinsic* and dependent on encouragement, for at times they, like all of us, doubt their ability to perform tasks. Clearly, then, one aspect of learning (and, necessarily, teaching) is the need for students to be intrinsically motivated.

It is essential that we devise ways to motivate and to maintain interest in our social studies classes. The ideas are limitless, but we need to consider (1) how to establish an interesting mental set at the beginning of a lesson *(set induction)* and (2) how to maintain interest *(stimulus variation)*. Set induction could be as simple as the earlier question about the archeologist, a

Learning requires motivation, but how do teachers motivate all students?

rearrangement of the classroom, or a new bulletin board motif. Stimulus variation could range from something as obvious as pausing or changing the inflection in one's voice to switching the mode of presentation from teacher talk to student talk, using the chalkboard or starting a new activity.

Sometimes motivation can be achieved with what appears to be a stroke of genius. For example, after getting nowhere with a lecture to a class of 10th graders, one student teacher hit upon the idea of asking his students to imagine themselves writing front-page articles about Europe in the so-called Dark Ages for a class newspaper. Although their abilities varied, all the students outdid themselves to write what they thought were clever or sophisticated articles. Whether or not we agree with students' self-evaluations, at least we can agree that when students are awake and participating, the opportunity to learn is available.

Conative Ability.   The third category of aptitude is the *conative*, which literally means attempting or striving but here refers to cognitive and learning styles. Good and Stipek (1983) recognize the "potential hazards of overemphasizing" learning styles as a single dimension (i.e., ignoring their relationship to the intellectual and affective domains) but argue that learning styles have "important educational implications" (p. 29). Cognitive styles, "information processing regularities that develop in congenial ways around underlying personality trends" (Corno & Snow, 1986, p. 617, quoting Messick), are concerned more with how, rather than what, a person learns (Good & Stipek, 1983, p. 29). As with intellectual ability, these differences in learning styles may help explain educational performance.

Learning Styles

Like the other categories of aptitudes, learning styles can be further classified. Among the theories about learning style are conceptual level, psychological differentiation, conceptual tempo, and image encoding.

Conceptual Level.   One class period, students were involved in an activity that illustrates the conceptual framework we have identified as the cognitive-disciplinarian approach. The class had divided into groups and, simulating anthropologists, were studying a site map and the accompanying key identifying artifacts found at the site. Melissa, one group leader, said to her group, "Let's take the artifacts just as they are listed, item by item. So let's start with artifact number one, located in the square represented by H8 on the map." Methodically the group set about determining the identity of the people who had occupied this site. Suddenly Wes blurted out, "Nomadic!"

Melissa and the other group members cocked their heads, looked askance at Wes, and simultaneously hollered, "What?"

"They are nomadic people," Wes responded.

Smiling inwardly, their instructor noted to himself: Melissa is a concrete-sequential thinker; Wes is concrete-random. No wonder teaching is so hard!

To what was the instructor referring? To the fact that Melissa and Wes clearly represented differences in the way we think. For example, how many *F*s do you see in the following sentence?

> THE FINISHED FILES ARE THE RE-
> SULT OF YEARS OF SCIENTI-
> FIC STUDY COMBINED WITH THE
> EXPERIENCE OF MANY YEARS.

Most of you will see either three or six, though some of you initially will see four or five. What accounts for the difference in the number of *F*s you see? One learning theory, *conceptual level,* argues that those who see only three *F*s are "right-brain dominant," while those who see six *F*s can be considered "left-brain dominant." Right-brain-dominant people tend to see the whole and not the parts; left-brain-dominant individuals see the parts sequentially or linearly.

Look again and see if you can find all the *F*s now:

> THE F̲INISHED F̲ILES ARE THE RE-
> SULT OF̲ YEARS OF̲ SCIENTI-
> F̲IC STUDY COMBINED̲ WITH THE
> EXPERIENCE OF̲ MANY YEARS.

This learning theory borrows from psychology and medicine, especially with respect to research into brain damage and the roles the left and right hemispheres of the brain play in our thought processes (see Figure 3.3). Research with recovering stroke patients "substantiate[s] the notion of bicameral specialization—people with left-brain damage have difficulty completing verbal tasks and people with right-brain damage have difficulty handling nonverbal, spatial tasks" (Sanders & Sanders, 1984, p. 14). According to this theory, insights tend to come from the right brain while explanations emanate from the left.

Sol Linowitz, counsel to Xerox Corporation and at various times a consultant to U.S. presidents, illustrates the distinction between right- and left-hemispheric dominance as follows:

> I live by general principles, which give order to the detailed information that comes to my attention. As a lawyer, I need the details, the facts of the case—for the case, for the moment. But I don't learn by accumulating details; I learn by discovering the right focus on the subject. [In contrast, President] Carter was always looking for the specific, for the precise—and he would remember it: if you gave him an answer on one occasion, it had better be the same answer when the question came up again. He learned by gathering details and putting them together. . . .*

*From *The Making of a Public Man: A Memoir* (pp. 209–210) by S. M. Linowitz, 1985, Boston: Little, Brown. Copyright © 1985 by Sol M. Linowitz. Reprinted by permission of Little, Brown and Company.

FIGURE 3.3
Hemispheric
Specialization

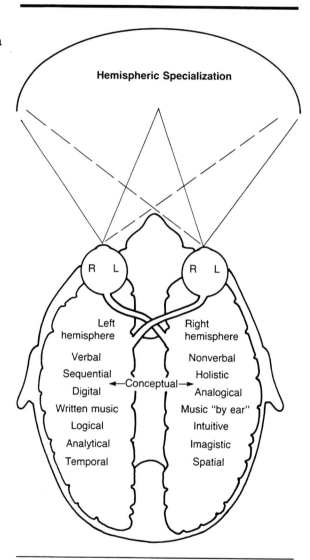

Source: From *Teaching Creativity through Metaphor* (p. 9) by
D. A. Sanders and J. Sanders, 1984, Boston: Longman.
Reprinted by permission of Donald A. Sanders.

From the above passage, we can see that Linowitz tends to be reflective
and analytical—in psychologist David Kolb's terms, an "abstract": or "right-
brain," thinker (Kolb, 1976). Former president Jimmy Carter, on the other
hand, appears to be a "concrete," or "left-brain," thinker, relying on his senses
and looking for specifics. Kolb would argue that all of us fall somewhere on a
continuum between the two extremes of "concrete" and "abstract":

Concrete — — — — — — — — — — — — Abstract
(Relying on senses)   (Reflective, analytical)

To Kolb's characterization of learning Anthony Gregorc (1979) adds two other dimensions, "random" and "sequential." The result is the matrix shown in Figure 3.4.

According to Gregorc's model in Figure 3.4, there are four types of thinkers:

1. *Concrete random:* makes intuitive leaps, employs trial and error, uses senses, and prefers independence
2. *Concrete sequential:* derives information through direct, hands-on experiences and prefers an ordered atmosphere, structure, and quiet
3. *Abstract random:* evaluates learning experiences as a whole and prefers reflection
4. *Abstract sequential:* is good with symbols and conceptual "pictures"; prefers to learn from authorities and vicarious experiences

Further, this theory suggests that most people fall into one or two of these modes. Thus, most teachers' instruction will adhere to the style most comfortable to them. Goodlad (1984) found that this is the concrete-sequential style. And typically this is the way social studies is taught.

"So what?" you might ask. The "so what" is that *inevitably there will be a mismatch between a teacher's style and a student's.*

Psychological Differentiation.   Another category of learning styles is *psychological differentiation.* This refers to *field dependence* and *field independence:* one's reliance on others versus one's reliance on oneself to learn. Like conceptual level (concrete-abstract continuum), psychological differentiation allows for "considerable within-person variation" (Good & Stipek, 1983, p. 31).

One student, when asked how she liked the way her teacher had taught a particular group lesson, bluntly replied, "I'd rather work alone." This student recognized that she was "field independent." Field-independent people

**FIGURE 3.4
Gergorc Model of
Thinking**

	Random	Sequential
Concrete	1	2
Abstract	3	4

Source: Adapted from "Learning Styles: Differences Which the Profession Must Address" in *Reading Through Content* (pp. 10–12), edited by R. Vacca and J. Meagher, 1979, Storrs, CT: University of Connecticut Press.

frequently are perceived as autonomous, impersonal, analytical, and even rude. In contrast, field-dependent people often are seen as warm, likable, and sociable and frequently rely on others for information. While researchers tend to ascribe these characteristics to individuals, there is evidence that such psychological differentiation cuts across cultures as well. For example, a hunting society may cultivate more autonomy and analytical skills than an agricultural society whose members value interdependence (Good & Stipek, 1983, p. 31).

In the context of schools and classrooms, we can infer that field-dependent students like working in groups, try to please the teacher, and prefer jobs that require social skills, such as social worker, teacher, or politician. On the other hand, field-independent students prefer working alone, seek more structure in what they are doing, perform better in mathematics and science, and choose careers demanding a theoretical and analytical orientation.

Given these variables, how is a teacher to "reach" all students? The obvious prescription is to use different teaching styles and activities during the course of the year. Clearly this is a big order for any social studies teacher, even the experienced, and too often we resort to rewarding styles that work *now* rather than *later* (Sternberg, 1990, p. 370). However, it is not necessary to *exactly* match styles with students; rather, we can capitalize on what Sternberg calls "points of entry" (p. 369) and help students move to another style.

Conceptual Tempo.   Jerome Kagan (1965, pp. 133–161) posited another dichotomy: one between "reflective" and "impulsive" thinkers, or *conceptual tempo.* To illustrate, imagine a class wherein the students tend to be active, waving their hands in the air and shouting out answers while the teacher tries desperately to get them to think about their answers before blurting them out. For example, Margaret, a student teacher, liked to pose questions that demanded higher-level thinking ("What if . . . " or "How else might this have happened?"). Her eighth graders seemed to be "off the wall," shouting out answers almost before she had framed her questions. Margaret, a reflective person, was ready to scream. Her students, in contrast, tended to be impulsive, a characteristic consistent with their developmental levels (Piaget, 1964). Obviously, a severe mismatch existed.

Now compare Margaret with a teacher who wants quick answers:

What were the dates generally given for World War II? Come on, now, class, you know the answer. Frank? Mary?

Right, what countries were involved initially in the war? You know this, class. Well? Sally?

Over what issues did these countries have a conflict? Let's go! You should have read about this last night. Carlos? Tina?

Our second teacher could be considered "impulsive," thereby matching styles with some students but likely causing frustration for other students who tend to ponder before answering—the "reflective" ones. Note especially the third major question the teacher asked ("what issues . . . ?"), which requires reflection.

Image Encoding. The teacher's task is complicated by the fact that we still know so little about how we think. For example, Karl Pribram (1983, pp. 29–40) suggests that information is encoded in the brain and parts encode the whole. Thinking involves mechanisms in the brain that organize the retrieval of information encoded and distributed in the brain. Pribram says, "[O]perations involved in thinking must invert the distributed memory into images—not necessarily visual images, but also kinesthetic/tactile, olfactory/gustatory and auditory/linguistic" (p. 36). Thus, according to Pribram, the teacher's job is to do two things: (1) communicate his or her own enfolded memory store to students and (2) engage students' enfolding/unfolding mechanisms that represent thinking.

More specifically, imagine trying to get students to learn a concept like balance of power or balance of trade. Learners who are visually oriented may close their eyes or look at the ceiling while trying to recall a mental picture of a balance and attach to it images of power or trade. Or you may recall asking someone to draw a picture of what that person was asking you to learn. Learners who are more comfortable with words—are "auditory/linguistic"—may move their lips or whisper as they try to verbalize what they are hearing. They hear something and enfold this information in some "word pictures" or "symbols."

To complicate this further, Pribram (1983, p. 37) has found that there are gender differences in terms of particular imaging. Males often are visual and kinesthetic, a trait more pronounced in elementary school. Females tend to be relatively auditory/verbal. More specifically, boys are predisposed toward objects, and their knowledge of objects is "gleaned by action." Girls tend to be biased toward persons and gain their knowledge through "nonaction"—by "tuning in" and suppressing motion (McGuinness, 1983, pp. 41–52). In other words, for boys language is a means to an end, while for girls language tends to become the end.

How do we as teachers handle such potential mismatches, especially in secondary schools, in which social studies teachers commonly are male? Or in middle and junior high schools, in which teachers more often are female? Our task is to help students structure their thinking. Therefore, it becomes imperative to find ways to structure our classes to accommodate our students' learning styles and to help them become more comfortable with other styles.

OTHER LEARNING THEORIES

Among the many theories that help explain learning are cognitivism, behaviorism, observational learning, and humanism.

Cognitivism

Simply put, *cognitivism* refers to the intellect and argues that learning is both genetic and environmental; that is, people have a central nervous system, glands, drives, capacities, and temperaments on which the environment acts. Cognitive psychologists such as Piaget, Gagne, Bruner, and Ausubel argue that we learn ("know" something) by acquiring, categorizing, and using information or, in terms of function, by observing and organizing information into a complex system. The key is processing and storing information, which sometimes is analogized to the computer's operations. Lefrançois (1985, pp. 90–91) illustrates this analogy by referring to inputs (sensory impressions) placed into short-term storage, then into short-term memory ("programmed operations"), and finally coded into long-term memory ("concepts" and "meanings") to become outputs.

Critical to placing information into long-term memory is the attention one gives to, or one's consciousness of, the information being received. "Encoding" of that received information must occur, and this requires giving meaning to the experience. Again using the computer analogy, long-term memory involves levels of processing (Lefrançois, 1985, p. 95) not unlike the "nesting" of which computer experts speak; that is, there is a hierarchical linkage to processing from the momentary, superficial recall to a complex of associated "nodes," "schema," "categories," or "subsumers."

Bruner, a leading cognitivist, emphasizes information processing, which involves abstractions (concepts) that are categorized into relationships—coding systems—which in turn would suggest classrooms wherein discovery learning would prevail. Teachers wedded to the process position introduced in Chapter 2 would tend to be attracted to this approach. In contrast, social studies teachers more attuned to the cognitive/disciplinarian position would be more comfortable with the theories of David Ausubel. Ausubel emphasizes expository teaching whereby students are engaged in meaningful verbal learning based on a cognitive structure that relies on relatively organized, hierarchical relationships among concepts.

Egan (1989, p. 457), however, challenges the computer analogy, arguing that "virtually nothing in human memory is stored in a stable condition over time." Rather, he argues, memory, the component necessary for learning, is vitally linked to imagination, the affect, which may be triggered by means of stories rather than such "procedural activities as problem solving, critical thinking," and so on, which often are "vacuous." Egan's position would appeal most strongly to social studies teachers who prefer the more traditional narrative history.

Behaviorism

Behaviorism assumes that behavior is

1. "Lawful" (suggests regularities) and subject to variability in nature

2. Observable, identifiable, and measurable

3. Adaptive and modifiable

4. Specific, discrete, and individualized

One view of behaviorism that enjoys varying degrees of popularity, especially for modifying behavior, is that of B. F. Skinner. Skinner emphasizes the notion of reinforcement:

Stimulus ⟶ Response ⟵ Reinforcement

In other words, we act in certain ways because we derive satisfaction from our responses to stimuli. In a school context, the teacher gives an assignment—the stimulus—which a (typically reluctant) student somewhat unexpectedly completes—the response—and the teacher praises the student—reinforcement.

The behaviorist theory suggests that a teacher can control the learning environment and students' behaviors by rewarding students' appropriate responses, thereby eliciting further (desired) responses from them. Alternatively, a teacher can reduce certain inappropriate behaviors by not responding to a student who, say, continually hollers out answers in class. These notions reflect the idea of *extrinsic motivation*—coming from without the student.

Skinner, however, believes that *intrinsic motivation* is a stronger and more durable influence on one's behavior than extrinsic motivation. A recent study (Story, 1986, pp. 86–90) seems to confirm this. Story's experiment attempted to determine what factors influence continuing motivation. Story found that if students perceive that they are able to perform a certain task, they are more likely to have subsequent interest in performing that task. Note that it is the students' perceptions of their own performances (intrinsic) more than the teacher's responses (extrinsic) that lead to a feeling of competence. Reinforcement comes from actually performing the tasks (inside) rather than from the teacher's praise (outside).

Another way to express this is "success breeds success." This implies that teachers need to be aware of students' capabilities and assign tasks that students will be able to perform. This does not mean "watering down" assignments; rather, it means manipulating assignments, creating situations in which students will succeed and build upon that success.

Observational Learning

"Copycat! Copycat!" is a taunt that can get under anyone's skin. No one wants to be seen as simply imitating another. Yet we are no longer startled to read about a rash of adolescent suicides, which clearly seems imitative behavior. So how do we explain the inconsistency?

Bandura (1986) and Bandura and Walters (1963) suggest that much of our behavior, including the enactment of sex roles, stems from observing others. Lefrançois (1985, p. 65) even recalls how his English setter learned how to imitate a basset hound, uncharacteristically baying and howling "very impolitely," after being left in a kennel with several dogs of that breed and the difficulty he had in trying to break his dog of this behavior.

Observational learning helps explain such behavior. This theory states that much of our learning involves modeling and reinforcement. The praise "good boy" or "good girl" given after a child imitates a desired behavior illustrates reinforcement. There is evidence that we tend to imitate (i.e., model and be reinforced for doing so) not only others' behavior but certain symbols. Consider the influence of television on our society, especially on clothing styles and even language.

Lefrançois (1985, p. 64) capsulized this theory into the following statements:

1. A great deal of human learning is a function of observing others' behavior.
2. Reinforcement encourages and maintains imitative behavior.
3. Principles of operant conditioning help explain observational learning.

The implications for teachers are similar to those identified under behaviorism: Modeling can be useful in the classroom, and direct reinforcement can influence the type and degree of modeling and extinguish undesirable behavior.

Humanism

One day eighth grader Malcolm Little, who stood near the top of his class, was alone with his English teacher, whom he greatly admired. Malcolm revealed that he wanted to become a lawyer someday. The teacher replied, not unsympathetically, "Malcolm, one of life's first needs is for us to be realistic. A lawyer is no realistic goal for a nigger." Malcolm recalled, "It was then that I began to change—inside"* (Haley, 1965, pp. 35–37). Years later, Malcolm Little became known as Malcolm X and a "Black Panther," an evocative description of a person who "aroused fear and hatred for the white man" as had "no man in our time" (Haley, 1965, p. ix). Malcolm X indeed had fulfilled a prophecy: to be somebody important.

Humanistic psychologist Carl Rogers (1969) might have explained the behavior of Malcolm X in terms of Malcolm's *self-actualization*, the emergence of his self as a result of private experiences and an inner direction. In other words, we learn to do things because of our uniqueness and our desire to become all we can. Malcolm Little could not become a lawyer, but he could become Malcolm X, a formidable black leader who challenged white society. He became what his experiences and sense of reality enabled him to become.

---

*Quotations from *The Autobiography of Malcolm X* (pp. 35–37) by Alex Haley, 1965, New York: Grove Press. Copyright © 1965 by Random House, Inc. Reprinted by permission of Random House, Inc.

Is there any doubt that a teacher influenced Malcolm X? All teachers influence students, for good or for ill, by their conscious or unconscious behavior toward them. Roy Williams (1972, p. 384) cites a poignant example:

> One day a child in the second grade drew a picture of a tombstone and put his own initials on it. Underneath he scrawled, "Sometimes I wish I was dead." The teacher's only response, in red, was to cross out *was* and to write in *were*.

Teachers have a profound impact on students' perceptions of reality and self-worth. Humanistic psychology would argue, then, that the most profitable approach to learning is to help foster in students a positive attitude toward the self, to care for students, and to offer a climate for learning that recognizes feelings and attitudes.

ASIDE TO THE READER: Given this cursory look at different learning theories, where do we stand? Which learning theory do we choose? Isn't a little ignorance a good thing? At least we would not be confused by competing theories of learning.

In this context, however, ignorance is not a good thing. We have an important responsibility for the students with whom we interact. Knowing our subject matter, the social studies, is necessary but not sufficient. Recall that earlier in the book we stressed that we as teachers are, of necessity, decision makers. We will have to make all kinds of decisions, often instantaneously, and it is better to be forearmed if we are to help our students to learn.

Theodore Sizer (1984, p. 151) wrote, "The only function of the teacher is to assist the student to learn. Any other kind of teacher performance is irrelevant. 'Did you teach a good class today?' is a miscast question. . . . ''* Instead, the question should be "Did your students learn what was expected of them and by them today?"

Summary on Learning

So how do we help students learn? Rather than attempt a lengthy section on diagnosing students' aptitudes, cognitive learning styles, motivation, and personality characteristics, we recommend that, as a starting point, you refer to Sternberg (1990), Carnine (1990), and Phi Delta Kappa (1980). Figure 3.5 summarizes the guidelines for adapting the classroom to meet the diverse learning needs of students.

FIGURE 3.5
Guidelines for Adapting Instruction to Learners

Social studies teachers have the obligation to:

1. Assess their students, especially in terms of developmental level, recalling that they are adolescents who suffer from role confusion and need self-esteem. It is particularly important to note students'
   a. Aptitudes
      (1) Cognitive (intellectual abilities)
      (2) Affective (motivation and personality)
      (3) Conative (cognitive and learning styles)
   b. Conceptual levels
      (1) Hemispheric dominance (left versus right-brain)
      (2) Concrete versus abstract
      (3) Gregorc's matrix
         (a) Concrete sequential
         (b) Concrete random
         (c) Abstract sequential
         (d) Abstract random
   c. Psychological differentiation
      (1) Field dependence
      (2) Field independence
   d. Conceptual tempo (impulsivity-reflectivity)
   e. Image encoding (Pribram, 1983)
      (1) Kinesthetic/tactile
      (2) Olfactory/gustatory
      (3) Auditory/linguistic
   f. Other learning theories
      (1) Cognitivism
      (2) Behaviorism
      (3) Observational (imitative) learning
      (4) Humanism
2. Structure learning environments to accommodate and help alter students' learning styles
3. Use a variety of methods (strategies) that involve different ways of thinking, i.e., adapt teaching to fit individual differences
4. Determine whether learning occurred (evaluation)

"SPECIAL" STUDENTS

It is becoming increasingly clear that many, if not most, of our notions about learning (and, correspondingly, about teaching) apply to students in general. However, we will encounter students who exhibit identifiable differences from the majority of our students, and these differences can pose problems for us.

The most difficult problem may be definitional. Terms and acronyms that were uncommon, if not unknown, less than a generation ago—gifted and talented, EMR, Option I or II, TMR, LD, PSEN, ESOL, PINS, at risk—are now part of every teacher's working vocabulary. More to the point, however, these terms represent individuals who populate our classrooms. Jim, the ex-convict we met at the beginning of this chapter, probably would be classified as "learning disabled (LD)" today, and likely it would have been evident much earlier in his schooling that he was destined to drop out of school ("at risk").

Let's look briefly at four classifications that might apply to some students in any school: gifted and talented, students with handicapping conditions, bilingual, and at-risk.

Gifted and Talented Students

Horowitz and O'Brien (1986, p. 1147) note that current estimates place from 3% to 5% of the American population into the "gifted" category. Note that these are just estimates. The typical criterion for classification as gifted has been an IQ of 130 and above, but this standard has been subject to increasing criticism. Today the primary focus tends to be on information-processing skills, especially "insight" or "selective encoding and combining of information that gifted and talented students demonstrate" (Horowitz & O'Brien, 1986, p. 1148). This measure looks at the way today's student population thinks rather than simply at IQs.

However, even this more recent criterion fails to satisfy many professionals, for it does not indicate whether giftedness is an isolated attribute or one that cuts across various domains. For example, Tina is obviously "gifted" in her ability to perceive relationships in math. But will this hold for social studies as well? Some researchers argue that yes, truly gifted students will show special information processing skills in multiple disciplines. To further complicate the matter, very little is known about how gifted and talented persons develop their gifts and talents—whether certain environmental opportunities nurture their abilities and whether current conditions must change if giftedness is to continue to develop (Horowitz & O'Brien, 1986, p. 1150).

For teachers, the problem becomes one of creating the appropriate environment for gifted and talented students and determining whether this environment must differ from that provided for other students. More specifically, does this mean "acceleration" (moving them into special groupings or changing them to a different grade level) or "enrichment" (offering them greater challenges within the current grade or classroom)?

It has been argued that all children should be treated as special, that enrichment should be offered to all students so that the gifted and talented will be accommodated in regular classrooms. In other words, we should offer all students the most challenging and stimulating learning experiences possible and treat all students as individuals; in that way, everyone will benefit. Others claim, however, that some students will not benefit from the enrichment because they are unable to learn what the more able—and, of course, the very small percentage of really bright students—can.

A more detailed consideration of this issue is beyond the scope of this text. We will simply note that *all* students will benefit from classes that are thought provoking and interesting.

Students with Handicapping Conditions

With the passage of Public Law 94-142, the Education of All Handicapped Children Act of 1975, came official recognition of the fact that millions of children suffer from disabilities that preclude their receiving the type of education enjoyed by the majority of students. The law was designed to address this situation. Two provisions were especially important: (1) All students with handicapping conditions were to be identified and (2) these students were to be placed in the "least restrictive [educational] environment."

These measures brought myriad problems, not the least of which was the identification and categorization of these students. An example is the category "learning disabled," or simply "LD," which has become a "catch-all" and consequently has experienced the biggest growth. The term "LD" has come to be viewed as a general, pervasive intellectual weakness. Often such students are "mainstreamed," that is, placed in regular classes with teachers whose training may not include working with special students. Commonly teachers who have LD students must seek out the help of special education or resource room teachers not only to prepare the individualized education plan (IEP) but to instruct students and test their learning.

However, research has begun to change focus, to "assessing partial or incomplete knowledge" (Brown & Campione, 1986, p. 1065)—that is, seeing LD students as lacking knowledge in specific domains rather than generally. This change in view could have significant social and educational consequences. One consequence is in terms of instruction, whereby "principles of naturally occurring instructional methods, repeatedly observed as being used by mothers with their children and master craftspeople with their apprentices . . . can be adapted to successful classroom instruction" (Brown & Campione, 1986, p. 1065). The significance of this for social studies teachers is that they can employ guided learning or cooperative peer interaction that "encourage[s] questioning, evaluating, criticizing and generally worrying about knowledge" (Brown & Campione, 1986, p. 1066), a topic we will cover in Chapter 6. This is the "stuff" of good teaching with *all* children: individualizing, guiding, fostering cooperative learning, and encouraging thinking. Moreover, it cracks some of the "mystique" of special education and enlists regular classroom teachers in teaching for greater learning.

One "fly in the ointment" has been the sharp division within the ranks of those dealing with LD students over the extent to which these students— indeed, *all* students with mildly handicapping conditions—can be taught in a general educational setting rather than being "pulled out" to receive instruction in resource rooms (Hallahan, Keller, McKinney, Lloyd, & Bryan, 1988, pp. 1–5; Viadero, 1988, pp. 1, 20, 21). More specifically, the issue over this

Regular Education Initiative (REI) is the extent to which the mildly handicapped can be "merged" into regular classrooms. A real concern for schools and teachers is to what degree LD students should be taken out of regular classrooms for special instruction ("pulled out"). Correspondingly, to what extent should provision be made for teaching LD students in regular classrooms ("merging")? For the regular classroom teacher, this imposes significant responsibilities: (1) to teach not only content but skills, (2) to aim instruction at and tolerate "difficult-to-handle" students, and (3) to find ways to compensate for the reform movement of the 1980s that stressed excellence and test scores in heterogeneous classes.

Again we can make the argument that good teaching is good teaching regardless of the audience, but it is necessary for the classroom teacher to make adjustments for the increasing numbers of students exhibiting individual differences.

"English as a Second Language" Students

Maria is warm, outgoing, and talkative when she babysits with her younger brothers and sisters. She lets her 3-year-old sister "help" her cook and makes a game out of it. But her teacher has never seen this Maria, only a withdrawn student who does poorly in her schoolwork. A less sensitive ESL teacher would see Maria as dull-witted and/or lacking in motivation.

Cummins (1984, p. 1) points out, "There has long been an unacknowledged relationship between bilingualism and special education as evidenced by the disproportionate numbers of immigrant and minority children 'deported' into special education classes and vocational streams in many countries." This is especially true for students for whom English is a second language. A large number of such students have been categorized as "learning disabled" on the basis of IQ tests and academic performance, typically reading scores. The percentage ranges from 2%, the federal definition of learning disabled, to 20% and, in some schools, up to 25%. The problem stems largely from misdiagnoses that allegedly illustrate test bias; that is, these students typically are tested and instructed through the majority language (English), so they do not perform well. And the number of students to whom this applies is soaring—the rate was over 60% between 1976 and 1986. Hispanics currently represent the largest minority population in the United States.

According to Cummins, however, given instruction in the minority language *all or part of a day*, these students will in time perform "in majority language academic skills as well as or better than equivalent students instructed entirely through the majority language" (Cummins, 1984, p. 150). The instruction would be equivalent, but in the minority language, until the students are ready for regular classrooms, at which point we can expect the same kind of performance we want from regular students.

A second remedy is for the regular classroom teacher to substitute a "reciprocal interaction model" for the more typical "transmission model of pedagogy" (Cummins, 1984, pp. 273, 274). In short, teachers will need to work with students—and students' families—on a more individualized basis rather than relying on the one-way instruction that often occurs in class-rooms. More longitudinal monitoring and greater interaction with the students' parents in home environments as well as with special education teachers will be required. This remedy is similar to one being proposed for at-risk students, discussed next. It means that regular classroom teachers—*we*—will have to extend our relationships with ESL students and abandon the typical mode of "telling." Again this puts a lot of pressure on the classroom teacher, but it suggests the role that will most strongly support learning regardless of the type of student.

At-Risk Students

Bill always sat in one of the back seats, never entered discussions, and tried to avoid at all costs answering a question directed at him. Fortunately, he and his teacher had an interaction—of sorts. Bill would write long poems on the backs of IBM answer sheets on major tests given in class. These poems were "stream-of-consciousness" pieces that revealed a lot about what he was think-ing. Bill's teacher fervently wished to get to know him so he could help Bill learn the material. But Bill chose not to reveal himself and eventually disap-peared from his teacher's memory. Did he finish school? It is hard to tell; he had slid through the cracks.

Except for his writing on the backs of exam sheets, Bill is simply a name in a grade book. But he does represent many students in schools and can be profiled:

He is 20.3 years old with fewer than nine years of schooling.

He lives with his mother, who has only an eighth-grade education.

His mother is unskilled or unemployed.

He left school because he was suspended, expelled, or "lost interest." (Walther, 1970; Fernandez & Shu, 1988)

Chances are that Bill and our profile (commonly it is a "he") have had scrapes with the law, possibly have served a prison term, and are poor readers. They represent the "typical" dropout.

Before Bill actually dropped out, though, there were plenty of signs that he was "at risk." Between 25% and 40% of those who leave school early make the decision to do so in 10th grade, but it is not a single, impulsive act (Schreiber, 1969, pp. 308–316). It is an act that has long been coming, especially if the student has been retained at a particular grade level in school at least once. The distinguishing characteristic of the at-risk student (the potential dropout) is not intelligence (one-half are intelligent enough to grad-uate from high school) but self-concept.

Jim, the ex-convict we met at the beginning of the chapter, had been a dropout before committing the felony for which he was sent to prison. A poor reader, slow to understand the material, he was a lost soul in many ways. But he was not unlikable or unsalvageable. With extra attention from his teacher, Jim had passed the required 12th-grade social studies course. His novice teacher simply felt she was doing her job. Jim was one of her charges, and he would have to be helped to learn the material. Would it have been different had Jim been identified as at risk much earlier? Probably, but we can only speculate.

The Education Commission of the States (1985) has argued that these youth pose a threat to the nation and a costly one, for they will have to be cared for at some point, and the costs increase with the years. For example, the costs to our society for Jim's incarceration has to be considered. And it is costly to pay unemployment insurance or to provide welfare payments. Jim is also a loss to the productive economy. But most important, it is a human loss.

At the risk of being repetitive, we must stress that most of the principles of learning that work with any population of students will work with at-risk students: active teaching, motivation, interaction between student and teacher (and student and student) and with the home environment, and the other prescriptions for working with ESL, LD, and gifted students. More specifically, there is a need for early identification of at-risk students (and of others identified in this section) as well as

- Reliance on prevention rather than remediation
- Greater involvement of parents as partners
- Careful monitoring of student progress
- Lower pupil-teacher ratios
- Emphasis on individual evaluations
- Creation of more cooperative learning opportunities

Thus, we can argue that the key to learning, regardless of the specific population, is the teacher who as decision maker plans to meet the needs of the diverse students who become her or his charges. Planning, in turn, requires applying models, or blueprints, for instruction that will accommodate the various learners in the classroom.

Summary

Secondary school teachers have a formidable job. They must work with a "breed unto themselves"—adolescents who psychologically need love. This love can come from peers as well as from family and, yes, from teachers. These adolescents, who represent great diversity but share certain attitudes and learning styles, are the teacher's responsibility. The issue, as Sizer claims, is whether learning is occurring, whether teachers can find ways to motivate and involve students in learning, recognize students' developmental levels (Piaget) as well as differences in how students learn, and can shape instruction to accommodate to and influence these diverse adolescent learning styles. As teachers, whatever learning theory we ascribe to—cognitivism, behaviorism, observational learning or humanism—we need to adapt our instruction to our students' cognitive and affective aptitudes. Further, this adaptation must address the needs of "special" students, whether labeled gifted, handicapped, bilingual or at-risk. And we argue, based on research, that effective instruction is adaptable to the range of students we will face in our social studies classes.

Decisions! Decisions!

1. How clearly do you recall being an adolescent? Was it a pleasant or difficult experience? With whom did you identify? What kind of influence did that person(s) have on you?

2. Given possibly 25 to 30 students per class and 150 students per day, how will you get to know your students? What can you do to get to know even some of them well?

3. To what extent *should* you know your students? Will not "familiarity breed contempt?" How can you get to know your students without losing necessary authority?

4. How do *you* learn? When does information take on meaning for you? Do you feel you have special aptitudes?

5. What learning style best characterizes you? Are you reflective or impulsive? Do you see the whole picture, or do you see individual parts connected to form a pattern? Do you prefer to work with others or alone?

6. How will you handle the many personalities and learners in your classes? What about the unloveable ones? The "slow" ones? How about those who challenge you and make you feel inadequate?

7. Where might you get help to work with the different learners in your classes?

8. What kind(s) or learning environment(s) will you try to create in your classroom? To what extent will you encourage students to help you create that learning environment(s)?

9. What kinds of classroom activities "turned you on" as a student? What types "turned you off?" What kinds of feelings did you have when you were really "into it?"

References

Bandura, A. (1986). *Social foundations of thought and action: A social cognitive theory.* Englewood Cliffs, NJ: Prentice-Hall.

Bandura, A., and Walters, R. H. (1963). *Social learning and personality development.* New York: Holt, Rinehart & Winston, 1963.

Brown, A. L., & Campione, J. C. (1986). Psychological theory and the study of learning disabilities. *American Psychologist, 41*(10) 1059–1068.

Bruner, J. (1960). *The Process of Education.* Cambridge, MA: Harvard University Press.

Carnine, D. (1990). New research on the brain: Implications for instruction. *Phi Delta Kappan, 71*(5), 372–377.

Corno, L., & Snow, R. E. (1986). Adapting teaching to individual differences among learners. In M. C. Wittrock (Ed.), *Handbook of research on teaching* (3rd ed., pp. 605–629). New York: Macmillan.

Cummins, J. (1984). *Bilingualism and special education: Issues in assessment and pedagogy.* San Diego: College-Hill Press.

deRosenroll, D. A. (1987). Early adolescent egocentricism: A review of six articles. *Adolescence, 22*(88), 791–802.

Dweck, C. S. (1986). Motivational processes affecting learning. *American Psychologist, 41*(10), 1040–1048.

Education Commission of the States. (1985). *Reconnecting youth: The next stage of reform.* Denver: Author.

Egan, K. (1989). Memory, imagination, and learning: Connected by the story. *Phi Delta Kappan, 70*(6) 455–459.

Erickson, E. (1950). *Childhood and society.* New York: Norton.

Fernandez, R. R., & Shu, G. (1988). School dropouts: New approaches to an enduring problem. *Education and Urban Society, 2*(4), 363–386.

Gagne, R. (1965). *Conditions of learning.* New York: Holt, Rinehart & Winston.

Good, T. L., & Brophy, J. E. (1987). *Looking in classrooms.* New York: Harper & Row.

Good, T. L., & Stipek, D. J. (1983). Individual differences in the classroom: A psychological perspective. In G. Fenstermacher & J. I. Goodlad (Eds.), *Individual Difference and the Common Curriculum* (pp. 9–43). (82nd Yearbook, National Society for the Study of Education). Chicago: University of Chicago Press.

Goodlad, J. I. (1984). *A place called school.* New York: McGraw-Hill.

Gregorc, A. F. (1979). Learning styles: Differences which the profession must address. In R. Vacca & J. Meagher (Eds.), *Reading Through Content* (pp. 10–12). Storrs, CT: University of Connecticut Press.

Haley, A. (1965). *The autobiography of Malcolm X.* New York: Grove Press.

Hallahan, D., Keller, C. E., McKinney, J. D., Lloyd, J. W., & Bryan, T. (1988). Introduction to the series: Questions about the regular education initiative [Special issue]. *Journal of Learning Disabilities, 21*(1), 1–5.

Horowitz, F. D., & O'Brien, M. (1986). Gifted and talented children: State of knowledge and directions for research. *American Psychologist, 41*(100), 1147–1152.

Kagan, J. (1965). Impulsive and reflective children: Significance of conceptual tempo. In J. D. Krumboltz (Ed.), *Learning and the educational process* (pp. 133–161). Chicago: Rand McNally.

Kolb, D. (1978). *Learning style inventory technical manual* (rev. ed.). Boston: McBer & Company.

Lefrançois, G. (1985). *Psychology for teaching* (5th ed.). Belmont, CA: Wadsworth.

Linowitz, S. (1985). *The making of a public man: A memoir.* Boston: Little, Brown.

Maslow, A. (1962). *Toward a psychology of being.* New York: Van Nostrand.

McGuinness, D. (1983). Males and females and the learning process. In K. E. Boulding & L. Senesh (Eds.), *The optimum utilization of knowledge* (pp. 41–52). Boulder, CO: Westview Press.

Messick, S. (1984). The nature of cognitive styles: Problems and promise in educational practice. *Educational Psychologist, 19,* 59–74.

Phi Delta Kappa. (1980). On mixing and matching of teaching and learning styles. *Practical Applications of Research, 3*(2). Bloomington, IN: Phi Delta Kappa Center on Evaluation, Development, and Research.

Piaget, J. (1964). Cognition and development in children: Piaget. *Journal of*

Research in Science Teaching, 2, 176–186.

Pribram, K. H. (1983). The brain, cognitive commodities and the enfolded order. In K. E. Boulding & L. Senesh (Eds.), *The optimum utilization of knowledge* (pp. 29–40). Boulder, CO: Westview Press.

Rogers, C. (1969). *Freedom to learn.* Columbus, OH: Merrill.

Sanders, D., & Sanders, J. (1984). *Teaching creativity through metaphor.* Boston: Longman.

Schneider, F. W., & Coutts, L. M. (1985). Person orientation of male and female high school students: To the educational disadvantage of males. *Sex Roles, 13*(1/2), 47–62.

Schreiber, D. (1969). Dropout—causes and consequences. In R. L. Ebel (Ed.), *Encyclopedia of educational research* (4th ed., pp. 308–316). Toronto: Macmillan.

Self, T. C. (1985) Dropouts: A review of the literature, project talent search. Monroe, LA: Northeast Louisiana University. (ED 260 307)

Sizer, T. (1984). *Horace's compromise.* Boston: Houghton Mifflin.

Skinner, B. F. (1953). *Science and human behavior.* New York: Macmillan.

Sternberg, R. J. (1990). Thinking styles: Keys to understanding performance. *Phi Delta Kappan, 71*(5), 366–371.

Story, N. (1986). Factors that influence continuing motivation. *Journal of Educational Research, 80*(2), 86–92.

Thinking strategically about the future. (1984, November 14). *Education Week,* 18, 19.

Viadero, D. (1988, February 24). Researchers' critique escalates the debate over "regular education" for all students. *Education Week,* 1, 20, 21.

Wagner, J. A. (1987). Formal operations and ego identity in adolescence. *Adolescence, 22*(85), 23–35.

Walther, R. H. (1970). *A study of negro male high school dropouts who are not reached by federal work-training programs* [Final report]. Washington, DC: Social Research Group, George Washington University.

W. Va. tightens its spec.-ed. criteria. (1988, March 2). *Education Week,* 13.

Williams, R. (1972). [Marginal note]. *Phi Delta Kappan, 53*(6), 384.

Chapter Four

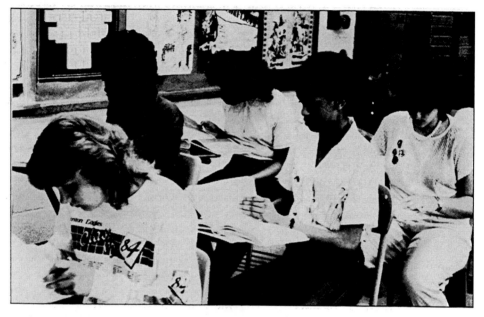

Models for Teaching

Effective teaching requires developing instructional strategies based on some conceptual scheme to match different student aptitudes to the greatest extent possible.

Reeling from what she recalled about learners and learning, Beth, a new teacher, slumped in her chair and looked out the window. But, as others had reminded her many times, she was not supposed to be a miracle worker. Instead, she was to do what she could to challenge her students. Maybe, just maybe, some of the "models" of teaching she had learned earlier would be appropriate.

Beth quickly remembered, however, that not everyone is as enamored of models as some of her instructors were. Indeed, one of the authors of this book cringes at the very mention of the term *model:* "We're just talking about strategies for teaching based on some clear, simple learning principles. Whom are we trying to impress with this whole business of 'models?' Models are just gimmicks to get kids interested in the material."

We do not completely disagree with our colleague, but we do believe that structuring and categorizing these "gimmicks" can help Beth and other teachers clarify their intentions. We are arguing that there are different ways to group the various instructional strategies, which we are referring to as *models,* borrowing the term from Kuhn (1970) and Joyce and Weil (1986). These models may serve as guidelines for organizing instruction appropriate for students' aptitudes, learning modes, and needs.

You may notice another bias: our preference for models that fall into the category of *information processing* (concept attainment, concept formation, and inquiry). That is, we prefer models that emphasize students actively involved in gathering, decoding, classifying, and synthesizing information, because we believe that, at the minimum,

- Learning is an active interaction between students and their environment.
- Learning is thinking, and thinking can be taught.
- Learning involves organization of information into schema that have meaning for students.
- Learning requires increasingly complex levels of thinking.
- Learning should be durable, and ways to learn can be transferred to different situations.

However, we do not deny that deductive models also are appropriate. Therefore, we will also examine direct instruction (Hunter, 1985), mastery learning (Carroll, 1971; Bloom, 1971), and advance organizer (Ausubel, 1968), which is usually listed as *information processing.* In addition, we will look at other models that more clearly reflect a process orientation: synectics (Gordon, 1961), group investigation, or problem solving (Dewey, 1961), role playing (Shaftel & Shaftel, 1967), and simulation (not attributable to a particular theorist).

It is likely that given a truly competent teacher, any model will prove effective. Indeed, this kind of teacher probably never stops to think about a model ("I use whatever works with my kids. I'll even stand on my head, if necessary."). But Beth, who is just starting out—and most of us—need some structure with which to organize our teaching strategies. So with these caveats in mind, we offer the following models, using Beth the novice as our foil.

Reflecting on the job ahead, Beth recalled a handout from her methods class that had impressed her (Calandra, 1968):

Angels on a Pin

Some time ago, I received a call from a colleague who asked if I would be the referee on the grading of an examination question. He was about to give a student a zero for his answer to a physics question, while the student claimed he should receive a perfect score and would if the system were not set up against the student. The instructor and the student agreed to submit this to an impartial arbiter, and I was selected.

I went to my colleague's office and read the examination question: "Show how it is possible to determine the height of a tall building with the aid of a barometer."

The student had answered: "Take the barometer to the top of the building, attach a long rope to it, lower the barometer to the street, and then bring it up, measuring the length of the rope. The length of the rope is the height of the building."

I pointed out that the student really had a strong case for full credit, since he had answered the question completely and correctly. On the other hand, if full credit were given, it could well contribute to a high grade for the student in his physics course. A high grade is supposed to certify competence in physics, but the answer did not confirm this. I suggested that the student have another try at answering the question. I was not surprised that my colleague agreed, but I was surprised that the student did.

I gave the student six minutes to answer the question, with the warning that his answer should show some knowledge of physics. At the end of five minutes, he had not written anything. I asked if he wished to give up, but he said no. He had many answers to this problem, he was just thinking of the best one. I excused myself for interrupting him, and asked him to please go on. In the next minute, he dashed off his answer, which read:

Take the barometer to the top of the building and lean over the edge of the roof. Drop the barometer, timing its fall with a stopwatch. Then, using the formula $S = 1/2at^2$, calculate the height of the building.

At this point, I asked my colleague if he would give up. He conceded, and I gave the student almost full credit.

In leaving my colleague's office, I recalled that the student had said he had other answers to the problem, so I asked him what they were. "Oh, yes," said the student. "There are many ways of getting the height of a tall building with the aid of a barometer. For example, you could take the barometer out on a sunny day and measure the height of the barometer, the length of the shadow, and the length of the shadow of the building, and by the use of a simple proportion, determine the height of the building."

"Fine," I said, "And the others?"

"Yes," said the student. "There is a very basic measurement that you will like. In this method, you take the barometer and begin to walk up the stairs. As you climb the stairs, you mark off the length of the barometer along the wall. You then count the number of marks, and this will give you the height of the building in barometer units. A very direct method.

"Of course, if you want a more sophisticated method, you can tie the barometer to the end of a string, swing it as a pendulum, and determine the value of 'g' at the street level and at the top of the building. From the difference between the two values of 'g,' the height of the building can, in principle, be calculated.

"Finally," he concluded, "there are many ways of solving the problem. Probably the best," he said, "is to take the barometer to the basement and knock on the superintendent's door. When the superintendent answers, you speak to him as follows: 'Mr. Superintendent, here I have a fine barometer. If you will tell me the height of this building, I will give you this barometer.' "

At this point, I asked the student if he really did not know the conventional answer to this question. He admitted that he did, but said that he was fed up with high school and college instructors trying to teach him how to think, to use the "scientific method," and to explore the deep inner logic of the subject in a pedantic way. . . . *

Beth likely will have no students as bright as the hero of this story, but the message is clear: She should try to provide a classroom environment wherein actively involved students will be permitted to use their varying aptitudes. Her task is to identify a useful model—a structure or pattern for organizing her instruction.

INDUCTIVE AND DEDUCTIVE THINKING

Seldom, if ever, do we stop to consider whether we are thinking inductively or deductively, recognizing that the combination of the two modes is the essence of thinking. But it is useful to distinguish between them. In the simplest terms, *inductive thinking* involves forming patterns or conclusions from specific observations, while *deductive thinking* reverses the process, starting with a pattern or generalization and working toward a specific illustration.

Inductive Thinking

Beth recalled how an auto mechanic had illustrated inductive thinking when she brought her car in with an engine-stalling problem. The mechanic began asking her for the symptoms: "Does the car usually start right off? Does it

*From "Angels on a Pin" by A. Calandra, 1968, *Saturday Review, 60.* Copyright 1968 by OMNI Publications International Ltd. Reprinted by permission.

stall immediately or after you put it in gear?" After a series of questions, he pinned the problem down to a fast idle. He had drawn a conclusion from a series of observations. He was thinking inductively. observations lead to pattern leads to conclusion

Deductive Thinking

One day, one of Beth's friends was trying to locate his adult son's apartment to leave a package. Once in the building, he could not recall the apartment number. His son was not home, and the mailboxes were not numbered. However, below the mailboxes were names and buttons for buzzing apartments. So Beth's friend had his daughter punch the button under the son's apartment number while he listened for the sound of the buzzer upstairs. He found the apartment through simple logic, to wit:

All apartments have buzzers.

His son's apartment had a buzzer.

Therefore, by punching the right buzzer, he could locate his son's apartment.

There was nothing sophisticated about this reasoning. He simply discovered a pattern and tested it. Pattern, specific part of pattern

Inductive versus Deductive Thinking

In many ways, inductive and deductive thinking are similar: Both require individuals to observe, to predict, and to make inferences, and both can be fostered in the classroom. However, they also differ in significant ways, as Figure 4.1 illustrates. Inductive thinking is more time consuming than deductive thinking, but it is also more affective, less structured, and more conducive to incidental learning. Also, it appears that learning of abstractions (concepts), rules, and generalizations occurs more readily from inductive thinking, although there is disagreement about this.

FIGURE 4.1
A Comparison of the Inductive and Deductive Models

Deductive Model	Inductive Model
Strong content orientation	Emphasis on thinking skills and affective goals
High structure	Less structure
More time efficient	Less time efficient
Less opportunity for incidental learning	Greater opportunity for incidental learning

Source: From *Strategies for Teachers* (2nd ed., p. 259) by P. D. Eggen and D. P. Kauchak, 1988, Englewood Cliffs, NJ: Prentice-Hall. Reprinted by permission of Prentice-Hall.

USING CONCEPTS TO FOSTER THINKING

Whether we personally prefer inductive or deductive thinking and, therefore, tend to use one or the other in our teaching, both forms should encourage the learning of concepts from which generalizations can be derived. In other words, one goal of schooling is to help students perceive relationships and recognize patterns in those relationships. As we do so, we apply labels to the resulting abstractions that summarize related phenomena, or *concepts*. This, in turn, demands modes of thinking in which we all, often unconsciously, engage at times but that all too often are not encouraged in the schools.

Concepts, which can be learned inductively or deductively, derive from recognizing related classes of events, ideas, or objects. They are products of identifying, classifying, and synthesizing related phenomena that help us construct a sensible totality out of seemingly unrelated experiences and data. Concepts, then, are a form of shorthand that we use to make sense out of what initially may appear simple accumulations of information.

To illustrate, try the following exercise, borrowed from Frank Smith (1975, pp. 51–52).* Look *briefly* at the following letters. Then close your eyes and try to recall how many *letters* you saw:

KYBVODUWGPJMSQTXNOGMCTRSO

Next, do the same with the following words:

READY JUMP WHEAT POOR BUT SEEK

Now try to do the same thing with this example:

KNIGHTS RODE HORSES INTO WAR

In the third example, you probably could count the letters easily with your eyes closed, given a second or two. The reason is that you now have a mental set and a scheme to organize what formerly was a bunch of scrambled letters. In other words, learning requires some organization of seemingly unfamiliar figures into a meaningful scheme.

To illustrate further, one of the authors recalls how one of his sons learned the "concept" of baseball. When barely able to swing even a plastic bat, the son enjoyed making contact between his bat and the thrown ball, but he was *thrilled* at being able to run. However, he was as likely to run to third base as he was to first—indeed, he ran just so his father would chase him to make the tag! Many years later, the son called to chide his father about the ineptness of the owner of the father's favorite baseball team. The owner had let a star pitcher escape his team as a "free agent." The son's concept of baseball, as we

*Excerpt from *Comprehension and Learning—A Conceptual Framework for Teachers* by Frank Smith, copyright © 1975 by Holt, Rinehart and Winston, Inc., reprinted by permission of the publisher.

would expect, had become considerably more sophisticated. He had accommodated and achieved what Piaget called *equilibration*. Because of his matured cognitive structure, the son was able to incorporate more sophisticated information and modify his conception of the term *baseball*.

Piaget (1952) explained this phenomenon in terms of *assimilation* and *accommodation*. His theory argues that to learn we need to (1) incorporate elements of the environment into our cognitive structures and then (2) modify our conceptions of the world based on that incorporation. In other words, the information becomes one's own rather than someone else's.

The problem is that too often students (as well as we) do not "see" the connections among the bits and pieces of information they encounter. Frequently, to students the world is a mass of unrelated data:

A	D	B		C
	B	B	C	A
	C	D	C	
B	A	C	B	A
D	B	D	B	

To many students, the world inside the school is often like a jigsaw puzzle. So the teacher's role is to help the students fit the pieces together. But how does the teacher go about helping students do this?

Look again at the confusing jumble of letters above. Imagine the letters rearranged and classified:

*A*s	*B*s	*C*s	*D*s
A	B	C	D
A	B	C	D
A	B	C	D
A	B	C	D
A	B	C	D

When students develop some scheme, they are forming their own "concepts." They are observing and gathering information, then sorting, selecting, categorizing, and summarizing it. Schematically, the process resembles a pyramid, as in Figure 4.2.

INFORMATION PROCESSING (INDUCTIVE MODELS)

The models we will discuss in this section—the concept formation, concept attainment, and inquiry models—focus on the "processing" of information,

FIGURE 4.2
Inductive Thinking

Observing,
gathering information
Collecting, sorting, selecting
Categorizing, classifying, synthesizing
Summarizing, concluding, generalizing, rule making

---

the intellectual operations in which humans engage to obtain knowledge. These models emphasize how one acquires information and what one does with it; that is, "knowledge becomes the vehicle rather than the destination" (Parker & Rubin, 1966, p. 2). Clearly underlying these models is the psychological notion of *cognition,* or thinking, and how it occurs.

The three models share the following characteristics:

- Reliance on studies of thinking
- Learning theories
- Research into the development of the human intellect
- Encouragement of discovery by the student

However, the models differ from one another as much as their proponents do. Concept formation stresses finding and organizing information, forming concepts, predicting (hypothesizing), and verifying the predictions. Concept attainment, as the term implies, asks students to discover the attributes of concepts that the teacher has identified and test their understanding by formulating their own examples of the concepts as well as by examining their thinking. The inquiry model evolved from the natural sciences and demands more formal causal reasoning, including asking questions and constructing and testing hypotheses; it is a problem-solving model.

Concept Formation Model

The *concept formation model* of information processing comes from the curriculum work of Hilda Taba (Taba, 1967). An important feature of concept formation is that students actively gather, sort, and summarize information. They must invent to the degree that they categorize related events, persons, and phenomena that characterize the abstract concepts to which we affix labels and distinguish them from things that do not represent the concept. Concepts, in turn, are "mental coat hangers" onto which we attach data so that we can manipulate them more easily. Concepts represent abbreviations for expressing complex ideas and relationships.

To illustrate, suppose Beth wants to help her students understand the concept of culture. The abstract of a series of lessons presented in Figure 4.3, though ostensibly aimed at fifth and sixth graders, might work (Mahood, 1981).

Advantages and Disadvantages of the Concept Formation Model. Clearly the concept formation model gets students actively involved. More important, it gets them working at a moderately high intellectual level. Students have to list, group, and label data so that they can identify and explore relationships and then apply principles drawn from those relationships. Further, the teacher, although very active in the design and conduct of the lesson, is more of a participant than an instructor in the usual sense. It is the students' *thinking* that makes the lesson effective. The argument is that students who have engaged in concept formation develop mental pictures that help them link information more effectively than they could if they were given information directly.

FIGURE 4.3
Sample Concept Formation Lesson

Nacirema, Weans, and Bushmen: Studying Other Cultures

Syllabus topic: Global studies (Africa)
Concepts: Culture, institutions, habitat, ethnocentrism

A. *Instructional objectives:* The students will
  1. List characteristics of the people described by the data cards and site map
  2. Describe the ways in which these people conduct their lives
  3. Draw inferences about the societies of these people based on the descriptions and inferences
  4. Contrast Nacirema society with those described as the "Weans" and the "Bushmen"
  5. Judge the correctness of their initial impressions and develop summary statements about the cultures
B. *Procedure:* To motivate the students, they were separated into groups of four or five, given the role of explorers, and asked to make some judgments about the society described on the data cards and based on "data" and "inferences."
C. *Concluding activity (Closure):* Students were asked to examine their conclusions in terms of accuracy of definitions and ability to define or state the attributes of the concept being studied.

On the first day, the teacher displays artifacts of different cultures and helps students define *culture*. Then she gives students, arranged in groups, the "data cards" and asks them to list characteristics of the people being described using categories such as "data," "inferences," and "conclusions."

On the second day, the students examine this culture more closely until the "joke"—that the Nacirema is "American" spelled backwards—is discovered, at which time the students can be introduced to the "Weans" ("US" or "U.S."), followed by a similar analysis. Finally, the teacher can ask the students to do the same with a genuinely "foreign" culture, the Bushmen of the Kalahari Desert, at which time comparisons can be drawn.

This lesson has a twofold purpose: to encourage students to collect, sort, and synthesize data—to think inductively—and to learn concepts that represent and foster higher-level thinking.

However, not all students are comfortable with a model that appears this open, especially those who were described in Chapter 3 as concrete sequential, impulsive, or field independent. The concept formation model is time consuming, it changes the teacher's role, and it could prove confusing for some students. Also, there is disagreement about whether students retain learning better from this type of inductive lesson.

ASIDE TO THE READER: The debate in Beth's mind—and likely in your mind as well—is how much time to spend on a lesson or series of lessons. Schools have curriculum guides, and typically students must be tested on their understanding of the curriculum. If it takes five to six days (or even three) to teach a particular lesson, will the teacher be able to "cover" the curriculum? Then the question becomes: What does it mean to "cover" the curriculum? Aren't we all necessarily selective in what we teach, given the breadth of most curricula? What should dictate how much time we spend on any particular information or model?

Another concern is how Beth (and we) can be certain that students are learning the material. When working in groups, it is easy for students to fool around, let others do the work, and enjoy the respite from the teacher's lectures. How can Beth assess student learning conducted this way?

We would argue that Beth can always resort to pencil-and-paper tests, to direct questioning, or to individual written papers to assess the attainment of lesson or unit objectives, but there are other goals that are more difficult to evaluate directly. In fact, using group activities with the concept formation model should present no distinct problems for Beth. She, like all teachers, will always have to use a variety of means to assess learning and trust that ultimately the learning will be demonstrated elsewhere and at another time—possibly in the next social studies class, while examining a newspaper cartoon or recognizing the ethnocentric remarks or actions of a particular person or group.

Concept Attainment Model

With these thoughts in mind, Beth recalled observing a lesson that might be considered representative of the *concept attainment model*, which is often attributed to psychologist Jerome Bruner (1961). The teacher had been trying to get the class to understand that relations among countries sometimes resemble relations among family members who create spheres of influence and that there is also a universalist way of living together. The teacher also recognized that this might be a good vehicle with which to examine the characteristics of power, a concept that pervaded the curriculum.

After writing the word *power* on the chalkboard, the teacher asked students to describe some situation that illustrated the exercise of power. The examples that emerged were not too surprising:

The taking of another hostage in Lebanon.

A dumb cop stopped me for going only 20 miles over the speed limit.

I got a can of soda pop out of a canteen by kicking the side of the machine just below the coin slot.

To these examples the teacher added some other illustrations on the chalkboard and asked the students to distinguish among the situations suggested:

Mohandas Gandhi calls for boycott.

Gai, the Bushman, divides the day's kill.

Queen Elizabeth reviews the guards at Buckingham Palace.

The U.S. Supreme Court affirms a lower-court decision.

A police officer directs traffic.

A gun-bearing masked person robs a bank.

President Bush appoints a new cabinet member.

Forty-niners quarterback Joe Montana says he will go to Disney World after Super Bowl win.

Magazine ad shows an attractive young woman modeling a miniskirt.

Nuclear war remains a threat.

Dr. Dogood prescribes a miracle drug.

Then the teacher asked the class how they might group these examples. Some of the answers were obvious:

Coercion (or pure force)	The taking of hostages
	Kicking soda pop machine
	Gun-bearing masked person
	Nuclear war remains a threat
Legal authority	President Bush appoints . . .
	U.S. Supreme Court affirms . . .
	Police officer directs traffic

Other answers were less obvious:

Tradition	Queen Elizabeth reviews guards*
	Gai divides . . .

The latter example took some coaxing and leading questions.

Other examples were even less obvious:

*Critics might argue that Queen Elizabeth is also exercising legal, persuasive, and even charismatic, influence, which suggests one difficulty often encountered in examining complex concepts.

Persuasion (influence)	Magazine ad with attractive model
	Joe Montana wins trip
Expertise	Dr. Dogood prescribes miracle drug

Here was the most difficult category:

"Charisma"	Mohandas Gandhi calls for boycott

Then it became especially tricky to get the students to develop a definition that would encompass these seemingly diverse examples ("Power is . . . ").

The next step was to have the students compare some examples that did not illustrate power. First, the teacher generated some "nonexamples" and the class identified critical attributes of the original examples. Then the students gave other examples and compared them with the definitions they had developed. Finally, the students were directed to return to their reading about the relations among countries and to distinguish the various ways in which countries exercise power. Most obvious were outright invasions by countries: Libya into Chad, the United States into Granada, the Soviet Union into Afghanistan, and Germany into France. Somewhat less obvious were the OPEC countries' hiking of oil prices and Japan's "dumping" of microchips on the open market. Less obvious still were former president Reagan's use of his personality to influence public opinion and Communist party chief Gorbachev's use of the media.

Success with such a lesson can be measured by the extent to which students bring in their own examples of "power," examples different from those illustrated in class and consistent with students' levels of maturation.

Advantages and Disadvantages of the Concept Attainment Model. Again we emphasize that evaluating the learning of concepts is no simple matter. The ultimate "test" is students' abilities to draw on the concept to comprehend and analyze other relationships: legislative-executive-judicial; economic and social interactions in their own society and lives; and social relationships among countries and regions within nation-states. For now, students can be asked to apply the concept of "power" to the immediate content.

Perhaps more significant is the issue of developing effective means of conveying concepts to students. Yoho (1986) suggests that concept learning involves considerably more than memorizing a concept's critical attributes and the most effective strategy of those tested emphasized focusing on the best example of a concept and elaborating on it with newly encountered examples. In all, the preferred strategy involved five steps: (1) introduction, (2) definitions, (3) best examples, (4) examples only, and (5) practice followed by presentations that stressed the best example. In contrast, the less successful strategies stressed critical attributes or critical examples in step 3 and examples and "nonexamples" in step 4.

McKinney, Gilmore, Peddicord, and McCallum (1987) report similar results. This study found no significant differences in the learning of concepts between groups of students who were presented prototypes (best examples) of concepts and those who were given critical attributes. In fact, the results appeared to support the claim that learners create a mental prototype of the concept and then forget the specific critical attributes (McKinney, et al., 1987)

As with the concept formation model, time is a factor. How much time should be spent developing the concept? Also, it is possible that students will view the concept in isolation, whereas concepts are supposed to be building blocks that incorporate data, which, in turn, lend meaning to what could be seen as isolated information.

Inquiry Model

Another information processing model Beth might use is the *inquiry model*, which involves two separate strategies.

The first strategy calls for the following steps:

1. The teacher explains the procedures and presents a discrepant event or problem.
2. Students attempt to understand the problem and then gather data.
3. Students experiment with variables (i.e., "hypothesize").
4. Students develop an explanation.
5. The teacher and the students analyze the strategy and students' explanations.

With this strategy, students are helped to develop ways to formulate questions with which they can resolve problems and dilemmas in classrooms as well as in their daily lives.

The first strategy has been used to examine cultural differences within the United States (Collins & Sawyer, 1984). It begins with a quote from Radar O'Reilly, a character from the television show "M*A*S*H":*

> We don't have a television. The nearest one is in the Grange Hall over at Mooseville. . . . That's about fifteen miles away . . . two hours by Chevy, one hour by foot. (Collins & Sawyer, 1984, p. 266)

TEACHER: How are other parts of the country portrayed on "M*A*S*H?" Where were the other characters from?

This can elicit amazing recall from students:

Hawkeye was from Apple Cove, Maine.

Colonel Potter was from Hannibal, Missouri.

*The following example is adapted from a lesson designed by student teacher Michael Courneen.

Klinger was from Toledo, Ohio.

Frank Burns was from Fort Wayne, Indiana.

Charles Winchester was from Boston.

TEACHER: OK, OK, I'm impressed. Tell me about Winchester. How did he live at home? Did his family have a television set?

Silence. (Now he had them.)

STUDENT: Probably.

TEACHER: Why do you think so?

Building on students' answers to this question about the lives of other characters, such as Klinger, another midwesterner, the next step would be rather obvious:

TEACHER: Well, which is the Midwest—Radar's, which was 15 miles from one television to the next, or Klinger's, which was made up of pool sharks trying to avoid the police?

This initiates analysis, just as a later question referring to Winchester's asking a high-ranking officer from whom he sought a favor: "Tell me about Montana. Does it have a city?" (Collins & Sawyer, 1984, p. 268).

So the rest of that class and the next was spent checking out various sources listed in the article by Collins and Sawyer, as well as U.S. Government Printing Office publications such as the *County and City Data Book, Statistical Abstract of the United States,* and the smaller version, *Pocket Data Book,* to develop and test hypotheses about differences and similarities among regions and states in the United States. But the ultimate goal—to dispel certain stereotypes—was not forgotten during the "diversion" into the geography lesson.

As in all teaching, planning inquiry lessons is critical; that is:

1. The lesson *goals* must be clarified. How does "M∗A∗S∗H" (or any aspects of our lives) reflect stereotypes? How do we test the validity of stereotypes?
2. The *problem* (or discrepant event) must be presented clearly to help students focus.
3. *Data gathering* procedures must be developed, including distinguishing and locating different sources, such as primary versus secondary sources.
4. *Hypothesizing,* or developing unverified generalizations ("educated guesses"), depends on whether content-specific learning or more open inquiry is being sought.
5. Student *explanations* should involve students in analyzing data and drawing some conclusions.
6. *Analysis* of both the explanation and the inquiry strategy must follow and be true to the model.

The inquiry model relies on the use of both primary and secondary sources.

A key element in the following inquiry strategy is for *students* rather than the teacher to ask the questions; this puts the shoe on the other foot (Suchman, 1962). Like the prior strategy, this approach begins with a problem or discrepant event. Students are asked to discover all they can about the problem or event by asking questions to which the teacher answers only "yes" or "no." Anyone can ask questions, continue until that line of questioning proves unproductive, and then "pass" to another. It is worthwhile to have a student record in shorthand the questions as they are asked, for this enables the students to check their lines of thinking as they go along.

The problem could be as a simple as this one, borrowed from a television movie based on John Jakes' popular *North and South*:

TEACHER: Two men in their mid- to late thirties, George and Orry, old friends and West Point classmates, are attending the West Point graduation of George's younger brother. George figures this is a good time to mention that his brother intends to ask Orry's sister's to marry him. Orry agrees that the two love each other, they do seem compatible, and George's brother is a fine young man with a bright future. But no, he won't agree to the marriage. Why?

The students might sit for what seems forever. But one can always be counted on to start the ball rolling:

STUDENT: Is Orry's sister underage?
TEACHER: No.

Then likely silence, followed by another student's question:

STUDENT: Does George's brother have some kind of disease?
TEACHER: No.
STUDENT: Pass.
                [The questioning continues.]

The intent of this example obviously is to encourage students to think, as evidenced by the nature of their questions. This strategy can be used to introduce, develop, or summarize a topic.

Advantages and Disadvantages of the Inquiry Model.   Inquiry lessons can be fun as well as productive. While the second version of the inquiry model (in which students pose questions) originally was created to help students think like scientists using a variation of the scientific method, it can be used in social studies classes as well. One advantage of using this method is that it turns the tables, allowing students to feel like they are running the class as much as the teacher is.

Like any inductive model, the inquiry model has its disadvantages. Jack Fraenkel (1973) cautions, "The purposes the teacher or student has in mind can influence the kinds of questions asked" (p. 163). In other words, students may well try to ask what they think the teacher wants to hear. Thus, the teacher is advised to "promote the purposes for which the strategy is intended."

Also, this type of lesson takes time to get going. With the second strategy, it would have been easier for the teacher to tell the story of George and Orry with the details or simply offer the notion of "brother versus brother" as an introduction to the lesson. While a number of the students are directly involved in questioning, not all are. (However, generally all are stimulated and follow the questioning.) But the students themselves are problem solvers, using the techniques that will help them in class and elsewhere.

On the other hand, it can be argued that the time an inquiry lesson requires is well spent. In the examples we saw, with both strategies the students had challenged their beliefs and thinking. At the very least, the teacher had the students' attention for a period of time, what in Chapter 3 we

~~ing time~~—"the simultaneous occurrence of allocated
, and high success rate" and time that is "positively
~~vement~~" (Denham & Lieberman, 1980, p. 66). The
in. ~~long~~ as the teacher remembers to do the necessary
hom. ~~ents~~ to gather information, and to challenge the
hypoth.

However. ~~bout~~ the role of problem solving and
inquiry in social stud. er the teacher or students should
formulate questions and whe. ular theoretical position should be
taken. Maxcy (1986) suggests that pr. ns to be examined can come from
the teacher's contexts but should be su. ct to "student revision and reinter-
pretation with the goal of seeking solutions, rather than building character
or yielding action upon the part of the students" (p. 305).

DEDUCTIVE MODELS

For many, if not most, teachers, the *deductive model*, typically viewed as
direct instruction, is more familiar and comfortable. Similarly, some students profit from a direct (or concrete-sequential) mode of learning, especially
those characterized as field dependent; that is, these students seek clearly
delineated, sequential teaching strategies wherein the lesson evolves linearly.

Direct-Instruction Model

A deductive strategy that has enjoyed considerable use is one espoused by
Madeline Hunter and associates (Hunter, 1985). While going under a variety
of labels, the one that seems most appropriate is *direct instruction*. Figure 4.4
illustrates the direct-instruction format.

The rationale behind direct instruction is that "teaching is now defined
as a constant stream of professional decisions made before, during, and after
interaction with the student; decisions, which, when implemented, increase

FIGURE 4.4
Direct-Instruction Format

Lesson objectives:	Objectives stated behaviorally
Anticipatory set:	A motivating device to introduce lesson
Pretest (if needed):	Formative evaluation
Input and modeling:	Spelling out what is to precede the lesson
Teaching:	Actual conduct of the lesson
Checking understanding and guided practice:	Lecture, discussion, activity
Posttest (optional):	Evaluate learning
Closure:	Concluding activity
Independent practice:	Start homework, for example

the probability of learning" (Hunter, 1985, p. 3). And Hunter analogizes the teacher's role to that of a coach. Advocates of direct instruction also argue that the model can efficiently teach facts, rules, and concepts.

Typically direct instruction takes the form of a lecture, with explanations and examples and, like the Hunter model, opportunities for practice with teacher guidance. It is teacher centered, with large amounts of information transmitted by the teacher. But presumably, unlike our recall of many college classes, considerable time is devoted to interactions with students through questioning and to review, practice, and correction of errors by students (Borich, 1988, p. 143).

Proponents of direct instruction view it more as demonstration than as monologue, stating objectives, focusing on one point, sequencing the presentation and ensuring its mastery, modeling the skill or process, offering specific examples, checking for understanding, and reteaching if necessary (Borich, 1988, p. 144).

Direct instruction gives considerable attention to identifying and matching objectives to the instruction and to providing students with information that is consistent with those objectives.

The suitability of direct instruction depends on the type of information to be learned, the particular timing of a lesson, and the degree of mastery sought. The last is particularly significant; that is, direct instruction borrows heavily on the notions underlying the mastery learning model.

Advantages and Disadvantages of the Direct-Instruction Model. Advocates of direct instruction, including Rosenshine and Stevens (1986), claim that the model, which often employs lectures and other teacher-directed activities, promotes higher learning achievement among students. This is attributed to the clarity of the goals, the ability to develop large amounts of material, especially material not readily available elsewhere, and the sequencing of highly organized material, notably algebra, science and reading. It is believed to be particularly useful for mastery of facts and rules. Not surprisingly, this model appeals to many teachers and students, especially those characterized as concrete-sequential learners, who tend to like material presented in a relatively straightforward, linear fashion.

On the other hand, the direct-instruction model tends to become highly didactic and to prove limiting to students who can more easily achieve higher levels of thinking—analysis, synthesis, and evaluation. Also, the model requires considerable monitoring and testing on the part of the teacher. It could prove frustrating for students who like to work on their own and who perceive relationships relatively easily.

Mastery Learning Model

The *mastery learning model* has its origins in the 18th-century writings of Comenius and Pestalozzi and experienced a revival in the early 1900s by Bobbitt (1918). Mastery learning is not one model but an amalgam of theories, which John B. Carroll (1971) and Benjamin Bloom (1971) have translated into a recognizable model.

Basic to the mastery learning model is the belief that each child has the right to learn everything the school has to teach and the school has the obligation to see that everything it has to teach is learned. Basic too is the notion that the time spent on teaching is directly related to the time needed to learn.

Achievement from mastery learning might be illustrated this way (Ryan & Schmidt, 1979, pp. 21, 22):

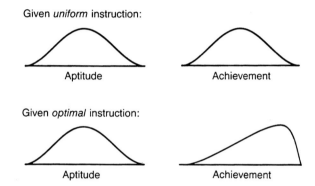

Given *uniform* instruction:

Aptitude   Achievement

Given *optimal* instruction:

Aptitude   Achievement

Clearly this is a behavioristic, systems model.

Figure 4.5 illustrates the steps in mastery learning. The teacher will have to consider the time it takes to develop lessons and units that closely adhere to the schematic illustrated in the figure, especially writing objectives, locating materials, assessing students' progress, and providing remediation.

The mastery learning model is somewhat radical in that it "modifies both the reward contingency and the instructional format" (Good & Stipek, 1983, p. 22). Instruction is paced and individualized, and performance is routinely evaluated and reinforced. The key is the individualization of instruction based on student aptitudes, which in principle should be most beneficial to lower-ability students. Positive rewards follow from successful performance.

Advantages and Disadvantages of the Mastery Learning Model. Questions have been raised about the mastery learning model's success with higher-ability students, who may well enjoy the competitive nature of the model. Because this model takes more time to implement than other models, such students may feel that they are being held back.

Another criticism of the model is that it tends to quash divergent thinking. The objectives may prove too narrow for students who cannot interpret them beyond a literal level.

But with a different model, the teacher might miss all the individuality that can emerge. Many students like mastery learning because it lets them work at their own pace. However, there remains the risk that bright students

FIGURE 4.5
Mastery Learning Model

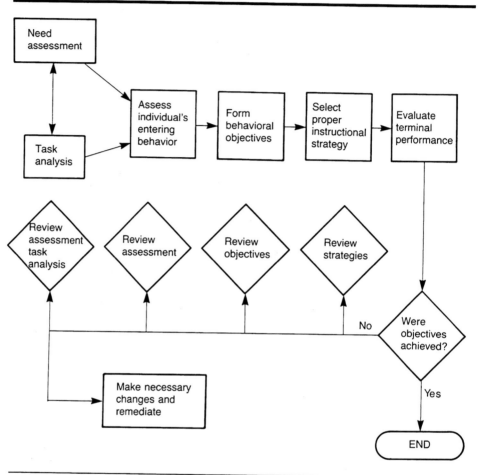

will be held back by slower ones; conversely, slower students, being forced to compete, can be intimidated by the brighter students. Nevertheless, self-motivated students can excel and can find more ways to do the assignments. To enthusiasts, however, intrinsic motivation is revealed when students are reinforced by their success, requiring less teacher praise and encouragement. They do it on their own.

Advance Organizer Model

The *advance organizer model*, proposed by David Ausubel (1968), claims to foster higher-level thinking. Indeed, Joyce and Weil (1986) categorize it as an information processing model, unlike direct instruction or mastery learning. The model shares with Piaget a recognition of developmental levels and a reliance on student accommodation of schemata; that is, it is receptive-discovery, not rote or telling. However, we find the structuring and notion of efficiency more suited to deductive models. That is, the teacher logically presents new information that is potentially meaningful to the students, who "discover" resulting meanings; the students integrate the new information into a means-end relationship that is their own.

According to Ausubel (1968), an advance organizer is:

1. "Appropriately relevant and inclusive introductory materials"
2. "Introduced in advance of learning"
3. "Presented at a higher level of abstraction, generality, and inclusiveness" (p. 148)

These are central ideas that introduce material to be presented and that take the form of concepts or statements of relationships. However, the presentation itself depends on the nature of the material, students' developmental levels, and their degree of familiarity with the material.

Two types of advance organizers have been identified:

- *Expository:* class relationships that subsume a new class
- *Comparative:* integration of new concepts with similar or familiar concepts (using analogies)

The key is to help students develop an "intellectual map" to anchor new learning.

Figure 4.6 presents an example of an advance organizer. This vertical hierarchy, with its gradual increase in detail and specificity, illustrates the progressive differentiation that the teacher helps students to learn.

The assumptions behind the advance organizer model are that (1) most of what anyone knows and understands derives from something discovered by others that is communicated meaningfully and (2) teachers are responsible for effective communication of information to students. Also, for anything to be meaningful, it must be perceived by the individual as having potential meaning, which is idiosyncratic.

Clearly Ausubel was challenging more inductive models, especially discovery models. However, Ausubel considered the advance organizer model equally appropriate for the learning of abstractions (concepts, rules, and generalizations), an objective less readily achieved with other deductive models such as direct instruction.

With the advance organizer model, both teacher and students are active. The teacher is responsible for identifying the advance organizer, logically ordering the content and anchoring the new learning to the old. The student is challenged to perceive relationships, especially between new and familiar material. The intent is to have students achieve higher levels of learning.

FIGURE 4.6
Advance Organizer

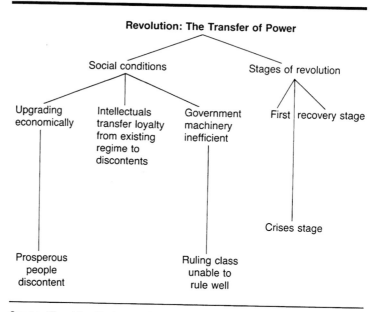

Source: "Teaching Students to Make Predictions about Events in History with a Graphic Organizer Plus Options Guide" by T. W. Bean, J. Sorter, H. Singer, and C. Frazee, May 1986, *Journal of Reading*, p. 741. Reprinted with permission of Thomas W. Bean and the International Reading Association.

Advantages and Disadvantages of the Advance Organizer Model. Ausubel, an advocate of verbal learning, distinguished passive reception (rote learning) from independent discovery, the latter being his advance organizer model. In other words, he argued that meaningful learning occurs when a mental set is established for the learner and when the new, potentially meaningful information logically relates to the learner's cognitive structure, that is, can be accommodated. This constitutes defensible, efficient learning if consistent with the learner's developmental level. Structures are identified for new information and combined with prior knowledge. Higher levels of learning, then, not only are possible but are attained.

Critics of advance organizers challenge Ausubel on a number of grounds. One point is that only some learners learn in a linear, sequential fashion while others are more intuitive, abstract-random learners. A structure that makes sense to one learner may not to another.

Also, many teachers may tend to perceive the model as a license to lecture—the simple transmission theory. Examples may be used to illustrate the content, and a question or two may be asked, but the mode is primarily didactic. Students become passive recipients—exactly what Ausubel, based on his research as a psychiatrist, sought to avoid.

The most enduring criticism of the model is that there is no clear agreement on what constitutes a good organizer (Dinnel & Glover, 1985). In addition, there is the question about students' abilities to encode, or find meaning in, advance organizers. Presenting clear organizers for students and getting students to recall them are two immediate problems. Linking the organizers (as students understand them) to subsequent material is a problem as well.

OTHER MODELS

Another model, an inductive one, may appeal to teachers and learners whose conceptual levels are characterized as abstract random, as well as to both impulsive and reflective learners, referring to Kagan's conceptual tempo in Chapter 3. But this model also demands considerable teacher confidence, for one cannot predict exactly how a class will react.

Synectics Model

Developed by William J. J. Gordon (1961, 1973), the *synectics model* purports to increase the probability of success in problem solving. The name derives from Greek, meaning "the joining together of different and apparently irrelevant elements." The model assumes that

1. The creative process in humans can be concretely described and taught.
2. The phenomena of invention in arts and science are analogous.
3. Individual and group creativity are similar processes. (Gordon, 1961, pp. 3, 5, 6)

The goal is to arrive at solutions in a fundamentally novel way. The process involves two strategies: making the strange familiar and making the familiar strange. The first strategy requires:

1. Describing the present condition
2. Direct analogy
3. Personal analogy
4. Compressed conflict (oxymoron)
5. Direct analogy
6. Reexamining the original task

The first step, describing the present condition, can involve brainstorming, which may free students from some of the usual constraints they encounter in the classroom. One activity involves asking students how many uses they can imagine for a brick or paper clip and having them write answers, no matter how strange, on the chalkboard. Once they cease being "reasonable," students become quite inventive.

Then, modifying this strategy somewhat, students are asked to think of some metaphors that we all use, often unknowingly: "planting the seed (or flag)," "reaping the harvest," "letting the idea germinate," or "cultivating a way of thinking." The intent is to have students transfer words from their original and familiar senses to new ones, thus drawing equations.

In an American history class, the synectics model could be used to examine Watergate, the scandal that rocked the country and led to the resignation of a president. John Dean, a White House counsel and principal in the affair, clearly was thinking metaphorically when he described the Nixon presidency in 1973–1974 as "cancerous" (Sternberg, Tournangeau, & Nigro, 1979); that is, the tactics of the Committee to Re-elect the President (CREEP) led to a number of "tricks," including a burglary of the Democratic Party headquarters in the Watergate office building in Washington and attempts to cover up the crime.

In describing the presidency as "cancerous," Dean was drawing a *direct analogy*, which in turn suggests a *personal analogy*—Dean's perception of himself as the surgeon who would remove the cancer. He would surgically heal the presidency—a *compressed conflict (oxymoron)*—by testifying about what he knew of CREEP's tactics. President Nixon's resignation, then, would represent a healing government—a return to the *direct analogy* just described. During this lesson, students would have to be encouraged to think metaphorically, as John Dean did, and to transfer their thinking to the powers of Congress (the House and Senate) during the impeachment process in 1974, 1866, or even earlier, at the time of the Constitutional Convention— say, the arguments made in *The Federalist 10*.

For another illustration of the synectics model, in which democracy is compared to the human body, see Joyce and Weil (1986, pp. 175–177).

Advantages and Disadvantages of the Synectics Model. The synectics model poses special problems in addition to that of deciding how much time to spend on particular material. It requires tolerance of ambiguity and invites confusion if not done well. Individual differences in verbal problem solving and, necessarily, metaphorical thinking, suggest that there is no simple, all-purpose way to develop figurative activity. Creativity is demanded as much by trying to make sense of someone else's metaphor as it is in attempting to construct a new one. Both interpretation and construction of metaphors are part of the creative process, and both arise out of a combination of systematic, analytical thinking, insight, and tension among ideas.

However, the synectics model offers a medium for encouraging creative thought that can be applied to a variety of topics in the social studies. It also helps students realize that the content of the social studies is not inert— something to be dug up from a dry textbook—but evolves from the interaction of individuals and events. Problem solving is critical to a functioning society, though it is often laborious and produces uncertain results.

Metaphorical thinking can be taught (Best, 1984). The research of Broderick (1984) indicates that while there are qualitative differences among students, youngsters comprehend and produce metaphorical language from the onset of their language development. Barell and Axman (1984), in their experience with 10th through 12th graders, found that metaphorical think-ing conforms to the basic process of inquiry, in which comprehension is a function of cognitive development with more creativity demanded by higher levels of abstraction.

However, the transfer and accommodation of two identities to each other, necessary for metaphorical thinking, may be affected by word order (Ver-brugge, 1980, 115–116); that is, the order of two noun phrases in a sentence strongly affects the directionality of transformation, for a metaphorical sen-tence is "not a symmetric equation or equivalent relation." The sentence subject typically fixes the "given" to which the predicate becomes the "new." For instance, in the Watergate example, the Nixon presidency would be the "given" and cancer the "new," and the transformation between the two may be problematic for some learners.

Also important, the teacher must be mindful that it is the students' point of view that is controlling; that is, students must make sense out of the problem and develop a conceptual scheme, starting with what and how something is known.

Group Investigation (Problem Solving)

Group investigation, one of the older models of teaching, can be attributed to John Dewey's descriptions of how we think and solve problems in a demo-cratic society (Dewey, 1961). This model appeals particularly to field-depen-dent learners. Recall from the previous chapter that field-dependent learners tend to be social and reliant on others for information. Generally they prefer less structure and like the opportunity to explore problems in interactive situations.

Keys to the model are active participation and experience-based inquiry. The classroom is seen as analogous to society, and, to the extent possible, problems students encounter should replicate society's problems.

The steps in group investigation are as follows:

1. The teacher or the students pose a problem.
2. Students, independently or in groups, study the problem and begin to collect data.
3. Students analyze the data and pose solutions.
4. Individual students or groups make reports to the whole class.
5. Results of individuals' or groups' analyses and solutions are examined for feasibility.

One example of group investigation emerged from a real-life experience; in fact, the students themselves posed the problem. As far back as anyone could remember, each winter a small pond near the school served as a community ice skating rink. But not this January. Some students who regularly walked by the pond and checked its readiness for skating were puzzled—and angered—by a posted sign warning against trespassing on the pond. The next morning, the students confronted their social studies teacher, who also happened to be the vice mayor. Rather than going on with his planned lesson, the teacher turned the problem back on the students: "So, what are you going to do about it?"

Momentarily this took the wind out of the students' sails, but shortly they were on the attack again, though no better informed or organized.

"Well," the social studies teacher–vice mayor asked, "does the owner have the right to post his property?"

Reluctantly, the students agreed that a property owner indeed had such a right.

"So who is the owner?" the teacher asked.

That stumped the group.

"Hadn't you better find out who owns the property? And then hadn't you better talk to the owner? Why, all of a sudden, is the property posted?"

Thus began a group investigation that lasted well beyond the school year, close to eight very exciting but frustrating months.

Obviously the teacher's direction—and considerable class time—was needed to resolve this very real problem. This included suggestions as to how to determine ownership of land. (In this case, the land was town property as a result of the original owner's delinquency in paying property taxes and subsequent forced sale to pay them. The posting had resulted from the town attorney's warning that the town might be liable for any injuries sustained while the property was being properly disposed of.)

The class was divided into groups to collect data, mostly on their own time but with teacher help. As they gathered data, they suggested and analyzed possible ways to challenge the town government (hypothesizing). The process took considerable time, including meetings with the town board, rewriting the zoning law, presenting it to the board, appealing to the town zoning board of appeals, and obtaining community support for their project.

Knowing better than to spend all class time on this project, the teacher continued with other lessons consistent with the curriculum but interrupted the lessons to allow the group to meet on strategy, analyze the steps they were taking, and agree to further steps.

The outcome was a happy one, for the students can now skate on the pond depending on safety conditions.

Not every issue for group investigation need be so time consuming or complicated. Compare this culminating project in a nine-week 12th-grade economics unit (Mahood, 1965, pp. 16–21). Given the analogy of a car (the economy) running along an uphill road (growth) with ditches of inflation and deflation on opposite sides, the class's goal was to keep the car running on all cylinders (growing smoothly) without swerving to either side despite both front- and back-seat drivers.

The first step was to review and discuss various proposals for encouraging economic growth without producing instability, including a tax cut, loosening of credit by the Federal Reserve System, and increased public spending.

Relying in part on a prior American history course, the students examined past economic cycles, monetary and fiscal policies, problems in stimulating the economy, and risks of foreign competition.

Then the class divided into three groups representing business, labor, and government, respectively. Each group was to study the issue and develop proposals. Ultimately, the class produced a final report. While the results were hardly sensational, they were the proud composite creation of 30 dissimilar students who had replicated a process that goes on continuously in our society. And it was the *students'* product, for the teacher's role had been merely to contribute suggestions on procedure, allude to other sources students might consult, or help them "test" an idea.

A related, though not necessarily different model is variously called *social inquiry* (Massialas & Cox, 1966) and *reflective thinking* (Hullfish & Smith, 1961; Dewey, 1933; Hunt & Metcalf, 1968). It refers to "thought controlled by an end . . . an attitude of mind and a generalized set of mental operations with which to approach all problems, whether social or physical in nature" (Hunt & Metcalf, 1968, p. 67). Again the basis for social inquiry, or reflective thinking, is John Dewey's analysis of thinking.

Like the group investigation and inquiry models we examined earlier, social inquiry begins with a problem. However, Hunt and Metcalf (1968) would begin by having students examine their beliefs consistent with their development and background to generate tension. Following this, the students would develop hypotheses for resolving the tension, test the hypotheses, and check their conclusions. Success with the techniques, whether teacher directed or not, depends on *how* the teacher uses the techniques, develops the classroom climate, and facilitates discussion. The content can be anything in the curriculum, but Hunt and Metcalf (1968) strongly encourage focusing on what they term the "closed areas," content areas "saturated with prejudices and taboos" (pp. 24, 26).

Advantages and Disadvantages of the Group Investigation Model. The most obvious advantage of the group investigation model is seen in our examples. In both instances, students were involved in real social problems, however minor in most people's eyes. Also, students resolved problems with their own data collection, analyses, hypothesizing, and hypothesis testing. In the first illustration they were participants in government, consistent with the Deweyian model, and in the second they learned how government and the economy work.

However, the amount of time required obviously is a consideration. The extent of participation is another factor for the teacher to assess. Will the participation and learning be sufficient to justify the time and energy expended? How will the learning be measured?

For the teacher who believes that teaching is more than "getting through the curriculum guide," however, this model offers real advantages.

Role Playing and Simulation Models

Role Playing. The *role-playing model* (Shaftel & Shaftel, 1967), as the name implies, has students portray other people, that is, "step into someone else's shoes." More important, role playing offers an opportunity to experience "firsthand" something about which students might only read or be told.

Role playing is thought to date back to at least the Peripatetic school in Athens in the late fourth century B.C. It is during this period that Theophrastus may have been influenced to write his treatise on characterization based on character portrayals in the comic drama popular during that era.*

The number of steps involved in role playing depends primarily on whether there is a reenactment, or second run-through, of the activity. Shaftel and Shaftel (1967) list nine steps, but these can be reduced to seven:

1. Warming up the group and explaining the task
2. Selecting role players
3. Setting the stage (restating roles)
4. Preparing observers
5. Enacting the role playing
6. Discussing and evaluating the role playing
7. Drawing conclusions or generalizations from the experience

An example of role playing involves the often ignored "Boston Massacre" and its aftermath (Mahood, 1980, pp. 212–217). The roles are Captain Thomas Preston, commander of a group of redcoats who found themselves trapped on King Street by an angry crowd of colonists; Royal Governor Thomas Hutchinson; Edmund Trowbridge, Superior Court of Massachusetts judge; John Adams, 34-year-old lawyer and representative to the General Court (the Massachusetts legislature) in Boston; and Josiah Quincy, the younger brother of Adams' good friend and prosecutor, Samuel Quincy.

Multiple sets of role cards allow the entire class to examine the situation more personally and to try to assess what *they* might do if they were these historical figures. Then the teacher suggests a scheme for decision making, allowing the students to review the choices and possible consequences of their decisions. Next, the teacher can introduce the actual outcome of the trial to check students' responses to the role play, followed by questions regarding the issues facing the colonists and England in 1770, the principles espoused, and the ultimate effects of the incident known as the "Boston Massacre."

An analogy has been drawn between this event and the tragedy at Kent State 200 years later. American history teachers might want to return to it in the latter context.

*Thanks for this background information is due Latin teacher Joseph Gerencser, Hornell, New York.

Simulation. The *simulation model* involves a recreation of something real that cannot be encountered directly in class.* (The word *simulation* comes from the Latin word *simul*, meaning "like.")

Simulation, a popular method of instruction in the 1960s, probably originated thousands of years ago. An early simulation was a war game developed about 3000 B.C. by the Chinese called *Wei-hai*. Another early war game, called *Chaturanga*, which some believe was a precursor to chess, was played in ancient India. In the United States, the first nonmilitary educational simulations may have been developed in business and management. The first widely used simulation was developed by the American Management Association in 1956. The object was to give players experience in carrying out business transactions and formulating management policies.**

The latest manifestation of simulation is the proliferation of computer games in arcades and virtually every place imaginable as well as in the classroom. An example is "Oregon Territory," created by MECC (Minnesota Educational Computer Consortium). New computer simulations appear daily.

Goals of simulations vary, but generally simulations are designed to help students comprehend certain specific information and apply that comprehension. Attitudinal changes on the part of students can be a goal as well. Important is the fact that students obtain immediate results ("feedback") that may be less readily available in other classrooms.

Assumptions underlying the use of simulations are that (1) it is possible to recreate realistic situations in the classroom in simpler form and (2) students can develop and test problem-solving skills.

Generally there are five steps in simulation:

1. Teacher preparation
2. Orientation of students
3. Assigning roles to students
4. Enacting the situation established by the simulation
5. "Debriefing," whereby students review the simulation and draw conclusions or generalizations

An example of a simulation appears in Mahood (1980). In this lesson, which worked especially well with eighth graders, students played "immigrants" seeking admission to the United States. "Doctors" were assigned to screen the immigrants based on a quota system. The "immigrants" formed lines and received role cards with biographical data, such as the following:

---

*The Link trainer, developed around World War II to train and wash out pilots, is still used to simulate flights.

**This brief history of simulation was provided by James Walter, another Hornell, New York, teacher.

VISA	VISA	VISA
Age: 68	Age: 25	Age: 7
Skilled, literate	Skilled, illiterate	Unskilled, illiterate
Poor health	Good health	Good health
Male	Female	Female
Protestant	Anglican	Roman Catholic
German	English	Slavic

At the conclusion of the simulation, the teacher conducted the critical "debriefing," asking students questions such as the following:

1. How did you feel standing in line waiting your turn? After you were admitted? Rejected?
2. What reasons might be offered for your admittance? Rejection?
3. What seemed to be the qualifications of those admitted? Rejected? Was there a pattern?
4. Would this pattern have existed in 1850? 1880? 1910? 1940? Now?
5. What effects might changes have on the United States? On the countries against which discrimination was shown? Economically? Socially? Politically?
6. Given the chance, in what ways would you revise the admissions policy?
7. What effects might your plan have?
8. Having done this simulation, what conclusions can you draw about the immigrant experience?

The preceding questions could lead to a discussion, extending well beyond the class period, about the nature of the American people and various theories about the effects of immigration on our country (e.g., do we have a "melting pot" or an "ethnic salad"?).

Advantages and Disadvantages of Simulation and Role Playing. Critical to the success of simulation and role playing in the classroom, especially the former, are teacher preparation, student orientation, and "debriefing." If the activities are realistically presented (albeit contrived for the classroom), historical events or situations come alive for students. The intensity of students' participation never ceases to amaze teachers who use these models.

Of course, poor preparation, orientation, and debriefing can lead to an aura of disorganized play in the classroom. Learning is then sacrificed, and time is lost unnecessarily. The hardest part is the teacher preparation, for it takes considerable time to develop the appropriate scenario, to ensure that students will identify with what they are to simulate or role play, and to introduce the necessary degree of reality. An increasing number of computer simulations that enable teachers to assign activities to students and monitor their progress are becoming available (discussed further in Chapter 6).

For the teacher more accustomed to dispensing information, these models may seem uncomfortable, even silly, and field-independent learners may feel the same. Constant performance of simulations and role playing can dull the excitement. But for some content and students, simulations and role playing offer a useful alternative to more typical lesson presentations. For the teacher they provide an opportunity to observe students interacting and thinking out their moves.

According to some curriculum specialists, Beth should have a "repertoire" of models from which to choose (Joyce & Weil, 1986, pp. 449–465). Further, we believe it is less likely that she will be dogmatic in the classroom if she tries to match models to her students' aptitudes, though this will require considerable work on her part.

Yet these adolescents who will occupy her classroom—so diverse in size, shape, and abilities—are her responsibility. Beth will be with them long enough this school year to get to know their needs (and moods) and recognize their different learning styles. She can, if she likes, vary her instruction accordingly.

What do you think? Which model most appealed to you? Which appealed least?

What do you regard as the most difficult aspect of selecting any model?

What might you do if you tried one of the models and found it was a failure as a lesson? Abandon the model? Modify it?

Summary

A comparative analysis of the teaching models discussed in this chapter is shown in Figure 4.7. The information processing models—*concept formation, concept attainment,* and *inquiry*—are largely inductive and are intended to encourage divergent thinking and problem solving. The student is prompted to "process" information, to actively engage in learning through observing, collecting, sorting, categorizing, and summarizing information generated as much by the student as by the teacher, although the teacher is equally active.

The deductive models, particularly *direct instruction* and *mastery learning,* argue that learning is the central objective of schooling and that every student can learn given the time and opportunity. These models also force teachers to clarify objectives for their classes, a task that should be, but is not always, routine. They also encourage students to complete assigned tasks because the activities are clearly identified and structured.

FIGURE 4.7
Comparative Chart of Teaching Models

	Student Role	Teacher Role	Advantages	Disadvantages
INDUCTIVE MODELS				
Concept Formation (Taba)	active participant; gathers, sorts summarizes, predicts	planner; moderator	encourages higher order thinking; abstract; random	time-consuming difficult to assess learning; minimal structure
Concept Attainment (Bruner)	active participant; classifies examples; invents own	planner, moderator: explains process; presents puzzle	encourates application, analysis, conceptualizing; abstract; sequential	time-consuming difficult to assess learning; isolates concept; requires structure
Group Investigation (Dewey, Thelen)	active participant; gathers data, hypothesizes, tests hypotheses	planner; explains strategies guides problem solving	encourages problem solving; use of scientific method; abstract sequential; field dependent	time-consuming teacher can subvert; hard to assess; less structure
Inquiry (Suchman)	active questioner; hypothesizes; tests hypotheses;	planner; establishes conditions; responds to students' questions	encourages questioning, problem solving; hypothesizing; field-independent	time-consuming; not all students involved
DEDUCTIVE MODELS				
Advance Organizer (Ausubel)	somewhat active; accommodate to teacher schema	planner; organizer; presenter at higher levels	promotes discovery; higher level thinking; more efficient than inductive; abstract sequential	disagreement about "good" organizers; limits intuitive learners

	Student Role	Teacher Role	Advantages	Disadvantages
DEDUCTIVE MODELS				
Direct Instruction (Hunter)	passive: practices skills	active; director; monitor: sequencer	efficient; linear; aims at mastery; concrete sequential	lower level thinking; tends to constrict thinking
Mastery Learning (Bloom, Carroll)	passive; practices skills	active planner, monitor, mediator	efficient: linear; aims at mastery; accommodates various learners	considerable revising, remediating, monitoring
SOCIAL/PERSONAL MODELS				
Synectics (Gordon)	active; responsible for learning creative process	planner; organizes initial analogies, parables	highly personalized; encourages analytical thinking; intuitive random	requires creative and interpretive skills; hard to assess
Simulation	active; discovers connections to real situations analogizes	planner; establishes scenarios and rules; "debriefer"	encourages student participation; recreates out-of-school events; field-dependent	time-consuming; assessment is difficult; inaccurate representations; risk of confusion
Role Playing (Shaftels)	active; helps create roles; must analogize	helps create roles and rules; "debriefer"	student involvement; affective; field-dependent	time-consuming; hard to assess; can lead to inaccuracy

The *advance organizer model,* while usually more deductive, illustrates many of the characteristics of the information processing models, particularly as it aims toward the learning of abstractions. The notion of intellectual scaffolding, or cognitive mapping, demands that students anchor new learning with old at increasingly higher levels.

Other models, which appeal more to field dependent learners, include synectics, group investigation, and simulation and role play.

Synectics is intensely personal. Students are encouraged to be inventive, finding something already existing but restructuring the information into something new to them, thus seeing new relationships. The usefulness of metaphorical thinking—employing analogies to represent familiar things in new ways, like John Dean's "cancerous government"—is illustrated daily. Using analogies (or parables) is one of the oldest teaching methods, and it still works.

Group investigation replicates decision making in society by requiring students to shape questions, gather data, and hypothesize and test "solutions." Getting a town to make an ice-skating pond available to residents is a real-life issue; in our example, the project succeeded because the teacher was willing to make the classroom more than a room in a building, thereby illustrating that schools are not isolated from the "real world."

Role playing and *simulation,* while not every teacher's cup of tea, recreate events that cannot be experienced directly and help these events come alive for students. Experiencing the immigrant's feeling of discrimination but coming to realize why government policies are made makes social studies more palatable for many students, however time consuming and demanding of a teacher's time the task may be.

What Beth has been wrestling with is the notion of matching models to environments, that is, diagnosing students' needs and planning appropriate instruction. While it may be difficult to fully appreciate the time and effort that goes into such planning, it is vital if teachers are to challenge their students.

Decisions! Decisions!

Following are four situations that you as a teacher might encounter. Examine each situation and answer the questions that follow.

Situation 1: You have a group of students who are definitely showing signs of ability to work and to empathize with others. The main problem your students have is staying on task because they are so concerned with others. However, it is clear that the students can name and distinguish attributes of concepts that you are introducing.

Situation 2: Your students tend to see things only in black-and-white terms (or right-and-wrong). Their relationships with others in the group tend to be one-sided, hierarchical, and egocentric. The students do understand rules and generally can follow them.

Situation 3: You have a group of students who can stay on task and work together generally well. They seem able to accommodate new information, handle abstract notions, analyze dilemmas, distinguish among related variables, and predict probable outcomes of complex relationships.

Situation 4: One group of students whom you teach challenges rules, is beginning to distinguish among alternative schemas for organizing information, and can integrate low-level structural properties. However, these students have a strong tendency to dichotomize relationships in the environment.

1. What model(s) might be most appropriate to use with each group of students?

2. How might you go about employing the model(s) in each situation?

3. What are the strengths and weaknesses of the model(s) in each case?

References

Ausubel, D. P. (1964). In defense of verbal learning. *Educational Theory, 14*, 83–92.

Ausubel, D. P. (1968). *Education psychology: A cognitive view.* New York: Holt, Rinehart & Winston.

Bailey, S. (1968). Untitled, unpublished paper read at the Symposium on Urban Education, Syracuse University.

Barell, J., & Axman, W. (1984). *Hi heels and walking shadows: Metaphorical thinking in schools.* New Orleans: American Educational Research Association. (ERIC Document Reproduction Service, No. ED 245 056)

Bean, T. W., Sorter, J., Singer, H., & Frazee, C. (1986, May). Teaching students to make predictions about events in history with a graphic organizer plus options guide. *Journal of Reading,* 739–745.

Best, J. (1984, May). Teaching political theory meaning through metaphor. *Improving College and University Teaching, 32*(4), 165–168.

Bloom, B. S. (1971). Mastery learning. In J. H. Block (Ed.), *Mastery learning: Theory and practice.* New York: Holt, Rinehart & Winston.

Bobbitt, J. F. (1918). *The curriculum.* Boston: Houghton Mifflin.

Borich, G. D. (1988). *Effective teaching models.* Columbus, OH: Merrill.

Broderick, V. K. (1985). *The development of metaphor comprehension.* Baltimore: Eastern Psychological Association. (ERIC Document Reproduction Service No. ED 246 698)

Bruner, J. (1961). *The process of education.* Cambridge, MA: Harvard University Press.

Calandra, A. (1968, December 21). Angels on a pin. *Saturday Review, 60.*

Carroll, J. B. (1971). Problems of measurement related to the concept of learning for mastery. In J. H. Block (Ed.), *Mastery learning: Theory and practice.* New York: Holt, Rinehart & Winston.

Collins, C. O., & Sawyer, C. H. (1984, November/December). Teaching from television: M*A*S*H as geography. *Journal of Geography,* 265–268.

Denham, C., & Lieberman, A. (Eds.). (1980). *Time to learn* (p. 66). Sacramento, CA: Commission for Teacher Preparation and Licensing.

Dewey, J. (1933). How we think. Boston: Heath.

Dewey, J. (1961). *Democracy and education.* New York: Macmillan.

Dinnell, D., & Glover, J. A. (1985, October). Advance organizers: Encoding manipulations. *Journal of Educational Psychology,* 514–521.

Eggen, P. D., & Kauchak, D. P. (1988). *Strategies for teachers* (2nd ed.). Englewood Cliffs, NJ: Prentice-Hall.

Fraenkel, J. (1973). *Helping students to think and value: Strategies for teaching the social studies* (2nd ed.). Englewood Cliffs, NJ: Prentice-Hall.

Good, T. I., & Stipek, D. J. (1983). Individual differences in the classroom: A psychological perspective. In G. Fenstermacher & J. I. Goodlad (Eds.), *Individual differences and the common curriculum* (82nd Yearbook, National Society for Study of Education, Part I, pp. 9–43). Chicago: University of Chicago Press.

Gordon, W. J. J. (1961). *Synectics.* New York: Harper & Row.

Gordon, W. J. J. (1973). *The metaphorical way of learning and knowing.* Cambridge, MA: Porpoise Books.

Horton, L. (1981). *Mastery learning.* Bloomington, IN: Phi Delta Kappa Foundation.

Hullfish, H. G. & Smith, P. G. (1961). *Reflective thinking.* New York: Dodd, Mead.

Hunt, M. P., & Metcalf, L. B. (1968). *Teaching high school social studies.* New York: Harper & Row.

Hunter, M. (1985). *Mastery teaching.* El Segundo, CA: TIP Publications.

Joyce, B., & Weil, M. (1986). *Models of teaching.* Englewood Cliffs, NJ: Prentice-Hall.

Kuhn, T. S. (1970). *The structure of scientific revolutions* (2nd ed.). Chicago: University of Chicago Press.

Kulick, J. A. (1982). Individualized systems of learning. In H. E. Mitzel (Ed.), *Encyclopedia of educational research* (Vol. 2, 5th ed., pp. 851–857). New York: Macmillan.

Mahood, W. (1965). The American economic order. *Economic Education Experiences of Enterprising Teachers II,* 16–21.

Mahood, W. (1973, January). Concepts in the social studies. *The Social Studies,* 25–35.

Mahood, W. (1980, January). The land of milk and honey: Simulating the immigrant experience. *Social Education,* 22–24.

Mahood, W. (1980, September/October). Boston on trial. *The Social Studies,* 212–217.

Mahood, W. (1981, July/August). Nacirema, weans and bushmen: Studying other cultures. *The Social Studies,* 184–187.

Massialas, B. G., & Cox, C. B. (1966). *Inquiry in the social studies.* New York: McGraw-Hill.

Maxcy, S. (1986, Fall). The conception of problem and the role of inquiry in social education. *Theory and Research in Social Education, 14*(4), 295–306.

McKinney, C. W., Gilmore, A. C., Peddicord, H. Q., & McCallum, R. S. (1987, Summer). Effects of a best example and critical attributes on prototype formation in the acquisition of a concept. *Theory and Research in Social Education, 15*(3), 189–203.

Parker, J. C., & Rubin, L. J. (1966). *Process as content.* Chicago: Rand McNally.

Piaget, J. (1952). *The origins of intelligence in children.* New York: International University Press.

Rosenshine, B., & Stevens, R. (1986). Teaching functions. *In M. C. Wittrock (Ed.), Handbook of research on teaching.*

Ryan, D., & Schmidt, M. (1979). *Mastery learning: Theory, research and implementation.* Ontario: Ministry of Education.

Shaftel, F., & Shaftel, G. (1967). *Role playing for social values: Decision-making in the social studies.* Englewood Cliffs, NJ: Prentice-Hall.

Smith, F. (1975). *Comprehension and learning—A conceptual framework for teachers.* New York: Holt, Rinehart & Winston.

Sternberg, R. J., Tournangeau, R., & Nigro, G. (1979). Metaphor, induction and social policy: The convergence of macroscopic and microscopic views. In A. Ortony (Ed.), *Metaphor and thought* (pp. 325–355). Cambridge: Cambridge University Press.

Suchman, R. (1962). *The Elementary School Training Program in Scientific Inquiry* (Report to the U.S. Office of Education, Project Title VII, Project 216). Urbana, IL: University of Illinois.

Taba, H. (1967). *Teachers handbook for elementary social studies.* Reading, MA: Addison-Wesley.

Verbrugge, R. (1980). Transformations in knowing: A realist view of metaphor. In R. Honeck & R. Hoffman (Eds.), *Cognition and figurative language* (pp. 87–126). Hillsdale, NJ: Erlbaum.

Yoho, R. F. (1986, Summer). Effectiveness of four concept teaching strategies on social studies concept acquisition and retention. Theory and Research in Social Education, 14(3), 211–223.

PART TWO

The Instructional Process

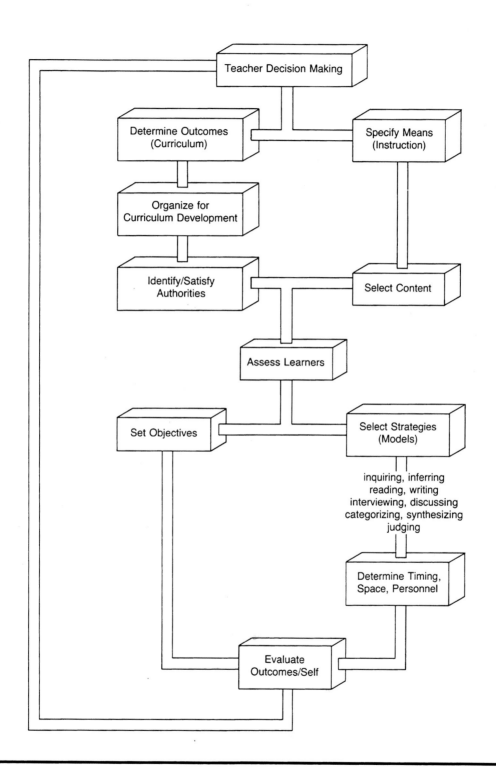

Chapter Five

Planning

Planning begins with the teacher developing a unit plan, which includes daily plans, based on a cognitive map that reflects the learning goals that match students' aptitudes and the content.

When Beth signed a contract to become a social studies teacher, there was no describing her excitement. Finally she was a teacher!

Then reality struck. *Now* what should she do? That first day of school, she would confront strangers, persons younger than she who would expect her to know what she was doing. Did she? Now she wasn't so sure. Would the students take her seriously? Would they see her as "the teacher?" The euphoria began to fade.

Beth is experiencing what Fuller and Bown found to be common concerns for teachers, and likely for any persons in what might be called the "helping professions": "Becoming a teacher is complex, stressful, intimate and largely covert" (Fuller & Bown, 1975, p. 25). According to their research, Beth is hovering between two levels of "concern": personal survival (Level One) and pressures of the job (Level Two). In time, given the necessary help, encouragement, and a combination of skills and ego strength, Beth will reach the highest level—concern about her students. At that stage, Beth will be much less apprehensive. She will be better able to adapt to her students' needs and try to fit the curriculum to the students rather than vice versa. Beth will succeed, as will many of you. She will not become a teacher "dropout," "never-in," or tyrannical bureaucrat.

"Where do I start?" Beth wondered. Maybe her department head could help. And so they met.

"First, Beth," the department head began, "recall that we have a district curriculum guide based on a state syllabus [see Figure 5.1]. Let's look at it."

But rather than reassuring Beth, the curriculum guide stunned her. What about everything she had heard about teachers as curriculum makers? What decisions was she to make when the curriculum was already formally laid out? Was she merely to be a slave to what someone else decided for her?

Anticipating Beth's reaction, her department head reassured her: "This is a *guide*, Beth, not a straitjacket. You still have to make decisions. There are only so many days in a year and hours in a day. You do have to be selective. And, in time, you will be comfortable with the content so that increasingly you will be making decisions. In fact, you will help revise the curriculum guide.

"Let me tell you a story that has helped me over the years," the department head continued. "When I was in elementary school taking piano lessons, my teacher, a master of pianos and people, posed the following question to me: 'How do you peel a *bushel* of potatoes?'

"I replied, 'You put them under cold water first?'

" 'No.'

" 'You boil them first?' I tried again, getting more confused.

" 'No.'

"After I don't know how many tries, I finally said, 'First you peel the first potato. Then you peel the second potato. And so on.'

"Every time I start a new project, I recall this simple question and the difficulty I had answering it. Now let's apply it to you. How do you start planning?"

Beth realized what was expected of her, but she could not figure out which step was the "first potato" in planning lessons for her classes.

"All right, Beth, let's do this logically," her new mentor said. On a sheet of paper, she drew the following continuum:

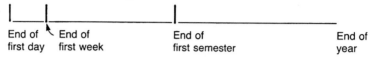

| End of first day | End of first week | End of first semester | End of year |

"Where do you want to be at the end of the semester? You don't have to answer now, but look at the curriculum guide, think about what you expect to have accomplished by the end of the year, and work backwards. Then peel the first potato."

In more academic terms, Beth's department head was arguing that "Achievement [of students] is maximized when teachers structure the material beginning with overviews, advance organizers or reviews of objectives" (Brophy, 1986, p. 1071). But however prescriptive this may appear, the fact remains that teachers need some mechanism to create order out of the overwhelmingly large and confusing amount of material that constitutes the social studies.

DEVELOPING A CONCEPTUAL FRAMEWORK

Educational philosopher Hugh Petrie, in terms similar to Brophy's, would begin with a "cognitive map" that uses meanings and key terms of the various social sciences (Petrie, 1976, pp. 9–15). Specifically, Petrie argues that we need to develop some ways to represent both the familiar and the unfamiliar to make sense out of the content we are to teach. To illustrate, he uses so-called "ambiguous figures," shown in Figures 5.2 and 5.3.

Let's focus on Figure 5.2(a). Suppose a teacher identifies it as a mailing envelope and begins discussing it with the class. One student, having just discussed drugs and alcohol in a health class, sees a martini glass instead. Another student, a male who clearly has arrived at puberty, is hopelessly lost in thoughts about the bikini he sees. A lesson on mailing envelopes will not go far with these students. Neither will a lesson in which the class, asked to discuss the rabbit in Figure 5.2(b), sees only a duck. Finally, imagine the confusion if students were asked to discuss the expression of the elderly woman in Figure 5.3. Many students might not see the elderly woman at all but only the younger woman.

FIGURE 5.1
Excerpt from Social Studies: Global Studies Syllabus

Unit Goals: By the end of this unit, students will be able to demonstrate knowledge of how diverse cultural influences affected national goals, political institutions, and foreign policy strategies for many centuries.

Unit Seven: The Soviet Union and Eastern Europe

Content	Major Ideas	Model Activities
II. The Dynamics of Change		
Content Objectives:		
To discuss the role trade played in encouraging cultural diffusion between the early Russians and the Byzantine Empire		
To understand and analyze the effect which the Roman Catholic/Eastern Orthodox split had upon the East/West relationships		
To appreciate the varied motives, both psychological and economic, which have encouraged the Russian/Soviet pursuit of a policy of defensive and economic expansionism		
To examine the origins of feudalism at a time when serfdom was beginning to disappear in the West		
To analyze the causes of the rise of Russia's centralized, autocratic state		
To evaluate the role played by the Russification policy in achieving national identity and unity		
To trace Russia's 19th century rise to world power status		
To examine the causes for dissension and opposition to the Romanovs' reactionary rule		
To appreciate Russia's contribution to the arts		
To identify and discuss the causes of the Russian Revolution		
To identify the stages in the Russian Revolution		

II. The Dynamics of Change

A. The cultural legacy of Byzantium

1. Basis of early Russian state formed by joining of two groups

  a. Slavs contributed language

  b. Varangians enforced law and order

    (1) Viking merchant princes

    (2) Seeking trade with Constantinople

The commercial *interdependence* between the Kievian State and Constantinople led to a *cultural* diffusion which helped to shape the modern *nation-state* of Russia.

Have students develop maps showing Viking trade routes and strongholds in Europe. They should locate the Byzantine Empire, the Black Sea, the Dnieper River, the Volga, the Baltic Sea, Novgorod, Kiev, Smolensk, and Constantinople. On the basis of this information have students assess the importance of Russia's rivers on trade links and cultural diffusion between the Byzantine Empire and the state centering in Kiev. Have students identify the items that were the basis of trade.

2. Introduction of Christianity

  a. Vladimir converted to Orthodox Christianity, end of 10th century

  b. Conversion of this Kiev prince brought in Byzantine culture and institutions

  c. Other Eastern European peoples converted to Roman Catholicism

Although Eastern Orthodox and Western Roman communions were not formally divided by *schism* until 1054, differences in style and emphasis were apparent from Christianity's earliest years and have served to shape *relationships* between Russia and its Catholic Slavic neighbors.

Russian *culture* attained distinct achievements in the fields of art and architecture.

Have the class examine a set of photographs of various street signs in Western Europe and the Soviet Union and identify similarities in the Western European signs; differences in the Russian signs.

3. Adoption of the Cyrillic alphabet

  a. Evidence of influence of Byzantine Empire

  b. Effect upon future relationships with Western Europe

An important difference between Western Europe and Russia was the *adoption* of the Cyrillic *alphabet* rather than the Roman *alphabet* in Russia.

Using encyclopedias and other resource materials, students may write a brief report on the Russian adoption of the Cyrillic alphabet and its origins, noting the influence of the Byzantine Empire upon Russian culture and the effect of that adoption upon relations with Western Europe.

B. Political/social legacy of the Mongols

1. Mongol rule had lasting implications

  a. Military organization

  b. Taxation

The harsh realities of the Mongol political system fostered a fear of foreign *exploitation* and *domination* among the Russians which has lasted to the present.

Despotism and *feudalism*, two major themes in subsequent Russian history, began under Mongol rule.

Have students examine a map of the Mongol Empire at its height and describe the global extent of Mongol power in Europe, the Middle East, and Asia. Have them locate the capital of the khanate of the Golden Horde.

Source: From *Social Studies: Global Studies* Syllabus, Field Test edition, New York State Bureau of Social Studies, 1986.

FIGURE 5.2
Ambiguous Cognitive
Maps (1)

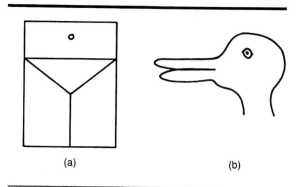

(a)   (b)

Source: From "Do You See What I See?" by H. Petrie, 1976,
Educational Researcher, 5(2), pp. 12, 13. Copyright 1976 by
the American Educational Research Association. Reprinted by
permission.

However enthusiastic, skillful in leading a discussion, or effective in
classroom management a teacher might be, if the students did not "see" the
mailing envelope, rabbit, or elderly woman the lesson would be a failure. The
problem is simply that the "field" is unclear. There is no "cognitive map," no
context for the teaching.

An example of a student creating his own context is humorously described
by James Herndon (1971, p. 117):

> Flax is what school is all about. In my own old-fashioned geography books I went
> to various countries in the company of Bedouin and Greek and Turkish kids and
> the thing that most remains in my mind now about those imaginary kids is that
> they always grew flax. . . . I never knew what flax was, but I knew that if I kept it
> in mind and wrote it down a lot and raised my hand and said it a lot, I would be
> making it.*

From this we can surmise that most of the time Herndon was not "on the same
wavelength" as his teacher, but he had a way of viewing the world in which
he thought his teacher lived. Clearly he and his teacher had failed to "connect."

Lefrançois (1985, p. 118) gives an example in which a "Dick and Jane"
text was used (at least until fairly recently) by a class of younger Eskimo
children:

---

*From *How to Survive in Your Native Land* (p. 117) by J. Herndon, 1971, New York: Simon &
Schuster. Copyright © 1971 by James Herndon. Reprinted by permission of Simon & Schuster,
Inc.

**FIGURE 5.3
Ambiguous Cognitive
Maps (2)**

Source: From "Do You See What I See?" by H. Petrie, 1976, *Educational Researcher, 5*(2), p. 14. Copyright 1976 by the American Educational Research Association. Reprinted by permission.

These children, who had never seen a city, an automobile, a telephone, or an indoor toilet, were asked to learn to read sentences similar to: "John goes for a drive," "Firemen, policemen, and college professors are our friends. . . . "*

And Lefrançois offers another notion that we might recall trying to learn: that "a demagog is 'an unprincipled politician who panders to the emotions and prejudices of the populace' " (p. 118).

So how does Beth build a conceptual framework, or "cognitive map," for her students? One way, referred to in Chapter 4 in our discussion of the synectics model, is the use of metaphors or, even more broadly, analogies. Recall John Dean, the White House counsel, who decided to "spill the beans" on the Watergate affair. The metaphor, Dean's cognitive map, pictured Dean as a surgeon who would remove the cancer that was eating away at the nation through the executive branch. The lens through which to view Watergate, then, depicted the American government as analogous to the human body. Or, looking at another period in American history, Beth might analogize the Cuban missile crisis and accompanying foreign policy to a chess game involving players, strategies, pace, structure, and outcome. "Players" are the "chiefs" (the president, secretaries of state, defense, and treasury) and so on. "Strategies" are the choices among moves that the players could make. Both of these examples offer students a structure, or cognitive map, based on something familiar to them that Beth can elaborate on as the students come to understand it.

Thus, for Beth the next step in "peeling potatoes" is identifying a structure that will work with her classes.

*From *Psychology for Teaching: A Bear Never Faces the Front,* 5/e, by Guy R. Lefrançois. © 1985 by Wadsworth, Inc.

ASIDE TO THE READER: We hasten to add that the notion of cognitive mapping has been challenged. Phillips (1987, pp. 137–157) stresses the "dark side": that cognitive structures can be misleading. The primary objection is that these structures tend to "have a reassuring atmosphere of reality and concreteness about them" (p. 153); that is, students may be led to believe that abstractions will appear exactly as depicted by the structures presented by the teacher.

The essence of this objection is that ultimately the student must organize material internally and then publicly express this organization. But will the public expression accurately represent the notions being learned? The individual remains the focus, and that individual must perceive a meaningful order to what is being learned so that he or she can translate it into some action. Given this objection, the teacher must be mindful that it is the students' perceptions that ultimately are controlling. In short, the teacher must exercise care when trying to offer students a conceptual framework for learning any material.

GOAL SETTING

Beth was strongly tempted to base a course outline on the textbook used previously with 10th graders studying global studies. The text provided a nice, tidy scheme, and the chapters appeared to correspond fairly closely to the school's curriculum guide. There were 20 chapters in the text, so 2 weeks per chapter would take her through the year. Then Beth remembered a story she had been told about taking the easy way out:

Processionary Caterpillars

Processionary Caterpillars feed upon pine needles. They move through the trees in a long procession, one leading, the others following—each with his eyes half closed and his head snugly fitted against the rear extremity of his predecessor.

Jean-Henri Fabre, the great French naturalist, after patiently experimenting with a large group of caterpillars, finally enticed them to the rim of a large flower pot. He succeeded in getting the first one connected up with the last one, thus forming a complete circle, which started moving around in a procession, with neither beginning nor end.

The naturalist expected that after a while they would catch on to the joke, getting tired of their useless march, and start off in some new direction. But not so. . . .

Through sheer force of habit, the living, creeping circle kept moving around the rim of the pot—around and around, keeping the same relentless pace for seven days and seven nights—and would doubtless have continued longer had it not been for sheer exhaustion and ultimate starvation.

Incidentally, an ample supply of food was close at hand and plainly visible, but it was outside the range of the circle so they continued along the beaten path.

They were following *instinct—habit—custom—tradition—precedent—past experience—"standard practice"*—or whatever you may choose to call it, but they were following it blindly.

They mistook activity for accomplishment,
They meant well—
But got no place. *

Beth was too idealistic to believe she would ever be a Processionary Caterpillar, but it was tempting to take the easy way out. Clearly she must have expectations for her students in terms of who they are, as well as what and how much they are to learn. And clearly the amount of learning depends on the opportunities provided her students, which in turn are influenced by:

1. Her ability to organize an efficient learning environment that includes the systematic pursuit of academic objectives
2. The activities she designs, which should be structured, run smoothly and help her students attain the objectives
3. The degree to which she provides appropriate, varied, brief, and orderly transitions among activities (pacing)
4. Her classroom management, which should not distract from opportunities to learn (Brophy, 1986, p. 1070).

Goals

Now Beth must prepare an overview of the course, specifying the *goals*, the long-range and general aims for courses she is to teach: statements of basic intent. For example, some of the goals in the 10th-grade curriculum guide on the Soviet Union and Eastern Europe (Figure 5.1) are as follows:

- Students will be able to demonstrate knowledge of the physical elements and history that have shaped the cultures of the peoples of Eastern Europe and the Soviet Union.
- Students will be able to demonstrate knowledge of the geographical and historical forces that led to centralization of authority in Russia and the Soviet Union.
- Students will be able to demonstrate knowledge of how diverse cultural influences affected national goals, political institutions, and foreign policy strategies for many centuries.

These goals are not discrete and measurable, as specific learning outcomes should be; rather, they are overall aims to structure units of study, which underlie any planning.

*Edward Lindsey, *REDESIGN* (June 1973), Educational Planning Office, BOCES #2, Spenceport, New York.

Good planners investigate the resources available to students before making assignments.

Goals and Unit Planning.   Given the task ahead, it appeared to Beth that she should try to break up the course into manageable segments, or units, as her department head had suggested. *Units,* she recalled, represent an organization of curriculum topics (lasting anywhere from a few days to a few weeks or even months) for which teachers can develop specific daily lesson plans. The daily plans, in turn, spell out in detail what students are to learn within the units, how the teacher will go about the teaching, and how the teacher will evaluate the learning.

One way for Beth to meet her goals is to develop a unit plan based on some cognitive map, such as Ausubel's (1960) advance organizer model, discussed in Chapter 4. Recall that an advance organizer incorporates the concepts and principles students are to learn. Like a scaffold, at the apex is the overall notion that students are to learn, built on concepts, subconcepts, and information subsumed by the subconcepts. For example, the advance organizer for the unit shown in Figure 5.1 might look like this (see Appendix A for an alternative unit overview):

Topic: The Soviet Union and Ukraine

The modern totalitarian Soviet state continues to scapegoat ethnic minorities and repress human rights to consolidate power and to transform the Soviet Union into a modern global power and is best illustrated by Ukraine.

Recall that a serious problem with advance organizers is disagreement about exactly what constitutes a good one (Dinnell & Glover, 1985). Here we have chosen to present an organizer in the form of a generalization based on concepts in the curriculum guide. Thus, it may be useful to review what is meant by a generalization and its relationship to concepts.

Generalizations.   A *generalization* is a broad, inclusive statement in complete grammatical sentence form that serves as a principle or rule and expresses relationships among concepts. Here are some examples of generalizations:

> Since natural resources are limited and human wants are unlimited, every society must develop a method for allocating its scarce resources.
>
> Every society has rules, written or unwritten, by which social control over people's conduct is maintained.
>
> The constants of history are change and continuity, and the goal is progress as society sees progress.
>
> A person's culture, its mores and traditions, affects that person's thinking, perceiving, and feeling throughout life.
>
> The more mature the society, the greater its reliance on formal institutions for maintaining social control.

Concepts.   In writing generalizations, it is important first to identify the concepts and subconcepts that comprise them. Recall that in Chapter 4 we defined *concepts* as the abstract body of meaning that a person associates with a symbol for a class of things, events, or ideas. An alternative definition of a concept is "a class or category all the members of which share a particular combination of critical properties not shared by any other class" (Markle & Tiemann, 1976, p. 54).

Concepts are mental constructs that help people classify experiences and that change with experiences. They are labels that evoke images in the minds of individuals, the synthesis of a class or group of things or actions having certain qualities or characteristics in common (Fancett, Johns, Hickman, & Price, 1968). The significance of concepts is that they serve as shortcuts to communication and comprehension, which purportedly aid in the transfer of learning (Fancett et al.).

Clearly these definitions are based closely on the work of Jerome Bruner and represent the cognitive/disciplinary curriculum position we examined in Chapter 2. Equally clearly, they are being challenged as inadequate, for there is a tendency to suggest that these "classical" definitions become fixed definitions for concepts, which can distort meanings. More important, those who would teach concepts must recognize the limitations in using these definitions (Stanley & Mathews, 1985, pp. 57–74).

Three specific limitations of the classical view of concepts are:

1. The possible existence of disjunctive concepts, "those for which there is no single set of necessary and sufficient defining features" (Stanley & Mathews, 1985, p. 59). For example, does the market system recognize government bailouts of corporations (loans to prevent bankruptcies of, say, Lockheed and Chrysler)?

2. A failure to define specific features of concepts, to list all the necessary attributes of a concept. For example, are the characteristics of Blacks, Mormons, and Cajuns included in the concept of ethnicity? (Stanley & Mathews, 1985, p. 69)

3. A lack of recognition of the "typicality" or extent to which examples of concepts are the best ones. For instance, to what extent do countries like Lebanon or Honduras represent sovereignty?

At best, teachers must recognize the fuzziness of some concepts, adjust instruction accordingly, and explain these concepts in a manner consistent with students' maturity.

Despite the limitations suggested by Stanley and Mathews, the fact remains that concepts are building blocks to higher learning, which the Ausubel model seeks to attain.

Figure 5.4 presents examples of concepts derived from the Curriculum Center at Syracuse University, a U.S. Office of Education–funded project that ran through the 1960s and used the classical definitions. There is no "magic" to these particular examples. A different list would serve just as well, but these help illustrate concepts that are appropriate to the social studies. They can also help Beth orient herself as she develops her advance organizer.

FIGURE 5.4
Examples of "Classical" Concepts

	Substantive	
Scarcity	Conflict	Nationalism
Sovereignty	Industrialization	Morality and choice
Modified market economy	Secularization	Habitat
Saving	Culture	Social control
Institutions	Compromise	Social change
Comparative advantage	Power	Ideology
		Leadership

Values	Methodological
Dignity	Historical method
Empathy	Geographical approach
Loyalty	Causation
Freedom and equality	Observation
Government by consent	Classification
	Measurement

Given examples of an advance organizer (or generalization, as used here) and concepts, Beth can now start to write her unit plan, based on the goals in the curriculum guide, specifically for the topic she has chosen, "The Soviet Union and Ukraine." Recall that goals are general and long range. The school curriculum guide lists a number of goals, one of which reads:

Students will become aware of social, political, and economic consequences of russification and collectivization of Ukraine.

Next, Beth might list the major and subordinate concepts incorporated in her generalization that are consistent with her goals:

Major Concepts:

Power	Justice	Culture	Change

Subordinate Concepts:

Political systems	Rights	Identity	Causation

Data from Which Concepts Are Drawn:

Lenin/Stalin	Empathy	Diversity	Conflict
Totalitarianism	Freedom	Social classes	Scarcity
Revolution	Repression	Diffusion	Purge
Statehood	Scapegoating	Cohesion	Ethnocide
Nationalism	Terrorism	Ethnic minorities	"class
Collectivization	Dekukalization	Reform	enemies"

Putting it all together, Beth's "cognitive map" for her unit will look like that in Figure 5.5.

WRITING OBJECTIVES

Now Beth faces the difficult task that was drummed into her in methods class and that she knows has to be done: write objectives that will clarify learning outcomes for individual lessons in her unit based on her objectives. *Objectives*, the short-range, specific statements that describe the learning behaviors or patterns of behaviors students are to demonstrate, are not only to guide her but to help her assess her students' learning (Mager, 1962; Bloom, 1956). Without objectives, Beth would have to guess what is in her students' heads or gauge the learning by referring to what students say in class. This could be done, but it would not be very reliable. Moreover, without objectives it is more difficult to prepare valid test items.

Basically, there are four characteristics of instructional objectives written in behavioral terms:

1. Action verbs, which describe what is to be learned
2. Identification of the learner or learners

FIGURE 5.5
Relating Goals, Generalizations, and Concepts

Topic: The Soviet Union and Ukraine

Goal: Students will become aware of social, political, and economic consequences of russification of Ukraine

Generalization: The modern totalitarian Soviet state continues to scapegoat ethnic miniorities and repress human rights to consolidate power and to transform the Soviet Union into a modern global power and is best illustrated by Ukraine.

Major and Subordinate Concepts:

Major:	Power	Justice	Culture	Change
Subordinate:	Political systems	Rights	Identity	Causation
Data:	Lenin/Stalin	Empathy	Diversity	Conflict
	Totalitarianism	Freedom	Social classes	Scarcity
	Revolution	Repression	Diffusion	Purge
	Statehood	Scapegoating	Cohesion	Ethnocide
	Nationalism	Terrorism	Ethnic minorities	"class enemies"
	Collectivization	Dekukalization	Reform	

3. Statements of the conditions under which the behaviors can be performed
4. Specification of some level or degree of performance

In fact, Beth often used a simple scheme from one textbook (Armstrong & Savage, 1983, p. 148) to help her recall the characteristics:

A = Audience (the student-learner)
B = Behavior (what the student-learner will do to illustrate that learning is occurring)
C = Condition under which the learning is to occur
D = Degree or level of learning

An example might be something like this:

Given a self-prepared list of items they would want as presents and a list of "assets" [condition], the 12th-grade students [audience] will (or will be able to):

place [behavior] each item into a column labeled "wants" or "resources" [degree] and *characterize* [behavior] the problem presented by the comparison [degree].

Beth was aware that, according to convention, she had to avoid non-measurable terms such as *know, understand, realize, see,* and *recognize.*

FIGURE 5.6
Writing Behavioral Objectives

I. Four characteristics of a behavioral objective:
   A. It provides a description of the learner.
   B. It provides a description of the behavior.
   C. It states the conditions under which the behavior is to occur or to be demonstrated.
   D. It states or provides minimal standards of acceptable performance.

II. In writing an objective, the leading question should be "At the conclusion of the class session, how will the student be expected to perform to demonstrate that learning has occurred?"

III. Action words used in writing objectives help ensure that learning will be demonstrated *behaviorally*. That is, something will be evident, visible, or performed.

IV. If you are interested in key words or phrases to employ when specifying conditions in your objectives, the following will be of assistance:

Given . . .	Starting with . . .
Using . . .	Beginning with . . .
Following . . .	Based on . . .
Provided . . .	With access to . . .
Faced with . . .	Without the aid of . . .
Placed in . . .	Having . . .

V. Examples of behavioral objectives:
   A. Having previously identified and named parts of speech and having listened to sounds played by a tape recorder, the 11th-grade writing class will:

   Describe in their own words each sound heard
   Arrange these descriptive words into phrases
   Organize these phrases into short sentences

   B. Given their self-prepared lists of items they would want as presents and of "money" they now have, the seventh graders will:

   Label the items as "wants" and "resources"
   Calculate accurately the value of each list
   Compare the dollar values of each list
   Describe the problem posed for them

Once more Beth searched around for a sheet she had been given to help her write instructional objectives in behavioral terms (see Figure 5.6). Also, she was encouraged to use the Bloom taxonomy (Bloom, 1956), which classifies goals in the cognitive domain, and the affective taxonomy (Krathwohl, Bloom, & Masia, 1964), both of which are viewed as hierarchical (see Figure 5.7). These taxonomies are intended as tools to help teachers identify cognitive and affective levels systematically and to plan accordingly. While there is some ambiguity and overlapping, the taxonomies serve as guides not only for researchers but for teachers preparing objectives at different intellectual and affective levels and testing attainment of them.

'onal Objectives for the Cognitive and

Objectives: Cognitive Domain (Bloom)

      Knowledge of specifics
.20   Knowledge of ways, means of dealing with specifics
1.30   Knowledge of universals and abstractions in a field
2.00 Comprehension
      2.10 Translation
      2.20 Interpretation
      2.30 Extrapolation
3.00 Application
4.00 Analysis
5.00 Synthesis
6.00 Evaluation
      6.10 In terms of internal evidence
      6.20 In terms of external criteria

A. Short-range objectives: 1 to 4 days

  1. Taxonomy code 1.0—knowledge

count	label	define	recite	draw
cite	identify	record	indicate	repeat
list	state	name	tabulate	point
trace	quote	write	read	

  2. Taxonomy code 2.0—comprehension

associate	estimate	infer	extrapolate
compute	interpret	decode	interpolate
describe	predict	translate	differentiate
rephrase	distinguish		

B. Intermediate-range objectives: 5 days to 2, 3, 4, or 5 weeks (unit coverage)

  1. Taxonomy code 2.0—comprehension

rearrange	predict	outline

  2. Taxonomy code 3.0—application

convert	employ	solve	calculate
examine	measure	illustrate	complete
practice	demonstrate	relate	

  3. Taxonomy code 4.0—analysis

group	compare	contrast	transform	differentiate	classify

C. Long-range objectives: 5 or 6 weeks to 1 semester or 1 year

  1. Taxonomy Code 4.0—analysis

analyze	separate	isolate	summarize
reclassify	reconstruct	categorize	distinguish

  2. Taxonomy code 5.0—synthesis

solve	develop	organize	combine	formulate
plan	create	generalize	conclude	design
integrate	prescribe	produce	propose	summarize

  3. Taxonomy code 6.0—evaluation

appraise	rank	select	assess
grade	test	critique	judge
recommend	determine	measure	evaluate
rate	prove	document	verify

VI. Taxonomy of Educational Objectives: Affective Domain (Krathwohl)
  1.00 Receiving (attending)
      1.10 Awareness
      1.20 Willingness to receive
      1.30 Controlled or selected attention
  2.00 Responding
      2.10 Acquiescence in responding
      2.20 Willingness to respond
      2.30 Satisfaction in response
  3.00 Valuing
      3.10 Acceptance of a value
      3.20 Preference for a value
      3.30 Commitment
  4.00 Organization
      4.10 Conceptualization of a value
      4.20 Organization of a system
  5.00 Characterization by a Value or Value Complex
      5.10 Generalized set
      5.20 Characterization

A. Short-range objectives: 1 to 4 days

  1. Taxonomy code 1.0—receiving

accepts	reads	names
expresses	looks at	listens
uses	asks	perceives

  2. Taxonomy code 2.0—responding

complies	observes	visits
reads	obeys	wears
labels	acquaints	writes

B. Intermediate-range objectives: 5 days to 5 weeks

  1. Taxonomy code 2.0—responding

engages in	recites	practices
cooperates	participates	accepts
helps	discusses	enjoys

  2. Taxonomy code 3.0—valuing

joins	compares	chooses
invites	devotes	communicates
develops	displays	challenges

C. Long-range objectives: 5 weeks to 1 semester or year

  1. Taxonomy code 4.0—organization

weighs	forms	determines
summarizes	generalizes	organizes
formulates	plans	rearranges

  2. Taxonomy code 5.0—characterization

serves	solves	integrates
modifies	practices	commits
judges	encompasses	reviews

FIGURE 5.8
**Behavioral Verbs Classified According to Bloom's Taxonomy
of Educational Objectives: Cognitive Domain**

Knowledge	Comprehension	Application	Analysis	Synthesis	Evaluation
define	translate	adapt	distinguish	produce	judge
locate	illustrate	develop	detect	constitute	argue
identify	give in own words	organize	classify	originate	validate
recall	prepare	use	discriminate	modify	assess
list	reword	employ	categorize	propose	decide
select	represent	transfer	contrast	plan	rate
label	transform	restructure	compare	design	rank
reproduce	rephrase	connect with	differentiate	derive	contrast
underline	restate	calibrate	isolate	develop	standardize
copy	interpret	convert	separate	combine	appraise
cite	reorder	compute	choose	organize	prove
name	rearrange	graph	sort	synthesize	verify
write	annotate	measure	dissect	classify	document
tally	match	codify	syllogize	deduce	umpire
point to	demonstrate	divide	dissolve	formulate	weigh
circle	estimate	locate	divide	solve	gauge
	infer	compose	parse	summarize	corroborate
	predict	calculate	sift	collect	substantiate
	determine	manipulate	group	evolve	confirm
	extend	revise		unite	
	interpolate			fuse	
	extrapolate			incorporate	
	fill in			merge	
	describe			conclude	
	outline			regroup	
	decode				
	verbalize				
	locate				
	pronounce				
	describe				
	estimate				

Beth still had a sheet to use as a "crutch" that listed words that fit into each level of Bloom's taxonomy and that she could use once she had determined the taxonomic level (see Figure 5.8). The actual objectives are to lead students toward the long-range goals, much the way one views a travel routing prepared by an automobile association; that is, the goal might be to reach, say, "Hernando's Hideaway" near Gallup, New Mexico. The objectives are points along the way, including the specific highways, cities, time zones, rest stops, gas stations, detours, and so on. If one follows the objectives, one should reach the goal.

However, merely knowing all of this will not get the job done. Beth still has to *write* the objectives for her unit on the Soviet Union and Eastern Europe (Ukraine). Moreover, the objectives should not only reflect the goal ("students will become aware of social, political, and economic consequences of russification and collectivization of Ukraine") but connect with the concepts listed previously—power, justice, culture, and change.

To begin, Beth should write the objectives aimed at helping students learn the concept of power. The results might be something like this:

Having read the text and discussed Soviet attempts to consolidate control, the 10th-grade students will:

1. *List* chronologically the major steps taken by the Soviet Union to centralize Ukraine.
2. *Name* Ukrainian ethnic minorities affected by centralization.
3. *Describe* in their own words at least three causes and means of Soviet centralization.
4. *Compare* conditions in Ukraine before and after centralization.
5. *Evaluate* the impact of Stalin's policies of collectivization on ethnic minorities in Ukraine in the period 1922 to 1934.

Then Beth will have to do the same for the other concepts—justice, culture, and change.

Questioning

After she has written her objectives, Beth could write some key questions corresponding to the objectives that in turn correspond to the concepts she has listed. Writing and asking questions is a skill unto itself—at least as important, if not more so, than writing objectives. Because an extended treatment of questioning appears in Chapter 7, we will simply introduce the topic here.

We suggest that if Beth prepares some guiding questions initially, she will have an easier time once she is in class. In time we hope that she will develop the proficiency that characterizes effective questioners who can ask good questions "in the heat of battle."

Recall the *inquiry model* from Chapter 4, in which lessons are conducted by relying primarily on questions initiated by either the teacher or the students. If Beth can anticipate the types, complexity, and timing of questions that will be used in class, she will have more confidence going into the lesson.

For her unit on Ukraine, here are some questions Beth might ask to get to the concept of power:

Under what kinds of political systems did Ukraine exist historically?

What kinds of power did Ukrainians traditionally exercise over themselves?

What effect did russification under the czars have on indigenous political systems?

In what ways did the Soviets alter the forms of centralization from those used by the czars?

Had Allied intervention in World War II occurred earlier, how might Ukraine's fate have differed?

Next, Beth would have to do the same for the other concepts identified earlier. It seemed like this was going to take forever, but at least Beth felt she knew what she was doing now. Beth had peeled the first potato.

LESSON PLANNING

The next potato Beth must peel is the lesson plan to begin the unit. This may be a harder task, for each lesson is an integral part of the unit.

Now Beth can shift her attention more specifically to the *quality* of her presentation. She must ensure that she actively engages her students in an emotionally supportive climate in which her presentation is clear, enthusiastically delivered, well structured, and "sufficiently redundant and well sequenced" (Brophy, 1986, pp. 1071, 1072). Artistry is especially relevant at this point.

A term that has been applied to this phase of teaching is *aptitude-treatment interaction*. In other words, Beth must identify the variety of aptitudes that characterize the students in her classes and vary her instruction accordingly. As Good and Stipek (1983) argue, "There are no generalizable methods to achieve optimal learning in a diverse group of children" (p. 10). Beth will have to be conscious of the cognitive levels—that is, students on a continuum from abstract to concrete—conceptual tempos—reflective versus impulsive—and psychological differentiation—field dependence versus field independence (Good & Stipek, 1983, p. 30). She will have to focus on and circumvent or compensate for differences to make the learning environment "nurtural" (Corno & Snow, 1986, pp. 606, 607). We will examine illustrations of this later in the chapter.

It remains, however, that there are some fairly standard elements in any lesson plan with which Beth can adapt her teaching to her students' aptitudes. Figure 5.9 presents a rather elaborate lesson plan outline. We readily acknowledge that there are probably as many versions of lesson plans as there are teachers. Figure 5.9 is one version.

First, Beth must review her unit goals, then her objectives, the short-range, specific statements of proposed learning outcomes. For example, she might begin with this:

Given readings for homework and a political map of Ukraine, the students will:

1. Locate Ukraine on the map of the Soviet Union.

FIGURE 5.9
Lesson Plan Outline

Grade level: _____   Name: _____

Time estimate: _____   Date: _____

Subject of the lesson: _____

1. *Preparation:*
    a. Purpose of the lesson (why are you teaching this lesson?)
    b. Resources used to prepare lesson (reading professional material, making charts, reading material to be presented, listing materials students will use)
    c. Teaching materials needed (test, handouts, transparencies, filmstrip, projector, etc.)

2. *Instructional objectives:* Having (given, using, or based on) . . . , the student(s) will:

3. *Procedure* (This should be your overview of the lesson):
    a. steps of the lesson: Spell out how you will carry out the instruction, illustrating the various steps.

	Questions, Comments, Directions

(1) *Introduction/motivation*
    Examples: (a) Show visual aid
    (b) State goal
    (c) Draw on students' backgrounds
    (d) Create a puzzling situation
    (e) Present a problem to be solved.
	State here what you plan to do to gain the students' attention and interest. What will you use to motivate them? Share the purpose of the lesson or what you plan to do in this lesson.

(2) *Body of the lesson*
List the major items or activities in the order they will occur
    Examples: (a) Brainstorm ideas from the group
    (b) Discussion of character and plot.
    (c) Review examples of types of rocks.
	List the *actual questions* you plan to ask.
	
	The questions should be included with the step related to the question. State any directions you need to give within the plan.

(3) *Concluding activity*
How will you conclude the lesson?
    Examples: (a) *Review* steps in experiment
    (b) *Preview* tomorrow's lesson
    (c) *Summarize*
	State here how you will bring the information together in relation to your behavioral objective(s). Summarize, review important points, draw conclusions, prepare for next lesson. The clock should not determine the conclusion of a lesson.

4. *Evaluation*
    a. *Of student learning:* to be written in the plan
        How will you determine the progress the students have made toward your objective? Discussion, worksheet, game, quiz, systematic observation, spot check
    b. *Of teaching process:* to be done after the lesson
        What were the strengths of your lesson? What parts of the plan worked well? What were problem areas? Why? How could you improve the lesson?

2. Name the major ethnic group in Ukraine and its primary language.

Then Beth can do some "homework," reviewing the content she is to teach and create or collect the materials she will need, including any handouts or audiovisual aids.

Introduction/Motivation

Next, Beth should consider how she will gain the students' attention at the outset of the lesson. A term we used earlier is *set induction,* which can be defined as "putting students into a receptive frame of mind to facilitate learning" (see Figure 5.10). Set induction also can be used to introduce new material within an ongoing lesson, although probably it is fairer to refer to this as *stimulus variation.*

Stimulus variation, as the term implies, consists of the teacher's actions, planned and spontaneous, to maintain students' attention during a lesson (Cooper, 1982, p. 121). Stimulus variation can take the following forms:

1. Pausing (silence)
2. Kinesic variation (the teacher's body movements)

FIGURE 5.10
Set Induction

Set induction means putting students in a receptive frame of mind to facilitate learning

Uses of Set Induction
1. To focus student attention on teacher's presentation by employing an activity, event, object, or person directly relating to students' interest
2. To provide a structure or framework for students to visualize lesson content
3. To aid in clarifying lesson goals
4. To introduce new material by building on the known

Examples of Set Induction
1. To introduce geographic barriers, the teacher places chairs blocking the classroom door, forcing students to navigate without disturbing the chairs
2. To introduce the character of George Washington, Richard Mulligan in the movie *Teachers* dressed as Washington. (By the way, Mulligan played a character who was recently released from a mental institution—so who is nuts?)
3. To introduce a lesson on chronology, the teacher asks students to express ways in which time can be stated and suggests they describe how long a particular class period is, following up with other examples of "objective" and "subjective" time.
4. To introduce a lesson or unit on law, the teacher asks students to play the "button game" or to recall ways in which law affects our daily activities.
5. To introduce graphing, the teachers asks students to name the types of part-time jobs they hold, the hours they work, and the money they earn weekly.

---

3. Focusing
4. Shifting interactions (from student to student, for example)
5. Shifting the senses (from lecture to, say, an overhead transparency)

Specifically, *pausing* is a break in the action, signaling students to prepare for something different, creating suspense or expectation, emphasizing a point, attracting attention, or indicating disapproval of what is occurring, especially an increase in noise in the classroom (Cooper, 1982, p. 127).

Kinesic variation, or changes in body movements, can be as dramatic as standing on one's desk, posturing to characterize an historical figure, or walking around the room or between the rows. However, Beth—and all of us—would do well to remember that pacing rapidly back and forth in front of students may be distracting. No one wants the students' heads to be turning as though they were watching a tennis match.

Focusing, an intentional act on the teacher's part to direct or control action, can take various forms, including verbal, gestural, and verbal-gestural (Cooper, 1982, p. 125). Verbal focusing can be anything from asking students to "look" or "listen." Gestural focusing may consist of nodding one's head, smiling, waving one's arms, or using a pointer. Verbal-gestural focusing includes pointing to something and asking students to look at the target or simulating some activity while describing it.

Shifting interactions is equally obvious and can involve switching from teacher talk to questioning, encouraging student-to-student talk, or changing from group work to individual work.

Shifting senses recognizes some learners' preference for using one sense. For example, "auditory" learners tend to prefer obtaining information through listening, while "visual" learners need to see diagrams, charts, or photographs to get the message.

While there is nothing mysterious or sophisticated about the notion of stimulus variation—and many effective teachers seem to vary stimuli naturally—the beginner may well need to consciously apply some of these techniques.

Body of the Lesson

Next, Beth should consider various modes of instruction, including changing the learning environment, which is illustrated in the lesson plan outline in Figure 5.9 under "Body of the Lesson." In other words, she should consider the use of particular activities to carry out instruction. The intent is to elicit performances from students by providing a specific activity, which alludes to the notion of models discussed in Chapter 4. Recall the lesson built on the *concept formation model* in that chapter. First, groups of students wrestled with data cards to learn more about the Nacirema, Weans, and Bushmen (see Figure 4.3 on page 89 for the complete unit.) Then they shifted to identifying the characteristics of culture, ethnicity, and ethnocentricism. Throughout the lesson, the teacher had students respond to questions and wrote some of their answers on the board.

Note that Beth can ask questions throughout the lesson, but it may be useful for her to write some specific questions tied to different parts of the lesson directly in the lesson plan. Compare some questions listed earlier for the unit on the Soviet Union and Eastern Europe (Ukraine), starting with questions at the knowledge level and thus likely to be considered less threatening and to elicit correct answers:

Where on the map is Ukraine located?

When does it appear that Ukraine was first recognized as a country?

Who might be considered a founder of Ukraine?

The advice to write out some questions in the lesson plan itself is sound even for experienced teachers, for effective questioning is a skill that must be developed. Likely teachers could start with knowledge-level questions to elicit correct answers and progress to higher-level questions (analysis, synthesis, and evaluation), keeping in mind that low-difficulty-level questions can stimulate higher-level thinking.

Concluding Activities

Finally, Beth needs to consider how to conclude her lesson to assess student learning. Concluding activities also can vary, but the key in all cases is to elicit responses from students that illustrate attainment of the lesson objectives.

Concluding activities can range from simply asking students to summarize the lesson to a full-scale project that summarizes the unit. For example, at the end of a specific lesson, the teacher could have a student randomly select a card from a batch of 3" x 5" cards containing individual students' names and ask the student so selected to recall what he or she learned from the lesson. Then the selected student randomly selects another card so that another student can summarize, and so on. Or students might respond to a question such as "What was the most important thing you learned today?"

Another way to conclude Beth's lesson on the Soviet Union and Eastern Europe might be to pose a question that either individual students or groups address:

Given events in Eastern Europe during the winter of 1989–1990, what are some of the major problems the Eastern European countries will experience? Make a list.

Given the fact that Eastern European countries have suffered under Soviet domination, what role might the United States play to help them adjust to greater autonomy?

Why might the Soviet Union strongly resist any attempt by Ukraine to declare its autonomy? That is, what factors make Ukraine so important to the Soviet Union?

When Beth completes her plan, she will have accomplished the task her department head set out for her earlier. She will have the first day planned. While "Murphy's law"—whatever can go wrong will go wrong—may still prevail, Beth will have a road map by which to check her progress.

In time, Beth will have to peel the remaining potatoes until she has developed enough units and plans to encompass the curriculum guide for her school district. But she knows that probably not everything in the curriculum guide necessarily will be included given all the things that happen during a school year.

Experienced teachers may balk at the seeming oversimplication of the linear planning illustrated here. Even logistics can be a problem. All of us can recall the fire drills that, by state law, must be called and the fire drills students "schedule" when the weather is too good to be in class. We are all too familiar with assemblies that wipe out classes periodically, as well as the days when nothing seems to go right—when students' minds are elsewhere. We also realize that many effective lessons occur spontaneously, such as the group investigation lesson in Chapter 4 in which the teacher made a unit out of the skating pond problem.

The following example illustrates another spontaneous lesson as well as how the difficult notion of chronology can be taught. It could also be a planned lesson using a similar format.

Teaching Chronology: A "Spontaneous Lesson"

"Hey, Elise, gotta second?"

"Hey yourself, Mike! I'm not a horse, and no, not now. Gotta run."

"Do you have any ideas for teaching 'time?' My kids don't think anything happened before 1976—actually, even before today!"

"I can't now, but I've had some luck with my classes. I'll talk to you later, I promise. 'Bye."

With that, Elise recalled a lesson on chronology one day. She was about to start class when a student, fumbling through her incredibly messy notebook, shouted out, "Wait a second, I can't find my notes—I mean *please!*"

So Elise paused and waited as patiently as she could when another student hollered, "Your second is up!" Then another student yelled, "C'mon, she's always late—she'll probably be late for her own wedding."

"Enough!" Elise commanded in her most authoritative but still pleasant voice. Recalling a problem that the same class had had with timelines and events, she decided to make a lesson out of what had just occurred.

"OK, smarties," she began, "how long is a second?" At the same time, she wrote *second* on an overhead.

"One-sixtieth of a minute."

"Yes. How else do we express time?"

The obvious came out: "An hour"; "A day"; "A month"; "A year"; "A century."

Elise wrote down all of these answers, carefully putting them in a column running down the left side of the transparency. Next, she asked, "How else do we express time? For example, when you were little, riding with your mother to visit someone in another part of the city or state, what did she say when you asked, 'How much longer?' "

There was a ripple of recognition from the class before one student answered, " 'Not much longer' " and another " 'We're almost there.' " Elise wrote both of these answers on the right side of the transparency.

Then Elise elicited other responses, recording them in the column she was creating on the right side of the transparency: "era," "eon," "shortly," "awhile back," and so on.

Finally, she said, "Let's stop now that we have two fairly long lists. How might we label these lists?" After some prodding by Elise, the class arrived at the result she had been seeking: "Objective" for the list on the left side of her transparency and "Subjective" for the list on the right:

Objective	*Subjective*
A second	Not much longer
1/60 of a minute	We're almost there
An hour	Era
A day	Eon
A month	Shortly
A century	Awhile back

Next, Elise began a brief discussion of the differences between the two columns, beginning with "Which column would be more useful for us in the social studies, and why?"

Following that, she had students use "objective" time to create a timeline corresponding to their lives. This timeline was simulated by a string on which the students attached note cards representing "significant" events in their lives. Of course, Elise had the students place the cards at appropriate intervals, based on drawing equations among the lengths of their lives, the string, and the note cards.

After the students completed the timeline, Elise asked them to identify some other events that had occurred during their lifetimes. This was not so easy for the class, and only a few "relevant" events were recalled. So Elise gave them some suggestions for obtaining more information about time periods.

The next day, Elise asked the students what they had found out overnight about other events in their parents' or guardians' lives. Then she distributed some materials in a packet given attendees at a National Council for the Social Studies conference in Chicago. It was a timeline done by the Chicago Neighborhood History Project (see Figure 5.11), supported by a grant from the National Endowment for the Humanities. Elise had modified the timeline

FIGURE 5.11
A Timeline of Chicago

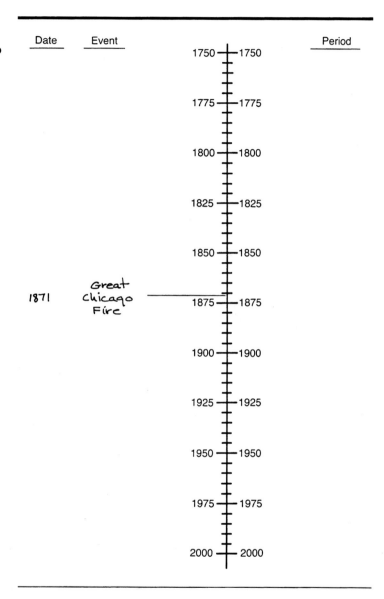

Date   Event   Period

1871   Great Chicago Fire

slightly for the community in which her school was located. Then she asked what was meant by a "period of time" and suggested some other ways to describe time periods, again borrowing from the Chicago Neighborhood History Project (see Figure 5.12).

However, from her outside reading Elise remembered that she would have to be careful about her students' readiness to tackle some of these notions about time. She recalled a chart (Thornton & Vukelich, 1988, pp. 72, 73) that illustrated findings about the ages by which students have developed the

FIGURE 5.12
Timelines by Periods

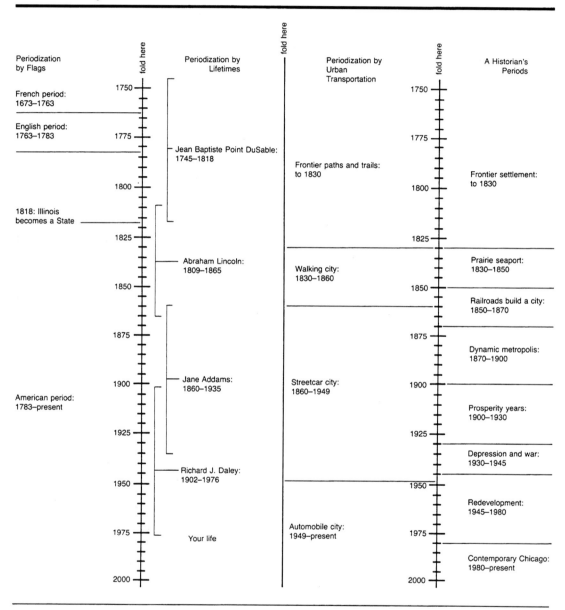

skills to handle the notions of "clock and calendar" (see Figure 5.13). By age 13, students should be able to match dates with historical events, persons, or periods. By age 14, students should have mastered "adult time vocabulary and concepts" such as generation and century. By age 15, students should be able to distinguish parts of centuries.

FIGURE 5.13
Acquisition of Time-Related Concepts or Skills

Age	Clock and Calendar	Historical	Researcher
4–5	Describes the sequence of a day's activities.		Friedman, W., 1978
	Uses terms *before and after, now and then.*		Harner, 1982
	Uses past and future verb tense		Harrison, Harner, 1934; 1982
6	Labels blocks of time as *lunchtime, playtime, naptime.*		Harrison, 1934
	Reads clock hour time correctly.		Elkind, 1960
	Recognizes time and distance as two different dimensions.		Elkind, 1960
7	Recognizes hours as being the same length of time.		Elkind, 1960
	Recites days of week, months, and seasons in order.		Friedman, W., 1978
		Places family members (self, parents, grandparents) in correct age sequence.	Jahoda, 1963
8	Names recent holidays.	Uses year dates but cannot accurately match year to person or event.	Oakden & Sturt, 1922
	Uses terms like *night, tomorrow, morning* to describe a point in time.	Given the dates 1750, 1850, and 1950, or 1970, 1980, and 1960, correctly orders them.	Friedman, K., 1944
	Names months, weeks, days.	Begins to match dates to significant persons or events.	Oakden & Sturt, 1922
9	Orders the holidays in a calendar year.	Uses general terms such as *a long time ago, way back when, once upon a time.*	Friedman, W., 1978
		Uses a specific number of years, for example, *about 100 years ago,* as a time referent.	Bradley, 1947
		Matches significant people with events.	Oakden & Sturt, 1922
10	Realizes that seconds, minutes, hours are the same length everywhere.	Labels periods of time, for example, Colonial times, the Civil War years.	Oakden & Sturt, 1922
11	Demonstrates mastery of clock and calendar time		Bullock & Gellman, 1979, Friedman, W., 1978
12		Matches dates with appropriate historical event, person, or period.	Oakden & Sturt, 1922
13			
14		Uses adult time vocabulary and concepts, for example, *century, generation, Pilgrim forefathers.*	Friedman, W., 1978, Harner, 1982
15		Distinguishes between parts of centuries	
16		Uses *the sixteenth century* and *the 1500's* interchangeably.	

Source: From "Effects of Children's Understanding of Time Concepts on Historical Understanding" by S.J. Thornton and R. Vukelich, Winter 1988, *Theory and Research in Social Education, XVI* (1), pp. 72–73. Reprinted by permission.

Elise recalled other ways to represent time. One was by industry, say, the automobile industry; to personalize the timeline, Henry Ford's lifetime might be highlighted (see Figure 5.14). Another approach included periods in world history ("Great Empires, 400 B.C.—A.D. 400"; "New Peoples, 400–900"; "Christian Europe, 900–1300"). Still another way was by rulers, such as in Great Britain ("Saxons and Danes, 829–1066"; "House of Normandy, 1066–1135"; "House of Windsor, 1910–present").

Elise also recalled discovering "Time Liner," the computer program by Tom Snyder Productions, with which she and her students could choose an already prepared timeline and add items to it or make their own timelines. One advantage of having prepared timelines was that it made it easier for some students having trouble creating timelines while giving more adept students the opportunity to modify prepared timelines. Elise also used the program to prepare and print timeline banners, which she taped above her chalkboard or tacked to her bulletin board when introducing particular time periods. The banners also provided a handy reference while conducting lessons.

Just then, Elise was abruptly brought back to the present by the arrival of her next class.

In the next chapter we will discuss various resources more fully, but now is a good time to get students into some "research" using an old standby, the almanac. Under the topic "World History" are listed events that affected the United States. Like Elise's students, you might look at events in your own lifetime and match them with other "historical" events.

Also, again like Elise's students, you are encouraged to extend the timelines to include parents or guardians, their parents' or guardians' parents, and so on and match events in their lives with world or American events.

FIGURE 5.14
Henry Ford and the Growth of the Auto Industry

1863	Henry Ford born
1891	Ford leaves farm, becomes mechanic
1893	Tests his internal combustion engine in kitchen
1896	Puts engine in quadricycle
1903	Sells his first car (July 15)
1913	Pays workers $5 per day, an industry high, revolutionizes car production
1947	Henry Ford dies

ALTERNATIVE PLANS

Whether conducting a planned lesson like the one described at the beginning of the preceding section or a "spontaneous" one like Elise's, Beth must consider different learners and their needs. Not all students (or teachers) like or do well with the neat, linear design suggested earlier. Therefore, Beth will need to consider other activities to try to match lessons to her learners.

Suppose Beth is teaching the following students: MARIA (M), LI (L), PETER (P), and CHRIS (C). As the profiles of these students presented in Figure 5.15 show, each has distinct needs, abilities, and personality characteristics. Again the lesson focus might be a syllabus topic or events taking place in Ukraine, Poland, China, Central America, or the Middle East. Here are some possible student activities:*

1. Referring to a recent newspaper as a guide, students might prepare an editorial page for a newspaper written in Hong Kong (or Tokyo, New York, or London) with at least six items, such as staff writer editorials, guest editorials, letters to the editor, and political cartoons about the above events.

2. Students might present to the whole class a live or videotaped "press conference" attended by individuals identified in the syllabus or closely connected with the above events.

3. Students could conduct a meeting of the U.N. Security Council called by the U.S. delegate to protest human rights violations. Students must recall which countries belong to the Security Council and suggest measures the member countries might propose to resolve the problem.

4. Students might make a bulletin board or collage using drawings, photographs, editorials, slogans, protest signs, and biographies to represent their perceptions of the topic under discussion. Or they might make the bulletin board or collage from original drawings.

To which of the students profiled in Figure 5.15 could Beth suggest or assign the above activities? With which activity might Li do best given his limited English but a strong ability to work alone and artistic talent? What about Chris, whose writing and spelling skills are limited? Peter? Maria?

What might be Beth's *objectives* (written in behavioral terms)?

- To state the problem presented by the topic identified above?
- To list the pros and cons of each position taken with regard to the problem?
- To propose, orally or in writing, a compromise position?

How might Beth start such a lesson if the students themselves introduced the specific topic?

---

*The following activities are adapted from *Mainstreaming Mildly Handicapped Students into the Regular Classroom* by P. B. Smith and G. Bentley, 1975, Austin, TX: Education Service Center.

FIGURE 5.15
School Psychologist's Appraisal

Methodical, needs structure	C L		M		P	Prefers flexibility, loose structure
Works independently	L			C M	P	Social
Slowly paced	C	L			M P	Rapidly paced
Intellectually directed	L M		C		P	Emotionally directed

Comments by other teachers:

Maria: One of the "bluebirds"; participates in every activity in class, answers questions readily, hands her work in on time, and likes "to do things right."

Li: Moved quickly out of ESOL class; very driven to succeed; has problems with nuances, slang, and things we take for granted; but has real art talent.

Peter: Tends to be "hyper," lacks concentration, prefers "hands-on" activities, losing interest in school, but likes to be center of attention.

Chris: LD in reading, writes and spells poorly, auditory learner, needs to watch others for reassurance.

"Spontaneous" lessons also arise out of an immediate event that demands attention. Many veteran teachers still vividly recall the assassinations of John Kennedy, Robert Kennedy, Martin Luther King, and former Egyptian president Anwar Sadat. Younger teachers have an equally vivid memory of the ill-fated Challenger space shuttle and its civilian passenger, Christa McAuliffe, a New Hampshire social studies teacher. With each of these events, it was difficult for social studies teachers to keep students "on task."

But each of these events no doubt formed the basis for a social studies lesson. For example, accompanying the shooting of President Kennedy was a false rumor that Vice President Lyndon Johnson also had been shot. "What if he died too?" was a question on many students' minds. It was inevitable— and useful—to examine presidential succession and the possible effects on American domestic and foreign policy given a president who had not been elected to that post. Immediate objectives might have included:

- Locating and stating the provisions for presidential succession
- Naming the individual who would succeed to the presidency and that person's governmental office
- Stating that individual's political party affiliation and philosophy
- Deciding whether that person "becomes" the president or simply "assumes the powers" of the president

The death of Martin Luther King set off a series of events that shook the nation. Racial tensions and their history, as well as the civil rights movement, its antecedents, and its likely future, immediately became the focus for unplanned lessons:

- What did Martin Luther King represent to African-Americans? Other minorities? Whites? The U.S. government, especially the FBI?
- What problems did the civil rights movement attempt to address?
- What effects did the civil rights movement have on American domestic and foreign policies?
- Who might be a rightful successor to King?

Because few teachers could jump right into a lecture on either presidential succession and its implications or the history and future of the civil rights movement, lessons took on a healthy reality: Teachers and students actually discussed issues for which there were no textbook answers. But in the first instance, teachers certainly could have asked students to examine the Constitution to find information about the presidential successor, the successor's powers, the limits of office, and so on. Obviously, today's students could have examined why the questions of ethics and the resignation of Speaker of the House James Wright in 1989 were so significant.

In these situations, the planning of a full-scale lesson obviously was out of the question. But imagine the interest these events stirred and the opportunities for learning social studies that they offered!

We are aware that this treatment fails to examine the issue of when to "abandon" a planned lesson. All teachers will need to resolve, often on the spur of the moment, the question of how significant an event must be to substitute a spontaneous lesson on that event for the planned one on another topic. Also, there are questions about the amount of time to devote to the topic of that spontaneous lesson, assignments for students, and evaluation of learning. Yet these questions should not make teachers refrain from substituting lessons that arise out of immediate interest. In fact, many teachers recall their "best" lessons being spontaneous ones. However, we caution about being, or even appearing to be, whimsical about the timing and nature of lessons taught.

Summary

Given the opportunity to prepare some lessons and having anticipated the need to think on her feet—to teach spontaneous lessons—Beth (and we) can well feel more secure. She will not (and should not) resort to "gimmicks" thought up the night before class because they "sounded good."

Let's review what Beth did. First, she developed a conceptual framework for a unit, the basic plan of teaching, which allowed for a variety of instructional models. That conceptual framework is an overview, or *cognitive map*, which can be stated as a *generalization* based on the unit *goals*, the long-range and general statements of intent. Recall too that a generalization is a broad, inclusive statement in complete grammatical sentence form that serves as a principle or rule and expresses relationships among concepts. These *concepts*, which are mental constructs that help people classify experiences and make sense of their world, also must be carefully chosen to reflect the more specific information and terms encompassed in the unit.

Next, Beth began preparing her daily lesson plans. For these she wrote specific learning outcomes, or *objectives*, employing the four characteristics of *audience, behavior, condition*, and *degree*. Note that she was encouraged to link these objectives to the concepts that comprise the generalizations she created. In addition, Beth wrote key *questions*, again tied to her concepts and reflecting what she knows about effective questioning.

Beth also was reminded that she is expected to demonstrate some of the artistry that characterizes teaching. In other words, she selected (or adapted) *models* aimed at students with various aptitudes, planned a suitable *set induction* to establish an interesting mental frame for the lesson, and developed *stimulus variations* to maintain students' attention. Further, she developed a variety of activities appropriate for the models and wrote questions to elicit student performance. Finally, she added some *concluding activities* to summarize the lesson and assess students' attainment of the lesson objectives.

Now Beth will have to think about the supportive climate that enhances student learning: the learning environment.

Decisions! Decisions!

1. Where can you find curriculum guides? Which guide is controlling, the school's or the state's (if your state has one)?

2. What would be appropriate goals for a course? Do curriculum guides always list them, or do they have to come out of our heads? Can some goals suffice for the entire course, or are they suitable only for the units within it?

3. How long should a unit or set of lessons take? Would a week-long unit be appropriate ? A six-week-long unit?

4. How do you go about developing an appropriate cognitive map for a lesson or

unit? What if your cognitive map proves unclear to your students?

5. Will it always take as long as it did Beth to write a lesson plan? Do all teachers write lesson plans?

6. What happens if a plan goes awry in the middle of class? What if it takes less than a class period to complete a lesson? More than a class period?

7. Should students be made aware of the teacher's objectives for a lesson?

8. Must you always think up clever ways to begin a lesson (set induction)? What about ideas for stimulus variation? Where can you get ideas if you want to plan a lesson ahead of time rather than counting on the right muse to visit during the process?

9. What is an appropriate way to conclude a lesson? Is there any particular format? Should you always ask students to summarize? Should you use some activity at the end of the class period?

10. How do you go about "establishing a climate" in the classroom? Are you necessarily limited to teaching in the classroom or the library? What other resources are available to you?

References

Allison, G. A. (1969). Conceptual models and the Cuban missile crisis. *American Political Science Review, 63,* 689–717.

Armstrong, D., & Savage, T. (1983). *Secondary education.* New York: Macmillan.

Ausubel, D. (1960). The use of advance organizers in the learning and retention of meaningful verbal material. *Journal of Educational Psychology, 51,* 267–272.

Bloom, B. S., Engelhart, M. D., Furst, E. J., Hill, W. H., & Krathwohl, D. R. (Eds.). (1956). *Taxonomy of educational objectives.* New York: David McKay.

Brophy, J. (1986, October). Teacher influences on student achievement. *American Psychologist, 41*(10), 1069–1077.

Cooper, J. M. (Ed.). (1982). *Classroom teaching skills* (2nd ed.). Lexington, MA: Heath.

Corno, L., & Snow, R. E. (1986). Adapting teaching to individual differences among learners. In M. D. Wittrock (Ed.), *Handbook of research on teaching* (3rd ed., pp. 605–620). New York: Macmillan.

Dinnell, D., & Glover, J. E. (1985, October). Advance organizers: Encoding manipulations. *Journal of Educational Psychology,* 514–521.

Fancett, V. S., Johns, E., Hickman, W., & Price, R. A. (1968). *Social science concepts and the classroom.* Syracuse, NY: Social Studies Curriculum Center, Syracuse University.

Fuller, F., & Bown, O. H. (1975). Becoming a teacher. In K. Ryan (Ed.), *Teacher education* (74th Yearbook, National Society for Study of Education, Part II, pp. 25–54). Chicago: University of Chicago Press.

Good, T., & Stipek, D. J. (1983). Individual differences in the classroom: A psychological perspective. In G. Fenstermacher & J. I. Goodlad (Eds.), *Individual differences and the common curriculum* (82nd Yearbook, National Society for Study of Education, Part I, pp. 9–43). Chicago: University of Chicago Press.

Herndon, J. (1971). *How to survive in your native land.* New York: Simon & Schuster.

Krathwohl, D. R., Bloom, B. S., & Masia, B. B. (1964). *Taxonomy of educational objectives: Handbook II. Affective domain.* New York: David McKay.

Lefrançois, G. (1985). *Psychology for teaching: A bear never faces the front* (5th ed.). Belmont, CA: Wadsworth.

Mager, R. F. (1962). *Preparing instructional objectives.* Palo Alto, CA: Fearon.

Markle, S. M., & Tiemann, D. W. (1976). Concept learning and instructional materials. In P. H. Martorella (Ed.), *So-*

cial studies theory into practice. New York: Harper & Row.

Petrie, H. (1976). Do you see what I see? The epistemology of interdisciplinary inquiry. *Educational Researcher, 5*(2), 9–15.

Phillips, D. C. (1987). *Philosophy, science and social inquiry.* Oxford: Pergamon Press.

Stanley, W., & Mathews, R. C. (1985, Winter). Recent research on concept learning: Implications for social education. *Theory and Research in Social Education,* 57–75.

Thornton, S. J., & Vukelich, R. (1988, Winter). Effects of children's understanding of time concepts on historical understanding. *Theory and Research in Social Education, XVI*(1), 69–82.

Chapter Six

Environments for Teaching and Learning

Effective teaching requires teachers to shape a truly productive learning environment. This, in turn, means making informed, careful decisions about time, resources, grouping of students, and general classroom management.

At first glance, the classroom seemed chaotic. A closer look, however, revealed intense, enthusiastic student activity. Yes, there was some shouting out of answers and interruptions of others' comments. But it was clear that these 10th graders, with their long lists comparing Rome before the fall with their own city's overcrowding, dirt, and shortsighted government, were *learning*. These students had succeeded beyond the teacher's wildest dreams.

Earlier, had this observer been in that same urban classroom in an old building, mutilated by time, graffiti, and litter, the impression would have been far different. Instead, it would have typified criticisms of stereotypical classrooms.

What had led to the change? An experienced teacher had simply suggested creating a *learning environment* that would extend beyond the classroom walls. And why not? Rome was a city like the students'. What did their city look like? What were its problems? Why weren't the problems being solved?

The answers had to come from many sources, including demographic data, city and school officials, local businesspeople, students' parents or guardians, and even students' textbooks. The *students* had to do the work rather than merely rely on the teacher. So the teacher became a manager rather than a dispenser of inert information.

Now what? you are no doubt wondering. First this book claimed we have to be skillful philosophers, social scientists, and pedagogues. Now it is telling us we must be skillful managers. What next?

But that's the way it is. Adding to your stress now will reduce it later. Teaching is many things, but it is also a very stressful career.

So let's assume that you have carefully and thoroughly deliberated about the social studies curriculum and content. You now know what you want to teach and why. Further, you have reflected on the nature of learning and learners. This has led you to make some difficult choices from a range of alternative and equally attractive models. But while you may feel overwhelmed by this new cog in the wheel, you are now competent enough to make the necessary decisions. Congratulations!

In this chapter, we will address some additional, often tough management-type decisions that you will inevitably have to make. One of these decisions concerns *time management*. For example, how much time will it take to attain your teaching goals? Which blocks of time will be most suitable? How should your precious time and that of your students be scheduled and organized?

A second decision relates to *space*. What sort of space do you want or need to foster the most productive teaching and learning possible? The classroom? The library? The computer lab? Other locations in the school? Or should this learning occur in the community, that is, in students' homes, a museum, a child care center, a construction site, a government chamber, an executive's office, or other source?

Third, what *resources* will you need to create the environment you want? Typically only a few social studies classrooms are adequately equipped for teaching and learning. While aspects of the environment are beyond your control, you can and should attempt to shape an advantageous social and physical setting for teaching and learning.

Fourth, how can you use available *technology?* What types of print, visuals, and nonprint materials and equipment will you need?

Fifth, how should students and instructional staff be *grouped?* As individuals working alone? In pairs, small groups, large groups, or some other arrangement? Should you use tracking or some other means to reduce variance among students? Why or why not? If your school uses such a system, how should you vary your instruction?

Finally, how will you control extrinsic conflicts—unproductive noise and confusion? How will you go about the often difficult job of keeping students on task? In other words, how will you practice *classroom management?*

All of these are profoundly important management issues and form the substance of this chapter.

CREATING PRODUCTIVE LEARNING ENVIRONMENTS

A social studies teacher was struggling to help ninth-grade students comprehend the land form known as "drumlin." The teacher had drawn several diagrams and used numerous verbal descriptions, to no avail. A colleague walking by the classroom, however, was dumbstruck. Outside the window of this school, not a quarter-mile away, was a real drumlin ("an elongated or oval hill of glacial drift," according to Webster)! Obviously the teacher had been relying on the classroom as the only available learning environment.

All too often we social studies teachers fall prey to the same mental trap: believing that the standard classroom is the only possible teaching arena. And all too often we convey to students that social studies can be learned only in the standard classroom, for that is where we spend most of our in-school time.

ASIDE TO THE READER: Think about this for a moment. Where do you think social studies is best taught? Conversely, where do you think social studies is best *learned?* Do you see our distinction?

Time Management

After 15 years of highly successful social studies teaching, Dr. Maria Alvarez had become a college supervisor and methods instructor. Currently she was planning the final weeks of her first semester in her new assignment.

Ten of her student teachers were about to return from an 11-week stint in various middle and high schools in the region. To make the final "wrap-up" meetings as valuable as possible, Maria reviewed her observation notes, students' journals, and other records.

Maria's study clearly pointed to the previously slighted issue of time management. Dozens of complaints centered on the use and abuse of time. Here are some examples:

There isn't enough time to cover the syllabus. What do you leave out in the social studies?

The time we have is too inflexible to accommodate many activities, such as field trips.

I never have enough time for planning, grading papers, previewing materials, and doing collateral reading, and I seem to have no time for my nonprofessional life. I've been neglecting my wife and kids.

Way too much of my classroom time is wasted on classroom management, recordkeeping, and interruptions from the office.

I seemed to spend all my time in pointless meetings.

Writing this journal and performing other assignments for the college have seriously undermined by efforts to find enough time for keeping up with the kids.

What with working, family responsibilities, and sports, my students just don't have enough time to do my assignments.

The department head visited today, and I completely ran out of steam. How do you determine how much time a lesson will take?

My desk and the floor around it became a disaster area! I didn't even open my mail.

When do teachers party?

Maria located some library materials on this topic, but, like her students, she was painfully aware of the powerful control of the clock and the desk. She was almost overwhelmed by the list of topics that needed to receive at least some attention when her students returned to campus. However frustrating, this activity increased her resolve to spend some of her time planning its wise use.

The purpose of the lesson she was planning was clear: to help her students better manage their time. Maria developed a skeletal outline of the lesson:

Outline of Issues on Time Management in Teaching

1. Issues largely beyond the control of individual teachers
   1.1 Spend more time in schools
   1.2 Schedule flexibly

2. Issues largely controllable by individual teachers
    2.1 Use classroom time more effectively
    2.2 Use extra-class student time more effectively
    2.3 Manage personal time better

Maria decided to assign a pair of students to each of the above five topics, give them some required reading, recommend additional study, and encourage the students to draw on their own experiences. Each pair would be asked to report to the larger group. Each presentation would be restricted to 20 minutes.

On the first day back on campus, Maria set the stage for the time management lesson by quoting from the students' papers and by reading the following passage from Ernest Boyer (Boyer, 1983, p. 142):

> Time is the currency of teaching. We barter with time. Every day we make small concessions, small tradeoffs, but in the end, we know . . . [that] the sense of the clock ticking is one of the most oppressive features of teaching. . . . [For example,] in a world history class students go over the worksheets on the Middle Ages they completed earlier. For the next thirty minutes, the teacher lectures on the following topics: Reasons why Constantinople was a good location for a capital, differences between the Greek Orthodox religion and the religion of the Western World, and characteristics of Gothic church architecture.*

Each topic might represent at least one class period in its own right. The challenge to the teacher seems to be to cover the material, to carry students from medievalism to the present, within the next five months. Fragments of information, unexamined and unanalyzed, are what is being transmitted here. Students suffer from information overload—not to mention boredom.

Maria went on to note that the compromise in Ted Sizer's insightful book on secondary schools, *Horace's Compromise*, is basically a race against the clock (Sizer, 1984).

Then Maria called attention to the following quote from Goodlad, which she had written on the chalkboard: "The availability of time . . . sets the basic framework for teaching" (Goodlad, 1984, p. 97).

Maria emphasized that Boyer, Sizer, and Goodlad were optimistic about the ability of teachers to improve their management of time. Believing that she had motivated her students, she gave the assignment.

Although interesting discussion followed each presentation, we will provide only the major findings from each group, using their own words.

---

*Quotation from *High School* by Ernest Boyer. Copyright © 1983 by The Carnegie Foundation for the Advancement of Teaching. Reprinted by permission of Harper & Row, Publishers, Inc.

Group 1: More Time Needed in School

1. The average American high school student is supposed to spend 179 days per year and 6.5 hours per day in school. Although we tend to think that schooling dominates the lives of adolescents, this is only about 13% of their time!

2. In contrast, as stated in *A Nation at Risk* (U.S. Department of Education, 1983, p. 9), "In England and other industrialized countries, it is not unusual for academic high school students to spend eight hours a day at school, 220 days per year."

3. In this country, the various states mandate the minimum number of hours to be spent in school. Only very rarely do local districts go beyond these requirements for their students. Recently, however, some school systems have increased the number of days required of staff, and there is some variability in the amount of time allocated to specific subjects and activities.

4. During the 1980s, we added many requirements for high school graduation and tried to increase the amount of content to be covered. In addition, most Americans have resisted the call to relieve the schools of socialization and psychological responsibilities.

5. All of the above have led many school "reformers" to argue that the school day and year must be expanded.

6. However, this has rarely happened. Costs, traditions, and widespread resistance from teachers' organizations are probably the major reasons why this effort has been blocked.

7. More efficient use of the time we have is likely to be the only politically acceptable answer. But even as beginning teachers, we have a responsibility to be involved in discussions of increasing required school time.

Group 2: Need for Flexible Scheduling

1. To divide the teacher's day into 50-minute periods, 5 times a day, 5 days a week, with 25 to 35 pupils in each class flatly *precludes curricular and instructional creativity* and even restricts opportunities for reasonable productivity.

2. For at least 20 years we have known how to schedule schools more effectively, efficiently, and humanely than the traditional arrangement just described (Dempsey & Traverso, 1983).

3. The most common label applied to such plans is *flexible modular scheduling.* It divides the day into 15- or 20-minute "mods" that can be arranged in a variety of ways.

4. While some schools have abandoned flexible modular scheduling on the grounds that (1) it is too complex and/or (2) it allows too much freedom for students, many others have been delighted with it.

5. While the literature contains many advantages, and some disadvantages as well, of mod scheduling (Swaab, 1974), here are the major pluses we found while we were student teaching in two local high schools using the plan:

a. Boredom was decreased because of the variety.
b. Time was readily available for field trips, simulations, lectures, long films, and so on.
c. Individual conferences with students were common.
d. Motivation was improved for both students and teachers due to their belief that they had greater control over the use of time.
e. Highly productive small-group seminars—12 students—were common. We also had groups of 90 or more, which are fine for disseminating information.
f. The library and resource rooms were widely used because students had a lot of independent study time.
g. Once every six days we had almost three hours of school time for planning and conferencing with our cooperating teachers.
h. Team teaching both within social studies and among disciplines was fostered.
i. Special remedial and elective courses were more feasible than with conventional scheduling,
j. Out-of-class assignments were more likely to get done because more school time was available to do them.
k. Since each department could recommend the amount of time needed for instruction, all staff were actively and cooperatively involved in planning.
l. Students regularly interacted with more than one social studies teacher, which is especially important in our field.

6. To make this more concrete, here is the schedule for one of our students [see Figure 6.1].

Group 3: Using Instructional Time More Effectively

1. During the 1960s and 1970s, there was a great deal of interesting research on using classroom time more effectively. Probably the best descriptor of this work is "time-on-task." We think the best source on this important effort is *Time and School Learning: Theory, Research, and Practice,* edited by Lorin W. Anderson (Anderson, 1984). A shorter but valuable and extremely practical reference is Chapter 5, "Academic Learning Time," in *Guide to Classroom Teaching* (McNergney, 1988).

2. There are differences among the many studies, but all seem to agree that (1) a large part of the school day is wasted as far as instruction is concerned, (2) schools in general and individual teachers in particular can significantly improve their use of time, and (3) time spent on-task increases student achievement.

3. Teachers should be involved in increasing classroom time by making breaks between classes, assemblies, announcements, opening and closing exercises, and so on as efficient as possible.

4. Even more important, teachers must ensure that the classroom time under their direct control is as productive as possible. Administrative tasks such as attendance, collection, and distribution of materials; disci-

FIGURE 6.1
Student Flexible Modular Schedule: Six-Day Cycle

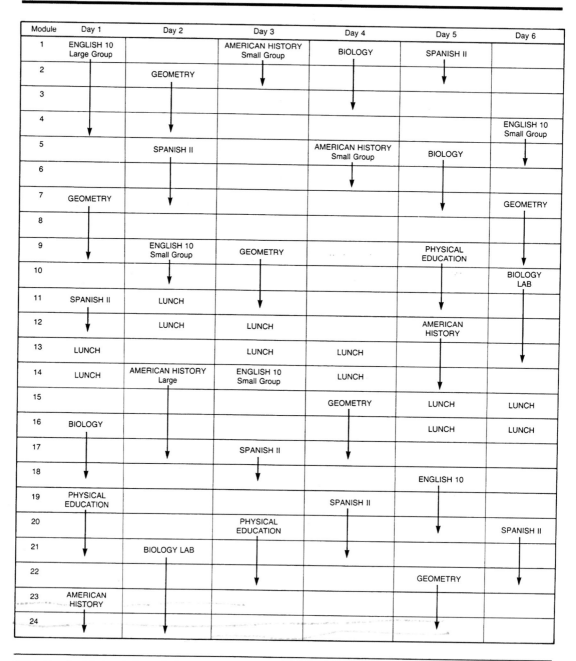

Module	Day 1	Day 2	Day 3	Day 4	Day 5	Day 6
1	ENGLISH 10 Large Group		AMERICAN HISTORY Small Group	BIOLOGY	SPANISH II	
2		GEOMETRY				
3						
4						ENGLISH 10 Small Group
5		SPANISH II		AMERICAN HISTORY Small Group	BIOLOGY	
6						
7	GEOMETRY					GEOMETRY
8						
9		ENGLISH 10 Small Group	GEOMETRY	. . .	PHYSICAL EDUCATION	
10						BIOLOGY LAB
11	SPANISH II	LUNCH				
12		LUNCH	LUNCH		AMERICAN HISTORY	
13	LUNCH		LUNCH	LUNCH		
14	LUNCH	AMERICAN HISTORY Large	ENGLISH 10 Small Group	LUNCH		
15				GEOMETRY	LUNCH	LUNCH
16	BIOLOGY				LUNCH	LUNCH
17			SPANISH II			
18					ENGLISH 10	
19	PHYSICAL EDUCATION			SPANISH II		
20			PHYSICAL EDUCATION			SPANISH II
21		BIOLOGY LAB				
22					GEOMETRY	
23	AMERICAN HISTORY					
24						

Note: Unscheduled periods are for independent study.

pline and control functions; transitions between activities; and interruptions and distractions must be carefully managed.

To help you appreciate the special importance of item 4, we recommend that you estimate how much of your own or a colleague's classroom time is spent on noninstructional activities and then compare your estimates with video recordings of some classes. We predict that you will be very surprised with the results. But improvements are possible.

---

5. Also, teachers must make certain that their instructional techniques are as effective in terms of the use of time as possible. Anderson provides a valuable summary of these key instructional elements (Anderson, 1984, 154–155):

> First, tasks should be chosen which are at an appropriate level for the students.
>
> Secondly, the task should be communicated directly to the students; that is, students should know what they are to learn and how they are to demonstrate that learning.
>
> Thirdly, behaviour settings and learning activities should be chosen which have a high degree of continuity (e.g., activities involving small groups working on a common goal, activities in which the students make or do something, activities in which the materials are continuously present, and teacher demonstration activities).
>
> Fourthly, teachers (or other adults) should monitor the learning. Such "monitoring" would involve, among other things, pacing the learning of students and indicating the nature and purpose of transitions between activities.
>
> Fifthly, behaviours such as those described in the categories of "with-it-ness", "smoothness", momentum and group alerting should be exhibited by the teacher during the activities in which he or she has direct involvement (such as recitations and classroom discourse), and during the monitoring of activities in which he or she is not directly involved (such as seatwork).
>
> Sixthly, appropriate task-oriented behaviours on the part of students should be reinforced.
>
> Seventh, feedback should be given to students concerning their attainment of the specified task.
>
> Eighth, and finally, errors and misunderstandings should be corrected before they are allowed to accumulate and interfere with subsequent learning.*

Group 4: Using Extra-Class Student Time Effectively
1. What we are talking about here is homework. We don't think teachers have any business trying to control the time of their students except for the assignments they make for their classes. Obviously, however, assigning homework is one way to attempt to increase the time-on-task.

*From *Time and School Learning: Theory, Research, and Practice* (pp. 154–155), edited by L. W. Anderson, 1984, New York: St. Martin's Press. Reprinted by permission.

2. Review of the extensive literature on the topic indicates that homework has caused heated controversy among educators, students and their families, and other citizens for at least 100 years. Revealingly, two recent doctoral dissertations (Foyle, 1984; Sullivan, 1988) reviewed this conflict.

3. However, many of the "reform" reports of the 1980s recommended giving more homework and insisted that homework increases student achievement, responsibility, good work habits, and self-discipline (*What Works: Research about Teaching and Learning*, U.S. Department of Education, 1987, pp. 52–53).

4. Partly as a result of the current reforms, most districts have quite specific mandates concerning the amount, kinds, and times for giving homework. Even if such policies don't exist in a school district, new teachers ought to be aware of general expectations in the school before they make many assignments.

5. Regardless of the findings mentioned in item 3 above, our experience causes us to be skeptical about most homework.

6. In any case, if homework is to be given, we think it should:
   a.   Relate directly and integrally to classroom work
   b.   Be carefully designed and prepared
   c.   Be fully explained and justified
   d.   Be interesting and require students to think
   e.   Attempt to individualize instruction whenever possible
   f.   Be closely examined and evaluated by the teacher

This presentation engendered vigorous debate in the seminar. Maria finally had to halt the discussion.

What do you think about assigning homework? What kind of homework should be assigned, and when? How much time should it take students? How and when will it be graded?

Group 5: Managing Our "Personal" Time.   Based on our reading and firsthand experience, we offer these assumptions:

• Teaching *is* stressful.
• Mismanagement of out-of-class teacher time contributes to stress and burnout.
• It is difficult to separate professional and nonprofessional endeavors, but we need to manage the time devoted to both very carefully.

Here is a list of hints for time management that we have culled from a variety of sources [see Figure 6.2].

Each of the five presentations took more time than anticipated, but Maria was pleased. These people were really becoming deserving of the title *teacher*.

MANAGING SPACE FOR PRODUCTIVE LEARNING ENVIRONMENTS

Typically students and teachers think social studies is learned in the standard classroom of 4 walls, 25 to 30 student desks in 5 neat rows, a teacher's desk, and perhaps a table. And they are half right. Much of the time, social studies teachers give the impression, by their actions, that they believe most social

FIGURE 6.2
Hints for Time Management

1. Make a "to-do" list for each day.
2. Do the toughest task first.
3. Become aware of your most efficient periods, and schedule your work load accordingly.
4. Learn to say no to extra tasks.
5. Use waiting time effectively. Take books to read, papers to grade, and assignments to write when waiting for your child or appointments.
6. Establish reasonable time limits for a task, and stick to them.
7. Delegate responsibilities.
8. Try to reduce the amount of work you take home. Do it at school whenever possible.
9. Increase students' responsibility for their own learning.
10. Handle each piece of paper only once.
11. Organize your desk and materials.
12. Keep meetings on-task and on time.
13. Avoid perfectionism.
14. Use break periods to restore energy.
15. Plan something exciting for each week.
16. Reward yourself for achieving difficult goals.
17. Take time to play. Plan to do something you enjoy each week.
18. Streamline your filing system. Label folders for each area you teach, assignments, articles, and so on. *File once a week!*
19. Team up with other teachers for special events and projects.
20. Use peer tutoring.
21. Keep a "mind joggle" notebook.
22. Acquire a lesson plan book, and use it for long-term plans.
23. Keep a bulletin board at home for notes to yourself and others.
24. Plan time for avocational interests.
25. Hire someone to do routine tasks at home.
26. Stay physically fit. Maintaining good health saves time.
27. Use the resources that are available, such as the teacher center, support personnel, professional library, support groups, and so on.
28. Read and write outside your field.
29. Save some private time.
30. Donate some time for community service. In the long run, this will save you time.
31. Make a list of your priorities. Use the list to plan your goals.

studies content can be learned only in the standard classroom, for that is where they and their students spend most of their time.

We are not saying that classrooms are inappropriate environments for learning; rather, we assert that they are not the *only* learning environments. But if you intend to use the regular classroom most of the time, think about ways to rearrange the furniture to match or to develop different learning activities. For example, you can place students in small groups for some activities, split up the class on days when you want a seminar format, or arrange students in a circle for more freewheeling discussion or brainstorming. Social studies lends itself to a variety of classroom formats.

However, you need to become familiar with the many other places inside and outside school where social studies can be learned. For example, we strongly urge you to make friends with the librarians/media specialists and computer coordinators, whose resources, expertise, and space are often essential. Remember that these people are teachers themselves and want to serve the students and other teachers.

Interviewing students and teachers in the hall or cafeteria, attending school board meetings and analyzing the power structure, and observing how children of different ethnic backgrounds interact with one another in the lower grades are just a few ways that you can use the school to promote active learning of social studies.

The larger community also is an excellent social studies environment. Extending the classroom into the community—some refer to this as "schooling without walls"—provides innumerable opportunities for active engagement in social studies. Local museums and art galleries, government offices and agencies, courthouses, city halls, senior citizens' centers, places of business, industrial complexes, factories, union halls, places of worship, day-care centers, cemeteries, and shelters for the homeless are just a few of the many locations in which social studies can be learned.

Even minor changes in classroom arrangement can create more effective—or at least novel—learning environments. For example, semicircular seating allows students to see and interact with others, often for discussion purposes. Another arrangement, albeit more common in elementary classrooms, is the establishment of "learning centers" in which different materials and assignments are located in various places in the classroom. Thus, some students might be assigned to the task of "data collection" from references (almanacs, *Statistical Abstracts of the United States*, or the *Pocket Data Book* from the Bureau of the Census). Other students might be required to compare or prepare maps and other descriptions of some geographic area. Still other students might be responsible for plugging their findings into a computer database in another corner of the classroom.

One teacher, whose students were studying human behavior, had them "observe" other students and faculty before and after school, during passing periods, and during lunch periods. These observations were recorded in various ways, including videotaping and reporting to the group and then comparing with findings in their textbooks. In this example, the "classroom" was the entire school.

Other teachers have team taught so that the same two groups of students had back-to-back classes. This afforded the teachers double time for assignments within and outside the classroom. This approach works especially well if the classroom is large enough to accommodate two groups of students and can be subdivided.

Hallways too can be used at times. Consider students who are learning about consumer behavior: picking up hallway litter and comparing the types and quantity of products represented. Or, if two class periods are available, students are generally responsive, and stores are near the school, students can do the same assignment, collecting litter outside the school. Or students can interview customers leaving the stores as to purchases and use of store coupons. They can also interview the store managers or clerks about best-selling items.

Many creative assignments can be done at sites other than a table or couch at home. Interviewing, observing, taking photographs, taping the sounds of the setting, and studying the architecture of a street are examples of activities that students can do within the community.

RESOURCES FOR PRODUCTIVE LEARNING ENVIRONMENTS: PRINT MATERIALS, VISUALS, AND NONPRINT MATERIALS

In addition to the community resources just described, the school itself offers a number of resources, including print, visuals, and nonprint materials such as computers. We strongly suggest that when you begin both your student teaching and your first paid teaching position you introduce yourself to the media specialists and obtain listings of all the equipment the school owns as well as procedures for obtaining and using it. Next, you might want to borrow catalogs from the librarian/media specialist to see what cassettes, films, or perhaps filmstrips the school owns. However, we caution you to check with your department head or principal to see how much money has been allocated to renting materials and with your colleagues, who may have already ordered the same materials.

Print Materials

The library/media center is a good starting point for finding *print* materials such as atlases, dictionaries (Webster's *Standard Collegiate, Dictionary of American History,* and biographical dictionaries, for example), almanacs, and thesauruses. Weekly newsmagazines and daily newspapers, as well as state and local historical society publications and other appropriate magazines and journals, are "musts."

Flexible modular scheduling allows students time to take advantage of resources outside the classroom and to share ideas.

Visuals

Visuals include maps (road maps, wall maps, and globes); photographs, slides, and paintings; political cartoons; charts, graphs, and tables in magazines and newspapers; posters; menus from foreign restaurants; and other "realia" one can find virtually anywhere (including drumlins!). Probably you already have started to build files of "everyday" visuals that may come in handy later.

Nonprint Materials

Also vital are the wide variety of resources that fall into the category of *nonprint* materials. For example, most schools, if not most classrooms, have overhead projectors on which to mount transparencies. Transparencies can complement a lecture by helping students with their notetaking or by providing them with a visual image of an abstraction or complex idea.

Let's say you want to illustrate the increase in Asian immigration. You can plot a graph using erasable pens on the transparency itself. Or you might find an appropriate chart in the daily local paper showing the effects Asian immigration is having on school enrollments. You can transfer the chart to the transparency by photocopying it and running the copy through a thermofax machine with a blank transparency. Or, on some copiers, you can insert a blank transparency into the paper tray.

Videocassette recorders, 16mm film projectors, slide projectors, and even filmstrip projectors also should be accessible.

Computers and the Social Studies Class

The computer already has begun to affect the teaching of social studies and likely will continue to do so. It is no substitute for the teacher, however, because "the computer cannot replace the uncanny ability and wit of a teacher who adds amusing and appropriate historical anecdotes (and gossip) at just the right moment of a lecture or discussion, nor can it communicate heartfelt feelings about people, places and events" (Kendall & Budin, 1987, p. 32).

Yet many teachers—and not just social studies teachers—do not make use of computers in the classroom. One study reports that fewer than 15% of all teachers in the nation use computers; thus, teachers may be considered computer illiterate (Bruder, 1989, p. 32). One reason may be that teachers simply have not taken the time to learn how to use computers. Also, other departments in their schools may control the use of computers, so access is limited. Some teachers have reported that the software they have seen is not "good social studies" or that they will have no time to "cover" the material if they add computer activities to their curriculum (Schug, 1988; Bruder, 1989, pp. 32–33; Budin, Taylor, & Kendall, 1987, p. 7).

Admittedly, incorporating the computer into the classroom takes time. Teachers who use technology in the classroom "spend a lot of time at it, in both preparation and class time" (White, 1987, p. 46). Most teachers have taught themselves how to use both the hardware and the software, although some school districts have conducted inservice training for their faculties. Unfortunately, it appears that new social studies teachers will be little better prepared than current ones unless colleges begin to include the study of computers in the classroom within their initial teacher preparation (Bruder, 1989, p. 32).

Are you computer literate? If your teacher preparation program does not require study of using computers effectively in the classroom, perhaps you had better sign up for a course anyway. After all, the students you will teach may know more about computer use than you do, and that may be an awkward situation for a new teacher.

Those teachers who have mastered the microcomputer, or personal computer (PC), find it an invaluable resource for themselves and their students. Many teachers use it as a tool to monitor student assignments and grades; to prepare tests, worksheets, and other handouts; or, along with their students, to write better (and sometimes more detailed) research reports. Other uses include skill/drill activities, simulations, and, more recently, databases.

Still, we hear many teachers complain that they cannot use the software because the hardware—the PCs themselves—is not available. Some teachers have only one computer in the classroom, while for others computer resource rooms have so few that two to three students must share one computer, if they can reserve the room at all. In some schools, there is such demand by the English department, which wants its students to write all of their papers on a word processor, or the math department, which wants its students to engage in skill/drill/instant correct answer activities, that the social studies teacher who has come late to the computer scene may have to wait weeks to get his or her students scheduled.

Many teachers seem to think that to make the most effective use of computers, each student must have one. Not so, according to former social studies teacher David Dockterman (Dockterman, 1989, p. 46). Dockterman has outlined three uses of one PC in the classroom: as a "smart chalkboard," as a discussion generator, and as a small-group activator.

Using the PC as a *"smart chalkboard"* means connecting it to the overhead projector and, with a PC Viewer, projecting the image on the monitor directly on a screen. Unlike the static images usually projected—cartoons, graphs, charts, lecture outlines, even dates—with a PC Viewer you can present changing images, such as tables that automatically change as you add numbers or the results of economic or political decisions. For example, you may look at a graph of wheat production in the United States since 1980 and notice that it has declined since the drought of 1986. The software package may have the capacity to predict production if the drought continues to 1995. You can add the extension to the graph in a few seconds. You could not do that so quickly with an overhead projector or in your head.

The second use of computers in a one-PC classroom, according to Dockterman, is as a *discussion generator* (1989, pp. 59–67). This involves role play and simulation, for students make decisions as though they were persons in history or government. An example is "Decisions, Decisions." Booklets with background information on several topics on which students make decisions are included in this software, which contains eight decision-making situations, from "burdens of world power" to "colonization" of the "new world." (These are available from Tom Snyder Productions, Inc., of Cambridge, Massachusetts. Snyder is a former teacher, and the software his company produces is among the best on the market.)

Group activator, the third category of benefits of using the computer in the classroom, involves the use of databases. A database is just what the term implies: hundreds of pages of information (data) that students can use to ask or answer questions. Databases can be purchased, or students can develop their own, although it takes a lot of time to gather information and then keyboard it. Tom Snyder Productions offers several ready-made databases, including *GeoWorld* and *The Social Studies Tool Kits*, which include *Our Nation* and *Our World*. *Our Nation* contains 280 separate data files; *Our World* has 88 files.

As mentioned earlier, we feel that in time computers will be in every classroom and more good software will be available. However, we caution against relying on skill/drill software except to acclimate the reluctant user, for this software tends to consist merely of activated worksheets.

Dockterman's clever book is well worth reading. It will convince you, by argument and by example, that a classroom really needs only one computer and a teacher who knows how to make the most use of it. So go sign up for a course, if you haven't taken one already, and even read Dockterman.

Also, note that we have drawn upon only a few of the numerous articles in social studies journals about the use of computers in the classroom. We suggest you peruse the May 1983 and January 1987 issues of Social Education, Current Journals in Education (CJIE), *and* Education Index *for additional articles.*

GROUPING STUDENTS

Teachers often are admonished to "individualize" their curriculum (ends) and instruction (means). They also are frequently reminded that each learner has unique interests, talents, skills, and needs and that a good teacher must tailor the teaching/learning process to accommodate and capitalize on these individual characteristics.

We believe this is sound advice. Further, we believe that far too little individualization—that is, varying the objectives, content, timing, instructional materials, and activities, including assignments and assessment procedures, on the basis of each student's strengths and weaknesses—occurs in the typical classroom. Throughout this text we offer suggestions for individualizing. But at this point, we will simply recommend a fine book on this subject, *Adapting Instruction to Individual Differences* by Margaret Wang and Herbert J. Walberg (Wang & Walberg, 1985).

However, learning—and, even more so, teaching—is also a social phenomenon. In school settings, it is impractical to learn exclusively by independent study. Moreover, nearly all of us learn from interacting, from shared or common goals and experiences. Indeed, the authors of this book find the currently popular description of the ideal school as a "community of learners" appealing. Hence, in addition to knowing how to individualize, effective teachers must know when and how to group their students.

In this section, we will provide some general thoughts on grouping students and offer more specific suggestions about an especially valuable form of subdividing, cooperative learning.

Some General Thoughts on Grouping

Much of what happens to students in all schools occurs in a wide variety of groups. Secondary schools typically have far more groups than do elementary schools. Participation is required in some groups and optional in others. As we saw in Chapter 3, peer relations, which are profoundly influenced by group membership, are particularly important for adolescents.

Most of the collective occurrences in secondary schools are not directly controlled by individual classroom teachers. Among the most important of these groupings are houses, grades, classes, tracks, sections, clusters, cliques, crowds, clubs, teams, councils, and pairs. We will resist getting into the thicket of trying to define these terms precisely; instead, we will rely on the reader's commonsense interpretations.

It is difficult for most of us to conceive of a secondary school, particularly a large one, in which all or nearly all of these groupings have not been implemented or at least considered. In other settings, such groupings are intended to serve significant organizational, educational, social, and psychological needs for the organization and its clients. In the schools, individual teachers should be well informed about these groupings and actively study their applications in their schools.

No doubt the most controversial element in all of these associations has to do with creating sections of a particular subject. For example, if there is more than one class in 11th-grade American history, some basis for assigning students must be used. Should the assignments be made randomly, or should an effort be made to reduce the variance among the students by utilizing the criterion of ability, interest, or some other variable or variables? Should sections be completely heterogeneous or partially homogeneous? Probably this issue has been more widely researched than any other schooling-related concerns. In a quite cautious attempt to summarize the vast evidence available, a recent *Harvard Education Letter* (1987) reported that, according to research and experience,

- Heterogeneous groups make sense in elementary schools.
- At the secondary level, it is worth trying less tracking than most schools now have.
- Teachers and counselors need to work harder at getting students to understand the consequences of their course choices.
- The results of homogeneous grouping in secondary schools do not justify its strong support among teachers.

We recommend that you read this source. For those of you who want a more detailed analysis, we suggest *Keeping Track: How Schools Structure Inequality* by Jeanne Oakes (Oakes, 1985). (Caution: Oakes is generally quite negative about the impact of between-class ability grouping.)

Other group activities, of course, occur within classrooms and can be controlled or strongly influenced by individual teachers. It is often advantageous to subdivide a class when a cluster of learners share a particular interest or need. Positive results may also come from grouping students with dissimilar strengths, as in peer teaching situations (see Chapter 7). One form of within-class group work deserves special mention here. It is variously called *small-group work, team learning, cooperative investigation,* and, most commonly, *cooperative learning.*

Cooperative Learning

The idea behind *cooperative learning* is simple but powerful. Nearly all examples of classroom practices are organized on one or possibly a combination of three fundamental motivational bases: *competition,* wherein learners compete with one another or with some type of group norm; *individualization,* described earlier in this chapter, wherein students work as individuals without being influenced by the group; and *cooperation,* wherein students work collaboratively to learn.

In most schools, the competition mode dominates. As we have said, individualization is uncommon in the typical classroom, and cooperation is exceedingly rare. We believe that all three modes should be used, but cooperation must receive the greatest emphasis. This need forms the foundation for cooperative learning.

Cooperative learning has received extremely strong evaluations. The following two paragraphs from an article by Robert Slavin, one of the most productive researchers in this area, are a fair summary of the evidence (Slavin, 1986, p. 8):

> Research on cooperative learning methods has taken place in grades two through twelve, in urban, suburban and rural schools, and in subjects ranging from mathematics to language arts to social studies to science. The findings are that certain forms of cooperative learning are consistently effective in increasing student achievement, usually measured by standardized tests. However, there are two elements that must be included in a cooperative learning method if it is to be instructionally effective. First, groups must be rewarded for doing well as a group. . . . Second, the group's success must depend on the individual learning of each group member, as when team members' quiz scores are added together to form a total team score. . . .

> Increased achievement is not the only outcome of cooperative learning. Researchers have also found that after participating in cooperative learning activities, students have improved attitudes toward their classmates, particularly those from different ethnic backgrounds. Attitudes toward students who are mainstreamed [pupils with handicapping conditions] have also been improved. Student self-esteem is typically significantly enhanced as a result of cooperative learning. Students learn how to cooperate to get a job done and come to see the value of cooperating with others. *

*From "Learning Together" by R. A. Slavin, Summer 1986, *American Educator,* p. 8. Reprinted, with permission, from the Summer 1986 issue of AMERICAN EDUCATOR, the quarterly journal of the American Federation of Teachers.

We think this high praise is well deserved. However, there are some potentially serious problems with introducing cooperative learning into unprepared classes. Classroom control can suffer. Large amounts of unproductive time can result. Some students, often the brightest ones, may be turned off because they have been quite successful using the competition mode. They may resent having to work with their slower peers.

To resolve these possible shortcomings, the teacher needs to engage in the demanding process of resocialization: changing behavior and, more important, altering attitudes toward appropriate behavior in the classroom. Students will need to be taught that competition is not the "name of the game" in these activities.

How do you feel about competition? Do you like to be the first one done with an assignment? Do you secretly rejoice when you receive a higher grade than others? Are you more comfortable working alone? Do others seem to "get in the way," sidetrack you, or tend to dominate you? You might want to compare your feelings with those of some of your classmates or friends.

In *Designing Groupwork,* Elizabeth Cohen goes into great and worthy detail to show how resocialization can be accomplished (Cohen, 1986). Here is the essence of her ideas:

1. The teacher must prepare students for group work by having them engage in activities that will cause them to discover and internalize new norms. They must be rewarded for sharing, helping, waiting, listening, relating, and so on. Each student must come to believe that the accomplishments of the team are in his or her best interests.
2. Each member of the group must be given a legitimate role to play. Managers, recorders, recordkeepers, reporters, resource collectors, checkers, safety officers, artists, typists, catalogers, and others are all needed from time to time. Each student must come to believe that each role is vital to the success of the group.
3. Following from the above, the teacher must give differentiated assignments that require a variety of competencies. In this way, the strengths of various members of the group may be recognized and used.
4. During cooperative activities, teachers must change their attitudes about their roles. They must pass along to students responsibilities that formerly they had assumed. For example, they can't and shouldn't try to answer every question; students should be answering one another's questions. Also, they must empower students to make mistakes without incurring penalties as they engage in their studies. They must be facilitators instead of disseminators.

Dee Dishon and Pat O'Leary (1984) have provided a simple inventory that may help the reader who is serious about trying cooperative learning (see Figure 6.3).

All of this talk about resocialization may lead one to believe that only those teachers whose top priority is socialization should use cooperative learning. We don't believe this is the case. It is true that for cooperative learning to be successful, you need to work on group-processing skills, but the long-term goal can be any of the five positions we presented in Chapter 2.

For example, let's say you are a cognitive/disciplinarian, that is, you want to be certain that your students have learned some principles from the disciplines that form the foundation for the social studies. Specifically, you have lectured on geographic and economic factors that were associated with, but not necessarily caused by, successful industrialization in the 19th and early 20th centuries. Availability of natural resources, a strategic location, inexpensive transportation, an educated labor force, capital, markets, and so on have been identified. You might divide your class of 28 into 7 teams of 4 persons each. You ask the groups to determine whether these factors were truly associated with industrial development in seven different countries. You will evaluate each team as a group on the bases of the quality of their research and their presentation skills.

In all probability, some learning of social skills will occur. But more important to you as a cognitive/disciplinarian teacher, students are likely to learn and retain information regarding the factors that were or were not associated with industrialization in some significant country of the world. (This activity could also have a devastating effect on the tendency to perceive geographic and economic factors as deterministic.)

In closing this section, we repeat that school authorities (and individual students) are and must be continually engaged in the highly significant process of grouping learners. Teachers must be active participants in this matter. Also, teachers should consider subdividing their own classes. In this regard, there is a special need to capitalize on the power of collaborative or cooperative learning.

More Conventional Groupings

Classroom groupings in the social studies can arise out of various needs and models of teaching: group investigation, synectics, role playing, and simulations. Questions for the teacher include when to group, what types of groupings, whom to group, and how to assess group work.

For the most part, there is nothing special about social studies that dictates answers different from what you have learned or can learn from more generic teacher preparation courses. However, we might note that students working in small groups can reveal considerably more about themselves than in large-group settings. The shy student may feel more relaxed, become more verbal, or even show leadership; the apathetic student may become animated; and the "class clown" will have a smaller audience for his or her "act."

FIGURE 6.3
Belief/Behavior Inventory

1. Put an N (meaning "Now") in the Me column on the side that represents your present beliefs and behaviors.

PRINCIPLE #1 Distributed Leadership			
Cooperative Groups	Me		Typical Classroom Groups
Belief: All group members are capable of understanding, learning and performing the tasks required for a group to complete a task and like each other when the task is done.			Belief: One group member, chosen by the teacher or the group, is responsible for seeing that the task is completed and everyone likes each other when the job is done.
Behavior: No leader is assigned or chosen. All group members perform the leadership skills when appropriate.			Behavior: One leader is assigned or chosen. That leader performs all leadership skills or assigns them to group members.

PRINCIPLE #2 Heterogeneous Grouping			
Cooperative Groups	Me		Typical Classroom Groups
Belief: The most effective groups are heterogeneous in terms of social background, skill levels, physical capabilities and gender.			Belief: The most effective groups homogeneous in terms of social background, skill levels, physical capabilities and gender.
Behavior: Selection of groups is made randomly or by the teacher to insure heterogeneity.			Behavior: The teacher selects groups based on similarities of group members.

PRINCIPLE #3 Positive Interdependence			
Cooperative Groups	Me		Typical Classroom Groups
Belief: All students are not willing to work in groups unless there is a built-in reason to do so.			Belief: Students will work together by being told to cooperate
Behavior: There is a group product, group or individual accountability, shared materials, and/or group reward.			Behavior: Group members create one or more products, sometimes share materials, are accountable only for their own learning, and have individual rewards.

PRINCIPLE #4 Social Skills Acquisition			
Cooperative Groups	Me		Typical Classroom Groups
Belief: The ability to work effectively in a group comes from skills that can be taught and learned.			Belief: Students come to school knowing how to get along and work in groups.
Behavior: Social skills are defined, discussed, practiced, observed, and processed.			Behavior: Groups are told to cooperate.

PRINCIPLE #5 Group Autonomy			
Cooperative Groups	Me		Typical Classroom Groups
Belief: Students learn to solve their own problems by resolving them on their own rather than being rescued from them by the teacher.			Belief: Group members always need the teacher's help to solve problems.
Behavior: In problem situations, the teacher suggests and prompts at the request of the entire group.			Behavior: The teacher directs and orders groups to solve problems according to the teacher's observation.

2. Analyze your position. If your N's are both on one side in each section, your beliefs are consistent with your behaviors. If your N's are not on the same side, you may experience stress because your beliefs and behaviors are inconsistent.
3. Now think about where you would like to be in terms of your beliefs and behaviors. We are asking you to experiment with new behaviors when you use cooperative groups, so it will be helpful for you to examine your beliefs to see if they coincide with your new practices. Go back through the columns and put an F where you would like to be in the future.

It may be useful to do activities in which students develop information (or use information, if a computer with a database is available) that ultimately can be used for large-group learning. For the study of artifacts, including census data, old telephone or city directories, or diaries in limited quantities, small groups may be especially appropriate.

In fact, the only limits on grouping are the teacher's imagination and the students' personalities. Some students, of course, are more field independent and prefer to work alone, and the teacher must be alert to this. There are other concerns as well, especially for middle school teachers: how to ensure that groups are functional, whom to group with whom, which boys are mature enough to work productively with girls and vice versa, and what kinds of assignments will be performed most effectively by small groups. Also, teachers need to consider optimal sizes for groups. with younger students, seven to a group is probably too large, two is too small, and an even-numbered group can result in a stalemate if group decisions are necessary. Five tends to be a good size, and three to a group could be workable.

As we have noted, because classroom grouping in social studies does not necessarily differ from that in other content areas, we are giving short shrift to this matter. We strongly recommend that you examine treatments of grouping in other sources. An example is Welton and Mallan, *Children and Their World*, pp. 368–376.

CLASSROOM MANAGEMENT

On January 5, 1864, a youth wrote in his diary, "Could not go out on akount of my [frozen] foot. It's best slaying [sledding] of the winter and I've got to miss it. . . . [At least I] can't go to school. That's something" (Polmenteer, 1980). To that entry, the next day he added, "If I freeze all my toes at a time maybe I can stay out of school for pretty near two weeks. . . .

Six days later he wrote, "Went skating. Played hooky from school."

On January 18 he bemoaned, "Very slushy. Wasn't anything to do and so I went to school. The teacher pretended she didn't know me. . . . I pasted her good with a paper wad blower. Had to stay after school."

Clearly, attending school was not this youngster's favorite pasttime. Imagine the poor teacher to whose class he was assigned! But maybe this goes with the territory. For example, more than 2,000 years ago, Socrates supposedly wrote that children "tyrannize over teachers." In 1830, a Massachusetts newspaper lamented the "dishonesty, fraud, and other wickedness among our boys and girls [which shock] the nation" (Williams, 1979).

Typical too are the comments that a social studies student teacher received from middle school students who had been asked to evaluate the teacher: "You were a good teacher but you know you didnt see us lighting matches. [S]omeone told you and thats all. [T]hiers more but I cant think now and Sue did cheat by changing a T to a F." And "I thought you were o.k. But you lied and said you saw us do things but you didn't. . . . Them boys were talking too! and I did not cheat on that paper."

Possibly the biggest pitfall for teachers, especially new ones, is the "big D": discipline. Fortunately, there is no dearth of advice, from presidents of corporations to popcorn vendors:

Don't smile 'til Christmas.

Select the biggest kid in class and give him a good licking so others will "fall in line."

Spare the rod, spoil the child.

Ignore it and it'll go away.

Try treats; reward good behavior.

In fact, it seems that everyone outside the classroom is an "expert," including Miss Manners, whose first bit of advice to a new teacher was to demand that "all feet belong on the floor at all times" (Martin, 1984, p. 24). However, the authors of this text are much more tentative about offering advice, because being teachers, we know better.

Classroom Management versus Discipline

While we may be reluctant to offer casual advice, we are quite clear about our distaste for the term *discipline*. We believe that the primary instructional decision teachers must make is how to ensure that learning occurs. This means being an effective manager of time, materials, and students—indeed, of the entire classroom environment. In short, we purposely use the term *classroom management* rather than *discipline*, which has a negative connotation and an inappropriate emphasis. Kearney and Plax (1987) found that teacher behavior tends to be influenced by student behavior, with teachers being especially attentive to active misbehaviors of their students. As a result, teachers reinforce passivity and apathy by ignoring "good behavior" (basically through silence). One can interpret this to mean that if discipline (control) is emphasized, passivity and apathy, not necessarily learning, will result.

Consistent with this notion is the research of Korth and Cornbleth (1982), who found that to increase cognitive learning opportunities in the classroom, teachers need to stress more than time-on-task and direct instruction. These researchers found that where the emphasis is on teacher authority, students tend to show mostly acquisition and reproduction of materials rather than comprehension and reasoning. "Unobtrusive strategies," more common in social studies classes than in, say, science or English, achieved better results.

Approaches to Classroom Management

Clearly the authors reflect their personal philosophies, just as you will in your classes. For example, do you see yourself as a conductor orchestrating disparate soloists or as controlling unwilling participants? To this end, we suggest viewing approaches to classroom management as a set of alternatives from which to choose:

– – –Permissive   Instructional   Authoritarian – – –

The *permissive* approach suggests a "live and let live," or "don't hassle me and I won't hassle you," philosophy. In fact, Powell (1985) seems to suggest that schools too often operate this way. Even within this approach lies a range of behaviors. In the extreme case, for example, the classroom appears to be "student controlled." Students do pretty much as they please; frequent trips outside the classroom occur, and incessant extracurricular talking dominates. We have seen such classrooms, but we consider this atmosphere more appropriate for a recreation or youth center.

Considerably less permissive is the notion of a "social system" wherein rules are established and enforced primarily by the students, but with teacher guidance. This can take the form of a contract: Offenders are identified, and punishments are meted out by the students. This approach requires a confident teacher and a relatively mature group of students.

The *authoritarian* approach lies at the opposite extreme. It relies on intimidation. The obvious advantage is that everyone knows who is boss—the teacher—and the students must necessarily adapt. Of course, the adaptations may take various forms, not all of which are particularly suitable for learning. Also, the authoritarian teacher may learn that the students are remarkably adaptable and clever, even making it *appear* that the teacher is in charge when in fact the students are.

Also toward the authoritarian side of the continuum is the teacher who employs a "bag of tricks": sarcasm, subtle intimidation, or, on the other hand, rewarding compliance with small favors, which Carlson (1964) calls "preferential treatment."

Another authoritarian device is behavior modification, which has found greatest use with special education students and borrows from the research of B. F. Skinner. Recently this approach has come under close scrutiny and received much criticism (Doyle, 1986, p. 423). In behavior modification, approved behaviors are reinforced and inappropriate behaviors are not, the goal being to elicit only desired behaviors in the classroom.

Toward the middle of the spectrum is the classroom that is viewed from an *instructional* rather than managerial viewpoint: teacher expertise, internalized rules, various teaching strategies, and students on-task. This we view as classroom management as opposed to discipline. Doyle (1986) has proposed that "the key to a teacher's success in management appears to be his or her (a) understanding of the likely configuration of events in a classroom, and (b) skill in monitoring and guiding activities in light of this information" (p. 424). The problem is that "teachers must meet students in groups on a daily basis for extended periods of time to achieve purposes that *do not*

**FIGURE 6.4
Client-Organization
Control in Service
Organizations**

Client Control over Admission

		Yes	No
Organizational Control over Admission	Yes	I	II
	No	III	IV

necessarily coincide with the immediate interests of the participants [emphasis added]" (p. 394).

Richard Carlson (1964, pp. 265–266) illustrated the problem for teachers, which increasingly has been codified and interpreted to the point where many critics have discredited it. However, it offers a useful beginning perspective for looking at schools in terms of the extent to which organizations and clients choose to do business. The matrix in Figure 6.4 illustrates this perspective.

In Figure 6.4, the ideal situation is the one in which both the client and the organization freely choose to interact or participate (type I). Examples are private universities, hospitals, and doctors' offices. The most problematic is type IV, wherein, in the extreme, neither the organization nor the client has any choice; each is forced to accept the other. Examples are state mental hospitals, prisons, and *public schools.*

In the latter case (admittedly an abstraction), students must be in school and the schools must accept them. In reality, however, students still have options: They can choose private, alternative, or other schools in the district (an increasingly popular option); find diversions (engage in athletics, be "student helpers," sleep in class, etc.); play truant; and, of course, drop out. But often these are *forced* choices.

Viewed exclusively from this perspective, discipline seems the only alternative. The rod, then, should be mandatory teacher equipment. Clearly, as Doyle (1986, p. 395) notes, the concern about order and control over pupils is a pervasive (and almost inevitable) concern of teachers. Yet we argue that teachers must be encouraged to think of ways to achieve and sustain involvement in classrooms rather than dwell on misbehavior. This means that teachers must pay attention to the almost infinite number of variables in the classroom.

Critical Features of Classroom Settings

According to Doyle (1986, pp. 395, 396), six critical features prevail in classrooms:

- *Multidimensionality:* crowded places characterized by a great deal of activity
- *Simultaneity:* many things happening at once

- *Immediacy:* rapid pace of events
- *Unpredictability:* distractions and interruptions
- *Publicness:* many witnesses to events
- *History:* an accumulation of a "common set of experiences" over a school year

Thus, teachers, particularly in elementary and middle schools, must work in a setting wherein there are many observers to multiple, simultaneous, immediate events involving individuals whose interactions over the course of a year predispose certain results. The makers of headache remedies have a ready group of consumers! Nevertheless, effective teachers manage this environment to ensure that learning occurs with regularity.

Guidelines for Classroom Management

Gettinger (1988) and Good and Brophy (1987) suggest that the key to classroom management is prevention, with particular attention to motivation in classrooms. Effective teachers focus on establishing order in the classroom rather than responding to problems of disruptive behavior. In addition, Good and Brophy distinguish between teacher attitudes and general management techniques (see Figure 6.5).

FIGURE 6.5
Guidelines for Classroom Management

1. Teacher attitudes
   a. Liking and respecting students
   b. Interacting privately with students
   c. Establishing credibility
   d. Assuming responsibility for student learning
   e. Valuing and enjoying learning themselves
   f. Communicating and modeling basic attitudes
2. Techniques
   a. Establishing classroom guidelines early
   b. Letting students assume responsibility
   c. Organizing lessons for independent activities
   d. Encouraging student effort
   e. Stressing, recognizing, and reinforcing desirable student behavior.
   f. Grabbing and maintaining student attention
   g. Pacing lessons
   h. Monitoring attention
   i. Terminating lessons at appropriate times.

Source: From *Looking in Classrooms* (pp. 228–255) by T. Good and J. Brophy, 1987, New York: Harper & Row.

FIGURE 6.6
Johari Window

	Known to self	Unknown to self
Known to others	Area of free activity (public)	Blind area
Unknown to others	Hidden or avoided area (private)	Area of unknown potential

Source: Adapted from *Of Human Interaction* by J. Luft, 1969, Palo Alto, CA: Mayfield.

Teacher Attitudes

Good and Brophy (1987) point out that the most important teacher attitude is *liking students*. We suggest that underlying this notion might be the admonition to each teacher to "know thyself." Many student behavior problems stem from teachers' inadequacies, known or unknown to the teachers themselves. An appropriate reference point might be the Johari Window (Luft, 1969), illustrated in Figure 6.6.

The most critical area, of course, is the "blind area," analogous to "The Emperor's New Clothes." In other words, whatever front we may desire to display to students, they see through us, which may prove especially embarrassing at times. We need to reduce the area that is unknown to us, to know ourselves better so that we can better relax with students without giving up the necessary ability to manage. The secure teacher—one who has reduced this blind area—can be a risk taker. Feeling relatively comfortable, such a teacher can allow his or her feelings to emerge, will respect students' feelings, and allow for variety in the classroom. This teacher, like the social studies teachers surveyed by Russell and Morrow (1986), recognizes that the major concern for teachers tends not to be with content, materials selection, grading, and other subject matter competencies but with motivation and classroom management.

Techniques for Classroom Management

The next important component of classroom management is employing appropriate techniques. The most critical is establishing guidelines, or rules of conduct, at the outset so that procedures are announced early on, demonstrated, and routinized (Doyle, 1986, pp. 410–412). We suggest that minimum, rather than maximum, expectations tend to have greater impact. Students, like one's own children, have a way of finding exceptions to rules anyway, so minimal rules spelled out clearly will tend to reduce the need for negotiations and arbitration.

We already discussed grouping and cooperative learning as techniques available to the teacher, and these techniques are receiving tentative approval as ways to reduce discipline problems. Greenwood et al. (1988) found that peer tutoring served as an effective procedure for both classroom management and direct instruction. Cohen and Lotan (1988) found that collective achievement among students from lower socioeconomic backgrounds occurred in classrooms that employed cooperative learning. In such classrooms, less teacher supervision was necessary and, conversely, more student cooperation resulted in greater test gains.

While the research base is still small, it appears that placing more responsibility for learning on students pays off. This is compatible with the notion that intrinsic motivation is stronger than extrinsic motivation. Students who feel they have some choice over their learning are more likely to buy into it. And the more varied the activities, the more likely it is that interest will be maintained.

Still, our experience with student teachers suggests that they and beginning teachers are insecure and hence are inordinately concerned about discipline. We are reluctant to suggest "gimmicks," because they may prove inappropriate, detract from concentration on instruction, and fail to consider all the idiosyncrasies that exist in a particular classroom. However, in Figure 6.7 we offer suggestions for classroom management borrowed from several sources.

FIGURE 6.7
Techniques for Classroom Management

1. Learn students' names promptly.
2. Be businesslike, that is, get down to work.
3. Attend to immediate problems, then get on with the class.
4. Consider different seating arrangements, and change students' seats when necessary.
5. Use the standards of the group when possible. This may mean overlooking some "undesirable" behaviors.
6. Avoid group punishments and singling out individual students as much as possible.
7. *Never* insist on public apologies.
8. Be prepared to back up "threats."
9. If uncertain about what to do, do the minimum until you are clearer about the situation.
10. Maintain a sense of humor and a smile—be human.
11. Clear the air as far as possible so the student can feel that the record is clean after the incident has been handled.
12. Vary pacing of the class and your delivery of information.
13. Recognize individual differences.
14. Be prompt about starting and ending a class.
15. Ask questions, then call on a particular student.
16. Ensure students' physical comfort.
17. Avoid unpleasant mannerisms—which means detecting them as early as possible.
18. Be sure students can see and hear what is happening.
19. Reward good conduct rather than punish bad.
20. Don't get mad—and *never* strike a student.

In summary, we believe that effective teaching requires attending to the classroom environment, including scheduling and timing, employing a variety of resources and appropriate technology, and judiciously grouping students for learning tasks. In short, the teacher must understand that learning is dependent on an encouraging environment. Such a setting is not defined solely as one in which the primary emphasis is on establishing and maintaining control. Instead, it is one that recognizes that learning depends on the teacher's configuration of events and activities and ability to improvise to ensure that comprehension and reasoning rather than discipline are the focus.

Summary

Effective learning demands effective teaching. Effective teaching, in turn, requires that the teacher be a good manager of the environment, that is, of time, space, resources, and groups.

Time management is crucial, for, as the old maxim goes, "Time is money." Increasingly it seems that our lives are being governed by demands on our time. This is especially true in the classroom, wherein so many things impinge on our time. There never seems to be enough time to "cover" the content. Thus, the teacher must be particularly alert to ways to use time wisely.

Space management is another concern. Too often we let the circumstances rather than instructional need dictate where learning will occur. We know quite well that learning takes place virtually anywhere, but we tend to feel constrained to stick to our classrooms. Yet we need not and should not. Libraries, museums, government offices, places of businesses, and numerous other locations can serve as "the classroom" equally effectively.

Resource management means using the wide variety of resources available. Certainly the library/media center has many ready resources for teachers' use—dictionaries, almanacs, atlases, films, videocassettes, and software programs. Computers are woefully underused, although software is only slowly beginning to fill the arena of potential educational uses.

Managing the environment means managing groups of students, for *grouping* is inevitable. The question is *how* to group and for what purposes. Antecedents of cooperative learning suggest opportunities that we are only beginning to reexplore, but research indicates the growing importance of grouping for learning.

Disciplining students could well come to occupy all of teachers' limited time. However, if we adopt the notion of *classroom management*, we will likely minimize what could be a major but exaggerated preoccupation. Organization, humor, and variety are highly effective tools in managing the classroom.

Decisions! Decisions!

1. How will you compress the content of your courses into 179 six-and-one-half-hour days? How will you find time to prepare exciting lessons? Grade papers? Be yourself?

2. Supposed you are saddled with only "low" sections? Must you count on seniority to get "good" classes? How difficult will it be to develop more flexible, modular scheduling of classes to accommodate and manage various learners?

3. If you want to "enlarge" the classroom environment to include museums, government buildings, and so on, what logistical problems are you likely to encounter? Approval from school authorities and parents? Bus scheduling? How will you find out what help you can get from individuals and groups outside the school? Are there published directories of museums and other resources?

4. Suppose your students cannot read some of the materials identified earlier in the text. Where can you go for help with translations of materials, especially for students whose native language is not English?

5. What if you cannot get into a computer course as recommended in the chapter? To whom or where can you turn? What if much of the available software is as bad as you have heard it is? Are there critiques of software that will help you make decisions?

6. If you choose to use different groupings of students, how will you find out about student relationships? How does one obtain a sociometry of a class (the leaders or followers, who likes whom, etc.)? If students in a particular class prefer competition to cooperation, how will you get them to engage in cooperative learning?

7. You are nervous about getting into the classroom. How do you know you will be safe? What kinds of policies and resources do the schools have to help you? What if you disagree with many of the school policies? What will happen if you ignore or "bend" the rules?

8. How will you learn about the "culture" of the school in which you might teach, that is, its traditions and ceremonies? As a teacher, in what ceremonies must you participate?

9. More than a half-century ago, educational sociologist Willard Waller observed that a class of students develops a collective personality. What if this "personality" and yours clash? Can you develop a "new," collective personality? Waller also stated that as a result of developing this collective personality, a class can become—that is, observe, feel, and act like—a mob. If this is an accurate representation, how can you prevent this from occurring? If you cannot, how can you learn to handle a "mob?"

References

Anderson, L. W. (Ed.). (1984). *Time and school learning: Theory, research, and practice.* New York: St. Martin's Press.

Boyer, E. L. (1983). *High school.* New York: Harper & Row.

Bruder, I. (1989, January/February). Future teachers: Are they prepared? *Electronic Learning, 8*(4), 32–39.

Budin, H., Taylor, R., & Kendall, D. (1987, January/February). Computers and social studies: Trends and directions. *The Social Studies, 78*(1), 7–12.

Carlson, R. O. (1964). Environmental constraints and organizational consequences: The public school and its clients. *Behavioral Science and Educational Administration* (63rd Yearbook, National Society for Study of Education, Part II), 262–278.

Cohen, E. (1986). *Designing groupwork.* New York: Teachers College Press.

Cohen, E. C., & Lotan, R. A. (1988, April). *Teacher as supervisor of complex technology.* AERA. ED 298945.

Dempsey, R. A., & Traverso, H. P. (1983). *Scheduling the secondary school.* Reston, VA.: National Association of Secondary School Principals.

Denham, C., & Lieberman, A. (Eds.). (1980). *Time to learn.* Washington, DC: U.S. Department of Education.

Dishon, D., & O'Leary, P. (1984). *A guidebook for cooperative learning.* Holmes Beach, FL: Learning Publications.

Dockterman, D. A. (1989). *Teaching in the one computer classroom.* Cambridge, MA: Tom Snyder Productions.

Doyle, W. (1986). Classroom organization and management. In M. C. Wittrock (Ed.), *Handbook on teaching* (pp. 392–431). New York: Macmillan.

Ferguson, J. (1989, March/April). Computing across the curriculum. *The Social Studies, 80*(2), 69–72.

Foyle, H. (1984). *The effect of preparation and practice of homework on student achievement in 10th grade American history.* Manhattan, KS: Kansas State University Press.

Gettinger, M. (1988). Methods of proactive classroom management. *School Psychology Review, 17*(2), 227–242.

Good, T., & Brophy, J. (1987). *Looking in classrooms.* New York: Harper & Row.

Goodlad, J. I. (1984). *A place called school.* New York: McGraw-Hill.

Greenwood, C., et al. (1988). The use of peer tutoring strategies in classroom management and educational instruction. *School Psychology Review, 17*(2), 258–275.

Hunter, B. (1987, January). Knowledge-creative learning with data bases. *Social Education, 51*(1), 38–43.

Johnson, D. W., & Johnson, R. T. (1975). *Learning together and alone: Cooperation, competition and individualization.* Englewood Cliffs, NJ: Prentice-Hall.

Johnson, D. W., & Johnson, R. T. (1984). *Cooperating in the classroom.* New Brighton, MN: Interaction Book.

Kearney, P., & Plax, T. (1987, Winter). Situational and individual determinants of teachers' reported use of behavior alteration techniques. *Human Communication Research, 14*(2), 145–166.

Kendall, D. S., & Budin, H. (1987, January). Computers in social studies. *Social Education, 51*(1), 32–33.

Korth, W., & Cornbleth, C. (1982, March). *Classroom activities as setting for cognitive learning opportunity and instruction.* AERA. ED 220 532.

Luft, J. (1969). *Of human interaction.* Palo Alto, CA: Mayfield Publishing.

Martin, J. (1984, November 21). Miss Manners: Rules for teachers, parents. *Education Week,* 24.

McNergney, R. (Ed.). (1988). *Guide to classroom teaching.* Boston: Allyn & Bacon.

Oakes, J. (1985). *Keeping track: How schools structure inequality.* New Haven, CT: Yale University Press.

Polmenteer, V. (1980, August 31). Oh, you naughty boy! *Rochester Democrat & Chronicle.*

Powell, A. G. (1985, December). Being unspecial in the shopping mall high school. *Phi Delta Kappan,* 255–261.

Roessler, M. (1987, January). Students design a depression simulation. *Social Education, 51*(1), 48–51.

Russell, T. E., & Morrow, J. E. (1986). Reform in teacher education: Perceptions of secondary social studies teachers. *Theory and Research in Social Education, 14*(4), 325–330.

Schug, M. C. (1988, May/June). What do social studies teachers say about using computers? *The Social Studies, 79*(3), 112–115.

Sizer, T. (1984). *Horace's compromise.* Boston: Houghton Mifflin.

Slavin, R. A. (1986, Summer). Learning together. *American Educator,* 6–11.

Sullivan, J. E. (1988). *Homework: The pied piper of the 1980s.* Ed. D. dissertation, University of Rochester, Rochester, NY.

Swaab, A. M. (1974). *School administrator's guide to flexible modular scheduling.* West Nyack, NY: Parker Publishing.

The Harvard Education Letter. (1987, July). Cambridge, MA: Harvard University Press.

U.S. Department of Education. (1983). *A nation at risk.* Washington, DC: Author.

U.S. Department of Education. (1987). *What works: Research about teaching and learning* (2nd ed.). Washington, DC: Author.

Waller, W. (1932). *The sociology of teaching.* New York: Wiley.

Wang, M., & Walberg, H. (Eds.). (1985). *Adapting instruction to individual differences.* Berkeley, CA: McCutchan.

White, C. S. (1987, January). Teachers using technology. *Social Education, 51*(1), 44–47.

Williams, J. W. (1979, January). Discipline in the public schools: A problem of perception. *Phi Delta Kappan, 60,* 385–387.

Chapter Seven

Listening and Speaking in the Social Studies

Most learning and all teaching involve communication. Listening and speaking are at the heart of communicating. Thus, all effective teachers must continually strive both to employ sound instructional strategies involving oral language and to improve listening and speaking competencies—their own and those of their students.

Talk often gets a bum rap. You've heard it:

Talk is cheap.

Put your money where your mouth is.

Action speaks louder than words.

Put up or shut up.

Verbal diarrhea!

Motor mouth!

He loves to hear the sound of his own voice.

While there is some truth to these denigrations, communication lies at the very core of our humanness. Language is a basic tool of the communication process, and oral language predominates over the written word.

Throughout our lives, we spend most of our productive time in verbal activities. A series of studies beginning with Rankin in 1929 repeatedly have shown that most adults, regardless of their occupations, spend approximately 70% of their waking hours using language. Of this time, on average, 42% is spent in listening, 32% in speaking, 15% in reading, and 9% in writing (Rankin, 1929). And this predates television! A similar ratio holds for students and teachers during school hours, but for students the listening portion is usually much higher (Wilt, 1950, p. 630).

Most of us first learn to listen and then to speak. Only later do we learn to read and, later still, to write. Although the vast majority of children enter kindergarten with sophisticated oral language, dialect or accent may differ from that of the teacher. The need to become more skilled in this area is ever present. Listening and speaking provide the foundation for reading and writing and indeed for all aspects of our ability to think, to know, and to feel—in other words, to be human.

Clearly, improving our use of oral language is far too important to be left exclusively to schools or to "language" teachers. All of us must continually be learners and teachers of communication. Still, language development often is said to be the school's most vital function (Boyer, 1983), and "the school years are a critical time for learning and refining speaking and listening" (Brown, 1981, p. 12). Further, we believe that middle and high school social studies teachers have an especially significant responsibility in this regard.

This chapter aims to help you meet a pair of closely and positively correlated responsibilities: (1) using effective oral language techniques in your classroom and (2) helping to develop the listening and speaking competencies of your students. We will begin with an overview of the goals and objectives of oral teaching activities in schools, followed by descriptions and illustrations of some of the most promising teaching strategies. We have broadly classified these overlapping activities as follows:

1. Reporting (including lecturing, reciting, questioning, interviewing, and tutoring)
2. Discussing in a variety of forms
3. Dramatizing (including simulation and gaming)

As always, your job is to analyze our suggestions, rejecting, refining, and adding as appropriate for your goals, situation, and teaching style.

NONVERBAL COMMUNICATION

Before we go on, we need to make one further important introductory point: Not all communication is verbal. *Nonverbal communication*—sending and receiving messages without the use of words—occurs in nearly all human interactions. Facial expressions, use of the eyes, posture, vocal intonation, touching, grooming and clothing, gestures, use of space, silence, and nonverbal artistic expressions, ad infinitum, often send very clear messages. When used in conjunction with words, they can support or refute the verbal messages. Indeed, if there is a contradiction between a verbal and a nonverbal message, the nonverbal one typically dominates. Further, many studies suggest that even without conflict, nonverbal behavior is far more powerful and durable than verbal communication in many situations, especially those involving the affective realm (Miller, 1988).

Unfortunately, interpreting nonverbal behavior is at least as difficult as (and probably more so than) gathering true meaning from words. Differences in age, ethnic background, race, class, gender, and so on between the sender and the receiver often result in misinterpretation.

We all need to be students of nonverbal communication, and there is a large and rapidly growing literature on the topic. Rather than try to review this scholarship here, we will strongly recommend an excellent pamphlet on the subject that is part of the National Education Association's *What Research Says to the Teacher* series, entitled simply *Nonverbal Communication* (Miller, 1988). In addition to summarizing the research evidence and providing an excellent bibliography, this pamphlet offers numerous practical instructional hints for teachers. Here are portions of Miller's concluding comments:

> If effective communication is to be achieved in today's schools, it must be an open process. . . . A good teacher is a good listener [and speaker,] not only to words, but to silent messages that signal agreement/disagreement, attention/inattention, boredom/interest, and the desire of the student to be heard. Teacher effectiveness is generally characterized by showing enthusiasm, varying facial expressions, gesturing for emphasis, moving toward students, spending more time in front of

the class than behind the desk or at the chalkboard, maintaining eye contact, displaying head nods, speaking with a clear voice and varied intonation, correlating between verbal and nonverbal messages, and exhibiting a sense of humor. . . . [Teachers must foster] positive characteristics, mannerisms, actions, and habits, as well as [overcome] negative ones that depress an atmosphere for learning.*

In short, we are saying that in addition to everything else good teachers must do, they must be very sensitive to nonverbal clues. They must analyze the signals they and their students are sending. "Body language" in its many forms is vitally important to this process.

GOALS FOR ORAL COMMUNICATION

By now you are well aware that we believe you should determine your own goals from among a variety of legitimate alternatives before proceeding any further in planning your teaching activities. To guide you, however, Figure 7.1 provides a brief but valuable enumeration of both broad goals and specific objectives of a process sort that you might profitably consult each time you plan an oral activity for your class (English Language Arts Syllabus K–12, 1988, p. 26).

REPORTING

Telling, disseminating, or reporting (and receiving) information primarily through the use of oral language is a basic element of teaching. This section describes a variety of reporting techniques ranging from formal lectures and oral reports through recitation and questioning, interviews, and tutoring. Teachers, students, visitors, and media presentations can and should share in performing the reporting function.

Lectures and Oral Reports

Lecturing—should you do it or shouldn't you? Opinions differ, but we believe that, with certain qualifications, you should lecture. In fact, we think lectures can accomplish some legitimate teaching aims better than any other technique in use today.

But first, what *is* a lecture? The American Heritage Dictionary defines a lecture as "an exposition of a given subject delivered before an audience or class for the purpose of instruction; discourse." In its pure form, a lecture is a well-organized, highly structured, thoroughly planned, and thoughtful analysis presented by an expert in which communication flows largely in one direction.

*From *Nonverbal Communication*, Third Edition. © 1988, National Education Association. Reprinted with permission.

FIGURE 7.1
Overview of Purposes and Objectives for Listening and Speaking, K—12

Purposes	Objectives—The Student Will:
I. Listening and speaking for social interaction: *Communicating in everyday interpersonal situations*	1. Practice the elements of good listening and speaking in conversation 2. Demonstrate principles of good listening and speaking in group situations 3. Participate in meetings as a member of an organization 4. Take and give messages with completeness and accuracy
II. Listening and speaking for information and understanding: *Acquiring, interpreting, applying, and transmitting information*	1. Follow and give oral directions 2. Listen for and relate essential information 3. LIsten for and use language of organization in formal presentations 4. Identify and use critical thinking and problem-solving skills 5. Identify and use vocal characteristics that influence the meaning of oral language 6. Identify and use levels of language, idiomatic expressions, and figures of speech that enhance oral communication 7. Interpret and use nonverbal cues, such as body language and visual aids, that enhance an an oral message
III. Listening and speaking for critical analysis and evaluation: *Evaluating and generating information and ideas according to personal or objective criteria*	1. Formulate and express judgments about the content, organization, and delivery of oral communication 2. Evaluate and generate statements of opinion, personal preference, and values 3. Evaluate and use persuasive techniques 4. Evaluate and present ideas and information transmitted by nonprint media and visual aids
IV. Listening and speaking for personal response: *Communicating for appreciation and entertainment*	1. Enjoy listening to and sharing personal experiences, stories, and drama 2. Appreciate and orally interpret sounds, words, imagery, repetition, rhyme, and rhythm patterns in language

Source: From *English Language Arts Syllabus K–12* (p. 26), 1988, Albany, NY: New York State Education Department. Reprinted with permission.

Doubtless there are far too many lectures that do not meet these tests. Also, lectures probably are overused, especially in higher education. However, the lecture approach has distinct advantages.

Advantages of Lectures.   Lectures offer the following benefits:

- Lectures are highly efficient in terms of the amount of class time they consume relative to activities that more actively involve students.
- Students often tend to be more active when listening to a lecture than they are while doing a reading assignment. A good lecturer can gauge the level of student attention quite accurately. Thus, there is immediate, albeit imperfect, verbal and nonverbal feedback for students and lecturer.
- Using lectures in secondary schools is valuable preparation and practice for college and for many workplaces in which the technique is widely used.
- A lecture frequently is a highly effective way to introduce a topic, that is, to motivate students by demonstrating the importance, the relevance, and especially the complexity of a subject that they are about to study in depth.
- Likewise, a lecture is a fine way to synthesize material that previously has lacked readily apparent organization. Lectures can be effectively used to present a significant but unpopular (or unfamiliar) view in a particular class on a controversial subject that otherwise might be overlooked or neglected. Indeed, a lecture can provide the speaker with a "bully pulpit," and a bit of preaching in a classroom may be a good thing.
- Control and discipline are more easily maintained during a lecture than in more active situations.
- Preparation for a lecture, while difficult, is far easier than in situations where the teacher has to plan numerous individualized activities.
- Lectures can communicate the interest, enthusiasm, and expertise of the speaker—and this may be contagious.
- Lectures can provide information that is not available in suitable print sources. For example, often a sophisticated idea is too complex in written form for some "poor" readers in the class, or the lecturer may have done some valuable research that has not yet been published.
- Communication by lecture offers economic advantages, because it reaches a large audience. Moreover, it may allow an opportunity for many students to "sit at the feet" of the recognized expert. A lecture can provide a modeling experience for the learner; that is, the presentation can demonstrate clearly how an expert tackles, organizes, and researches a problem.
- A lecture may give some students a sense of security, because they know precisely what is expected of them.

Disadvantages of Lectures.   Like all techniques, the lecture approach has its disadvantages, many of which overlap with its benefits:

- Despite nonverbal clues, a lecture by itself usually doesn't give the instructor systematic knowledge about what the student is learning.
- Students can be quite passive and even lethargic during the lecture.
- Attention spans are short—20 minutes is pushing it for adolescents. This may not be enough time to develop the argument.
- Good lectures require a great deal of preparation, although advance work is far from limited to this approach.
- Even with attentive listeners, information learned in a lecture tends to be forgotten quickly—more quickly than in more active situations.
- Some students just don't learn well by listening. Lectures, by their very nature, do not account for this reality.
- Lecturing is probably best suited to lower levels of knowledge or understanding. If you want students to apply, analyze, value, or evaluate, the lecture may tend to emphasize *the* answer instead of engaging listeners in a search for alternative views.
- Effective lectures require effective public speakers—people with verbal fluency, good timing, pleasing voices, and self-confidence in public settings. Some of us, even those reputed to be good teachers, may lack these attributes.

Planning and Executing a Lecture. Sam had intended to omit the military aspects of his unit on the Civil War largely because he thought his eighth-grade students were too interested in violence as it was. In fact, he was certain that some of his kids were gang members. They probably had been involved in turf wars in the neighborhood. But then Sam began to have second thoughts. Perhaps he should try to capitalize on the students' interest in warfare—maybe that interest would spread to other areas. Perhaps he could use some of the Civil War battles to demonstrate certain principles of leadership that he had been trying to teach. Even more important, maybe he could convince some of the kids that war is not glamorous—quite the contrary. Besides, the state exam usually included some questions on military events.

So, after some careful reading, Sam collected some interesting instructional materials, including a couple of recordings of Civil War songs. He planned three 20-minute lectures on some of the major battles in the eastern theater of the war around the two capitals. He interspersed these lectures with recitations based on more general reading. Maps were used, diagrams were drawn, songs were played—there were even a few moments of singing. Bull Run, Antietam, Chancellorsville, Gettysburg, the Wilderness, and so on came to life. So did a typology of leadership styles. The class was alive.

Subsequent evaluations proved that these lectures were among the most productive sessions of the semester. Further, it was evident that Sam's students understood the more important aspects of the Civil War thanks to the "digression" into the violence of battle.

FIGURE 7.2
Guidelines for Planning and Executing a Lecture

1. Know your audience. What are their interests and backgrounds?
2. Limit your topic. A few points clearly made work better than trying to cover the whole field.
3. Be organized. Have an outline and share it with the listeners—you can use a handout, a transparency, or the chalkboard. The logic of the order should be clear to both speaker and listener. Chronology and causality are especially valuable means for providing the structure.
4. Give examples, but beware: It is easy to get "carried away" and devote far more time to the example than you intended.
5. Use illustrations—a graph, picture, film, map, chart, artifact.
6. Supplement with sounds other than your voice—a recorded speech, music, noises evocative of the setting being described.
7. Unless you are "preaching" (which is acceptable at times), try to be balanced in terms of controversies.
8. Speak clearly, loudly, and slowly. If you are going to lecture often to this group, agree on signals that they will give you when you break these rules.
9. Pause for questions and comments. If you don't get them, raise them yourself. Provide regular changes in the pace. Break for an example, break for a story, break for any legitimate change—but break often.
10. Avoid distracting mannerisms and verbal tics. It is always worth the time to listen to or view a recording of your lecture or to have a colleague point out these flaws.
11. Give a succinct, motivating introduction. Get students' attention before going on. Within reason, say something shocking if necessary.
12. Emphasize the crucial, and minimize the trivial. If there is any doubt, tell your class, "Now this is really significant." Repeat the material that truly counts two or three different ways.
13. Use humor, but don't be silly. Achieving this distinction is not easy, but it is well worth the effort.
14. Pause frequently. Give your listeners time to think.
15. Talk, don't read. Rarely is reading justified.
16. Look at your listeners, not at your notes, as much as possible. Eye contact is enormously important.
17. Build in response mechanisms, e.g., thumbs up for "yes," thumbs down for "no" in terms of agreement.

Years ago one of the authors was teaching, or trying to teach, the meaning and significance of the Bill of Rights to a group of 11th graders. Simultaneously, the McCarthy hearings were being televised, and the students had been encouraged to watch them as part of current-events instruction. Things were going reasonably well with the main lesson until the class encountered the Fifth Amendment. Probably because of the hearings, the students were absolutely convinced that anyone "who took the Fifth" was a crook and had something terrible to hide. The teacher tried to counter this reaction without success. Finally, he mentioned his frustration to a friend who taught constitutional law at the university. She offered to lecture to the students.

This instructor had the kids on the edges of their chairs. She outlined the history and purposes of the prohibition against self-incrimination, got some

18. Recognize valuable questions or comments.
19. Work continually on reception skills, e.g., teach your students the artful science of notetaking. Give them practice in outlining material gleaned from an oral source.
20. Give and/or get accurate summaries.
21. Invite well-informed guests to lecture. Many districts have lists of community people who would want to be invited, e.g., a union leader, a conservationist, a local historian, a political party chairperson. If your district doesn't have such a file, work with your colleagues to start one. And don't overlook the valuable resources within the school. Administrators, guidance personnel, fellow teachers, librarians, and nurses often can provide just the right balance.
22. Use students as presenters—students from your class or from other groups. For example, invite students from the previous year to come back to share their most valuable work when they themselves were studying the topic. Of course, you need to be careful: Students at all levels, including those who are preparing to teach, may well read pages from the encyclopedia if you don't give them help in lecturing. All the disadvantages of lecturing can be magnified tenfold if you have clusters of ill-prepared students doing the work. Still, having students do some lecturing can be interesting and worthwhile.
23. Get regular evaluations from students (and from others when possible). It can be as informal as a show of hands in response to a couple of questions or as formal as requesting, "Please write the three major points of my lecture, and leave your papers with me before the end of the period." It may well go further and become a systematic long-term activity. For example, in a team-taught class in American history, the four instructors formed a lecture committee composed of students and one of the teachers to analyze all of the large-group presentations in the course. Those involved were convinced that this practice led to improvements.
24. Even more important, engage in regular self-evaluation. Mechanical recordings can be very valuable, albeit rather devastating at times. You might want to keep a journal of impressions following your lectures.

Source: From *Improving Lectures* by W. Cashin, 1985, Manhattan, KS: Center for Faculty Evaluation and Development, Kansas State University. Adapted with permission.

fine questions, and then launched into some fascinating examples. The instructor and the students learned a great deal.

We hope these two examples have convinced you of the value of the lecture method. Figure 7.2 presents several guidelines for planning and delivering a lecture, drawn mainly from the work of William Cashin (1985).

Recitation and Questioning

Recitation. For many of us, the word *recitation* connotes a 19th-century schoolmaster with his hickory stick and rows of docile students on wooden benches who would jump to their feet when called upon to give their memorized lessons. The dictionary reinforces this image. *The American Heritage Dictionary*, for example, defines *recitation* as "the act of reciting memorized materials in public performance."

However, this is *not* what we are talking about, and it was probably not what most 19th-century teachers did. In fact, a delightful, if quaint, source from 1914, by Charles A. McMurry and a group of other distinguished early leaders in the field of pedagogy, describes the functions of recitation as follows:

> A recitation has several functions. First, it must test the preparation which the pupils have made. . . . Second, it must give whatever new information is necessary [so] that the pupil may understand his lesson and get a wider view of the subject. Third, it must review the lesson. . . . Fourth, it must relate to other lessons of the past. Fifth, it must apply the information gained to practical purposes. . . . Sixth, it must prepare the way for the future. (McMurry et al., 1914, p. 114)

McMurry goes on to describe the kinds of recitation that a good teacher may use and puts at the top of his list informal conversations with the students. He places the focus of productive recitations on questioning: "It is doubtful if any one of the teaching devices is more powerful than questioning in the hands of the skillful teacher" (McMurry et al., 1914, p. 116).

If the flow of communication in the lecture is largely from the teacher to the students and in discussion it is multidirectional, we see the recitation as a midway point. The teacher clearly is in control during the recitation, leading the students by using conversation and questioning to predetermined ends. Typically, the students have been given an assignment, perhaps for homework or for supervised study during class time. Usually they also have been given some study questions as part of the assignment. Then the group is led by the use of questions and answers to analyze the assignment.

In using recitation, the teacher needs to consider: What did they learn? Where does confusion still exist? What new information is needed, and how should it be obtained? How do these understandings and appreciations relate to past studies and to future activities?

We hypothesize that recitation is the most widely used technique in secondary classrooms (perhaps even overused in some cases). There are valid reasons for its popularity. The technique offers some of the advantages of both the lecture and the discussion. Further, it is usually an efficient consumer of precious class time. To be sure, recitations can be dull and dry, but at their best they are effective—and fun. Many worthwhile goals, including the development of speaking and listening skills, may be achieved by their use.

The key to effective use of recitation is the teacher's ability to ask questions, to which we will turn next.

FIGURE 7.3
Suggestions for Effective Questioning

1. Effective teachers phrase questions clearly.
2. Effective teachers ask questions which are primarily academic.
3. Effective teachers ask high cognitive level questions.
4. Effective teachers allow 3–5 seconds of wait time after asking a question before requesting a response, particularly when higher cognitive level questions are asked.
5. Effective teachers encourage students to respond in some way to each question asked.
6. Effective teachers balance responses from volunteering and non-volunteering students.
7. Effective teachers encourage a high percentage of correct responses from students and assist with incorrect responses.
8. Effective teachers probe students' responses for clarification, support for a point of view, or to stimulate thinking.
9. Effective teachers acknowledge correct responses from students but are specific and discriminating in their use of praise.

Source: From "Effective Questions and Questioning: A Research Review" by W. Wilen and A. Clegg, Spring 1986, *Theory and Research in Social Education*, pp. 153–161. Reprinted with permission of the National Council of the Social Studies.

Questioning. How do teachers ask effective questions? Figure 7.3 offers one set of useful criteria.

However, Brophy (1986, p. 1071), in summarizing research on effective teaching, raises some issues that complicate the task, especially with respect to the level of difficulty (see item 3 in Figure 7.3.). First, "optimal question difficulty probably varies with content"; that is, questions should be phrased to elicit correct answers most of the time, even fast-paced "drill and practice" questions. But teachers should also ask students to generalize and evaluate, which may result in few or no correct responses.

Given what at first blush seems an impossible task, it remains that teachers must employ some scheme for asking questions. Perhaps the most obvious way is to key questions to the Bloom taxonomy, which reflects a hierarchy of difficulty. Figure 7.4 presents an example that has made the rounds of methods classes for years.

Although the questions in Figure 7.4 show an obvious link to the Bloom taxonomy, other schema for questioning exist. The following sections identify *types* of questions to ask, including closed, open, descriptive, divergent, convergent, higher-order, and probing (clarifying, focusing, redirecting) questions. Obviously there is some overlap among these question categories, but the typology nevertheless is useful.

Types of Questions

Closed Questions. Closed questions, which often are factual, tend to use words like *who, what when,* and *where.* Recall Beth and her unit on

FIGURE 7.4
Applying Bloom's Taxonomy: "Goldilocks and the Three Bears"

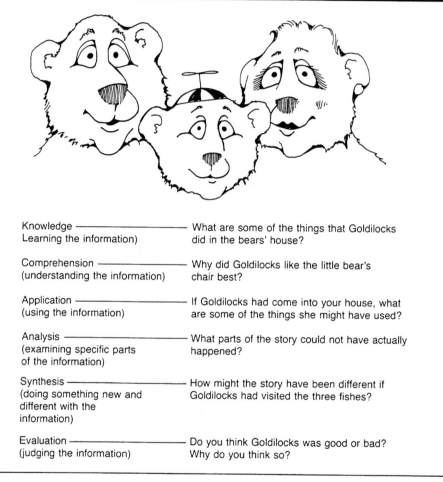

Knowledge —————————— What are some of the things that Goldilocks
Learning the information)   did in the bears' house?

Comprehension ———————— Why did Goldilocks like the little bear's
(understanding the information)   chair best?

Application ————————— If Goldilocks had come into your house, what
(using the information)   are some of the things she might have used?

Analysis ——————————— What parts of the story could not have actually
(examining specific parts   happened?
of the information)

Synthesis —————————— How might the story have been different if
(doing something new and   Goldilocks had visited the three fishes?
different with the
information)

Evaluation ————————— Do you think Goldilocks was good or bad?
(judging the information)   Why do you think so?

Source: This adaptation is from Charlotte Brummett.

Ukraine from Chapter 5. Here are some examples of closed questions that
Beth might use:

Who could be considered a founder of Ukraine?

What was the population of Ukraine in 1930?

Where is Ukraine located?

Closed questions tend to appear less threatening than open questions
and thus are especially helpful in getting a discussion started. These lower-

level—typically knowledge-level—questions tend to test memory, but they also develop the information on which concepts are built.

Open Questions. The purpose of *open questions* is to allow students to volunteer answers and obtain different kinds of responses. Here are some open questions that Beth might use:

> Given a choice of climatic regions, where in Ukraine would you prefer to live?
>
> Of the reasons given for the creation of Ukraine, which seems most likely to you?

Although open questions are not necessarily higher level, they generally are considered more threatening when used to begin a recitation because the answers are not obvious.

Descriptive Questions. *Descriptive questions* both test memory and require some organization of the answers. Often they are at the comprehension level of the Bloom taxonomy. They require more thought on the students' part and necessarily, suggest a longer answer:

> How did the feudal castle in Ukraine serve the community?
>
> How did the barter system work in the early days of Ukraine?
>
> How might a transaction have occurred between tradespeople in Ukraine?

Divergent Questions. *Divergent questions*, sometimes called *heuristic divergent questions*, have no "right answer." They are open ended and require students to think at higher levels, often abstractly:

> How might Ukraine's history have differed had Kerenski and the White Russian revolution succeeded?
>
> What might have happened in Ukraine had Gorbachev's policy of "openness" existed in 1932 and 1933 (the time of the great famine)?
>
> What might have been its relationship to the Soviet Union had Ukraine had fewer natural resources?

Often a divergent question is followed by a long silence, which can make both students and teacher uncomfortable. Another difficulty is that divergent questions often lead students into the unknown.

Convergent Questions. As the term implies, *convergent questions* tend to draw a lesson together, for they ask students to summarize or synthesize the lesson. They often follow analysis-level questions and seek principles or conclusions:

In what ways were Ukraine, Georgia, and Latvia alike?

What conclusion can we draw from the lesson today?

Of the forces we studied regarding the rise of Ukraine, which might be considered the most important?

Higher-Order Questions.   *Higher-order questions* demand answers that go beyond mere memory. They also require abstract thinking, reflecting levels of the Bloom taxonomy above application, that is, analysis, synthesis, or evaluation. Typically higher-order questions begin with *why*. Higher-order questions may require students to infer, to make comparisons, to apply principles or generalizations, to perceive causes and effects, and to evaluate outcomes.

Here are some higher-order questions for Beth's unit:

In general, what factors rendered Ukraine unable to avoid centralization?

How might Ukraine have maintained a separate state in Eastern Europe?

What form of power was lacking in Ukraine in the period 1918 to 1921?

Assuming that Western reporters could have had freer rein to report on the famine of 1932–1933, what might have been the result?

Probing Questions.   The purpose of *probing questions* is to encourage students to go beyond superficial answers. The teacher can ask higher-level questions directly or follow up a superficial answer with a probing question. This takes considerable skill, for probing questions are asked in the heat of a lesson, based on the students' answers. Probing questions can ask for clarification ("What do you mean by that answer?"), an increase in the complexity of answers ("What are you assuming?"), refocusing ("How does your answer differ from the answer just given?"), or redirecting ("Frank, what can you add to Sarah's answer?").

Other Considerations.   Despite the best intentions, many teachers fall into traps in their questioning and ask questions like:

Who is buried in Grant's tomb?

Is the Pope Catholic?

Certainly no one asks such questions intentionally, but it is all too easy to ask questions mindlessly. Teachers should avoid asking questions that are so obvious or rhetorical that students will not bother to answer them or will find them confusing. They should also be aware of unintentionally asking questions to which no answer can be posed, such as "Would you rather walk to school or take your lunch?" In all cases, it is important to think carefully about which questions will best reflect students' intellectual levels and are relevant to the unit being covered.

The frequency and timing of questions are another consideration. Teachers can expect more incorrect answers at the beginning of a lesson. Later, as students learn the material, the rate of correct responses should increase.

Obviously asking good questions is hard work, but it is essential for an effective recitation (and, for that matter, for an effective discussion).

Interviewing and Oral History

The interview is, of course, a widely used technique in social science research. It is employed in a wide range of disciplines for numerous kinds of studies. Thus, as we would expect, there is a substantial body of literature on this subject in the research methodology field.

Likewise, in history the process of interviewing subjects who have had noteworthy experiences is a respected and growing research technique. This activity is usually called *oral history*. Here too there is a significant body of how-to-do-it literature; for example, see the work of Louis Starr (1977) or James Hoopes (1979).

We believe that the interview is also an extremely useful teaching technique. Unfortunately, it is all too often neglected and also tends to be slighted in the literature about teaching.

As the term suggests, an *interview* is an interaction between two or more people or groups wherein one person or group tries to uncover what the other person or group knows, feels, believes, or has experienced. It is an exchange for the purpose of increasing understanding. Most people who have been interviewed report that they learned something valuable in the process, but the basic intent is for the interviewer and those who examine the results of the exchange to obtain expanded knowledge. Face-to-face and telephone approaches may be used.

Interviews used for instructional purposes usually are combined with other teaching techniques, including lectures, recitations, and discussions. The interview can follow or precede reading and writing assignments. It can be the culminating experience flowing from individual or group work. There are numerous other possibilities for using interviews.

Of course, interviews can be conducted by scholars, including teachers. They can be live exchanges before a class or recorded ones that are played (and possibly viewed as well) in their entirety or edited for the class. Or a teacher can describe and analyze a single or a series of interviews in a lecture. It is also possible to have students study the written text of interviews. For example, one of the authors recently observed a student teacher who had asked pairs of his students to read aloud excerpts from Stud Terkel's oral history account of the Great Depression (Terkel, 1986). It was a highly effective lesson that combined aspects of the interview and dramatization.

Students also can do the interviewing, using any of the presentation strategies identified earlier. Again the technique provides the opportunity for access to a wide range of valuable sources. Further, it gives students a valuable opportunity for active, inquiry-oriented learning. In the process, the interview can significantly enhance opportunities for development of interpersonal and communication skills.

One disadvantage of interviewing is that it tends to be a very sophisticated procedure, requiring a lot of savvy and practice. Obviously there is little point in conducting an interview if the information thus obtained is of dubious reliability and/or validity.

What can teachers do to increase the likelihood of getting accurate data in a usable form? First, we think social studies teachers should systematically study research methodology, including interviewing, at some point in their preparation for teaching. Furthermore, we believe all teachers should engage in independent and collaborative research activities throughout their careers.

Following are some broad (and sometimes overlapping) guidelines for preparing a successful interview:

1. *Know the purpose of the interview.* After studying the subject, you will need to determine exactly what you want to know and why. You should write a detailed "interview guide" or "interview schedule" to document your intentions.

2. *Based on your purpose, select the appropriate format or type of interview.* Will it be a *nondirective* (uncontrolled, unguided, or unstructured) interview? That is, will the subject merely be encouraged to talk about any aspect of the topic under investigation without direction from you? Or will the interview be *directive,* whereby the interviewee is asked a series of carefully structured predetermined questions—a kind of oral questionnaire? Or will it be something in between? It might be useful to think of a continuum, with directive interviews on one end and indirective ones on the other in terms of flexibility. Again, to select the interview type wisely, you need to be clear about your purposes. What kinds of data do you need? Are you seeking facts, opinions, feelings, impressions, descriptions, or reactions? (Many other types of interview are specified in the literature, but this dichotomy will probably suffice for our purposes.)

3. *Select your sources thoughtfully.* Will the subject(s) be willing and able to provide the information you want? Because good interviews consume a lot of time and energy, you will want to reach the best available sources.

4. *Prepare and protect the subject(s).* Prior to the interview, you must inform your subject(s) about your purposes, the amount of time required, whether or not recordings will be made, whether there will be opportunities for corrections, and the use to which the data will be put. If you are interviewing a person who may not understand the consequences of being forthright, you must explain any and all possible risks involved. If you will be interviewing a child for any systematic purpose— that is, for anything more than an informal, unplanned conversation—

you must obtain permission from a responsible adult (parent, guardian, or professional).

5. *Be on the lookout for often vitally important nonverbal reactions.* We noted the importance of this point in all forms of oral exchanges at the beginning of the chapter, but nowhere are nonverbal clues more important than in interviews. Alfred C. Kinsey, in his landmark work on human sexuality, details the importance of what he calls "involuntary reaction" in interviews:

> A minute change of facial expression, a slight tensing of a muscle, the flick of an eye, a trace of a change in one's voice, a slight change in one's rate of speaking . . . a hesitancy . . . a spontaneity . . . or any of a dozen and one involuntary reactions [may be far more important] than words. (Quoted in Young, 1966, p. 215)

6. *Encourage, but don't "put words in the mouth" of, the respondent.* Be friendly, direct, open, supportive, and stimulating, but don't tell the subject what you think or know. In fact, don't do any more talking or signaling of any kind than is absolutely necessary. Yes, the interview is a social exchange, but the bulk of the verbal and nonverbal information should come from the interviewee.

7. *Employ good questioning skills.* (See the section on recitation and questioning.)

8. *Record the interview unless the logistics or the source make this impossible.* In some oral history projects, a mechanical recording is absolutely essential, because any written statement can detract from the richness of the oral language. Thus, in this type of activity, one must listen to the evidence instead of reading it. Of course, you must always obtain the subject's permission to record the interview.

9. *Keep good notes.* This is especially important if mechanical recordings are not possible. You can also get another person to take notes while you conduct the interview.

10. *Control digressions, if possible.* Of course, sidetracking may sometimes get you where you want to go faster than your original course of action.

11. *Make an objective written recording of the interview as soon after the session as possible.* Analyses and editorials come later. At this stage, what you need is a record of what actually happened and was said. (This report, at least in a written form, may not always be essential when an interview is being used for teaching purposes. However, except in instances such as item 8, it is mandatory in the research process.)

12. *Analyze the interview.* Look for themes. Check for inconsistencies. Match the words with the nonverbal clues and with the interviewee's actions. Compare and contrast the results with previously examined sources. Write about the interview. Discuss it. Go back to the source if this seems warranted; for example, conduct a second interview if some

significant change in the circumstances has occurred. Most important, check the results against your original goals for the interview.

The following story may help you appreciate the value of interviewing. Although Willie's family had lived in the same neighborhood of a large Ohio city for three generations, Willie continued to proudly identify himself with the Appalachian culture of eastern Kentucky. While attending elementary and secondary schools, later in his factory job, and still later when he labored through a local college at night, Willie's peers tended to recognize him as an Appalachian and sometimes stereotyped him as a "hillbilly" or a "ridge runner." While Willie had moved to the suburbs, he had carefully striven to retain many of the mores, beliefs, and speech patterns of his forebears.

After college, Willie entered teaching. He was a good bit older than is typical. Quite deliberately he was assigned to a school in his old neighborhood. The seventh-grade course he taught had a major unit on the local community. This beginning teacher thoughtfully developed the unit around one question that troubled him deeply: Why had so many Appalachian folks made such a poor adjustment to urban life? Willie employed an oral history approach with his students. They interviewed dozens of Appalachians and others who had regular contact with this group, including politicians. Each of three of Willie's classes wrote an insightful report, one of which bore the highly significant title "From Being a Social Problem to Becoming an Ethnic Group."

Willie and his supervisors were delighted with the positive results for both his students and the interviewees in the community. Many recognized and applauded the work, including a group of university scholars who were studying Appalachians. (For an extremely valuable analysis of urban Appalachians, see *Too Few Tomorrows: Urban Appalachians in the 1980's [Obermiller, 1987].)*

ASIDE TO THE READER: What exciting examples of the teaching interview can you develop? You might want to begin by examining the "local" section of a newspaper serving your school district or college. After reading it, make a list of the persons mentioned who might provide valuable information for your students on any of the topics you think you might be teaching next term or next year. We think you will be surprised by the wealth of possibilities that present themselves.

Further, we are certain that most or even all of these people would be pleased to be interviewed. Most of us, no matter how busy we think we are, are delighted to be asked for the opportunity to be listened to, to be taken seriously. In a few instances, logistics may pose insurmountable problems. Sometimes certain issues have been placed "off limits" (that should tell you a lot). Sometimes the intended source will recommend a substitute. However, two of the authors of this text who have relied heavily on interviews in their teaching for many years have never encountered a potential source who refused to comply with a properly crafted request for an interview to be used for teaching purposes.

Tutoring

One might think of tutoring as simply an addendum or a supplement to a lecture, a recitation, or even an interview. In fact, the word *tutoring* is sometimes used interchangeably with *teaching.* But we believe tutoring is sufficiently distinctive and important to warrant separate treatment in this chapter.

Tutoring usually means one-on-one or very-small-group instruction in which the tutor gives and the tutee receives. Many social studies teachers tutor daily in a variety of contexts, especially, as they "make their rounds" of a class during individual assignments. They may ask a question or respond to one. They may simply raise an eyebrow or point to an offending sentence after looking at a student's paper. They may encourage a small group whose members seem to be having the same difficulty to come to the desk for a recitation, some special instructions, or a review. All of this suggests that the line between teaching and tutoring is quite thin. A further implication is that good teachers routinely engage in tutoring.

However, *peer tutoring,* in which students of the same age instruct one another, and cross-age tutoring, in which students of different ages work together, are valuable forms of tutoring that are all too rarely employed. Instead, teachers commonly admonish students *not* to help one another with schoolwork. We offer this section in an effort to encourage you to try the tutoring technique.

Lilya Wagner has written an interesting book on the history of students tutoring other students (Wagner, 1982). She begins as follows:

> Helping relationships between students in formal and planned school settings have been utilized by teachers for centuries. This concept can be traced to the first century A.D.; since that time, peer teaching has alternatively lapsed into obscurity or seen a resurgence of interest. During the last two decades, many educators in the United States have again promoted the use of peer teaching, and considerable literature and research on this topic have resulted.*

The impetus for the revival of tutoring in the 1960s was to help economically disadvantaged students who needed special compensatory assistance. Today reformers tout the idea for all students, from those with serious handicapping conditions to the gifted and talented.

---

*Lilya Wagner, *PEER TEACHING: Historical Perspectives* (Greenwood Press, Westport, CT, 1982), p. 3. Copyright © 1982 by Lilya Wagner. Reprinted with permission.

Empirical research heavily supports this renaissance. For example, Benjamin Bloom reported that having a trained tutor in itself leads to astonishing academic achievement results—98% of the students who had had a tutor outperformed those who were taught in a conventional classroom without a tutor (Bloom, 1984). And the cognitive gains for the tutees is only a small part of the glowingly positive story. Relying heavily on the work of Diane Hedin (Hedin, 1986), Figure 7.5 summarizes some cognitive, psychological, and social benefits of students teaching students in a one-on-one format. These benefits add up to marked advantages for the local community and the larger society.

What are the necessary conditions for an effective tutoring program? A definitive and solidly researched list does not exist, but here are some ideas to consider when planning a peer or cross-age tutoring effort. Again we rely

FIGURE 7.5
Benefits of Tutoring

Benefits for the Tutor
1. *Developing personally, psychologically, and socially.* Being a tutor has been shown to add to the sense of competency and self-worth of persons who previously lacked these attitudes. Further, playing this role seems to add to the feelings of empathy for others and even to operating at higher and more mature levels of thinking.
2. *Learning or reviewing basic content.* The tutor has a face-saving way to learn material that he or she should have known earlier or to review forgotten material. In the process, the tutor's skills and competencies often improve.
3. *Applying or transferring learning.* Tutors benefit from the opportunity to apply or transfer what they have previously learned to a new context while working with other students. This reinforces what they already know.
4. *Learning about learning.* It has been shown that tutoring offers the potential for tutors to better understand the learning process—a clear advantage for their future growth and development.

Benefits for the Tutee
1. *Learning what was missed earlier.* Tutoring greatly increases the likelihood of increased academic achievement for the tutee. The success rate is often dramatic.
2. *Developing personally and socially.* One commonly cited benefit is that the tutee develops a more positive attitude toward teachers and toward the learning process. Another is that the tutee can and often does find a positive role model in the tutor.

Benefits for the Teacher
1. *Improving the classroom climate.* The change in the usual routine that tutoring affords often leads to improved discipline. Also, having a cadre of helpers leads to fewer control problems.
2. *Allowing more time for curricular and instructional planning.* By employing tutors, the teacher is no longer constantly engaged with a classroom full of students. Thus, there is more time to plan and reflect on curricular and instructional goals.

Source: From *Students-as-Teachers* by D. Hedin, 1986, New York: Carnegie Forum on Education and the Economy. Adapted by permission of the National Center on Education and the Economy.

on Hedin's summary of the research, but her ideas are supplemented with our own experiences:

- Tutees seem to experience greater gains if the tutor is older than they are.
- Tutees tend to prefer same-sex tutors, and since there doesn't seem to be any difference in terms of gains, it might make sense to honor their preferences. Of course, if one of the teacher's objectives is to provide increased opportunities for students of different genders to work together, this admonition should be ignored.
- Short programs seem to work better than long ones; that is, on average, relationships between tutors and tutees of a few weeks' duration seem to be more effective than semester- or year-long ones. Similarly, short sessions—a maximum of 30 minutes—appear to produce better results than than longer sessions.
- Structured sessions in which both tutor and tutee are aware of specific goals and activities generally are more effective than unstructured episodes. Thus, the tutor should say, "Let's do A and B today to help with X" rather than "Let's read something interesting together."
- While the research evidence on this point is mixed, the majority of studies seem to suggest that training tutors results in a higher success rate. For example, untrained tutors seem more likely to use negative approaches, such as sarcasm, than trained ones. Thus, they might need coaching to remind them to abandon such tactics. Many teachers can use help with skills such as giving clear directions, confirming correct reactions, correcting flaws, and avoiding overprompting. It stands to reason that students can too.
- While prior training may not always be necessary, the existing research shows a very clear relationship between supervision of tutors and success of the tutoring program. Tutors left on their own don't seem to function as well as those who receive some assistance and encouragement. At the very least, a well-prepared educator should be available to answer the tutor's questions. Also, more formal observations of the tutor at work and then follow-up conferences with a supervisor seem to lead to improved results.
- To ensure the greatest chance of success, school and community leaders must understand the potential value of the program and support it. Political endorsement from the "right" people clearly is facilitating. Related to this point, research shows that many educators who play key decision-making roles are unaware of the positive research results on tutoring. In sum, a successful tutoring program, depends on some good public relations.
- Tutoring programs that are available during the regular school day have a far better chance of reaching those who need it most than do after-hours programs.
- When students from different schools are involved, transportation can be a serious headache. This issue always needs careful consideration. Obvi-

ously you can't just turn children loose and hope that they get to another building safely.*

The issue of whether or not to provide tangible rewards for tutors has received a good bit of attention. Should student tutors be paid? Should they receive credit that will count toward graduation? Should this experience be used to satisfy a "community service" requirement—often as a part of the social studies program—that a growing number of districts have instituted? Should tutors receive "points" that they can cash in for privileges in a token "economy," as used in some schools?

The answers to these questions seem to be tied to local conditions, and therefore we cannot offer a general response. But they do deserve consideration. Fortunately, Hedin (1986) provides a number of references that will be useful to a system that is considering a large-scale tutoring program.

Management skills are required for a teacher to operate a successful tutoring program. Moreover, the management process takes a good bit of time from teachers, who already work long and stressful hours. Some teachers need help with these operational matters.

At least one teacher center of which we are aware has instituted a program to assist teachers in developing these capacities. We also know of a district that has given one teacher, a strong advocate of tutoring efforts, some release time to assist other teachers in matters such as scheduling, transportation, supervision, and public information.

Following are two examples of tutoring programs that one of the authors has observed. We hope they will encourage you to experiment with the idea.

The first illustration concerns Thomasina, a sixth-grade social studies teacher in an inner-city middle school. Recently her district instituted an "extended home room" program. The idea behind this effort is that every child have a close relationship with at least one teacher, who becomes that child's mentor or counselor. A group of no more than 20 youngsters stay with the same teacher for the three years spent in the middle school.

Thomasina has a sister who teaches second grade in a primary school about two blocks away. The two have worked out a tutoring program that uses some of the extended home room time. On a voluntary basis, a sixth grader is assigned to work with a second grader. At least one afternoon each week (some go twice a week), the older children read to the younger ones or help them with tasks suggested by the second-grade teacher.

Both Thomasina and her sister are delighted with the results. Most of the student tutors have volunteered. Both tutees and tutors now seem more serious about their schoolwork. The tutors have enormously positive feelings about what they are doing. While the focus is on improving reading skills, the content used for this purpose is drawn largely from social studies. The two

---

*From *Students-as-Teachers* by D. Hedin, 1986, New York: Carnegie Forum on Education and the Economy. Adapted by permission of the National Center on Education and the Economy.

teachers enthusiastically agree that the goals of the social studies program are being well served.

Our second example takes place in a suburban school district in the same metropolitan area. An "alternative" high school program has been established for a group of 20 youngsters who wanted to drop out. Joe, a social studies teacher and coach, convinced the district that he could "save" these students. With parental agreement, in most cases enthusiastic, the program began last year.

Initially the youngsters were assigned to Joe all day long. He met with each student and together they worked out a "contract" aimed at meeting the student's individual goals. Twenty very different programs have evolved. Most youngsters take a few self-selected regular courses in the school. Some are transported to a vocational technical school for a part of each day. Others have arranged independent study experiences with nonschool personnel. One is working half-time under school supervision. There are numerous other variations. The only common aspect among the 20 programs is that all students take social studies from Joe.

It is clear that these students won't earn a diploma during the conventional four-year period. But they have remained in school.

While it is too soon to accurately assess the successes and shortcomings of the program, the teacher-in-charge believes that of all of its features, the most successful element has been peer tutoring. In close cooperation with other teachers in the building (and in the regional vocational program), whenever one of the youngsters in the alternative program takes a "conventional" class, an effort is made to find a student in that course who will serve as a tutor. It has not been difficult to get volunteer tutors, and the tutees have, by and large, reacted quite favorably to offers of assistance. Only one youngster has refused to have a tutor. Some pairs have become quite close. As an example of an interpersonal success, one tutor has convinced his partner to become a manager for an athletic team. The high-risk tutee has been successful in this role and has formed a productive relationship with a coach.

Furthermore, in the common social studies class, members of the group themselves took the initiative to set up a peer tutoring situation; that is, the students asked to form pairs within their own group to assist one another in the social studies classwork. Needless to say, Joe is delighted. But he does report that if he gives a youngster a "bad time" about his work in the course, he nearly always has some "explaining to do" to the other member of the pair.

DISCUSSION

Definitions for *discussion* in school settings and elsewhere abound. The one we like best was written over three decades ago by William Howell and Donald Smith (Howell & Smith, 1956, 5):

Discussion is that form of discourse which occurs when two or more persons, recognizing a common problem, exchange and evaluate information and ideas in an effort to solve the problem. Their efforts may be directed toward a better understanding of the problem or toward the development of a program of action relative to the problem.*

This definition encompasses all the necessary and sufficient conditions of a genuine discussion: There must be a *shared concern* by all of the participants; there must be an *exchange* and *evaluation* of data; there must be a *sincere effort* to better *understand* or take appropriate *action* to resolve the problem; it is a unique *collaborative* approach in which people are trying to solve a problem, the solution to which is *not yet known* by any of the discussants.

In addition to being unique, discussion is a frequently attempted form of discourse. In our roles as family members, neighbors, workers, citizens, consumers, students, teachers—whatever—we Americans are, necessarily and continually, required to be discussants. Further, even in many of our passive and solitary functions, such as reading or watching television, we need to assess the discussions we are experiencing indirectly. The frequency of attempts at discussion in our society is based on our political ideology. We profess that we believe in shared decision making and that "two heads are better than one." Obviously, if we are required to engage in discussion so often, we ought to try to be good at it.

Further, the frequency of the need to discuss is only one justification for becoming skillful in the process. It has been demonstrated repeatedly that this form of discourse is consistent with the principles of learning. Properly executed, a discussion is active rather than passive, highly motivating, immediately and positively reinforcing, multi- rather than single-sensory, ordered and organized, geared to the capacities of the participants, transferrable to other situations, readily subject to evaluation and measurement, and so on. Clearly it is an ideal technique for a learning environment.

Thus, it is not surprising that students of teaching and schooling are very enthusiastic about using discussion in classrooms. Mortimer Adler, in the widely acclaimed *The PAIDEIA Proposal: An Educational Manifesto*, says that discussion "stimulates the imagination and intellect by awakening the creative and inquisitive powers. In no other way can children's understanding of what they know be improved, and their appreciation of cultural objects be enhanced" (Adler, 1982).

However, discussion, the genuine article, is rare because it is difficult to achieve. We are surrounded by pseudodiscussion in such forms as advocacy, groups dominated by certain individuals, talk in which minds are closed,

---

*Reprinted with permission of Macmillan Publishing Company from *Discussion* by William S. Howell and Donald K. Smith. Copyright © 1956 by Macmillan Publishing Company; copyright renewed © 1984 by William S. Howell and Donald K. Smith.

recitations or question-and-answer sessions, and lectures. As we have seen, these forms of discourse have legitimate uses, but they are not cooperative problem solving. They don't meet the tests presented in the above definition. Participants in these activities easily sense the difference; they resent the charade of being told they are participating in a discussion when they are not.

We think the major stumbling blocks to achieving genuine discussion can be summed up in two propositions. First, discussion absolutely demands a tremendous expenditure of time and energy. Often even those who are authentically searching for solutions to problems are unable or unwilling to commit the necessary resources. The needed skills, knowledge base, sources of information, and time just may not exist. In a classroom, if you decide to discuss a topic rather than use some other technique, you must start with the assumption that some other topic(s) will get passed over.

Second, productive discussion cannot occur unless a delicate balance between critical-thinking and human relations processes is achieved. If one set of skills is emphasized to the neglect of the other, the results will be flawed. For example, if a particular participant consistently and sharply carps, even if the criticism is valid, the search for truth is likely to fail. Hostile, egocentric, and defensive attitudes and behavior will develop and will inhibit the process. On the other hand, if a participant continually engages in a popularity contest, the discussion will be equally jeopardized. Figure 7.6 demonstrates this crucial equilibrium.

In both of these examples, a skillful leader may reduce, or even eliminate, the unproductive values and behavior. However, this is exceptionally difficult. Sometimes even the most effective leader will fail.

Improving Skills as Discussion Participant and as Leader

As a teacher, you must continually strive to be an effective member of discussion groups. In addition, you will often have to be a discussion leader. Figure 7.7 presents some guiding questions that will help you play both of these demanding roles.

Usually good discussions require leadership. But too much leadership is as debilitating as too little. Yet there is a wide acceptable range of leadership styles between the unproductive extremes of authoritarianism and anarchy. Figure 7.8 lists some recommendations for improving your discussion leadership skills.

Types of Discussions

Discussion in classrooms can employ many different formats. Two of the major types are large-group and small-group discussions.

Large-Group Discussions. At times, we may ask an audience to participate in a discussion. Members of the large group are encouraged to question,

FIGURE 7.6
Balancing in Effective Discussion

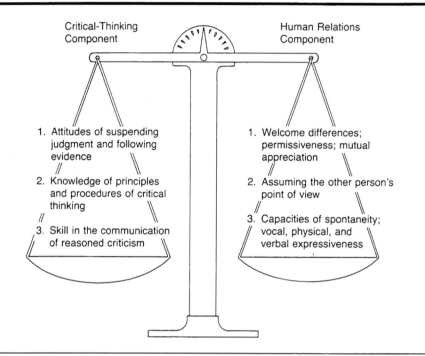

Source: Reprinted with permission of Macmillan Publishing Company from *Discussion* by William S. Howell and Donald K. Smith. Copyright © 1956 by Macmillan Publishing Company; copyright renewed © 1984 by William S. Howell and Donald K. Smith.

challenge, comment, and so on. Typically, of course, a large group is less directly involved in the interaction than are participants in a small-group investigation.

The broad name for the large-group approach is the *forum*. It is stimulated by a presentation in which opposing views are provided: a lecture, a debate, a film, a recording, a discussion by a smaller group, and so on.

If *debate* is used, it can be either formal, using all the procedural rules that are necessary for this approach, or informal. In either case, a debate involves two or more well-prepared individuals who give the pros and cons on some controversy while trying to convince members of the audience of the correctness of their views. A debate can be a highly stimulating event, but it is also a very demanding technique for a leader. Emotions can easily carry the day. One point of view can readily dominate. Some worthy positions not favorable to the stance of either speaker may be ignored altogether. The leader clearly has a responsibility to deal with these issues.

Sometimes in a large group it is advisable to get all members of the audience more directly engaged in the give and take. The buzz group is a

FIGURE 7.7
Guidelines for Conducting Effective Discussions

Reporting
1. Do I present worthy evidence? Is it pertinent, plentiful, and well documented? Does it neglect and/or cope satisfactorily with contrary evidence? Have I consulted appropriate authorities?
2. Do I recognize and admit the limitations of the evidence I present?
3. Do I supply information that will supplement or test data offered by others?

Thinking
1. Do I stay on track with one point at a time?
2. Do I understand questions put to me? Do I answer them directly, specifically, and succinctly? Do I admit my inability to answer questions when I don't know?
3. Do I test all contributions, my own included, by critical analysis? For example, do I accept single interpretations of data when others are plausible? Do I weigh the relative importance of facts or ideas? Do I use language in such a way that criticism is silenced or meaning is obscured?
4. Do I separate facts from opinion while recognizing both are important?
5. Do I distinguish differences based on semantics from more substantive ones?
6. Do I seek and find a viable plan of attack? Do I abide by the plan when I have determined it?

Cooperating
1. Do I listen?
2. Do I try to understand others?
3. Do I change my views when warranted?
4. Do I support necessary leadership?
5. Do I accurately define areas of real or potential agreement?
6. Do I try to promote group harmony while I am disagreeing or criticizing?
7. Do I recognize useful contributions from others?
8. Do I avoid self-serving and self-aggrandizing activities except in cases where they contribute to solving the problem?
9. Do I try to contribute to the mutual enjoyment of the discussants?

valuable way to accomplish this. In a *buzz group*, the topic to be discussed is a small portion of the larger question under investigation. The leader breaks the group into subgroups of from three to six, gives a very specific assignment, appoints a leader and possibly a recorder, restricts the groups to a given amount of time (usually a relatively short period), and announces a system for reporting back to the large group.

As an example, let's assume that the presenter for the large group has identified five major possible courses of action to take to control the booming costs of health care in the United States. The leader recognizes that it would take a great deal of time to uncover the known advantages of each position. There are 25 students in the group, so the leader breaks the large group into 5 sections of 5 members each. *Each group is responsible for one of the five potential courses of action.* The leader tells them that they have 10 minutes to come up with the major positive features for their assigned

FIGURE 7.8
Guidelines for Improving Discussion Leadership Skills

1. *Build a permissive climate.* You can contribute to climate building by displaying enthusiasm for the topic, appearing optimistic that goals will be accomplished, being responsive and open, avoiding impatience and contempt, and being impartial.
2. *Have and follow a plan.* There must be a generally accepted agenda, time table, and recordkeeping system. As leader, you are the flexible guardian of these essential details of housekeeping. The plan must also prepare you to deal with necessary interruptions and distractions to eliminate unnecessary ones.
3. *Give or get accurate summaries.* Throughout a productive discussion, there is a need for "taking account" of where participants have been and what they have accomplished. If other members of the group do the summarizing, fine; if not, you must. Further, you must be certain that the members accept the accuracy of the summaries.
4. *Give or get clarification of ambiguous statements.* This is, of course, far easier said than done. Dangerous distortion can result from inaccurate restatements or from insistence on "linguistic purity."
5. *Promote critical evaluation by the participants.* Again, danger lurks behind good intentions. Perhaps the greatest threat to the needed equilibrium between sound thinking and good human relations presents itself in the performance of this essential task.
6. *Protect minority opinion.* This necessary role often can conflict with rule number 1 regarding building a permissive climate. As leader, you may at times need to stifle the majority so that minority views can be truly heard and thoughtfully considered.
7. *Minimize extrinsic conflict.* True discussion is founded on conflict, but the different views must be based on significant substance, not on personalities or other irrelevancies. The effective leader encourages substantive conflict that is intrinsic to the problem at hand but discourages pointless procedural or other forms of extrinsic conflict.
8. *Evaluate the discussion.* Almost every good technique of evaluation can be used in assessing the quality of a discussion: observation, paper-and-pencil tests, participation charts, before and after questionnaires, attitude surveys and scales, sociometric devices, descriptive compositions (written or oral), interviews, analyses of recordings by participants, and others. Both process and content evaluations are in order. Likewise, placement, diagnostic, formative, and summative evaluation should all be used (see Chapter 11.) But remember the basics: All sound evaluation must start with the objectives and should be aimed toward the highest form of the art—self-evaluation.
9. *Help students become effective participants and leaders in discussion.* Clearly you must teach about discussion—that is, go over these suggestions with students—as well as having discussions.
10. *Avoid all other functions!* A good leader stops with the above nine roles and, then, gets out of the way. Your own status or popularity must not be an issue. In the successful classroom, the teacher as leader should consume increasingly smaller percentages of the time. Leadership should be increasingly shared. In some settings, a designated leader won't even be necessary.

courses of action. Then the total group comes back together, and a representative of each group goes over his or her group's findings. With this system, the buzz group has saved time, provided a change of pace, and actively involved more people in the forum.

Small-Group Discussions.   There are many kinds of small-group discussions. We will examine the two major types: the roundtable and the symposium. (In Chapter 6, we described small-group investigations known as *cooperative learning*.)

In the *roundtable*, four to seven people have agreed on a topic of shared concern, a designated leader. and an agenda for solving the problem. (More people could be used, but this would diminish the involvement of each individual.) The problem may deal with factual, policy, or speculative matters. A general approach may be used, or the discussion could center on a particular case. In a case discussion, the group may focus on how one region coped with a particular problem rather than look at the country as a whole. The case method of discussion is extensively used in legal education. Likewise, over the years it has been widely used in values or moral education. In any event, despite a lot of necessary preparation and continuing research, the roundtable should be informal and open.

The roundtable may be public, that is, conducted so that others may observe. It may even be broadcast by the media. If so, time constraints become a major concern.

The *symposium* replaces the informal character of the interaction with set, short, and well-prepared speeches. The broad topic has been subdivided into smaller parts, and each person agrees to prepare and deliver a talk on his or her portion. Then a roundtable usually follows. The symposium can also provide an excellent springboard for a forum when a large audience observes the presentation.

Sources for Discussion Topics

Rather than give specific examples of general discussion beyond those already mentioned, we will simply note two good sources to stimulate your thinking about suitable topics. One is an exciting series of paperbacks published by Greenhaven Press Library (577 Shoreview Park Road, St. Paul, Minn. 55126) entitled *Opposing Viewpoints*. These books and pamphlets cover a very wide range of issues of contemporary importance. Some recent titles include *Aids*, *The Soviet Union, Latin America and U.S. Foreign Policy, Drug Abuse*, and *The Mass Media*. They are inexpensive, easy to read, and generally balanced. We have seen them stimulate wonderful discussions.

Another series of a far more detailed and scholarly sort was originally developed by the "Amherst Project" (the Amherst College Committee on the Study of History) and published by Addison-Wesley. Amherst College, Hampshire College, and the Newberry Library were involved in the project. The units used authentic historical scholarship to examine important and especially controversial events in American history. They are superb tools for stimulating discussion. Unfortunately, some of the titles are out of print; however, some are being reissued. Contact the Social Science Education Consortium, 855 Broadway, Boulder, Colo. 80302 for details.

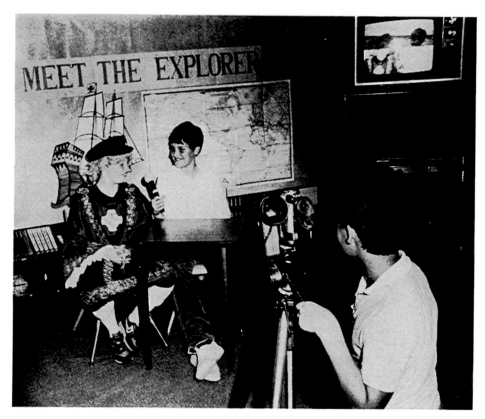

Role playing brings historical characters to life, motivates students, and helps combine study across subject areas.

DRAMATIZATION

Selma is a former student of one of the authors in the Five-Year Teacher Preparation Program. She is bright, articulate, personable, and diligent. She also has two exceptional characteristics: She has a remarkably active social conscience and volunteers a great deal of her time to work with inner-city children, and she has an extraordinary flair for drama. In voice and movement, she has the style and manner of an accomplished dramatic actress. As an undergraduate, she "double-majored" in drama and social studies. Her academic advisers perceive her as a "natural" teacher. The "problem" is that Selma can't decide whether teaching or acting is the more appropriate place to devote her primary efforts.

While engaged in the teacher preparation sequence, Selma and her peers were asked to teach two lessons in the "methods seminar." Predictably, Selma elected to teach her two classes on the use of drama in secondary social studies classrooms. She received "rave reviews" from both her peers and the instructor.

We wish that instead of merely reading about dramatization you could experience Selma's lessons firsthand. Since this isn't possible, we offer her "Outline of Content" in Figure 7.9.

For each of the 10 overlapping forms identified in item 2 of Figure 7.9, Selma provided at least one vivid example. As illustrations, she displayed

FIGURE 7.9
Outline of Content (Dramatization in the Social Studies)

1. Rationale and Purpose
   1.1 Exciting, active, motivating, fun
   1.2 Develops expression skills, oral and written, while harmonizing body and voice
   1.3 Develops and focuses energy and powers of concentration
   1.4 Teaches, through active experiences, the fundamentals of human behavior—depending on the vehicle, increases understanding of self, peers, other contemporaries or individuals, and groups from the past
   1.5 Increases the understanding of and skills in interpersonal relations, including an awareness of the effects we have on others
   1.6 Increases self-esteem
   1.7 Exercises and channels emotions
2. Major Dramatic Forms*
   2.1 Creative or dramatic play [imaginative manipulation of artifacts or objects such as tools, coins, or toy soldiers]
   2.2 Movement to sound—music, rhythms, or recorded speeches [individuals or small groups gesturing or moving in response to sounds]
   2.3 Pantomime [conveying ideas through acting without words— becoming someone else or something else]
   2.4 Improvisation [using words or dialog to convey meaning without scripts; in therapy sessions, this is frequently called *psychodrama* or *sociodrama,* which are *not* recommended for most classroom teachers]
   2.5 Puppets and masks [creating and using these devices to assist in improvisation]
   2.6 Enactment of a story or event, including role playing [developing and performing a play]
   2.7 Rehearsed readings, e.g., choral reading [individuals or groups engaged in careful oral reading of texts to obtain the author's intended meaning more fully]
   2.8 Simulation/gaming [see below]
   2.9 More formal speech activities, including storytelling, monologues and media presentations [Selma is enraptured with the learning potentialities of telling stories, and she has research evidence to support her view (U.S. Department of Education, 1987). She claims that many adults in most communities are anxious for the opportunity to tell stories to children.]
   2.10 Enacting scripts [See *Plays* magazine for dramas written especially for children. Most schools include drama teachers who want to assist their colleagues with the production of plays.]
3. The only significant problem of using dramatizations in classrooms [from Selma's perspective] is the need to overcome the fears and inhibitions of teachers and, to a lesser extent, older children.

---

some puppets created by some of her sixth-grade students and glowingly described how they had been used. She engaged several of the women in the class in a pantomime of their reactions to a potential rapist in a subway car. She passed around a tool from the 18th century with an unknown use and asked small groups to demonstrate a possible use for it. The students studied and then orally read a familiar passage from the Kennedy inaugural speech in unison. They discussed both its meaning and reasons for its impact.

Selma had the ability to "win over" people who initially viewed dramatization as silly or at best appropriate for young children only. She recommended some relaxation and concentration exercises that members of the class could use to reduce their inhibitions (McCaslin, 1984). She identified several sources for additional examples (Joyce & Alleman-Brooks, 1979; Moffett & Wagner, 1983; Lee, 1974).

Are you now thinking about using dramatizations in your classroom? We are willing to wager that you would had you had the opportunity to interact with Selma.

SIMULATION

We described simulation in Chapter 4, but we give it some attention in this section because of the prevalence of this form of dramatization. Although there was a decline of interest in instructional simulations in the late 1980s, from the mid-sixties to the early eighties they were highly promoted. Simulations have been widely recommended because of their congruence with elements of the principles of learning, including motivation, activity, involvement, transferability, and relevance.

Conflict exists among the authorities in the field over the precise definition of simulation, that is, how to distinguish among instructional games, role playing, and simulation. We will attempt to avoid this controversy by simply saying that in an instructional context, a *simulation* is a representation or simplified model of the reality of a social situation or event designed for teaching. Students use simulations to discover principles and strategies that will help them understand real-world phenomena.

As you would expect, simulation has its critics. Opponents cite these disadvantages: (1) an oversimplification of complex reality; (2) an overemphasis on competition (usually, but not necessarily, there are "winners" and "losers" in simulations); (3) overly complicated rules; (4) a lack of demonstrated transfer; and (5) inappropriately high costs in terms of time and money. In our view, simulations that avoid these pitfalls can be designed and used.

Any worthwhile simulation, whether commercially prepared or teacher made, needs to have clear and specific objectives that the teacher and, eventually, the students will understand. The educational aims need to outweigh the entertainment ones; that is, the content and the techniques involved in playing the game should be truly significant. There must be opportunities for positive interaction among the players; no participant should be placed for very long in a high-risk social situation, even in a game. In fact, playing the game should be voluntary. Defensible and realistic roles should be the norm. The rules must be understood and followed by all players. Most important, there must always be a follow-up discussion or debriefing in which both the substance and the process of the activity are carefully examined.

We think that some instructional developers in the social studies went overboard in their promotion of simulations, but we also believe this approach can be quite effective in the right circumstances. The annual *Data Book* (Social Science Education Consortium) provides useful reviews of commercially available simulations. The methods texts by John Lee et al. (Lee, Ellenwood, & Little, 1973) and William Dobkin et al. (Dobkin, Fischer, Ludwig, & Koblinger, 1985) provide valuable analyses of their use. Fannie and George Shaftel (Shaftel & Shaftel, 1967) offer a great many examples of stories to use as springboards for role playing in the social studies.

Summary

In this chapter, we indicated that listening and speaking lie at the very heart of successful teaching and learning. All teachers need to employ a variety of sound strategies (pun intended) that focus on oral language and to continually engage in efforts to improve listening and speaking abilities. We also emphasized the importance of nonverbal communication.

Lectures, recitation, questioning, interviews, tutoring (by students for other students), *discussion* (in many forms in both large- and small-group situations), *dramatization,* and *simulation* were described and analyzed. Each of these techniques has its benefits and shortcomings.

The chapter did not provide an exhaustive catalog of all the oral language approaches to teaching, but it offered a place for you to begin serious consideration of suitable strategies for your learning environment.

Decisions! Decisions!

1. Which of the oral language techniques discussed in the chapter do you plan to use? Why? Under what circumstances? How will you use these techniques to meet your instructional goals?

2. How can you make the techniques you selected in question 1 as effective as possible? How much time will they take? What resources will you need? How should you organize your students? What content should be emphasized? What managerial problems must you consider and resolve?

References

Adler, M. (1982). *The paideia proposal: An educational manifesto.* New York: Macmillan.

Bloom, B. (1984, May). The search for methods of group instruction as effective as one-to-one tutoring. *Educational Leadership,* 4–17.

Boyer, E. (1983). *High School.* New York: Harper & Row.

Brophy, J. (1986, October). Teacher influences on student achievement. *American Psychologist,* 1069–1077.

Brown, K. L., et al. (1981). *Teaching speaking and listening skills in the elementary and secondary school.* Boston: Massachusetts Department of Education.

Bureau for English Education. (1988). *English language arts syllabus K–12.* Albany, NY: New York State Education Department.

Cashin, W. (1985). *Improving lectures.* Manhattan, KS: Center for Faculty Evaluation and Development, Kansas State University.

Dobkin, W., Fischer, J., Ludwig, B., & Koblinger, R. (Eds.) (1985). *A handbook for the teaching of social studies.* Boston: Allyn & Bacon.

Hedin, D. (1986). *Students-as-teachers.* New York: Carnegie Forum on Education and the Economy.

Hoopes, J. (1979). *Oral history: An introduction for students.* Chapel Hill, NC: University of North Carolina Press.

Howell, W. S., & Smith, D. K. (1956). *Discussion.* New York: Macmillan.

Joyce, W. W., & Alleman-Brooks, J. (1979). *Teaching social studies in the elementary and middle schools.* New York: Holt, Rinehart & Winston.

Lee, J. R. (1974). *Teaching social studies in the elementary school.* New York: Free Press.

Lee, J. R., Ellenwood, S. E., & Little, T. H. (1973). *Teaching social studies in the secondary school.* New York: Free Press.

McCaslin, N. (1984). *Creative drama in the classroom.* New York: Longman.

McMurry, Charles A., et al. (1914). *Public school methods: Vol 3.* Chicago: School Methods Company.

Miller, P. W. (1988). *Nonverbal communication.* Washington, DC: National Education Association.

Moffett, J., & Wagner, B. J. (1983). *Student-centered language arts and reading, K–13: A handbook for teachers.* Boston: Houghton Mifflin.

Obermiller, P. J., & Philliber, W. W. (1987). *Too few tomorrows: Urban Appalachians in the 1980's.* Boone, NC: Appalachian Consortium Press.

Rankin, P. (1929). *Listening ability.* Columbus, OH: Ohio State University Press.

Shaftel, F., & Shaftel, G. (1967). *Role playing for social values: Decision-making in the social studies.* Englewood Cliffs, NJ: Prentice-Hall.

Social Science Education Consortium. (Annual). *Data Book.* Boulder, CO: Author.

Starr, L. M. (1977). Oral history. In *Encyclopedia of library and information science.* New York: Marcel Dekker.

Terkel, S. (1986). *Hard times: An oral history of the Great Depression in America.* New York: Pantheon.

U.S. Department of Education. (1987). *What works: Research about teaching and learning.* Washington, DC: Author.

Wagner, L. (1982). *Peer teaching: Historical perspectives.* Westport, CT: Greenwood Press.

Wilen, W., & Clegg, A. (1986, Spring). Effective questions and questioning: A research review. *Theory and Research in Social Education*, 153–161.

Wilt, M. E. (1950). A study of teacher awareness of listening as a factor in elementary education, *Journal of Education Research, 43,* 626–636.

Young, P. (1966). *Scientific social surveys and research.* Englewood Cliffs, NJ: Prentice-Hall.

Chapter Eight

Reading in the Social Studies

Learning involves students' comprehension—linking a conceptual map to new information introduced in various ways, including textbooks and other print and nonprint materials.

Probably most social studies teachers assign a reading passage as homework nearly every day. Some also ask students to briefly answer end-of-chapter questions orally in class or in writing. Typically these are low-level questions that ask the students merely to regurgitate the main factual points of the chapter. However, good teachers go beyond the textbook, using it as one of many tools to help students learn content or, better yet, cull meaning from the content. In other words, good teachers ask students to reconstruct passages to incorporate the gist of the reading into their own knowledge base.

In *The Politics of Education*, Paulo Freire (1985) says, "When reading a book, we subject-readers should be . . . looking for a connection between the main idea and our own interest" (p. 3). Students do not come to a reading assignment *tabula rasa;* rather, they incorporate their own experiences into the reading. If we don't help them see this, the reading becomes meaningless busywork, and no comprehension occurs.

Reconstructing meaning, or reading comprehension, is what we teachers need to help our middle and secondary school social studies students to do. Our task is to provide students with learning experiences that will build on what they already know, think, and feel. We do this by guiding their reading: first by engaging them in prereading activities and second by providing them with reading guides to use as they read the assigned material.

ASIDE TO THE READER: We are not trained reading teachers, so we do not engage in diagnosis and prescription of reading problems. A few students will need remedial reading assistance. But as social studies teachers, we are not expected to provide that service; most schools have reading specialists to perform this function.

WHAT IS READING COMPREHENSION?

Specialists in the area of teaching reading comprehension define *comprehension* as "relating new experiences to the already known" (Smith, 1975, p. 10) or "building bridges between the new and the unknown" (Pearson & Johnson, 1978, p. 24). Thus, in order to fully comprehend a reading selection, students must do more than merely read it. As they read a passage, they draw on their own prior knowledge and experiences—the old—and integrate them with what they glean from the reading—the new (Nelson-Herber, 1986). Research over the past decade has fairly well documented the positive relationship between prior knowledge and reading comprehension (Anderson, Reynolds,

Schallert, & Goetz, 1977; Johnston & Pearson, 1982; Pearson, Hansen, & Gordon, 1979; Reynolds, Taylor, Steffenson, Shirey, & Anderson, 1982).

When we read, we always bring our own knowledge to the new material, but we experience difficulty comprehending reading materials in which we have no conceptual or semantic background. For example, consider the following passage from an undergraduate textbook in engineering:

> Gaskell has considered the hydrodynamic problem in the rolling system assuming Newtonian flow. He has pointed out that the pressure developed by the squeezing of the material past the nip of a pair of rolls actually must carry beyond the nip, regardless of whether the material is elastic or not. He showed that equations can be developed to describe flow conditions through the nip, and pointed out that it is feasible to do so for a Bingham body as well as for a Newtonian flow.

With little experience or knowledge to bring to the above selection, the concepts seem unfamiliar and the vocabulary alien. However, second-year engineering students would be able to read it with much less difficulty because of their background of study—knowledge and experiences—in engineering.

ROLE OF THE TEXTBOOK

Most social studies teachers use a textbook; in fact, they rely on it heavily. Others go so far as to allow the textbook to determine—or even *be*—the content of the course. If an event, a person, or a perspective is not in the textbook, students usually don't learn about it. You may have been that bright 11th grader who dared to ask about Mexicans' views on the "Mexican War," to which the teacher responded that since these views weren't discussed in the text, the class wouldn't be concerned with them. (By the way, Mexican students study the "Mexican War" as the "Great American Invasion.")

However, as teachers we should consider the textbook as only one of many tools of learning in the classroom. Further, how we use that textbook needs improving. Reading researcher Joan Nelson-Herber (1986) writes, "A textbook is not really designed for independent reading. It is a tool for teaching vocabulary, facts, concepts, and values that are beyond the current knowledge and experiences of the reader" (p. 629). Research has shown that "up to fifty percent of the students in an upper-grade class cannot read their textbooks" (Estes & Vaughan, 1978, p. 8.) That does not mean that such students are illiterate, that is, incapable of reading; rather, they may well have mastered word attack skills and be able to read the words, but they have difficulty comprehending the material. And if they are unable to comprehend, they are in fact not reading and not communicating with the textual material.

When we assign a reading, we have students engage in learning both content and process. The *content* includes the main ideas, the facts, the relationships among events, and so forth. But we should be teaching *process* as well—the learning process—through teaching the skills of reading comprehension. Most students enter middle and secondary schools with basic word attack skills fairly well in place. Primary school teachers have done a good job of teaching the introductory reading skills. Those of us who teach children at the upper grades, though, have faltered in continuing from where the early-grade teachers left off. In other words, although we expect students to comprehend the reading we assign, we do not help them learn the *higher-order* reading skills—the various skills involved in reading comprehension. We will discuss these skills in detail later in the chapter.

INTRODUCING THE TEXTBOOK

Before we have students begin to read a textbook, we should introduce them to that typically mammoth tome. You might argue that students already know what a textbook is; they've been in school for years and have used, or at least lugged around, those heavy, dull things since fourth grade. Indeed we agree. But if students understood from the start the organization of their social studies text—each text differs to a varying degree—they would find it easier to use.

First, there is the title. Ask the class what it means and what they think they will learn. For years a book called *The Record of Mankind* was the standard world history (i.e., European) text, but few students understood the title. To them, a *record* meant the Rolling Stones, Bruce Springsteen, or The Clash. How disappointed they were when they read the table of contents! But the teacher could have exploited their interest in rock music to explain the intended meaning of the word *record*. With the onset of the women's movement in the 1960s, a "feminist" teacher—male or female—could have used the title as a springboard for discussion: Why *The Record of* Mankind? Students could have scanned the index to see if there were any references to women in the text and then discussed whether *mankind* was an acceptable generic term.

Looking at the table of contents might be the second step: What are the scope and sequence of the text? (Will we really get to learn about World War II this year?) Students need to have some sense in September of where they might be (that is, in what country, decade, or anthropological dig site) come January or June.

Did you ever get to Vietnam in your high school text? That reminds us of the "Shoe" cartoon in which Skyler tells his uncle that you can always tell that the end of the school year is coming when it takes only 10 minutes to cover the Truman administration.

Next, take a chapter—any chapter—and have students examine headings, boldfaced and italicized words, and visuals, including maps, charts, tables, graphs, political cartoons—all those items that break up the monotony of the printed word. Students need to learn that they can outline the chapter from the headings (though we're not advocating that they do so). By reading headings—noticing those in solid caps and those in lowercase letters—students can determine what the textbook author(s) considers most important.

Now have students go to the back of the book and find the appendix, the glossary, and the index. The Declaration of Independence and the U.S. Constitution typically are located in the back of American history texts. Maps, as well as comparative tables of economic production (agriculture, industry, natural resources), are in geography texts. Because students will be using them during the academic year, it makes sense to let them see where they are at the outset.

We'll wager that even you will learn a lot about the textbook from having your students examine it. We suggest this teacher-student activity for one of the first days of school, preferably the day the books are distributed. Turn students on to *reading* the text—the words as well as the visuals—from day one.

Do you ever examine one of your college texts as we suggested here? Why or why not?

VARIETIES OF PRINT (READING) MATERIALS

Thus far, we have discussed only the social studies textbook. However, we don't want you to think for a minute that that's the only reading source you should use with students. As we said earlier, a textbook is one of many tools to use in the social studies classroom, including tools that don't emphasize reading: films, audio- and videotapes, artifacts, computers and appropriate software, games and simulations, guest speakers, and visuals (maps, globes, charts, tables, graphs, and cartoons). We will discuss the use of the nonreading tools in Chapter 10.

Primary Sources

Primary sources such as letters, diaries, journals, government documents, and speeches lend a flavor, a realism, to the social studies. The use of these materials also gets students into the inquiry mode of learning, letting them determine what happened during a certain historical period and then compare their hypotheses with the textbook's generalizations. Primary sources must be carefully selected to (1) blend well into the day's objectives, (2) be interesting to students, (3) complement the text reading or other learning tools to be used, and (4) be readable, a point to which we'll return shortly.

Other types of reading materials include case studies; newspaper and newsmagazines (old or current); novels, biographies, and poetry; reference works; and miscellaneous items such as posters, advertisements, deeds, court records, wills, tax rolls, and census data. Case studies lend themselves nicely to small-group discussion, problem solving, and inquiry learning. They are available in some books or you can make them up yourself based on either real or imaginary situations. In fact, developing them yourself is probably preferable, because you can tailor them to fit your objectives and your students' needs. For example, for a government class you might have students read a case study (Figure 8.1) based on a newspaper item which concerns a small city's opposing views on group homes for mentally handicapped adults. You could ask students to role play the town meetings, thereby encouraging an active learning situation. Other case studies can be based on historical situations. For example, in 1872 a few women in a small upstate New York community decided that they should have the right to vote according to the 15th Amendment, which reads: "The right of citizens of the United States to vote shall not be denied or abridged on account of race, color, or previous condition of servitude." Deciding that this amendment could refer to females, the women tried to vote. With this case study, you could have students, in groups, determine if these women were right according to the Constitution.

Old or current newspapers and newsmagazines are another type of non-textbook print material. Journalists write to sell, and there is more competi-

FIGURE 8.1
Using a Case Study in the Classroom

Mental Health in Harmonyville

The State Commission on Mental Health has established new clinics, or homes, for those suffering mental or emotional problems. These group homes enable people with mild retardation or emotional problems to live together and receive help from one another and from specialists, based on the idea that all people need to feel that they can contribute to society and perhaps earn enough money to support themselves. Having accepted this idea, one community helped establish three group homes. Sensing no problems with these facilities, all of which are within one residential area of the city, the county mental health department now sees a need for another home. The county legislature has selected for the new facility a fourth building within the same area as the other three. It is owned by a local lawyer whose offices occupy only part of the building, a former residence.

But the neighbors are now getting upset. "Enough is enough!" they say. "Why not another part of the city or county?" Some young parents fear that "these people with problems" may harm their children who play outside at home or at the playground nearby. The county legislature and the mental health staff have several reasons for wishing to use the lawyer's building. But opponents have hundreds of names on petitions opposed to the site, and the vocal residents are attending both city council and county legislature meetings in which the new group home is being discussed.

The decision to be reached is: Should the new center be at the lawyer's offices?

Source: Adapted from Linda Biemer, *New York and its Western Hemispheric Neighbors* (pp. 185–188), 1988, Salt Lake City, Utah: Peregrine Smith Books. Copyright 1988 by Peregrine Smith Books. Reprinted by permission.

tion for their writing than there is for textbooks. Like primary sources, old news journals give students a sense of how people at the time viewed current events, which we now call "history."

But don't assign just the news articles in these old journals. Have students read the want ads to see what types of jobs people had, study the food and automobile ads to compare prices then with those now, and dig into articles on the society page. Who were considered the social and charitable leaders of society? Why were they featured? Use of current magazines and newspapers constantly updates our textbooks, which typically have a school life of five years. Also, these sources help students see their lives as part of tomorrow's history.

"But the newsmagazines aren't written at the 8th-grade level, the reading level of the slower 10th graders," your cooperating teacher reminds you. "How can you assign these materials if your students won't be able to read them? And lots of the primary sources too were written for adults, not your junior high kids." Indeed, maybe some of these nontextbook materials *will* be too difficult. But let's not jump the gun here. These materials tend to turn youngsters on, and you may be surprised when certain low-ability students are able to read these frequently more interesting materials.

All students need to have their minds stretched. Using interesting materials that may be above their instructional reading levels is one way to do it. If, on the other hand, you sometimes feel that these primary sources are indeed beyond your students' reading levels, determine the materials' general reading level before rushing to decide whether or not to use them. You may be surprised at the results.

DETERMINING READABILITY OF PRINT MATERIALS

Several readability guides are available. The one we will use here was developed by Edward Fry, a reading educator at Rutgers University. Fry's guide (Fry, 1972), like many others, looks at length of sentence and length of words within those sentences in a particular passage. The longer the words and the longer the sentence, the more difficult the reading level. Students lose track of the main idea, or they just get turned off if the sentence is too long. If you don't believe us, just keep reading. Following are similar passages from two different American history textbooks, the first for middle school students and the second for senior high ones. Pay particular attention to the length of the sentences and the words, for they tend to indicate the complexity of the vocabulary.

First, here is the junior high passage:

> Congress passed the Northwest Ordinance (1787). In spite of its limited power, Congress did manage to pass one important law. This was the Northwest Ordinance, sometimes called the Ordinance of 1787. An ordinance is a law. The Northwest Ordinance, as you may have guessed, was a law that referred to the Northwest Territory.

Several states claimed to own all or part of the Northwest Territory, which George Rogers Clark and his men had won. The conflicting claims made it impossible for anybody to govern the region. The states finally agreed to give up their claims and let Congress govern the territory.*

And now the senior high passage:

The Northwest Ordinance of 1787 was probably the Confederation Congress's most important piece of legislation. Under this ordinance, the Northwest Territory became a single unit with a governor appointed by Congress. When 5,000 free male inhabitants had settled in the territory, those who owned at least 50 acres were to elect a territorial legislature whose acts would be subject only to the governor's veto. The voters would also send a nonvoting delegate to Congress. No less than three and no more than five states were to be carved out of the territory. The boundaries of three future states were laid out.**

We think you can see the differences quite easily.

Now let's try to determine the reading level of the two passages. Using the readability graph in Figure 8.2, count the number of sentences in each of the two 99-word passages (yes, it's supposed to be 100, but we're so close!). Then count the number of syllables in each reading selection. Next, plot those two numbers on the graph. Where they come together is the approximate reading level of the material. Go ahead, try it. The answers are printed upside down at the bottom of this page, but don't cheat! It's important that you learn how to determine readability.

Other guides have been developed by both Alton Raygor and G. Harry McLaughlin. Raygor's (1977) is similar to Fry's, but in addition to counting sentences you count only the number of words of six letters or more rather than syllables. McLaughlin (1969) developed what he calls the *SMOG formula*. Using this formula, you choose three passages containing ten sentences each and then count every word of three syllables or more. You then round off to the nearest perfect square the total of the words containing three or more syllables and then determine its square root. Next, you add 3 to the total. The result will be the approximate grade level.

Today, however, there is a much easier way to determine the reading level of materials: using a computer and readability software. An example is the School Utilities software package from MECC (Minnesota Educational Computer Consortium), which enables teachers to ascertain reading levels in just

*Excerpt from *Story of Our Land and People* by Glen W. Moon and John H. MacGowan, copyright © 1955 and renewed 1983 by Holt, Rinehart and Winston, Inc., reprinted by permission of the publisher.

**Winthrop D. Jordan/Leon F. Litwack, THE UNITED STATES, Combined Edition, 6/e, © 1987, p. 138. Reprinted by permission of Prentice-Hall, Inc., Englewood Cliffs, New Jersey.

Answer: The first passage has 8 sentences and 151 syllables, making it just between the 7th- and 8th-grade reading levels. The second contains 6 sentences and 162 syllables; thus, it is just between the 10th- and 11th-grade reading levels.

FIGURE 8.2
Graph for Estimating Readability

Average number of syllables per 100 words

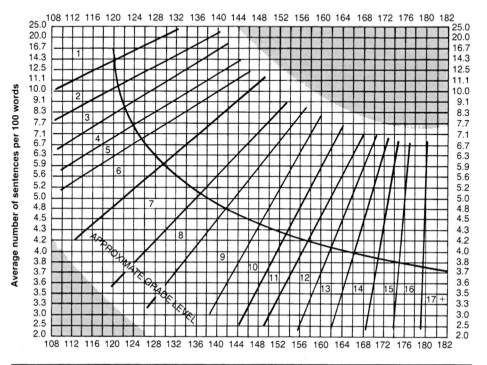

Source: Adapted from Fry (1972).

a few minutes. Figure·8.3 presents a sample computer-generated readability analysis.

Check with your methods professor, the teacher materials center on campus, or the school in which you expect to work to see what software is available. Then try it. Not only will it be a valuable time saver; it probably will be more accurate than you are (some of us do have trouble with syllabication).

Note that the formulas or graphs used with these software products yield only approximations of reading levels of materials, so use them as guides only. The computerized guides will come in handy for determining the reading levels of nontextbook materials you bring to class, such as primary sources, newsmagazine articles, and others mentioned earlier in this section. As for textbooks and textbook-related materials, their publishers usually provide reliable indications of the intended reading levels.

FIGURE 8.3
Computer Analysis of Readability

```
            "CAMP LIFE" BY RWM, Passage 2

     THE LAST DAY OF THE MONTH WAS A BIG REVIEW BY
GENERAL CASEY, WHO RODE HIS IRON-GRAY PACER. AS #WYMAN
STOOD IN FORMATION, HE COULD SEE SMILES CREEPING ON THE
FACES OF SOME OF THE MEN. CASEY RODE SO FAST THAT HIS
STAFF HAD TO GO ON THE GALLOP TO KEEP IN SIGHT OF HIM.
MOST OF THE STAFF WERE NOT VERY GOOD HORSEMEN, SO THEY
KEPT LOSING THEIR BALANCE. EVEN THEIR HATS FELL OFF.
THAT AFTERNOON #WYMAN SAT DOWN IN HIS TENT TO WRITE A
LETTER TO #CONNIE. DEAR BROTHER. I HAVE JUST RECEIVED
YOUR LETTER. I WAS GLAD TO "END"


SYLLABLE COUNTS:


  1   THE              1   LAST

  1   DAY              1   OF

  1   THE              1   MONTH

  1   WAS              1   A

  1   BIG              2   REVIEW

  1   BY               3   GENERAL

  2   CASEY            1   WHO

  1   RODE             1   HIS

  3   IRONGRAY         2   PACER

  1   AS               2   #WYMAN

  1   STOOD            1   IN

  3   FORMATION        1   HE

  1   COULD            1   SEE

  1   SMILES           2   CREEPING

  1   ON               1   THE

  2   FACES            1   OF

  1   SOME             1   OF

  1   THE              1   MEN

  2   CASEY            1   RODE

  1   SO               1   FAST

  1   THAT             1   HIS

  1   STAFF            1   HAD
```

FIGURE 8.3
continued

```
1   TO              1   GO
1   ON              1   THE
2   GALLOP          1   TO
1   KEEP            1   IN
1   SIGHT           1   OF
1   HIM             1   MOST
1   OF              1   THE
1   STAFF           1   WERE
1   NOT             2   VERY
1   GOOD            3   HORSEMEN
1   SO              1   THEY
1   KEPT            2   LOSING
1   THEIR           2   BALANCE
2   EVEN            1   THEIR     SUMMARY FOR PASSAGE 2:
1   HATS            1   FELL
1   OFF             1   THAT      NUMBER OF SENTENCES:  8
3   AFTERNOON       2   #WYMAN    NUMBER OF WORDS:          102
1   SAT             1   DOWN      NUMBER OF SYLLABLES:      130
1   IN              1   HIS       WORDS OF 6 OR MORE LETTERS:16
1   TENT            1   TO        3 OR MORE SYLLABLE WORDS:  5
1   WRITE           1   A         % OF 3 OR MORE SYLLABLE WORDS: 4.9
2   LETTER          1   TO        AVERAGE SENTENCE LENGTH:  12.8
2   #CONNIE         1   DEAR      AVERAGE LETTERS PER WORD:  3.9
2   BROTHER         1   I         AVERAGE SYLLABLES PER WORD:1.3
1   HAVE            1   JUST
2   RECEIVED        1   YOUR      THERE ARE 10 WORDS NOT IN THE
2   LETTER          1   I         DALE-CHALL WORD LIST.  CORRECTED
1   WAS             1   GLAD      DALE-CHALL GRADE LEVEL:  5th-6th
1   TO              1   END
```

236

READING GUIDES

Despite the availability of reliable measuring instruments for assessing readability levels, reading experts warn that even if students' reading levels (which the school may make available to you from end-of-year tests) match the levels of the materials, there is no guarantee that reading comprehension will occur. Students may not understand the relationships inherent in the reading, such as cause and effect, and they may lack the sophistication required to draw inferences from the reading. Thus, we recommend developing reading guides for students to use both before they read and as they read.

Prereading Guides

Standing in the school hallway outside a social studies classroom as the dismissal bell rang, one of the authors overheard the teacher announce, "Your assignment for tomorrow is to read the next chapter in your text. Come prepared to discuss it." The listener's immediate reaction was "Now come on, teacher, what kind of assignment was that?" The answer was that everything was wrong with it, including the timing. We doubt that most students even heard it! Of course, maybe there was no need for them to hear it if they kept getting the same type of assignment every day.

The fact is that teachers need to spend considerable time explaining an assignment, especially a reading assignment, and preparing students for it. We need to turn students on to the reading, to help them become interested in it. Research tells us, not surprisingly, that teaching is more effective when students have a personal interest in what's being taught. So how do we do it? One effective way is to develop and use prereading guides. A *prereading guide* has a twofold purpose: (1) It prepares students to engage in the reading, and (2) it provides the teacher with information about the students' prior knowledge or experiences with the content of the material. Recall our earlier statement that comprehension means bridging the gap between what students already know and what we seek to have them know; that is, the more they realize that they have some familiarity with the content to be read, the more comfortable—and interested—they will be in engaging in the reading.

Figure 8.4 presents an example of a prereading guide. The scenario is an eighth-grade social studies class of 25 average-ability students. The subject to be covered is immigration, and the specific topic is immigration to the United States in the late 1800s. Some of the students no doubt have retained some knowledge of the topic from having studied immigration to their state the year they "did" (to use their word) state and local history. But their teacher is not sure how much they remember, how many of the students attended school in the state that year, or how thoroughly the topic was examined. The prereading guide in Figure 8.4 is to be used before doing any reading about immigration. A different guide will be used when it's time to do the actual reading.

The prereading guide in Figure 8.4 is called an *anticipation/reaction guide*. The first activity gives students the opportunity to *anticipate* what the reading will be about and to *react* to the statements based on just their own experiences and prior beliefs. Because there are no "wrong" answers at this point, students should have no fear of failure. After the second activity, the teacher acts as facilitator, asking several teams to share their responses with the rest of the class. The teacher thus gleans a sense of what the students already know about immigration and some of their conceptions (or misconceptions) about the topic.

It's a good idea to have students keep prereading guides in their notebooks and refer to them near the end of the chapter to see whether they want to change their minds about any of their earlier views.

Structured Overviews

The anticipation/reaction guide is only one of several forms of prereading guide. Another type is modeled on the advance organizer of David Ausubel (Ausubel, 1960), referred to in Chapter 4. An *advance organizer* presents the student with a semantic map (or "map of words") of the material to be studied in the new chapter or chapter section. Ausubel believes that a person's "existing cognitive structure is the foremost factor governing whether new material will be meaningful and how well it can be acquired and retained" (Joyce & Weil, 1986, p. 72).

Reading comprehension specialists have adapted Ausubel's cognitive structure model into a type of prereading guide often referred to as a *struc-*

FIGURE 8.4
Anticipation/Reaction Pre-reading Guide: Immigration

Directions: Place an A (Agree) or a D (Disagree) on the line in *column 1* before each of the following statements. Draw on your past study of immigration: newspaper articles you have read, TV news items related to the topic, and your personal opinions.

1	2	
____	____	1. All people who wish to immigrate to the United States should be allowed to do so.
____	____	2. Immigrants have made outstanding contributions to American society.
____	____	3. Immigrants take jobs away from U.S. citizens.
____	____	4. Immigration increases the number of people on welfare.
____	____	5. Only immigrants with immediate family members who are already U.S. citizens should be allowed to come here.
____	____	6. Only immigrants who are political refugees in communist countries should be allowed to enter.

Now share your responses with a partner, and try to reach consensus between the two of you, placing an A or a D on the line in column 2.

tured overview (Barron & Stone, 1974). A structured overview may be used in one of two ways depending on the topic or the amount of class time available. Returning to the topic of immigration used in the preceding section, one way to use the structured overview would be for the teacher to complete most of it prior to class and present it to the students on an overhead transparency (students should have their own paper copy of it, too.) The second way would be to have the students as a full group complete it during class. We'll use the second method to illustrate.

Let's assume that the teacher has a transparency that contains only the word *immigration*. He asks the students to which questions they want answers, which questions about immigration they think the unit should answer, and how they can categorize those questions. Typically the students will respond with the following:

Why did they come?

Why did they come to the U.S. instead of Canada, England, or Australia?

When did they come?

From where?

Did they have problems adjusting to the United States?

Where did they settle in the U.S.?

Why there?

No doubt they will come up with others, but these are enough for illustration purposes.

Next, the teacher leads the students in a discussion aimed at categorizing these questions. Then the teacher fills in possible categories, or clusters, on the transparency, while the students fill in their blank paper copy. The completed overview will look something like Figure 8.5.

A second way to use the overview is to provide students with it already filled in and ask them what other questions they want answered, what they feel is missing from this semantic map, and what answers they already have in their heads for some of the questions.

Keep this structured overview, or semantic map, in mind, for later we will refer to both it and the anticipation/reaction guide in Figure 8.4 to help students learn more (and better) as they read.

Are you ready to attempt a structured overview? Try it using a chapter from this text.

In this section, we discussed only two of the many types of prereading guides available. We suggest that you refer to the references at the end of this chapter and seek out general books on teaching reading comprehension to find other examples.

FIGURE 8.5
Structured Overview
Guide for Teaching
Reading

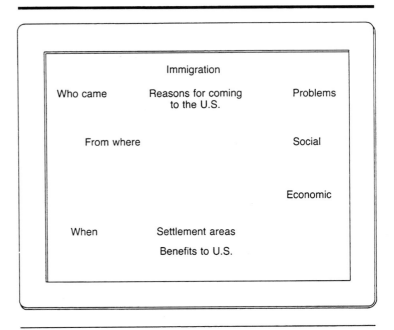

Guides to Use During Reading

Textbooks are difficult to read for a variety of reasons:

- Typically they are written in an expository style rather than in an easier-to-read narrative style.
- Students often are just not interested in the subject matter.
- Frequently each page introduces an overwhelming number of concepts and vocabulary terms. (Smith & Dauer, 1984)

Also, much of the information textbooks contain is new and therefore probably unfamiliar to students. As we saw earlier in the chapter, as teachers we need to help students learn how to learn the unfamiliar in the text by drawing on what they already know. The use of prereading guides is a start, but we can't leave off there. We also need to develop guides to assist students *as* they read.

These guides will focus on exactly what we want our students to learn from reading the text. We want them not only to glean facts, new vocabulary, and new ideas but to be able to interact with the reading to interpret and infer from the text. We even want them to go beyond that and relate these new ideas or inferences to other situations they have experienced. In other words, as Frank Smith has put it, we want students to develop "an ability to link internal knowledge or beliefs about the nature of reality with the information supplied by print" (Smith, 1978, p. 122).

This hierarchy of comprehension has picked up various labels and recently has come under question. Frequently the comprehension levels somewhat parallel Bloom's taxonomy and nearly always consist of three strands, collapsing Bloom's six levels into three. Davey thinks this is stretching it a bit and agrees with Rosenshine (Rosenshine, 1980) that this hierarchy, these levels, are not necessarily accurate (Davey, 1986). We will examine her criticism later in the chapter, so hang in there if the trinity of comprehension levels bothers you.

Three-Level Guides.   So what are these three comprehension levels? The three most commonly described levels are, quite simply,

- Reading for direct factual information
- Interpreting the reading to acquire more meaning
- Using the students' experience by looking at similar situations to better understand the reading.

Do these sound somewhat vague? Let's use some examples to unmuddy the waters.

For level 1, let's say the student read in the assigned chapter: "President Lincoln issued the Emancipation Proclamation effective January 1, 1863, to

Students must interpret their reading to acquire meaning.

free all the slaves in those states in rebellion against the Union." That statement of fact may be one that the teacher wants the students to acquire from
the reading. But the teacher also may wish the students to go beyond that and
begin to interpret the meaning. Thus, we're now on level 2. For example, some
students may attribute Lincoln's action to his personal feelings against slavery. Others may feel he did it only to encourage slaves to run away from their
masters and go north. A third group may infer from Lincoln's action that
Lincoln believed that by freeing the slaves he would gain the support of Great
Britain, which had freed its slaves in 1833.

Level 3 uses the text reading as a basis for studying situations that have
like characteristics or pose similar dilemmas. For example, the teacher asks
if the students themselves have ever been in a predicament in which they had
to make a decision that ran counter to their own beliefs but was for a greater
good. Using the Emancipation Proclamation as a model, some students might
conjecture that the president really was not against slavery (he never owned
any slaves because he couldn't afford to, they'd add). But because Lincoln felt
that the war would end sooner if he made a statement that appeared to decry
human bondage, he issued the Proclamation to respond to a greater good: an
end to war casualties and justice for Black Americans. In his level 3 section,
Herber (1978) tends to use declarative statements with which students may
be familiar. An appropriate statement for the Emancipation Proclamation
example might be: "All men are not equal, but their rights are."

Readence, Bean, and Baldwin, a trio of reading specialists (not lawyers),
define the three levels as (1) the textually explicit level, (2) the textually implicit
level, and (3) the experientially based level (Readence, Bean, & Baldwin, 1981).
Reading specialist Harold Herber (1978) refers to level 1 as the literal level, 2
as the interpretive level, and 3 as the applied level. Gray (1960) defines them
as reading the lines (level 1), reading between the lines (level 2), and reading
beyond the lines (level 3). But regardless of their labels, the idea behind the
three comprehension levels is basically the same.

Figure 8.6 presents an example of a three-level guide that tends to follow
the Herber model, stating the directions as if the students are using it.
Remember that this is to be a group activity, so students are interacting with
one another rather than alone with the reading.

Three-level guides are fairly easy to make. Here are the basic steps:

1. Select a passage to assign. Read it carefully, and decide which key facts
    you want your students to learn from it.
2. Put the facts into declarative statements. Throw in a few false ones as well,
    of course.
3. Reread the passage and determine what the author has said between the
    lines that lends itself well to discussion among your students. Develop a
    second section (level 2), using statements that are on the interpretive or
    inferential level.

FIGURE 8.6
Three-Level Guide for Teaching Reading

Part I. Directions: Listed below are three statements. With your group, read each statement and then individually read the passage below the statements. Next, decide with your group which statements contain the same information as the passage, either in exact words or in a paraphrase, and place a check mark on the line in front of those statements. Be ready to support your opinion with evidence. After your group has reached agreement on the first three statements, go on to Part II.

____ 1. Over 1,000 thousand female factory workers in Lowell went on strike in 1834 because of a cut in wages.
____ 2. The Factory Girls' Association was opposed to the strike.
____ 3. The striking women had to move from the boardinghouses owned by the company.

   In 1834 a thousand or more Lowell girls walked out in protest against a 15 percent wage cut. "One of the leaders," reported the Boston Transcript, "mounted a stump, and made a flaming . . . speech on the rights and the inequities of the 'monied aristocracy' which produced a powerful effect on her auditors, and they determined to have their way, if they died for it." The strike was broken, and many of the women went home. Those who stayed, however, continued to fight back, forming a Factory Girls' Association in 1836, with a membership of 2500. They declared: "As our fathers resisted unto blood the lordly avarice of the British ministry, so we, their daughters, never will wear the yoke which has been prepared for us." When they went out on strike they were evicted from the company-owned boarding houses and starved into defeat. But the struggle inspired other women textile workers, whose strikes were later successful.*

Part II. Directions: Read each of the statements below and think about how each relates to the passage just read. With your group, place a check mark on the line in front of each statement that says what the authors meant by what they wrote. This is sometimes called "reading between the lines."

____ 1. The Lowell women were in favor of rights for women.
____ 2. Included among the "monied aristocracy" were the Lowell factory owners.
____ 3. The women were successful in their strike.
____ 4. The Factory Girls' Association was the forerunner of a labor union.

Part III. Directions: Read through the following statements and think about experiences you have had that relate to the reading passage. Check each statement with which you and your group members agree because of its similarity to an experience one of you has had and to the reading selection. Be ready to support your decisions with evidence.

____ 1. If at first you don't succeed, try, try again.
____ 2. It's the little people in the world who make the changes.
____ 3. Right triumphs over all in the end.

---

*Winthrop D. Jordan/Leon F. Litwack, THE UNITED STATES, Combined Edition, 6/e, © 1987, p. 218. Reprinted by permission of Prentice-Hall, Inc., Englewood Cliffs, New Jersey.

4. Determine the main ideas of the passage. Using *Bartlett's Familiar Quotations, Treasury of Thought,* or similar references, create a few statements that relate to the reading but are not content bound to it. Like the statements in level 2, these should be provocative, debatable, and not necessarily true or false.

Reread the three-level guide in Figure 8.6 and review the above steps. Then try to make your own guide. You will find it's not as formidable a task as you expected.

Textbook Activity Guides. Earlier we stated that the hierarchical three-level guides recently have come under attack. Davey feels that those guides "are based on rather restrictive and possibly inaccurate notions of hierarchical levels of comprehension in learning from textbooks" (Davey, 1986). Davey does not always see in textbook reading passages the clear, coherent organization patterns suggested by Herber's internal organization guides. Instead, Davey prefers her *TAGs,* or *textbook activity guides,* which involve students, always working with a partner, in a variety of reading and learning activities. Students may answer questions, predict an outcome, draw a semantic map, or merely discuss a fact or idea with their partners.

Figure 8.7 illustrates a textbook activity guide using the same idea of the early labor unions in the 1830s used in Figure 8.6. Students will hand in their work when completed and after full-class discussion of some of the reading passages or activities with which they had difficulty (? or –).

In addition to three-level guides and TAGs, several internal organizational guides are also valuable. We don't have space to go into them here, so we suggest that you find yourself a copy of Herber's *Teaching Reading in Content Areas* (1978) or Niles and Memory's *Reading Tactics, Teacher's Guide* (1977). These sources will help you create guides that will assist students in ferreting out internal reading organizational patterns such as cause and effect, comparison and contrast, time order, simple listing, or a fifth that Readence, Bean, and Baldwin (1981, pp. 45–47) have added to the list—problem solution.

Whichever type of reading guide you decide to use, remember that you are helping your students learn both content and process—the higher-level learning process—through reading activities.

TEACHING VOCABULARY IN THE SOCIAL STUDIES

Earlier we mentioned that one of the difficulties students have in reading textbooks is the heavy vocabulary load. So many unfamiliar words, some of them concepts, are introduced into each new page of reading in social studies that

FIGURE 8.7
Textbook Activity Guide for Teaching Reading

Strategy codes: DP = Read and discuss with your partner
PP = Predict with your partner
WR = Each of you write your response on a separate piece of paper
Map = Complete the semantic map
Skim = Read quickly; discuss with partner

Self-monitoring codes: + I understand this information
? I'm not sure if I fully understand
– I do not understand this

1. ___ PP pp.215–219: Using the headings, predict at least five ideas, events, or people you will learn about.
2. ___ DP p. 215: Explain why eastern industry developed and grew.
3. ___ Skim section entitled "First Factories," pp. 215–216.
   ___ WR: Describe in a sentence or two the first factories in the U.S.
4. ___ Skim section "The Entry of Big Capital" to find the source of big capital and why those with capital elected to invest in new northeastern industry.
   ___ WR: As though you were a capitalist, explain in a few sentences why you would be investing in industry. Read your writing to your partner for comments and revisions.
5. ___ Map: With your partner, develop a semantic map of the early labor union movement.

Source: Adapted from "Using Textbook Activity Guides to Help Students Learn from Textbooks," by B. Davey, March 1986, *Journal of Reading, 29,* pp. 489–494.

students are frightened away from trying to comprehend the reading when they can't even pronounce the words they encounter. (Recall that paragraph from the undergraduate engineering book that we looked at earlier.)

How do students learn new vocabulary? For years we have had them memorize lists of words, often for a Friday quiz. Or we have felt that students would figure out unfamiliar words from the words' context, a process called *indirect* or *incidental learning.* However, according to a publication by the National Council of Teachers of English way back in 1935, the direct teaching of new terms by having students memorize a list for the end-of-week quiz leads only to good scores on the quiz. There is little or no carryover; that is, students do not use the new words in their speaking or writing assignments. Further, Nelson-Herber cautions that "[e]ven though students can learn vocabulary incidentally through reading, it appears that the new vocabulary load in content area materials is so heavy that it prevents students from comprehending the materials and thus impedes vocabulary learning from context" (Nelson-Herber, 1986, p. 628). Let's take a look at the vocabulary load from just three sentences in a fairly standard social studies textbook:

Schools dropped the German language from the curriculum. A peak in <u>absurdity</u> was reached by restaurants that renamed sauerkraut 'liberty cabbage' and kennels that <u>rechristened</u> dachshunds 'liberty pups.' But <u>pacifists, socialists</u> and <u>left-wing workers</u> suffered the worst <u>repression.</u> Congress made <u>intolerance</u> <u>official</u> by <u>adopting</u> the <u>Espionage</u> Act of June 1917 and the <u>Sedition</u> Act of May 1918.*

All of the underlined words (14 in just those three short sentences—a mere 1/20th of a typical reading assignment!) are ones that students will probably have some difficulty with unless they know the meaning; that is, they likely will not learn them incidentally. Nor will looking them up in a dictionary lead to mastery. We all know that dictionary definitions are not easy to comprehend, and that students are not always sure which of multiple definitions is the correct one for the unfamiliar word. Many of the terms typically found in social studies texts have meanings unique to the social studies context. For example, in the above passage students probably have heard of *absurdity, (re)christened, intolerance,* and *adopting* within different contexts that will not necessarily help them with the social studies meanings as used in the passage.

So back to the problem at hand: How do we relieve students of the frustrations they face when encountering so much unfamiliar vocabulary within social studies reading assignments? In other words, how do we get them to do their reading assignments? To answer this, refer to the section on prereading activities and develop some activities that emphasize the vocabulary within the passage to be read.

One possibility is the structured overview, or semantic map. Students have their own paper copy, and the teacher uses the overhead projector to complete the prereading vocabulary guide with the students. The example in Figure 8.8 returns to our immigration topic. Students are to explain the terms in the space underneath each term. (On 8 1/2" x 11" paper, more space will be available for the students' remarks.) If necessary, they can refer to their texts while doing the assignment.

Another way to introduce vocabulary and have students work with it in small groups prior to the reading is to use a multiple-choice-type exercise. Figure 8.9 presents an example, again borrowing from the immigration topic. As in the semantic map activity, students can refer to their texts if necessary.

In the activity in Figure 8.9, students probably will not develop the same groupings. That's OK, for they may see different connections that even you didn't think of. As long as they can justify them, fine; after all they are learning vocabulary in this activity by interacting with the words and their peers; there are no pat answers.

---

*Winthrop D. Jordan/Leon F. Litwack, THE UNITED STATES, Combined Edition, 6/e, © 1987, p. 292. Reprinted by permission of Prentice-Hall, Inc., Englewood Cliffs, New Jersey.

FIGURE 8.8
Semantic Map for Teaching Reading

IMMIGRATION   EMIGRATION

[   ]   [   ]
   New immigration   Migration

[   ]   [   ]
   Old immigration

[   ]
                       Cultural diffusion   Political oppression
   National origins   [   ] [   ]

[   ]   Cultural mosaic   Religious conviction
   Quota systems   [   ] [   ]

[   ]   Acculturation   Economic instability
                      [   ] [   ]
       "Tossed salad" ⟵——— Assimilation ———⟶ "Melting pot"

> To wrap up the activity in Figure 8.9, the teacher leads a full-class discussion, drawing on different groups to respond. Again, the students will interact so vigorously with the vocabulary terms (many of which are social studies concepts) that by the time they do the reading (their homework for the next day, perhaps with an "as-you-read" guide to assist them), they will have an easier time and comprehend more of it.

> This section has illustrated only two of the many vocabulary guides available. Refer to the references at the end of the chapter for additional sources of such guides.

FIGURE 8.9
Learning Vocabulary Through Word Association

Directions: In your group of 3 to 4, decide which word does not belong. Refer to your text and a thesaurus or dictionary if you need to. Circle the word that is out of place, and under each list of terms, explain why the three you chose should be grouped together and the fourth is inappropriate for the grouping.

IMMIGRATION
1. refugee political oppression cultural diffusion quotas
2. acculturation assimilation migration "melting pot"
3. economic instability political oppression wars socialization
4. "new immigration" National Origins Act quotas customs
5. cultural mosaic cultural diffusion assimilation emigration

When selecting print materials, teachers must be alert to biases, stereotyping, and distortions.

SELECTING PRINT MATERIALS*

As teachers, we are especially obligated not to use materials that blatantly or insidiously discriminate against women, racial and ethnic minorities, the handicapped, and the elderly. In addition, civil rights legislation, P.L. 94-142 (the Education for All Handicapped Children Act), and state laws imply or demand outright that there be no discrimination in reading materials. Social pressure for change has also come from the groups that traditionally have been the targets of discrimination.

We also need to be wary of the biases of authors, editors, journalists, publishing companies, and governments. The following categories are particularly important to be aware of when checking books and materials for bias: (1) authors, (2) indexes, (3) illustrations, (4) use of role models, (5) language, (6) so-called "problems," and (7) methods of inclusion.

Authors. Is the author qualified to write on the subject? Does the author exhibit bias based on sex, race, political views, or other perspectives? Check that female authors do not slight males and that males do not slight females, that African-Americans do not slight whites nor whites African-Americans. For example, compare the following perspectives:

*Material for this section draws heavily on *Stereotypes, Distortions and Omissions in U.S. History Textbooks*, 1977, New York: Council on Interracial Books for Children.

To live in the South was to live in the daily fear of slave violence.

To live in the South was to live in the daily hope of a successful rebellion against slave owners.

While the people were trying to live, farm, and hunt peacefully in their homeland, they had to constantly be on guard against marauding and invading whites.

Alone in the wilderness, the pioneer and his wife had to protect themselves from wild animals and unfriendly Indians.

Indexes.   Check to see whether the index includes women, African-Americans, and ethnic minorities. Also note how some topics are outlined. For example, one index we've seen lists the following subentries under "immigration": "problems," "hostility," "language," "poverty," and "unemployment."

Illustrations.   Count the number of photographs of males and females, of whites and ethnic minorities, of Northern Europeans and Asians. Check the photo content. For example, are slaves or sweatshop workers depicted as happy? Are there only pictures of white cowboys? (Incidentally, there were also Black cowboys and Indian cowboys.)

Use of Role Models.   Who are represented in the biographical studies in textbooks? White men? White women? No women? Women in stereotypical "female" roles?

Language.   Are derogatory terms or connotations used? Is "he" used to mean both male and female? Did Columbus "discover" America? Were the natives he found "savages?" Are welfare recipients described as "lazy" or "docile?" Is "primitive" used only when referring to people outside the United States of America, with the exception of Native Americans? Is the women's movement referred to as "Women's Lib?" Is the standard of living of mainstream whites in the United States used as the standard for people in the rest of the world? Are African, Asian, and Latin American nations referred to as "underdeveloped?" Are "nonwhite" and "non-Christian" used as though "white" and "Christian" were the "norm?"

"Problems."   Are there implications that only low-income people, immigrants, minorities, and women have problems? Or are these groups depicted as the victims of other people's problems (e.g., those of wealthy white males)?

Methods of Inclusion.   Are non-native-born residents of the United States seen as contributors to someone else's culture—for example, Native Americans gave "us" corn, African-Americans gave "us" jazz, Chinese Americans helped build "our" railroads?

Are victims blamed for their misfortunes? For example,

Native Americans lost their land because "they did not understand the concept of private land ownership."

Asian workers received low wages because "they were willing to work for very little."

African-Americans could not find jobs because they were unskilled and uneducated.

Hispanics faced problems because they were not fluent in English.

Filipinos and Puerto Ricans were colonized because they were not ready for self-government.

Few women worked in "traditional male" occupations because they lacked physical strength.

Even if books and other printed materials already have been selected and you find biases such as those described in the preceding categories, incorporate the discriminatory language and authors' biases into your lessons. After all, you want to develop critical readers and thinkers, and this is an obvious way to begin doing so.

Summary

Teaching content reading is an integral part of the social studies teacher's job. Merely giving reading assignments does not constitute effective teaching of reading. Students need assistance in learning how to learn independently in school and on their own later. The learning that must occur in social studies classes is both process learning (the "how-to") and content learning (the "what").

Learning involves students' *comprehension,* the linking of their own knowledge or conceptual map to new information introduced in various ways, including by *textbooks* and other *print* and *nonprint materials.* These materials, the *content,* can be primary sources (letters, journals, speeches, newspapers, and so on). The *process* asks the teacher to use (1) *prereading guides,* (2) *three-level guides,* and (3) *textbook activity guides.* We also recommended using *checklists* for print materials in terms not only of readability but also of the qualifications and biases of authors, the usefulness of indexes and illustrations, the inclusion of role models, and the language used to describe various groups, especially minorities.

Decisions! Decisions!

1. When you were in secondary school, did you always do the *entire* reading assignment or did you just find the answers to the questions at the end of the chapter? Why or why not? Will you expect your students to read an entire assignment? How will you encourage them to do so?

2. Before reading this chapter, did you think of yourself as a reading teacher as well as a social studies teacher? Do you now?

3. Explain the value to students in using three-level guides.

4. Underline the content-load vocabulary in three paragraphs in a standard middle or high school textbook. How heavy is it?

5. How can you tell if material is biased? Bring a sample of some biased material to class.

References

Anderson, R. C., Reynolds, R. E., Schallert, D. L., & Goetz, E. T. (1977). Frameworks for comprehending discourse. *American Educational Research Journal, 14,* 367–382.

Ausubel, D. P. (1960). The use of advance organizers in the learning and retention of meaningful verbal material. *Journal of Educational Psychology, 51,* 267–272.

Barron, R. F., & Stone, V. F. (1974). The effects of student-constructed graphic post organizers upon learning vocabulary relationships. In P. L. Nacke (Ed.), *Interaction: Research and Practice for College-Adult Reading* (23rd Yearbook, pp. 172–175). Clemson, SC: National Reading Conference, 172-175.

Davey, B. (1986, March). Using textbook activity guides to help students learn from textbooks. *Journal of Reading, 29,* 489–494.

Estes, T. H., & Vaughan, J. L. (1978). *Reading and learning in the content classroom.* Boston: Allyn & Bacon.

Freire, P. (1985). *The politics of education.* South Hadley, MA: Bergin & Garvey Publishers.

Fry, E. (1972). *Reading instruction for classroom and clinic.* New York: McGraw-Hill.

Gray, W. S. (1960). The major aspects of reading. In H. Robinson (Ed.), *Development of reading abilities* (Supplemental Educational Monograph No. 90, pp. 8–24). Chicago: University of Chicago Press.

Herber, H. L. (1978). *Teaching reading in content areas* (2nd ed., pp. 43–49). Englewood Cliffs, NJ: Prentice-Hall.

Johnston, P., & Pearson, P. D. (1982). *Prior knowledge, connectivity, and the assessment of reading comprehension* (Technical Report No. 245). Urbana, IL: University of Illinois, Center for the Study of Reading.

Joyce, B. R., & Weil, M. (1986). *Models of teaching* (3rd ed.). Englewood Cliffs, NJ: Prentice-Hall.

McLaughlin, G. H. (1969). SMOG grading—A new readability formula. *Journal of Reading, 12,* 639–646.

Nelson-Herber, J. (1986, April). Expanding and refining vocabulary in content areas. *Journal of Reading, 29,* 626–633.

Niles, O. S., & Memory, D. (1977). *Reading tactics, teachers guide.* Glenview, IL: Scott-Foresman.

Pearson, P. D., Hansen, J., & Gordon, C. (1979). The effect of background knowledge on young children's comprehension of explicit and implicit information. *Journal of Reading Behavior, 12,* 201–209.

Pearson, P. D., & Johnson, D. D. (1978). *Teaching reading comprehension.* New York: Holt, Rinehart & Winston.

Raygor, A. (1977). The Raygor readability estimate: A quick and easy way to determine difficulty. In P. D. Pearson & J. Hansen (Eds.), *Reading theory, research and practice* (26th Yearbook, pp. 259–263). Clemson, SC: National Reading Conference.

Readence, J. E., Bean, T. W., & Baldwin, R. S. (1981). *Content area reading: An integrated approach.* Dubuque, IA: Kendall-Hunt.

Reynolds, R. E., Taylor, M. A., Steffenson, M. S., Shirey, L. L., & Anderson, R. C. (1983). Cultural schemata and reading comprehension. *Reading Research Quarterly, 17,* 353–356.

Rosenshine, B. V. (1980). Skill hierarchies in reading comprehension. In R.

Spiro, B. Bruce, & W. Brewer (Eds.), *Theoretical issues in reading comprehension.* Hillsdale, NJ: Erlbaum.

Smith, F. (1975). *Comprehension and learning.* New York: Holt, Rinehart & Winston.

Smith, F. (1978). *Understanding reading.* New York: Holt, Rinehart & Winston.

Smith, R. J., & Dauer, V. L. (1984, November). A comprehension-monitoring strategy for reading content area materials. *Journal of Reading, 28,* 144–147.

Thompson, L. C., & Frager, A. M. (1984, November). Teaching critical thinking: Guidelines for teacher-designed content area lessons. *Journal of Reading, 28,* 122–127.

Chapter Nine

Writing and Thinking
in the Social Studies

Effective social studies teachers emphasize the connection between thinking, especially higher-order thinking, and writing, which aligns content and process.

The social studies department had been all abuzz lately about the new program the principal wanted to implement in both the middle and high school: writing across the curriculum. The principal had attended a workshop on this topic recently and had since asked one teacher from each academic area to meet with her to discuss what she had learned. Will Wright volunteered to be the social studies department delegate, and he was to inform the other social studies teachers about the new program. Will himself had attended a few workshops on the topic that had been held at the local and state social studies conferences over the past couple of years, and some of the ideas presented there had excited him. Excerpts from his meeting with the social studies department follow.

WILL: Well, the meeting with the principal was a good one. Except for one teacher, we agreed that we all need to work on teaching more writing.

ELLEN: Will, I've been teaching writing for years! My kids have had to do reports, including book reports on historical figures every now and then, and all my tests include at least one, maybe two essays. I grade them with a fine-tooth comb.

ANDY: Well, I guess I've been teaching writing, too, then, if giving essay questions is teaching writing. I'm not into grammar, punctuation, and making corrections, though. I just grade for content. I'm not an English teacher. That's what those folks are supposed to do.

WILL: Wait! We all have assigned reports and given essays on tests and then graded them, but look at what we haven't done: taught the kids *how* to write, that big chunk between assigning and evaluating their writing. In the meeting I attended, this very topic was discussed, and the research we were shown indicates that the only way we teachers have tried to "teach" writing is by the comments or the grades we put on the students' writing [Bader & Pearce, 1983, p. 102].

ANDY: Will, obviously you didn't hear me. We are social studies teachers, not English teachers. I couldn't begin to teach about form, style, structure, and whatever else English teachers cover when they teach writing. I'm embarrassed to admit this, but I didn't do so well in English comp in college, and I haven't written much since. I had an anxiety attack last year when I had to write the report to the Board of Ed on the new Grade 12 syllabus and got my wife to revise it for me. She sure made a lot of good changes.

WILL: Andy, I'm glad you brought up the point about revising. Real writers spend hours revising, yet most of us accept the first draft from students. We accept it and return it either all marked up—some would say we do an autopsy on each student's paper—or with just a letter grade assigned. Some of us grade on mechanics, others on content, and some on both. But I'll bet none of us really grades the students' writing *ability.*

MARTHA: Will, the bell is going to ring in a few minutes, but I want you to know that I do support everything you've said, and I'm willing to go along with a writing plan if the whole school does. Otherwise, we'll just be lumped along with the English teachers as those who are to teach writing, whereas kids need writing work in all their classes. What's our next step?

WILL: Thanks, Martha. I'm glad you're interested in this writing-across-the-curriculum plan. But I need support from the rest of you. Are we all willing to get involved as a department in an inservice program on better teaching of writing? [The usual silence (the "I'm not so sure now is the right time") and moans and groans followed. But Will pressed and got a positive response after Sarah reminded the group that they had been complaining all along about the poor writing of their students on essay tests, and it wasn't going to change until and unless the teachers learned how to teach writing more effectively. "We have nothing to lose," she reasoned.]

As the preceding dialog points out, the study of the teaching of writing is a fairly new topic for social studies teachers. Yet for language teachers, it has been a concern for hundreds of years. Rhetoric, or the study of the principles and rules of speaking and writing, was a major focus of the Greeks, for effective communication then, as now, enables one not only to learn but to pass on knowledge—to teach ideas to others.

Unfortunately, American schools have not viewed writing as having that purpose. Think about it: Most of what you wrote in junior or senior high school was written for teachers, and it was telling those teachers what they already knew. In other words, the emphasis was not on writing as a learning tool but on displaying acquired knowledge (Applebee, 1981, p. 101). Thus, there has been little emphasis on using writing as a vehicle for learning or thinking.

This chapter focuses on the purposes of writing by (1) examining the connections between writing and learning and writing and thinking, (2) reviewing some of the research on the teaching of writing, and (3) giving some suggestions on how to develop effective writing activities for your social studies classes.

CONNECTIONS BETWEEN WRITING AND LEARNING

Again think back to those writing assignments you had in middle school social studies. No doubt they were what the teacher referred to as a "report" or a "project." The latter usually meant projects to which you added pictures, a colored folder, and several extra pages front and back to make it appear longer. Often the writing was copied verbatim from a magazine article (*National Geographic* was usually a first choice) or, more likely, from an encyclopedia. You probably didn't copy the entire article; you copied only what you understood and found interesting. David Welton refers to this type of writing as "pseudowriting" and reminds us that the only learning that came from such assignments probably was incidental at best (Welton, 1982, pp. 444–445).

Another common type of writing assignment was the high school term paper, perhaps done for Honors English in preparation for college. You learned how to develop a bibliography, take notes on cards, write a draft, and revise (and, having no idea what was expected, you checked the spelling of a few words and asked your mother about the commas). At last you handed in the final draft, thoroughly sick of the whole thing. By then you had probably convinced yourself that you'd never write another term paper ("If that's what college is about, maybe I'll work in a factory instead"), or at least never read another word on the topic you wrote about. Then came the days of waiting for the paper to be read, graded, and returned by your teacher. It was returned with few comments and an unexplained grade ("C? Why C? What's wrong with this?"), or it looked like it had just come off the operating table, dripping with red. Instantly it occurred to you that you would never make it in college (and factory work did pay well).

Those writing activities—called "essays"—that always followed the multiple-choice questions on a social studies test were another dread for some and a waste of time for others. You may have been one of those students who "froze" when you got to that part of the test because you never did well on "essays." On the other hand, your best friend never understood your panic, for she felt the essays were easier than the multiple choice: "Just tell the teacher everything you remember that relates to the topic in the question, and write neatly. She'll think you know it. That's what I do, and I always get a good grade."

After looking at some of those "essay questions," we agree with your friend. The questions really don't ask students to do any thinking and thus no new learning. Most social studies essay questions ask for a regurgitation of facts that were emphasized in class; students who simply connect some facts in sentence form generally do well. For example, here is a typical "essay" question:

Immigrants came to the U.S. in the late 1800s from several European countries and for many different reasons. List any five countries immigrants came from during that time, and *explain* three reasons why they came.

Hardly any thought had to go into answering that question. Students were no doubt given a list of countries as well as reasons for immigration during the teacher's lecture on the material. Or they gleaned the information from their textbooks as they answered the end-of-chapter review questions.

In this chapter, you will learn how to develop writing activities that will make your students use the higher-order thinking skills of application, analysis, synthesis, and evaluation and help them to learn on their own. We will discuss the composing process and what research tells us about how to improve the teaching of writing.

RESEARCH ON TEACHING WRITING

"Performance in writing in our schools is, quite simply, bad," says Archie Lapointe, executive director of the National Assessment of Educational Progress, in his introduction to *The Writing Report Card: Writing Achievement in America's Schools* (Applebee, Langer, & Mullis, 1986, p. 3). This survey, mandated by Congress, has been conducted every five years since 1969 with 4th, 8th, and 11th graders. In 1984, 55,000 public and private school students completed the test. The survey consists of four main areas: analytic writing (compare and contrast), persuasive writing, short responses based on personal experiences, and story writing. Only 18% of all eighth graders tested were rated adequate or better, with 82% only minimal or better. For 11th graders the number increased somewhat, with 25% writing adequately or better but 85% doing only minimally or better (Applebee, Langer, & Mullis, 1986, p. 9).

The report also notes that "students at all grade levels are deficient in higher-order thinking skills," but higher writing performance came from students who did more planning, revising, and editing, that is, used the composing process and wrote three or more reports and essays during a six-week period (Applebee, Langer, & Mullis, 1986, pp. 10, 11). Further, writing must be expected in *all* classes, not just English class. Thus, in addition to using the composing process and writing more frequently, the remedy consists of implementing "writing across the curriculum" and teaching students how to think more effectively as they write (Applebee, Langer, & Mullis, 1986, pp. 11–12).

Other research on student writing illustrates similar results and prescriptions. In sum, students must write more frequently and use different forms. The typical essay question mentioned earlier will not help students either learn how to write or learn how to learn using higher-order thinking skills.

THINKING SKILLS

Educators typically organize thinking skills into different categories or camps, including (1) critical-thinking and creative-thinking skills, (2) convergent, divergent, and evaluative thinking skills (Orlich et al., 1985, p. 169), and (3) deductive or inductive (inquiry) skills (see Chapter 4). Beyer (1987) refers to these skills as skills of problem solving, decision making, conceptualizing, microthinking, and specific critical-thinking skills.

In the 1980s, critics claimed that most students do not know these skills and those who do do not know how to use them. Some would say that too many teachers involve students in only convergent thinking skills, which actually entail little thinking beyond mere recall. Questions that demand convergent thinking tend to have an implicit correct answer; "student responses converge or focus on a central theme" and "elicit short responses from students" (Orlich et al., 1985, p. 169). Divergent thinking, on the other hand, gives students opportunities to formulate several new answers to a question. Divergent questions demand that students think at a higher level: analysis, synthesis, and evaluation. For example, a writing assignment in which the student plays the role of a public policy expert and prepares a speech for the Democratic National Convention Platform Committee comparing and contrasting the merits of a national health insurance plan involves divergent thinking. There are no pat answers; the assignment requires the student to analyze, synthesize, and evaluate when preparing the speech.

The above assignment is indeed an evaluative one, for the student makes a *judgment*, in this case a potential policy. Another example would be to have the student assume the role of a freelance journalist in New York City who is assigned to write a column for a midwestern newspaper examining the increase of acid rain in New York State's Adirondack Mountains. The student would have to make a judgement about the situation in which the Midwest is seen as the villain in creating acid rain in the East.

The connection between thinking and writing is thus quite obvious. Students don't just learn to think; they must think about something, that is, *content*. Writing helps one to think, for writing forces one to organize one's thoughts, to think logically and sequentially, to develop a stand or opinion on a topic, and to communicate those thoughts to others. Indeed, "writing is thinking" and we must remember that writing "is not simply a reflection of learning, but an important road to it" (Rosenberg, 1984, pp. 57, 58).

Elbow (1983, pp. 37–38), in stressing the connection between writing and thinking, feels that we teach thinking by teaching writing. However, he has his own terms to describe thinking skills. *First-order thinking*, he writes, "is intuitive and creative and does not strive for conscious direction or control." It is this type of thinking that "brings out people's best and most intelligent thinking." Elbow sees prewriting, especially free or expressive writing, as first-order creative thinking. This is followed by *second-order thinking*, "conscious, directed, controlled thinking" that is committed to accuracy and strives for logic and control. Revising and rewriting involve second-order thinking, for students are consciously criticizing their work to improve it. *

---

*Quoted material from "Teaching Thinking by Teaching Writing" by P. Elbow, September 1983, *Change*, *15*, pp. 37–38. Reprinted by permission of Heldref Publications.

Writing is recursive (see page 263), and some researchers feel that both "thinking and writing are recursive processes" (Olson, 1984). Like Elbow, Olson sees the thinking and writing processes as directly connected. Using Bloom's taxonomy, Olson argues,

> [T]he thinking process recapitulates the writing process and vice versa. . . . To produce a composition, writers must tap memory to establish what they know, review the information they have generated and translate it into inner speech or print, organize main ideas into a logical sequence, discover specific support for those main ideas, re-see the whole to find a focus, construct a structural framework for communicating an intended message, transform this network of thought into a written paper, and evaluate the product.*

So how do we begin to teach students how to write so that they will learn as they write, develop higher-order thinking skills, and rid themselves of "write fright" to the point of even enjoying writing?**

ASIDE TO THE READER: Did you ever have "write fright?" If so, how did you deal with it?

FUNCTIONS OF WRITING: EXPRESSIVE, TRANSACTIONAL, AND POETIC

Research from England shows that most of the writing that teachers assign students falls into the category of *transactional* writing—writing that is typical of "planning, reporting, instructing, informing, advising, persuading, arguing and theorizing" (Martin, D'Arcy, Newton, & Parker, 1976, p. 25). However, students may feel too far removed from this type of writing; that is, they may be unable to "get into it."

The second category of writing established by Martin et al. is *expressive* writing, which allows students to use their own "voice" and, perhaps, their own experiences. It is also a form of prewriting, giving students an opportunity to get their own "juices" flowing about a topic in preparation for a piece of transactional writing.

The third category of writing, according to Martin et al., is *poetic* writing. This means writing in a different genre, which permits students to go above and beyond transactional writing by experimenting more heavily with language while remaining within the social studies content.

---

*From "Fostering Critical Thinking Skills Through Writing" by C. B. Olson, November 1984, *Educational Leadership,* 42, p. 32.

**"Write fright" is a term coined by Richard Ross, M.S.Ed., State University of New York at Binghamton, who is an English teacher at Livingston Manor, N.Y.

FIGURE 9.1
Illustrative Writing Assignments

Writing Activities for a Unit on Religion in the Middle Ages*
Expressive writing assignment: *(Students engage in this writing activity a few days before the transactional assignment or even before a study of the Middle Ages.)* In your own words, describe one experience in your life that was influenced significantly either directly or indirectly by religion.

Transactional writing assignment: *(Students do this writing activity following a study of the Middle Ages.)* In our study of the religious, political, and cultural activities of the Roman Catholic Church during the Middle Ages, it became evident that the church exerted significant influence within the community. You have just been elected Pope. The feeling among the church hierarchy is that the community is losing faith. Create a church doctrine to change the tide of community sentiment. Include in your doctrine (1) the use of excommunication and the Inquisition to restore order and (2) the social and economic consequences of breaking wtih the church. You will present this new doctrine to the College of Cardinals.

Poetic writing assignment: *(This would be assigned either in place of the transactional assignment or as a supplement to it.)* During the Middle Ages, the Roman Catholic Church was both a unifying force and a divisive force within the community. You are a medieval poet. Write a poem in either rhyme or free verse with the title "Nurturant Parasite." Express in your poem the contradiction between church belief and church practice.

Writing Activities for a Unit on Unions/Labor Relations**
Expressive writing assignment: *(Students engage in this activity prior to studying the topic.)* You have just landed your first job. You will be working for General Motors on the truck assembly line. Write a letter to your brother or sister that describes your job. Tell him/her how much you expect to be paid, what kinds of benefits you will receive, and what working conditions are like in the factory.

Figure 9.1 presents illustrative assignments using the three categories of writing in various social studies contexts.

THE COMPOSING PROCESS

There is a specific process geared to writing well—to producing a final product. *Composing* emphasizes the process of writing rather than just the final draft. The version of the composing process that we will examine here consists of from four to six parts, falling under three main rubrics: the prewriting stage, the drafting (the actual writing) stage, and the postwriting stage (see Figure 9.2).

Prewriting Stage

The *prewriting stage* is the getting-ready-to-write phase, or the rehearsal. There are many ways to get ready for writing.

Brainstorming is an effective technique. It is best used in small groups or in full class, but it can also be used individually. Following is a three-step

Transactional writing assignment: You are a member of the union at General Motors. You go to a union meeting and take your tape recorder. The topic of discussion is grievances and the new contract. You tape the meeting and play it back. Write down what you hear on the tape.

Poetic writing assignment: Find a book that reprints the lyrics to songs written by Pete Seeger, Woody Guthrie, etc. Find a song that deals with workers or labor protests. Using this song as a guide, write words to the music that deal with another aspect of labor unrest.

Writing Activities for a Miniunit on Political Campaigning
Expressive writing assignment: *(This activity is assigned prior to studying campaigning.)* Imagine that you are going to run for office in your city, county, state, or the U.S. Jot down some of the campaign slogans you might develop to bolster your candidacy.

Transactional writing assignment: *(To be done after studying campaigning.)* You have been hired as campaign manager for a local, state, or national candidate. Develop the campaign strategy you will present to the candidate.

Poetic writing assignment: Your candidate wants to use a popular song for a theme song. Write the words for a campaign song using a popular tune.

*Writing Activities for a Miniunit on Political Campaigning***
Expressive writing assignment: *(This activity is assigned prior to studying campaigning.)* Imagine that diary of someone working at the worst type of job you can think of.

Transactional writing assignment: *(Students do this activity after studying the Industrial Revolution.)* Write a journal entry for your first week in a workhouse of a 19th-century English factory.

Poetic writing assignment: Write a play about children working in a 19th-century London factory.

*These lessons were developed by Michael Piccirillo, M.A.T. candidate at the State University of New York at Binghamton and social studies teacher at the Pottersville Middle School, Pottersville, New York.
**These lessons were developed by Rebecca Hemzik, M.A.T., 1987, State University of New York at Binghamton, who teaches at Chenango Valley (New York) High School. The lessons were written for a high school class of slower learners.

prewriting activity for an assignment to establish the pros and cons of giving aid to the new goverments in Eastern Europe.

Step 1: Brainstorming: Individually, students develop a list of the pros and cons of U.S. aid to the new governments in Eastern Europe.
Step 2: Students meet in groups of three to share and modify lists.
Step 3: The teacher leads a full-class discussion on the students' results.

Following this activity, students write a first draft.
Other prewriting techniques include the following:

1. *Free writing:* Students engage in a content-related, but not content-bound, writing activity, letting their words flow as in the expressive writing example on the Middle Ages in Figure 9.1. Another example, this

FIGURE 9.2
The Composing Process

Stage 1: Prewriting
• Free writing, expressive writing, journals
• Questioning
• Discussion
• Role play, simulation
• Use of visuals, media

Stage 2: Drafting
• Definite purpose for writing
• Definite audience for writing

Stage 3: Postwriting
• Self-evaluation
• Peer evaluation (paired learning)
• Small-group writer's workshop
• Revising/rewriting
• Editing
• Publication

time for a writing activity on cities of the Middle Ages, might be: "Describe your perfect imaginary city" or "Write a few paragraphs about why you would like to live in _____ (any city you choose)."

2. *Questioning:* This could be part of a full-class or small-group activity. An example for the Middle Ages unit might be: "What factors would make a city a worthwhile place in which to live? What are some problems that all cities have? What are some advantages of living in cities over living in rural areas or small towns? What are some disadvantages?"

3. *Discussion:* In either small-group or full-class discussion, students could engage in debate on any of the questions listed above or on other questions. A possible example relating to the Middle Ages topic is: "In what ways and why was the Roman Catholic Church able to gain so much control over so many people?"

4. *Role play or simulation:* The teacher has two student volunteers sit up front facing each other. One will be a Catholic priest, the other a dissenter. For about five minutes, the two students discuss the increasingly tight control of the people by the Church. (For a review of role play and simulation, see Chapter 4.)

5. *Use of visuals and media:* The teacher passes around or projects several pictures or slides of different scenes in cities of the Middle Ages. Students comment on the pictures/slides, perhaps comparing and contrasting them to cities today.

Drafting Stage

After students have engaged in a prewriting activity, it's time for them to write the first draft—and we emphasize *first*. Often teachers accept a student's first draft as the final draft because (1) they haven't encouraged students to write more than one draft and (2) they haven't given them the opportunity to learn how to improve the first draft. But the composing process gives students that opportunity.

In the *drafting* stage, students begin their drafts, drawing on notes, ideas, or a piece of free writing created during the prewriting stage. But during the drafting stage, the writing activity is *recursive*; that is, students continually revise as they write. They go "in and out of" the writing as they think—again, the connection between writing and thinking—changing a word or a phrase or perhaps even a sentence as they prepare the first draft. Indeed, writing *is* thinking. As Donald Gray has written, "Writing is a record of the mind in the act of knowing" (Gray, 1988, p. 729).

Historically, the drafting phase of the composing process has been the most difficult for students. Just putting pen to paper (or fingers to keyboard) has been particularly arduous in the case of "school writing," that is, writing to fulfill an assignment. Applebee reminds us, however, that it is not the writing that is difficult but the "nature of the writing task" (Applebee, 1981, p. 2).

No doubt you have noticed that most students have no problem whatsoever writing notes to pass to classmates or writing long letters to boyfriends or girlfriends whom they see 10 or more times a day in school.

Therefore, we need to assign students better prewriting and drafting tasks—not the bland "essays" of the past but activities that students will perform more willingly because they see the activities (assignments, if you will) as ones that will stretch their minds, that they can succeed at, or that will be just plain fun to do. Thus, our writing assignments must meet these criteria.

What types of assignments should these be? First, the assignment should be interesting enough that students will see it as worth doing. Second, it must have an audience other than the teacher. Several studies show that student assignments that have a real or even imaginary audience other than the teacher are better written (e.g., Martin et al., 1976, pp. 132–140; Applebee, 1981, p. 5). Yet Martin et al. (1976, p. 21) found that in history and geography classes, 69% and 81%, respectively, of writing was for the teacher/examiner only. Thus, the message to students is that the real purpose for writing is grading, not learning (Martin et al., 1976, p. 22). We will turn to evaluating student writing later in this chapter.

In middle and high school, what did you think were the purposes of the writing assignments you were given?

Postwriting Stage

Contrary to what students probably think based on experience, the writing is not over once they have completed the first draft. In fact, the real work of writing has just begun, for this final stage, *postwriting*, has several components.

Sharing the First Draft.   The first step in the postwriting stage is sharing the draft with peers. This may occur in a paired learning situation (two students working together), small-group writer's workshop, or writer's circle (to be explained shortly). One of the best ways to begin is to have the author read his or her draft aloud to a partner or small group. A major advantage of this procedure is that the writer will self-correct while reading. Long, convoluted, or even run-on sentences will first be picked up here as the writer/reader becomes aware of the errors.

Peer(s) will serve as the first reactor(s) to the spoken or written word; that is, students may exchange papers and read their partners' papers silently. Often, however, students don't know what to look for or what kind of advice to give their classmates. Therefore, the first few times you have students review one another's papers, you may wish to prepare a reader's review guide. This can be as simple or as complex (but not too complex) as you feel they need to be. You should phrase them so that they emphasize positive, constructive comments. For example, at first the guide may pose only three to five questions, such as

1. What do you like best about your classmate's paper?
2. Which part of the draft needs the least amount of work?
3. What suggestions for improvement can you make?

Besides the paired-learning review, students may engage in small-group discussion of one another's papers. This technique is often called a *writer's circle* or *writer's workshop*. An example of this is *cycle writing,* based on an idea from Ann Gebhard (Gebhard, 1983). Here students meet in groups of three after they have written their first drafts. Each member of the group, in turn, enacts all three roles: reader, reactor, and prescriber. The *reader* reads her own draft to the group, self-correcting as she goes along. The *reactor* summarizes what he believes are the reader's main ideas and gives a general, holistic reaction to the draft—what he likes, what needs improvement, and so on. Then the *prescriber* makes suggestions for the second draft. For example, the prescriber might suggest that the writing have a more forceful beginning, get to the point sooner, or provide more descriptive details of a particular portion. The reader has an opportunity to respond to her critics before writing her second draft, which typically is an in-class or homework assignment.

Then the three students exchange roles: The reactor becomes the reader, the reader the prescriber, and the prescriber the reactor. To complete the first cycle, the third person in the group reads his or her draft and listens to the reactions and directions from classmates. After the three students have revised their drafts, they meet again to do the same activity for cycle two and, if time permits, cycle three.

By the time the teacher receives the final draft, all the students have had the benefit of advice from their peers and time to edit their drafts for mechanical errors such as spelling, punctuation, and syntax.

Have you ever engaged in a writer's circle? If so, what was your reaction?

Revising and Rewriting. The revising/rewriting component of the post-writing stage has been considered the most important one, the one in which students really learn how to write: "Revision is the key to the writing process" (Balajthy, 1986); "[R]evision may be the most crucial part of the process for encouraging mature writing" (Gebhard, 1983, p. 211). Yet research indicates that this is the component that most teachers do not teach.

Although we emphasize that revision occurs during the postwriting stage, it actually occurs throughout the three stages in a recursive manner (Butler-Nalin, 1984, p. 121; Farris, 1987; Applebee, 1984; Balajthy, 1986). But what precisely do we mean by *revision*? Do students interpret that process the same way their teachers do?

Two research studies on revision indicate that fewer than half of all students ever revise (Abrams, 1988, pp. 27, 29; Butler-Nalin, 1984, p. 123). They may edit, however, correcting mechanical mistakes—spelling, punctuation, word choice, and maybe sentence structure—for students see editing as revising. While editing is a part of revising, revising itself is a developmental, complex skill that teachers appear not to teach (Flower, Hayes, Carey, Schriver, & Stratman, 1986, p. 15).

Revising means to resee, to take a second look at, to go back and survey, "to read over carefully and correct, improve, or update; to change or amend," according to Webster. One student has put it succinctly: "To say what she meant to say and to say it so the reader could understand her better" (Hauser, 1986, p. 153). In other words, one revises for intention and convention— *intention* to make a point, to convince the reader of the writer's point of view, and *convention* to follow the rules of writing so that communication will occur between the writer and the reader.

Yet students have difficulty revising, because they don't know what it means to revise or how to do it (Calkins, 1986, p. 185). Butler-Nalin (1984) has proposed that for the most part students are concerned only with what they see as the "proper presentation of material"—the conventions of writing. However, the more demanding the task, the more revising occurs. In general, that is tied to the notion of audience; nearly 60% of all papers addressed to an audience other than the teacher were significantly revised (Butler-Nalin, 1984, p. 123).

A study by Abrams (1988), a middle school teacher, illustrated that revising must be taught: Students do not learn how to revise on their own. Unless we teach them how to revise, students will merely edit their papers. Abrams analyzed the first and second drafts of a social studies writing assignment of 19 fifth graders. His students had used the process approach to writing for over a year, and they had written the second draft after they had met in groups and were told "to revise their writing" in groups. Abrams compared the first and second drafts and then interviewed each student about the revision process. The 19 first drafts had contained a total of 159 sentences. But after the group revising process, 111 sentences (or 70%) remained exactly the same in meaning from first to second draft. However, 71 of the 159 sentences showed improvements that did not alter the meaning of the text. The improvements were in word choice or corrected spelling only—the conventions of writing.

Abrams' interviews with the students inform us that "each student operated with a different understanding of what revision meant." Most saw it related to correcting spelling and punctuation. Twelve of the 19 expressed negative views about revision. The only real reason they perceived for seriously revising their work was to communicate with an audience other than the teacher. Then they would be more concerned about intentions and not just writing conventions (Abrams, 1988, p. 38).

Evidently, teachers have emphasized the conventions of writing rather than the intent of a piece of writing. The role of the audience—a real audience—is important to students' writing.

So how do we teach revising? Several writers agree that it is important that the "real" writing come through the revising. Elbow (1981, p. 9) refers to this part of writing as the *critical* act as opposed to the *creative* act, which the prewriting and first draft constitute.

Elbow (1981, pp. 123—124) suggests two major steps by which students can learn how to revise. First, students should practice revising one another's work (this is easier than hacking away at one's own). Then they can see what does and does not work for someone else's writing and apply this knowledge to their own work. Second, students should engage in collaborative writing, revising one another's work in groups of three.* But this differs from the usual writer's workshop approach. In Elbow's prewriting stage, the three students first discuss their ideas. Then student A writes the first draft. Next, all three students discuss the draft and student B writes the second draft. All three discuss the second draft, and then student C writes the next-to-final

Writing with Power (pp. 123—124) by P. Elbow, 1981, New York: Oxford University Press.

draft. The group revises and edits this draft. Then either A, B, or C writes the final draft, the result of all students' contributions.

Abrams (1988) concluded that to improve writing,

- All assignments must have an audience other than the teacher.
- If a writer's workshop (composed of small revising groups) is used, students should receive written guidelines to help them help one another. These guidelines should deemphasize the mechanics of writing.
- The teacher needs to provide assignments that require students to use the higher-level thinking skills, which will demand more of them while allowing them to be more creative. (pp. 35–39)

How many drafts do you typically prepare before the final one? Where did you learn to revise? What revision techniques can you offer students?

Editing. As indicated above, to most students revising/rewriting and editing are the same. But in fact they are not, for in the editing stage one merely checks to see whether a word is used or spelled correctly and whether other standard conventions of writing have been followed. It is better if a classmate edits a peer's paper. Even professional writers have editors who go over their submitted drafts.

Publishing. The final component of the postwriting stage is publishing. Now that does not mean that the teacher is expected to help students write so well that their work gets into *Social Education* (although once in awhile some may). We are talking about a different type of publishing wherein the writing gets a real audience, that is, an audience other than the teacher: Other people receive it, read it, hear it, or see it.

Recall that earlier in this chapter we presented the results of studies showing that most of the writing students do—what we call "school writing"—is for the teacher only. We also said that students write better if they are writing for an audience other than the teacher (Martin et al., 1976). So the type of publishing we are talking about "connects" with an audience, real or imaginary people to whom the students' writing is addressed.

An example in a typical social studies class would be to have students "role play" recent immigrants and write letters to their "families" back in the old country about their experiences in the United States. In a government class, students might write and mail letters to their congressional representative complaining about the lack of a national health care system. Still another type of publishing would consist of posting the writing in the classroom or even in a school showcase for all to see. It is amazing how much interest students take in reading one another's work. At the same time, they learn more about writing and content by seeing how someone else puts words together.

The postwriting stage, which includes "publishing," begins the real work of composing.

Figure 9.3 illustrates a lesson using the composing process. Note that in the second example we have the first mention of evaluating writing for a grade. Evaluating writing in the social studies class is a complex area, to which we now turn.

ASSIGNING AND EVALUATING STUDENT WRITING IN SOCIAL STUDIES

Assigning Student Writing

Did you notice that the writing assignments illustrated so far in this chapter have not specified a particular length or emphasized the teacher's grading criteria? There are some definite reasons for that. Let's look at two all too typical social studies writing assignments, one for middle school and the other for high school.

First, here is middle school assignment (the students have been learning about the settling of the Thirteen Colonies):

Write an essay describing the New England, the Middle Atlantic, and the Southern Colonies. Make sure you write in complete

FIGURE 9.3
Illustrative Lesson Using the Composing Process

Example 1*
Concept/content area: constitutional government
Skills to be developed: synthesizing and evaluating in group
Purpose: students will work successfully in small groups to develop a constitution for the school
Audience: classmates, school faculty and administrators

Prewriting: Students review and discuss the constitutions that they have studied. They discuss the difficulties of framing such a document and how constitutions affect their lives. They can also brainstorm ideas about what makes a good constitution.
Drafting: Working in groups of three or four, students attempt to write a viable constitution for students in their school. The document must not contradict education law, state regulations, or school policy (research in each area will be necessary). Together students decide what should be included in their constitution using those they have studied as models. After getting the basic idea into writing and agreeing on what will be included, each student writes a constitution. As a group, students combine the best parts of each student's constitution and create a complete constitution incorporating a preamble, bill of rights, and any amendments they deem necessary.
Postwriting. This constitution will be presented to the other students in class, the student government, faculty, and administrators as a viable constitution for the school.

Example 2 (A Middle School Lesson)
Concept/content area: women's history, discrimination
Skill to be developed: letter writing, persuasive writing
Purpose: Students will become aware of sexism in the past and present; students will be able to explain why women should be allowed to become doctors
Audience: medical school admissions office

Prewriting: The class has been studying famous women in history, including Dr. Elizabeth Blackwell. Either in full class or small groups, students are asked to name as many famous women from the past as they can think of; then they are to name as many of today's famous women as they can. The teacher compiles the two lists on the board and leads students in a discussion of why their list of women years ago is so much shorter than their list of today's women.
Drafting: The teacher tells students, "Pretend that you were Elizabeth Blackwell in 1848. Write a letter to a medical school explaining why you should be admitted."

---

*This lesson was developed by Laura Atwell, M.A.T., 1985, State University of New York at Binghamton, New York, and a teacher at John Jay High School, Katonah, New York.

sentences, have at least 200 words, and use correct spelling, grammar, and punctuation.

So what's wrong with this? At least three things.

First, the word *essay.* What does that mean? *Essay* is one of those words so misused in schools, for it is used to mean an answer composed of several sentences or a few paragraphs. However, an essay really is "an analytical or interpretive literary composition usually dealing with its subject from a lim-

FIGURE 9.3
continued

Postwriting:
1. Revising/rewriting: Each student selects a partner. Working in pairs, each student either reads his or her draft aloud or reads the partner's draft silently. Students make constructive comments about their partners' content and the writing itself. The teacher may provide students with some written guidelines to use during the process. Then students rewrite based on the input from their classmates.
2. Editing/proofreading: In the same paired-learning situation, students help each other correct spelling and punctuation. Dictionaries, thesauruses, textbooks, the teacher, and other students may be consulted as resources.
3. Evaluating: Using written guidelines, students meet in pairs or trios and review their partners' papers by either reading them aloud or exchanging them and reading them silently. The teacher will later collect and evaluate the papers according to the assignment.
4. Publishing: Volunteers read their papers to the entire class. Letters will be posted on the bulletin board.

Example 3**
Concept/content area: feudalism
Skill to be developed: descriptive/instructional writing
Purpose: students will better understand the role of the knight in feudal society
Audience: a "squire"; classmates

Prewriting: All students have read the text and an additional selection on knights, such as tales from King Arthur, an excerpt from *Men of Iron,* or other writings on knighthood. Individually or in small groups, students list the duties of a knight.
Drafting: Each student writes a short instructional manual from a knight to a squire to help in the latter's training.
Postwriting: Students divide into two or three groups. Each manual is read, and a different student is chosen to play the role of the squire in each case. After the reading, the role player acts out or describes what he or she sees as the role player's duty according to the manual.
1. Revising: The writer will become cognizant of weaknesses and strengths in his or her writing from the preceding activity and be able to revise accordingly.
2. Editing: Editing is done in pairs in class. Dictionaries, thesauruses, and grammar handbooks are available. The teacher also serves as a resource.
3. Publishing: All final drafts are put on the classroom bulletin board and identified with a number to facilitate student ranking by secret ballot. The teacher assigns grades in accordance with this ranking.

**This lesson was developed by Robert Bowker, M.S.T., 1988, State University of New York at Binghamton, New York, teacher at Christian Academy, Harford, Pennsylvania.

ited or personal point of view" (Webster's *New Collegiate Dictionary,* 1981). The above assignment hardly demands analysis; thus, it is not, in strictest terms, an essay question.

Next, the question itself is poor. In answering it, the student will create nothing new or original. It is a low-level, total-recall question demanding a response in sentence/paragraph form that could just as easily be given in list form. In other words, the student could just as well list attributes, both positive and negative, instead of wasting time writing the answer in composition form. The student is not being asked to learn anything or even to think about anything while forming a response to this "essay" question. Can you imagine a duller weekend than one during which you, the teacher, have to read 125 of these answers? They all will be the same. Reading them will be almost as boring as writing them was!

But there's more. Did you notice that the criteria the teacher provided as a guide for the student writer had nothing to do with social studies content? The teacher's message is that grading will be based on the mechanics of the paper turned in. A "complete sentences" request almost guarantees that the teacher will read nothing but short, choppy sentences. Students will dare not play around with language and perhaps try to put into practice all those comma rules they learned in English class, for they might make a mistake. Similarly, the "200-word minimum" will lead students to continually count while trying to get up to 200 words. Again the emphasis on content—social studies—has been put to side stage. "Correct spelling, grammar, and punctuation" will only reinforce students' reliance on short, familiar words (which probably will not include any new social studies vocabulary) that they know they can spell correctly. Likewise, they will fall back on short, single-independent-clause sentences bereft of commas. Thus, the teacher will get a poor essay—which is really what he or she has asked for. Yet the teacher will complain that the students "can't write well," use abrupt, simplistic sentences, and produce dull essays.

So how can the "essay" assignment be improved? Look at the following assignment, which requests basically the same content but in a more original way. The student can "get into" the writing, have fun with it, experiment with different forms of language and sentence structure, and ensure the teacher a more exciting "grading weekend":

> You are an agent for a land company in the Thirteen Colonies. Write a brochure that attempts to convince people to buy land or come to the area you represent (the New England colonies, the Middle Atlantic colonies, or the Southern colonies) rather than to the other two areas. You may wish to use drawings, pictures, colored paper, a small map, etc.

Wouldn't *you* prefer to read those "essays" over the weekend?

Now let's look at two assignments on the same topic for a high school class. Here is the first example:

> In a well-developed essay, explain why the U.S. should or should not give aid to the new East European governments. Use complete sentences, logical arguments, correct spelling, grammar, and punctuation, correct facts, and no fewer than 300 words.

Now here is the second assignment:

> You are a member of Congress opposed to (or in favor of) aid to the
> new east European governments. A vocal minority in your district
> disagrees with you and has won several voters to its point of view.
> Write the speech you will give back home in your district to
> convince your constituents of your view without losing their
> support. Hecklers are expected to attend.

We're sure you've already guessed why the second assignment is the better
one. Look at the higher-order thinking skills the students are to apply:
analysis, synthesis, and evaluation. As a result, they have to give facts and
organize their thoughts well or risk heckling or even losing the next election.
Doesn't the second question offer a more exciting prospect for both writer and
reader?

Evaluating Student Writing

After peers have reviewed the drafts and the writer has completed the final
editing, the teacher receives the paper for the summative evaluation. For the
most part, teachers in content areas say that they don't like to evaluate
student writing, even though they do it all the time. Their reasons are twofold:
(1) It takes too much time (recall that the typical high school teacher has
classes totaling 125 to 150 students), and (2) they feel unqualified to evaluate
writing, an area they see as the English teacher's bailiwick (Pearce, 1983, p.
212).

But evaluation comes with the territory. A better reason for evaluating
student writing is that it "helps students continue to learn content and skills
and helps them improve their writing" (Beyer & Brostoff, 1979, p. 195).

On the other hand, students tell us that they are not taught *how* to write;
rather, we simply give them directions on what *content* to write about and
what *form* to use. Therefore, is it fair to have teachers grade students' written
work? Students do expect a grade for their efforts, but in general they "are
rarely impressed by the helpfulness of their teacher's comments" (Marshall,
1984, p. 106). Most teachers grade the writing conventions—focusing on
form at the word and sentence level—and provide little to no guidance for
improvement.

Elaine Maimon (1988, p. 734) states that despite the emphasis on the
writing process over the final product, teachers tend to evaluate only the last
draft, the one that goes to the teacher-as-examiner. Of course, at this point it
is too late to be of any help. If, on the other hand, the teacher looked at the
first or second draft and saw it as "what you can make this become" (not "what
this is not"), his or her constructive comments would actually be an effective
way to teach writing.

Beyer and Brostoff (1979) agree with Maimon and urge teachers to comment on earlier drafts so that improvement can occur. They suggest that for

both earlier drafts and the final papers teachers read student papers holistically, that is, "read quickly through a written statement as a whole and judge it by our impression of the whole."* Teachers may also wish to cut down on the time it takes them to read so many papers while simultaneously improving the comments for students by engaging in a "primary trait evaluation," focusing, for example, on the main point of the assignment (Did the student respond adequately to the question? Did the student use appropriate persuasion techniques?). Third, teachers probably should focus on only one area of concern and not riddle the drafts with so many criticisms that students feel they will never be able to rewrite them adequately. For example, teachers can focus on the logical flow of students' arguments rather than on sentence structure, topic sentences, or use of writing conventions.

Maimon (1988, p. 738) and Pearce (1983, p. 215) also follow Beyer and Brostoff and recommend that teachers ask questions of the draft instead of making lengthy negative statements or shorthanding the comments. "Awk," "WC," "frag," and other such remarks do little to help the student correct the problem. If the student knew why the phrase was awkward, he or she probably wouldn't have used it.

Have you ever felt that professors' comments on your papers were a waste of your time? Were they ever beneficial? Think of some examples.

Finally, teachers should provide positive comments. Writing is so personal that pages and pages of negative feedback only discourage students from attempting to improve their writing, not to mention decreasing their self-esteem by several notches.

Earlier we referred to both self-evaluation and peer evaluation as steps in stage 3 of the composing process, the postwriting phase. We see no reason why the teacher has to read, evaluate, and grade each piece of completed written work. Students can learn to improve their own writing from reading other students' work, as Elbow (1981) reminded us earlier.

Summary

Although writing is not an easy task—for students *or* teachers—learning how to write using the process approach helps students begin to feel competent as writers. In addition, writing in the social studies is one more way that students learn to think, using higher-order thinking skills as they acquire social studies content. This meshing of content and process in writing—using language for a real purpose—enables students to see the value of writing: to persuade, to describe, to tell a story, and enjoy doing it. As

*"The Time It Takes: Managing/Evaluating Writing and Social Studies" by B. K. Beyer and A. Brostoff, March 1979, *Social Education,* 43, p. 195.

teachers, we must offer students exciting writing activities that will be read by persons other than the teacher-as-examiner. Research tells us that students' writing improves more readily as a result of peer evaluation than of teacher evaluation. Peer evaluation also helps students shed the "write fright" that they develop once their writing becomes content specific.

Decisions! Decisions!

1. Think back to your most exciting or stimulating writing assignment in middle or high school. Why was it so good?

2. Develop some convergent and some divergent questions. Then turn them into writing assignments.

3. Using any topic you like, prepare an expressive, a transactional, and a poetic writing assignment.

4. What type of help do you think you still need to effectively teach writing in the social studies? Where will you look for it?

5. What criteria will you use in evaluating students' writing? Why?

References

Abrams, J. (1988). *Teaching revision.* Unpublished master's thesis, State University of New York, Binghamton, NY.

Applebee, A. N. (1981). *Writing in the secondary school: English and the content areas.* Urbana, IL: National Council for Teachers of English.

Applebee, A. N. (1984, Winter). Writing and reasoning. *Review of Educational Research, 54,* 577–596.

Applebee, A. N., Langer, J. A., & Mullis, I. V. S. (1986). *The writing report card: Writing achievement in America's schools* (Report No. 15-W-02, National Assessment of Educational Progress). Princeton, NJ: Educational Testing Service.

Bader, L., & Pearce, D. L. (1983, May). Writing across the curriculum, 7–12. *English Education, 15,* 97–106.

Balajthy, E. (1986). *Do writers really revise? Encouraging unnatural acts in your classroom.* Paper presented at the Conference of Language and Literacy, Geneseo, NY. (ERIC Edu 274 997)

Beyer, B. K. (1987). *Practical strategies for the teaching of thinking.* Newtown, MA: Allyn & Bacon.

Beyer, B. K., & Brostoff, A. (1979, March). The time it takes: Managing/evaluating writing and social studies. *Social Education, 43,* 194–195.

Butler-Nalin, K. (1984). Revising patterns in students' writing. In A. N. Applebee (Ed.)., *Contexts for learning to write: Studies of secondary school instruction* (pp. 103–119). Norwood, NJ: ABLEX Publishing.

Calkins, L. M. (1986). *The art of teaching writing.* Portsmouth, NH: Heinemann.

Elbow, P. (1981). *Writing with power.* New York: Oxford University Press.

Elbow, P. (1983, September). Teaching thinking by teaching writing. *Change, 15,* 37–40.

Farris, C. R. (1987, October). Current composition: Beyond process and product. *English Journal, 76,* 28–34.

Flower, L., Hayes, J. R., Carey, L., Schriver, K., & Stratman, J. (1986, Fall). Directions, diagnosis, and the strategies of revision. *College Com-*

position and Communication, 37, 16–55.

Gebhard, A. O. (1983, December). Teaching writing in reading and the content areas. *Journal of Reading, 27,* 207–211.

Gray, D. J. (1988, June). Writing across the college curriculum. *Phi Delta Kappan, 69,* 729–733.

Hauser, C. (1986, February). The writer's inside story. *Language Arts, 63,* 153–159.

Maimon, E. P. (1988, June). Cultivating the prose garden. *Phi Delta Kappan, 69,* 734–739.

Marshall, J. D. (1984). Schooling and the composition process. In A. N. Applebee (Ed.), *Contexts for learning to write: Studies of secondary school instruction* (pp. 103–119). Norwood, NJ: ABLEX Publishing.

Martin, N., D'Arcy, P., Newton, B., & Parker, R. (1976). *Writing and learning across the curriculum, 11–16.* London: Ward Lock Educational.

Olson, C. B. (1984, November). Fostering critical thinking skills through writing. *Educational Leadership, 42,* 28–39.

Orlich, D. C., et al. (1985), *Teaching strategies: A guide to better instruction* (2nd Ed.). Lexington, MA: Heath.

Pearce, D. L. (1983, December). Guidelines for the use and evaluation of writing in content classrooms. *Journal of Reading, 27,* 212–218.

Rosenberg, V. M. (1984). Writing instruction: A view from across the curriculum. *Journal of General Education, 36,* 50–66.

Welton, D. A. (1982, October). Expository writing, pseudowriting, and social studies. *Social Education, 46,* 444–448.

Chapter Ten

Geography and Map Skills
Graphic Skills: Graphs, Charts, and Tables
Using Available Printed Resources
Teaching from Pictures, Photographs, Art, Artifacts, and Other
   Realia

Special Skills in the Social Studies

Learning the content of the social studies demands the use of skills consistent with inquiry to interpret, discern relationships, and draw conclusions from data represented by visuals and realia.

In teaching social studies, we ask students to learn not only the content but the skills derived from the social sciences, that is, to learn *from* content as well. For example, in teaching students map skills, we want students to learn not only the information on a map, such as the particular land forms of East Africa, but how those land forms have affected the culture of the people of East Africa.

In this chapter, we will examine the four basic special skills areas in social studies:

- How to teach map skills and other graphic skills using charts, graphs, and tables
- How to teach with pictures, photographs, artifacts, and other realia
- How to use political cartoons effectively in class

MIKE: Say, did you all see the latest issue of *Social Education,* the one on skills? I read some of the articles over the weekend. Am I out of touch, or are the authors? I always saw social studies teaching as emphasizing content, but those articles say we need to teach skills just as we teach content. They sure opened my eyes!

PEDRO: Where have you been? How have you been teaching social studies anyway? The kids have to do something with content, you know. You're probably one of those guys who still has kids color in maps.

MIKE: Isn't that how one teaches geography? That's all my teachers ever did when I was a high school student. But you're an expert, Pedro, because you went to one of those National Geographic Summer Institutes.

PEDRO: Come on! But would you like to sit in on one of my classes to see how I now teach geography? I'll admit I used to teach it the old way, too, because I didn't know better.

YASUKO: Well, guys, geography skills aren't the only social studies skills. I hope you are also teaching your students not only how to read and analyze charts and graphs but to make them, too.

ELISE: And don't forget political cartoons. My kids love them! Come on in and see my political cartoon bulletin board. The students bring cartoons in almost every day. In fact, we start class with them.

The preceding dialog suggests that there are certain skills we help students learn in social studies class:

1. Skills of inquiry necessary for making, reading, and analyzing maps, charts, graphs, and tables
2. Skills in interpreting political cartoons
3. Skills to learn from photographs, paintings, and artifacts
4. Critical-thinking skills (e.g., making inferences, drawing conclusions, separating fact from opinion, discerning relationships between cause and effect)
5. Reference and research skills

The last two skill areas are not unique to social studies, although they may be more heavily emphasized in social studies classes than in other content area classes. Math teachers may emphasize making and learning from charts, graphs, and tables, but social studies teachers use these visuals more often (or at least they should). However, learning from visuals, realia, and political cartoons is endemic to social studies.

We argue that all of the above skills should be taught in social studies. But how should we teach them? All too often students are not taught how to use maps, photographs, charts, political cartoons, and the other visuals or realia. Teachers are quick to demand that students glean meaning, analyze, and evaluate these visuals, when in reality that process is step 2 of the following three steps necessary to teaching these social studies skills:

1. Simply reading what is there, that is, looking at the visual
2. Analyzing the visual—pulling meaning from it
3. Going above and beyond the visual itself, relating it in some way to students' prior experiences.

We will examine this three-step process in greater detail later in the chapter.

GEOGRAPHY AND MAP SKILLS

Before going into specifics about teaching map skills, we should describe what we mean by *geography* and *geographic literacy*. According to Pedro, the ninth-grade social studies teacher who attended a summer geography institute,

> Too many students—and teachers, like me before I attended the summer geography institute—equate geography skills with finding places on the globe or on maps or knowing where countries or capitals are. That may have been OK in the past, when physical geography was the only geography emphasized in our schools—and here I'm citing one of the authors we read—[Welton, 1988, p. 11]—but literacy in geography is more than knowing place names and capitals.

Over the past decade, we have broadened our definition of the purpose of studying geography based in part on the ideas of the National Council for

Geographic Education (NCGE) and the Association of American Geographers (AAG). The Joint Committee on Geographic Education of the NCGE and the AAG (1984) have developed guidelines for geography education, which state that:

> A sound geographic education provides the perspectives, information, concepts and skills to understand ourselves, our relationship to the earth and our interdependence with other peoples of the world. . . . [W]e must know where and why events are occurring if we hope to apply our intelligence and moral sensitivity toward improving the quality of human life on this planet.*

Further, the study of geography involves the development of inquiry skills stimulated when students ask, "Why are such things located in these particular places, and how do those particular places influence our lives?"**

Fundamental Themes of Geography

Drawing on the NCGE and AAG guidelines further, we find that there are five fundamental themes in geography: (1) location; (2) place; (3) relationships within places; (4) movement; and (5) regions.*** Figure 10.1 presents a sample lesson using the themes of location and relationships within places. (A lesson can also use just one or several of the themes.)

Location. *Location,* or the position of people and places on the earth's surface, can be either absolute or relative. *Absolute location* means the exact location, usually latitude and longitude, of a particular point on the earth's surface. For example, we can use latitude and longitude to locate absolutely the city of Santo Domingo in the Dominican Republic. *Relative location,* on the other hand, is the position of people or places in relation to the location of other people or places.

Pedro would advise us to ask several questions or make several hypotheses about Santo Domingo because of its location (you may wish to find Santo Domingo and look at its relative location as we discuss it; it is at 18 N, 69 W):

> How does its location on the Caribbean Sea affect its economy?
>
> How does its location on Hispaniola (the island occupied by the Dominican Republic and Haiti) affect its people?

*From *Guidelines for Geographic Education: Elementary and Secondary Schools* (pp. 1–2) by the Joint Committee on Geographic Education of the National Council for Geographic Education and the Association of American Geographers, 1984, Washington, DC: Author. Reprinted with permission.

**Ibid., p. 2.

***The following discussion is based on material from the Joint Committee on Geographic Education of the National Council for Geographic Education and the Association of American Geographers (1984).

FIGURE 10.1
Sample Lesson for Incorporating Location and Place Relationships

Setting: High school social studies class in European history

Topic: Italy in the Renaissance. A large map of the United States and a map of Italy during the Renaissance are available (or the two maps can be shown on an overhead projector).

Instructional objectives: Based on viewing and discussing maps of the United States and Italy, students will be able to:

1. State reasons why Italy was a loosely knit group of city-states
2. Describe the political and economic features of Italy
3. List ways in which and summarize why the city-states warred against one another

Rationale: Students know that the United States consists of several states strongly linked together, but typically their main perception of other nations is that of one homogeneous state. This lesson will help them understand that some foreign countries not only were and still are divided into states, or city-states, but they often warred against one another as did the states in the United States during 1861–1865. Geographic locations can help explain the reason for the differences among city-states. The geographic theme of location will be used to help students see the divisions within Italy. Relationships within places will help them understand how climate, location, and physical features could produce city-states opposed to one another.

Student involvement: While looking at the maps of the United States and Renaissance Italy, students will compare and contrast the states of the United States with the states of Italy and discuss why the United States engaged in the 1861–1865 Civil War.

   Next, students will split into groups of five. Each group will be assigned a feature of Italy that explains the division into city-states and the friction it caused: absolute and relative location, climate, politics, economy, and language. (Students may refer to their text, maps, and other materials.)

Teacher role: The teacher serves as facilitator, moving from group to group to assist students, answer and ask questions, and provide additional materials.

   The teacher also conducts a formative oral evaluation (see Chapter 11 for a review of evaluation), for example, by asking each group for at least one comparison or contrast between the United States and Renaissance Italy. A continuing and follow-up activity to the day's group work is to have each group of students cooperatively develop a two-page analysis of the reasons why their assigned feature of Italy led to the development of city-states and wars. As an example, the group assigned economic features might discuss why the economies of Milan and Naples differed so widely.

Source: This lesson was developed by Eric Schafer, M.A.T., 1989, State University of New York at Binghamton, New York.

What political problems might it have because it is near Puerto Rico? Because it is near Cuba?

Place.   According to the Joint Committee on Geographic Education of the NCGE and the AAG (1984), "All places on the earth have distinctive tangible and intangible characteristics that give them meaning and character and distinguish them from other places. Geographers generally describe places by their physical or human characteristics."*

Physical characteristics of a *place* include the land and water forms, such as mountains, plains, plateaus, rivers, bays, and so on, plant and animal life, climate, and soils. *Human characteristics* of a place refer to the lifestyles of the inhabitants—languages, religions, political organizations, education, communication networks, health and medical status, population distribution, and so forth.**

Geography often can explain why some people are nomadic while others are sedentary and why some languages are spoken only in certain parts of the world.

Relationships Within Places. *Relationships within places* deal with how humans interact with their cultural and physical environments. Places where people live have advantages as well as disadvantages for human habitation, and thus people adapt to the physical and cultural conditions of an area. These adaptations are rooted in the inhabitants' cultural values and mores and in their economic, technological, and political abilities to modify the environment to meet their survival needs or desire for a higher standard of living. Using Brazil, for example, teachers and students could use these sample questions:

Why were the rain forests of the Amazon removed? Who was responsible?

How have the inhabitants of the rain forests of the Amazon adapted to the removal of the forests and the resulting soil erosion from the heavy rains?

Were the inhabitants of the area consulted about the deforestation? Why or why not?

What has been the role of the Brazilian government in deforestation?

What has the Brazilian government done to aid the people whose homes have been flooded away?

Movement. How humans interact as they move from place to place on the earth, how they communicate with one another, and how they depend on goods, services, and ideas from environments other than their own further explain the *movement* concept. Topics such as emigration, immigration, and migration, as well as the obvious topic of transportation, really deal with movement of people. Movement may also include the transfer, or communication, of products, ideologies, technology, and new ideas and ways of thinking.

---

*Ibid., p. 5.

**For an excellent reference on human characteristics of women in different parts of the world, see *Women in the World: An International Atlas* by Joni Seager and Ann Olson (New York: Simon & Schuster, 1986). To acquire more background on teaching geography, see Natoli (1988).

Practical examples of studying movement in geography in social studies class might include a study of immigration. For example, students could develop the following questions:

Why did people emigrate from Italy and the Netherlands to Canada after World War II?

What goods and services were missing in Toronto that people were used to in Italy and the Netherlands?

What goods might they have imported from Italy and the Netherlands after they settled?

What ideas, goods, and services might they have infused into Toronto and Canadian societies?

What cultural changes might have occurred in the lives of the Canadian-Italians as they settled in Toronto?

Regions.   *Regions,* or areas of land, may be determined by political, physical, sociocultural, or economic criteria. Typically regions are bound by a common characteristic, such as a government, mountains, a seacoast, language, religion, or the growing of certain crops. We divide the world into different regions in order to study it as a whole, to look at its interrelationships with other regions, and to dissect it carefully.

Often our study of social studies is regional; that is, we learn about a particular region but not about the interrelationships regions have with other regions. Instead, however, we should compare and contrast regions of like characteristics throughout the world to discover and analyze their similarities and differences. For example, why do Americans refer to the main sugar-producing regions of the world, such as the Philippines and the Caribbean Basin, as "Third World" countries? Does raising sugar keep a region in the Third World? How do you explain why the southern and western regions of the United States, which are major sugar-producing areas, are not considered Third World? Are all Spanish-speaking regions of the world members of the Third World? Why or why not?

ASIDE TO THE READER: Are the five geography themes new to you? Do you see how you can incorporate them into your social studies lessons?

Map and Globe Skills

It is obvious from the preceding section that Mike indeed has been "out of touch" in his perception of geography instruction as place names and capitals. We have seen that a good social studies program includes the five themes of geography discussed earlier.

How does a teacher go about incorporating these themes while teaching map and globe skills? We propose that students will learn these skills not only by studying maps and globes but by learning how to make maps themselves. First, we will discuss why maps are useful and examine the different types of maps. Then we will identify the map and globe skills that students should be learning, including the use of scales and legends.

Purposes of Maps.   Maps are useful because they provide a simplified symbol of reality. They enable us to "look at" a place on the earth's surface by viewing a greatly reduced image of that place. Maps thus show spatial distribution as well as relationships.

However, because maps are an oversimplified and highly condensed representation of the earth's surface or a part of it, they are necessarily distorted. We all know that the earth is spherical, and to reduce something in that shape to a flat representation (called *projection*) leads to distortion.

Map Projections.   Currently an intellectual battle is being waged among cartographers and geographers about which map projection of the more than 250 developed is the most accurate. However, both sides agree that no projection can ever be totally accurate, that is, free from distortion. Teachers are involved in this controversy in that they are the ones who teach children geography skills and incorporate the use of maps into social studies classes.

The first projection, that of Marinus of Tyre, developed about 120 C.E., was challenged by Ptolemy, who developed two alternative methods for showing the world on a flat surface (Robinson, 1987). In 1568, the Flemish geographer Gerhardus Mercator came forth with his projection, the one still most commonly seen in schools. Most teachers were brought up on the Mercator projection (see Figure 10.2), the large, flat map that shows Europe in the center of the world.

This Eurocentric depiction was objected to by Reverend J. Gall, who in 1855 came forth with his own projection. The Gall projection was adopted by German journalist-historian Arno Peters as his own in 1973 (Figure 10.3). Peters suggests that his projection "corrects" Mercator because it shows a more accurate representation of the size and shape of the world's nations, especially the Third World, or the world south of the equator (Robinson, 1987).

However, geographers and cartographers of the 1980s preferred the newest projection, that of geographer-cartographer Arthur Robinson (see Figure 10.4). The National Geographic Society reviewed over 20 projections in late 1987, and their unanimous choice was Robinson's because it "matches reality" more closely than any other and has the least amount of distortion at the north and south edges (Garver, 1988, p. 913).

The use of different maps with different projections depending on the purpose of the map activity is the only recourse for the teacher, for no projection is perfect. Thus, "the map user must exercise care in selecting the

FIGURE 10.2
The Mercator Projection

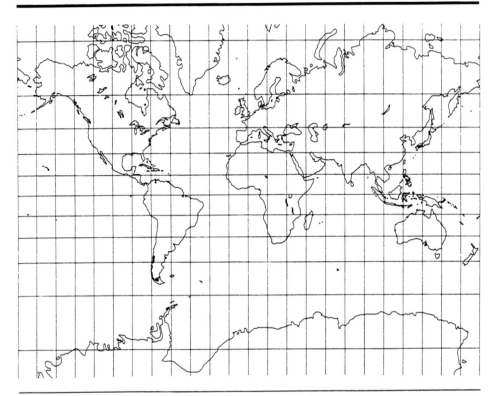

Source: From *Which Map Is Best?* Falls Church, VA: American Congress on Surveying and Mapping, 1987. Reprinted with permission of ACSM.

projection most suitable for each mapping project" (Natoli, 1988). Further, the teacher must use the map type most appropriate for meeting the goals of the particular lesson.

Types of Maps.   A globe tends to be only a *political* map; that is, it indicates the political, or nation-state, boundaries on the earth's surface. *Topographical* maps indicate the earth's physical surfaces. Sometimes topographical maps are in relief, with mountains and other highlands raised on the surface. (That's the kind of map we usually made in elementary school with papier-mâché.)

Atlases tend to contain the greatest variety of maps. Some atlases are historical, meaning that they contain *historical* maps, which show sections of the world at different times in history. For example, an historical atlas of

FIGURE 10.3
The Peters Projection

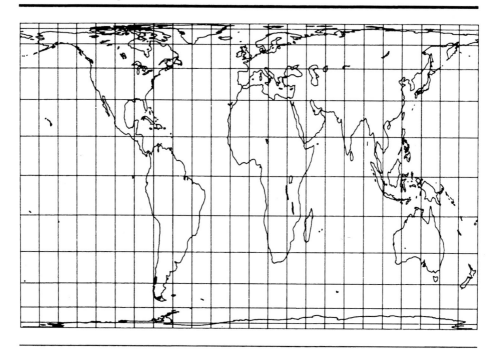

Source: From *Which Map Is Best?* Falls Church, VA: American Congress on Surveying and Mapping, 1987. Reprinted with permission of ACSM.

FIGURE 10.4
The Robinson Projection

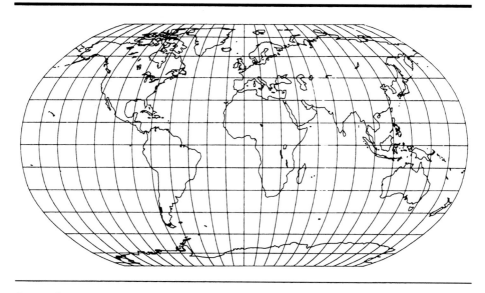

Source: From *Which Map Is Best?* Falls Church, VA: American Congress on Surveying and Mapping, 1987. Reprinted with permission of ACSM.

the United States might contain maps of the United States during 17th-century colonization, the Revolution, the Civil War, and other periods.

Special-purpose maps show industrial production, agriculture, languages, natural resources, population density, temperature, literacy, and other unique characteristics of a nation-state or area of the world.

Most social studies educators would agree that there are some basic map and globe skills of which all students should have a working knowledge. We can place these skills into the categories of acquiring and using information. We locate places on maps and globes not merely to know where they are but to learn more about each place because of its absolute and relative locations. Thus, one skill in using both maps and globes is the use of *latitude* and *longitude*. Once students understand longitude, they will be able to learn how to determine time throughout the world as well as the daily length of daylight and darkness. Once they comprehend latitude, they can be introduced to learning how latitude affects temperature, climate, length of the growing season, and so forth.

Using a *scale* and *legend* (or *key*) is the next skill to learn. By looking at the scales listed on maps (e.g., 1 inch = 200 miles), students will be able to determine the distances between places. Thus, students acquire information—that scale represents miles—and then use that information to determine distances. The next step is for students to inquire constantly. One valuable type of inquiry is the "so-what" question. An example would be "So what if Columbus and Dayton, Ohio, are 72 miles apart?" One possible response is that because a major highway connects the two cities, one can drive there in less than two hours. Another is that goods produced in Dayton, such as cash registers and computers, are easily shippable by truck to Columbus for sale there. Another question type is "what-if" ("What if Dayton and Columbus were 372 miles apart instead of 72?"; "What if New York City and Madrid were on the same latitude?"). Still another example is provided by a special-purpose map on "illness and health" in Seager and Olson's *Women in the World: An International Atlas* ("Why do women in the world live longer than men?").

A map *legend* also provides students with information, but students need to learn how to *use* that information, going beyond the details of the legend. Maps that require legends typically are considered special-purpose maps, because they provide special information only, such as rainfall, population density, or agricultural production.

As an example, look at the map and legend in Figure 10.5. Notice again what information the legend contains. By color code, it tells you the population of the various Indian (Native American) reservations. The most heavily populated reservations are salmon colored and the least populated ones lilac colored.

Students will also use the information in a legend to acquire new knowledge as they apply the legend to the map. Using the legend in Figure 10.5, for example, they might ask themselves: Why are some reservations so lightly populated and others so heavily populated? Why would Native Americans

FIGURE 10.5
Identifying and Using a Map Legend

POPULATION OF INDIAN RESERVATIONS, 1883

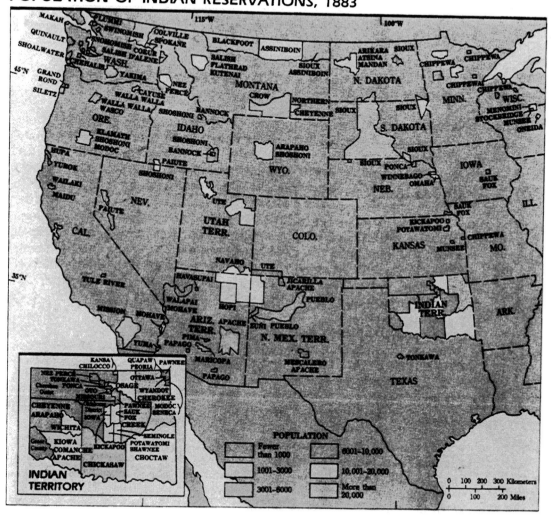

Source: From The United States: Vol. 2. Reconstruction to the Present (p. 67) by H. N. Drewry, R. P. Green Jr., T. H. O'Connor, L. L. Becker, and R. E. Corviello, 1986, Columbus, OH: Merrill. Copyright 1986 by Merrill Publishing Company. Reprinted by permission.

choose to live on reservations? Is life better there than in the rest of the United States?

To summarize, students should learn the map skills just described for three reasons:

1. To learn what types of information latitude, longitude, scales, and legends provide
2. To apply that information to a map or globe
3. To acquire additional information, typically by asking questions such as "So what . . . ?" and "What if . . . ?"

Making Maps. We feel that the three reasons for learning location, scale, and legend just described are basic to helping students learn how to make their own maps as well as read maps and globes developed by their classmates, their teachers, and commercial map and textbook publishers. An easy map activity for middle school students is to make a map of their walk or ride to school. They can learn to work with scale by asking a parent or bus driver the distance between home and school. They can develop a legend that contains a symbol for streets or roads, sidewalks, homes, businesses, and places of worship and then locate these places on their map. They can then give their map a title, date it, and sign it. Or they might make a map of their neighborhood, village, or city. This activity is especially good for students working in pairs or groups of three. They can use large posterboard to create a flat map or make a relief map.

High school students can make more complicated maps. Because we don't expect them to be artists, they can trace the exterior boundaries of a continent, region, nation, state, or city by using the overhead projector. (Students can simply duplicate the desired map, make an overhead transparency of it, or tape their paper or posterboard to the wall or chalkboard and draw the map's outline as projected on the paper.) Then they should title, date, and sign the map and develop a scale and legend.

Learning from Maps. Ideally, students will obtain a better understanding of the value of maps and how to learn from them as a result of making their own. In addition, there are certain consecutive steps students need to take to get the most from maps. As we said at the beginning of the chapter, teachers frequently ask more of students than students can answer because they have not been taught how to read, or learn from, maps. We like Rose Sabaroff's analogy: Opening a book no more equals reading it than looking at a map equals understanding and reading the map (Sabaroff, 1969, p. 330).

There are at least three steps students need to take to learn how to learn from maps:

1. *Reading* the map, both outside and inside, including its title, legend, date, and what one actually sees

2. *Interpreting* the data on the map
3. *Applying* the newly acquired knowledge to other situations

Figure 10.6 presents a map activity that shows how a lesson incorporates these three steps.

GRAPHIC SKILLS: GRAPHS, CHARTS, AND TABLES

MIKE: Say, Yasuko, I recall your saying in the social studies department office a few weeks ago something about teaching charts and graphs. Do you think you could help me analyze a lesson on graphs that I just taught? Actually, it was a lesson that just bombed; I don't think they learned anything!

YASUKO: We all have lessons that bomb. Don't let that get you down. But sure, I'd be glad to help you out. I love teaching with all those non-textbook-reading activities—graphs, charts, and tables. And the kids really have fun with them while learning a lot. They too like the break from reading the text. Let's see your lesson.

[Figure 10.7 shows Mike's lesson. If you were a student in his class, would you have learned from it? Would you have enjoyed the lesson? See if you can figure out what is wrong with it before reading the rest of this section. As you read, refer to Mike's graph in Figure 10.7 and see where he needs to make changes in his lesson.]

YASUKO: Oh, I think I see some of the problems, Mike.
MIKE: That quickly? OK, let's go over it.
YASUKO: Let's do it one question at a time. Basically, there's nothing wrong with the graph; it's the lesson, the questions you're asking them.
MIKE: Oh? Like what?
YASUKO: Well, number one is vague. I think you want the answer to be "an increase in union membership, especially since 1936," right? But asking them what happened to labor unions is not the question for the answer you want.
MIKE: OK, I get it. "Vague"—I agree.
YASUKO: Moving on to number two, the kids won't know from reading the graph why more people joined, which is what your directions tell them you want them to do. The question is good, because it gets them thinking beyond the graph itself, but hold off and ask that later. The same is true for question three—see?
MIKE: Yes. And I bet you're going to tell me that four is no good either.
YASUKO: Well, what's the point of it? Do you really care how many were members in each of those years?

FIGURE 10.6
Lesson on Reading, Interpreting, and Applying Data from Maps

POPULATION DENSITY

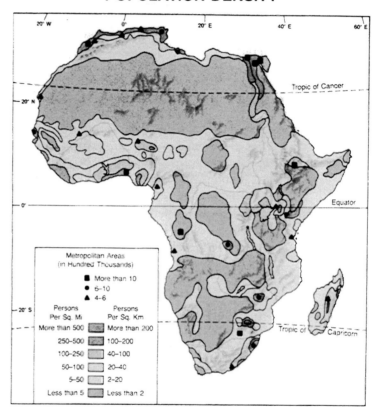

Part A. Reading the Outside of the Map
1. Looking at the title and the map itself, explain what this map is about.
2. What continent is this?
3. What information does the legend, or key, provide?

Part B. Reading the Inside of the Map
1. What regions of the continent are very sparsely populated?
2. What regions are very heavily populated?
3. Most of the continent falls into which of the six categories indicated in the key?

Part C. Reading Above and Beyond the Map
1. How do you explain the areas of sparse settlement? Of dense population?
2. Why do you feel the most heavily populated areas are where they are?
3. Is there a connection between geography, climate, and population on the continent? If so, what? If not, explain why not.
4. How do you think the population density affects Africa and its people's way of life?
5. What, if anything, might cause the population to shift to the sparsely populated regions?

Source: From Global Insights (p. 19) by J. N. Hantula, T. O. Flickema, M. A. Farah, A. B. Karls, E. Johnson, K. A. Thuermer, A. Resnick, P. W. Kane, 1987, Columbus, OH: Merrill. Copyright 1987 by Merrill Publishing Company. Reprinted by permission.

**FIGURE 10.7
Labor Union Graph
Lesson**

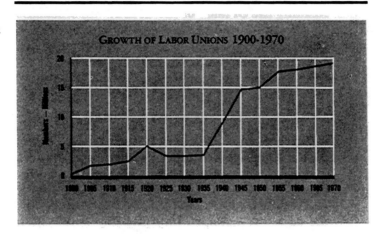

Directions: Use the graph to answer the following questions.
1. What happened to labor unions from 1900 to 1970?
2. Why did more people join unions in 1936?
3. Why were there so few unions in 1900?
4. How many people were members of unions in 1910, 1920, 1930, 1940, 1950, 1960, 1970?
5. Will you join a union once you start working?

Source: From *One Nation Indivisible.* (p. 497) by L. R. Heller, Jr. and N. W. Potter, 1971, Columbus, OH: Merrill. Copyright 1971 by Merrill Publishing Company. Reprinted by permission.

MIKE: No, I guess not. I don't know why I even asked that now that I look at it. And I guess five is an OK question, but another one that cannot be answered from the graph alone—right?

YASUKO: You're a quick study, Mike. I always use a three-step format when teaching graphs. If you've got a minute, let me explain; I think it will help you.

Teaching Graphs

Earlier we said that students need to make their own maps so that they will be better able to read and analyze professionally made maps. The same is true for graphs—and, as we will see later, for charts, and tables (Anderson & Winston, 1977, p. 75; McCune & Pearson, 1964, p. 206).

As the preceding dialog indicates, Yasuko typically uses a three-step process in teaching graphs:

1. Reading the *outside* of the graph
2. Reading the *inside* of the graph
3. Reading *above and beyond* the graph

Reading the Outside of the Graph. As students make their graphs, they need to give them titles, date them, and provide the sources for the data the graphs contain. As you can see, the graph Mike made for his class (Figure 10.7) has a title, but it is not current, which may mislead the students. Also, the graph doesn't indicate the source of the data. Whether these are government statistics or union figures for recruiting purposes might affect the data's validity.

The *title* of a graph is important because it tells the students what the graph is about so they don't become frustrated trying to puzzle it out. The *date* is equally important, for without a date students will tend to think the data are current. In Mike's case, the students might wonder why there are no figures for 1975 through 1990; have there been no union members since 1970? Finally, the *source(s)* is necessary to alert students to possible bias in the data. For example, they probably would interpret Mike's graph quite differently if the data came from a pro-union organization rather than from the government.

Reading the Inside of the Graph. What does the graph tell us? With the students and teacher working on this together, the graph "tells" them information on two levels—the literal and the interpretive. Notice, however, that Mike's question goes straight to the second level, the interpretive, when he asks students, "What happened to labor unions from 1900 to 1970?" As Yasuko said, this is a vague question. A better question would be: "What trend do you see in labor union membership from 1900 to 1936 and from 1936 to 1970?"

Do you see why this is a better question? State the reasons.

Reading Above and Beyond the Graph. We need to carry the graph activity one step further if students are to really make meaning of the graph by asking questions that relate the graph to them. Mike has done that in his fifth question (Figure 10.7), "Will you join a union once you start working?" But there are so few good questions leading up to it that we cannot be sure whether students will be ready to answer that question.

Mike's entire lesson would be better if he

1. Rewrote the directions
2. Introduced the graph more gradually with questions about the outside of it (e.g., "By what is growth in unions measured on this graph?")
3. Made his questions clearer
4. Asked questions that forced students to wrestle with the data the graph contains
5. Made the graph more relevant to the students' own lives

Now it is your turn to improve on Mike's lesson. Go ahead—make up some questions with a classmate. Ours aren't the only ones that would work.

YASUKO: Well, Mike, I've really taken your lesson apart, but I hope you see what I mean about how I teach graphs. This three-stage format works for me. I've been doing it this way for so long that I can't remember for sure where I even learned it, but I think it was in my undergrad social studies methods class.

MIKE: Well, I wish I'd been in that class. I had never learned as much about teaching graphs as I have in the last 15 minutes, Yasuko. I really appreciate the time you have spent with me, and so will my kids.

YASUKO: Really, I was glad to do it, Mike. It makes me feel good about myself to be able to share what works for me with a colleague and for you to be so receptive. Tell you what: I'll gladly pass on to you some other lessons I've developed that teach kids how to learn from graphs, if you like.

MIKE: I'll take them all! Do you have one that will correspond with the unit I'm working on in my fifth-period class, the Industrial Revolution? I'd like to try one out as soon as I can.

Within a few days, Yasuko had gone through her course files and provided Mike with lessons that she had developed as well as ones that she too had collected from others. One of those lessons is presented in Figure 10.8.

Types of Graphs. The four main graph types are, in order of simplicity, the picture, bar, pie or circle, and line graph.

Picture graphs are easy to read and interpret because the information is presented in pictorial rather than abstract form. Figure 10.9 presents a picture graph from a standard textbook. *Bar graphs* are more abstract. In Figure 10.10, the vertical bars represent population growth in the People's Republic of China. *Pie,* or *circle, graphs,* such as those in Figures 10.11(a) and 10.11(b), give students a sense of the whole and of the relative size of each part of the pie. Thus, students can see relationships among parts of a whole (Hawkins, 1980, p. 5). *Line graphs* are more abstract. They neither provide a sense of the whole nor present clear delineations among the graphed items, but they offer another way to present abundant information efficiently. Figure 10.11(c) illustrates a line graph.

Did you enjoy learning social studies from these types of visuals? Why or why not? How might you make their use more worthwhile for your students?

FIGURE 10.8
Using the Three-Stage Format to Teach Graphs

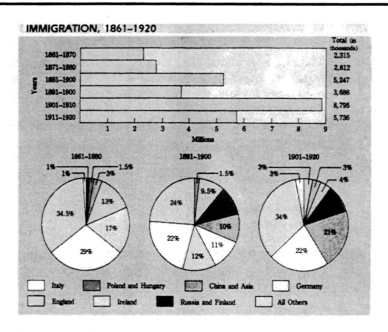

Directions: Using the graphs entitled "Immigration, 1861–1920" and your knowledge of social studies, answer the following with two other classmates.

Part A. What Information Is Being Presented?
1. With what topic do the graphs deal?
2. How many types of graphs are used? What are they?
3. What information does the bar graph attempt to convey?
4. What time period does it cover? How is this time period segmented?
5. What does the length of each bar represent?

Teaching Charts and Tables

ELISE: I couldn't help but overhear you talk about graphs, Mike and Yasuko. I don't use them as much as I do tables and charts, but I do teach them much as you do, Yasuko, using the three different levels. I tell my kids that the three levels, or steps, are (1) what do you see?, (2) what does that mean?, and (3) so what? They had some difficulty with number three at first, but once they got the hang of it, they loved doing charts and tables.

6. With what time periods do the three circle graphs deal?
7. What information do the circle graphs attempt to convey?
8. What do the colored wedges of the circles represent?

Part B. Analysis of Information Presented
1. In the time period under review, what 10-year period saw the largest influx of immigrants to the U.S.? What period saw the smallest amount of immigration?
2. Can you discern any overall pattern of immigration from the bar graph?
3. What group does the largest wedge of each circle represent?
4. After the category "all others," what three groups are most heavily represented in the time period 1861–1880? What percentage of the total does each represent?
5. What percentage of the total did each of these groups represent in 1901–1920?
6. After the category "all others," what three groups are most heavily represented in the period 1901–1920?
7. How does this compare with the percentage represented by each group in the period 1861–1880?
8. Immigration from which area of the world remained relatively stable over the period under review?
9. What pattern is represented by the changing native origins of immigrants to the U.S.?
10. What are some aspects of immigration that the graphs do not address?

Part C. Developing Hypotheses from the Information
1. What factors do you think accounted for the spurts in immigration in the periods 1881–1890 and 1901–1910?
2. Why do you think each of these periods was followed by one of sharp decline in immigration?
3. How could we test our answer to questions 1 and 2?
4. Why do you think the native origin of immigrants shifts from Western to Eastern and Southern Europe? How could we find out?
5. What might be some of the consequences in the U.S. of such a shift in immigration?
6. Do you think the later immigrants from Eastern and Southern Europe faced the same problems that the earlier immigrants from Western Europe faced? Why or why not?
7. What countries do you think contribute the largest number of immigrants to the U.S. today? How could we find out?
8. What might be some of the consequences for the U.S. of this latest shift in the pattern of immigration?

Source: This lesson was developed by Kirk Darling, M.A.T., 1987, teacher at the Chenango Forks, New York, high school. Graphs reprinted from *The United States: Vol. 2. Reconstruction to the Present* (p. 132) by H. N. Drewry, R. P. Green, Jr., T. H. O'Connor, L. L. Becker, and R. E. Corviello, 1986, Columbus, OH: Merrill. Copyright 1986 by Merrill Publishing Company. Reprinted by permission.

MIKE: I don't use charts and tables much, because I just don't think about them. Maybe if there is one in the textbook we'll study it, but I don't go out of my way to make them. You probably think I should, right, Elise?

ELISE: Well, my kids like them and really learn from them. My poorer readers especially do well with them because there is so little reading.

FIGURE 10.9
Picture Graph

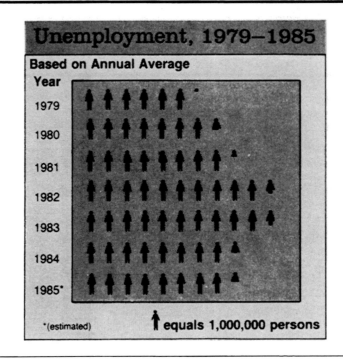

Source: From *America Is* (p. 713) by H. N. Drewry and T. H. O'Connor, 1987, Columbus, OH: Merrill. Copyright 1987 by Merrill Publishing Company. Reprinted by permission.

FIGURE 10.10
Bar Graph

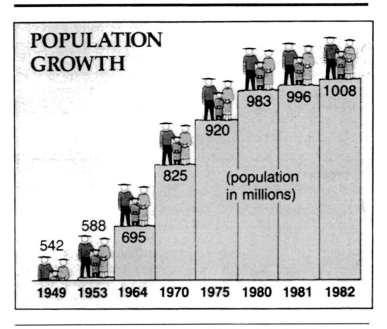

Source: From *Global Insights* (p. 214) by J. N. Hantula, T. O. Flickema, M. A. Farah, A. B. Karls, E. Johnson, K. A. Thuermer, A. Resnick, P. W. Kane, 1987, Columbus, OH: Merrill. Copyright 1987 by Merrill Publishing Company. Reprinted by permission.

ERICA AT WORK

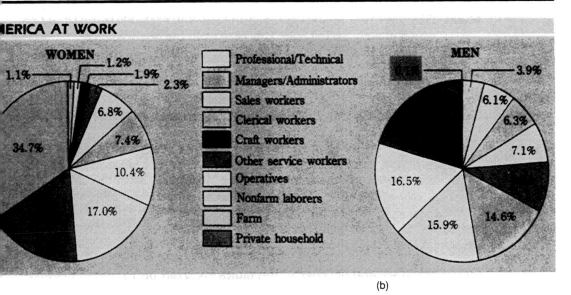

(b)

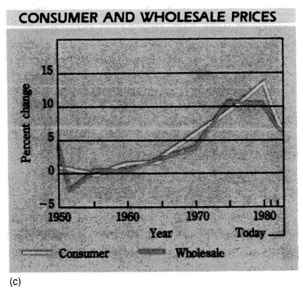

(c)

ce: From *The United States: Vol. 2. Reconstruction to the Present* (p. 600) by H. N. Drewry, R. P. Green, Jr., T. H. O'Connor,
Becker, and R. E. Corviello, 1986, Columbus, OH: Merrill. Copyright 1986 by Merrill Publishing Company. Reprinted by
"ission.

MIKE: And you're saying that I can teach them using the same three levels that Yasuko just taught me?

ELISE: Sure. Want to see some of my lessons?

MIKE: Why not? Gee, you two are shaming me! You probably think I don't do much in class except have kids read from the textbook.

ELISE: Well, now that you mention it . . .

[*Two days later:*]

ELISE: Here you go, Mike. A lesson on teaching social studies using a chart [Figure 10.12]. It's from my sociology class.

YASUKO: And here's one of mine [Figure 10.13]. We're doing recent U.S. history, and this table looks at the pre-Reagan years. My students will then ask the same questions of people now in the 1990s and extend the table, comparing each decade and deciding in what ways Reagan made a difference.

Why Use Graphs, Charts, and Tables?

Students will see graphs, charts, and tables every day on TV and in newspapers and magazines. Thus, they need to know how to read and analyze them as well as think beyond them to develop civic literacy. These skills are easy to master once students learn how. Recall that Yasuko mentioned earlier that her slower readers love to do graphs, charts, and tables in class because they find them easy to read. Think about how difficult the information on the chart on suicide rates in Figure 10.12 would be to read and make sense of if it were presented in narrative rather than chart form.

Another, related reason for using these visuals is that they are efficient: A chart, table, or graph can present a great deal of data in a compact form. Also, they break up the monotony of the printed word and give students alternative ways to obtain information.

Making Graphs, Charts, and Tables

When educators speak of broad, general categories of social studies skills, they refer to the skills of locating, gathering, organizing, interpreting, and evaluating information. In this presentation of visual skills for learning from maps, graphs, charts, and tables, we will concentrate on reading, interpreting, and evaluating information. If those materials are already available for students, these three broad skill areas will be most relevant. However, we feel that students will obtain a better understanding of the value of visuals if they make some themselves. Thus, they need to learn how to locate, gather, and organize information, and teachers need to provide opportunities for them to acquire those skills.

FIGURE 10.12
Sample Lesson Using a Chart

Suicide Rates, by Sex, Race, and Age Group: 1970–1979

Rates per 100,000 population in specified group. Excludes deaths of nonresidents of U.S. Deaths for 1979 classified according to the ninth revision of the *International Classification of Diseases*.

Age	Male								Female							
	White				Black				White				Black			
	1970	1975	1976	1979	1970	1975	1976	1979	1970	1975	1978	1979	1970	1975	1978	1979
All ages*	18.0	20.1	20.2	20.0	8.0	10.0	10.8	11.6	7.1	7.4	6.9	6.6	2.6	2.7	2.8	2.8
5–14 years	.5	.6	.7	.6	.1	.1	.3	.3	.1	.2	.2	.3	.2	.1	.2	.1
15–24 years	13.9	19.6	20.8	21.0	10.5	12.9	13.4	13.4	4.2	4.9	5.0	5.1	3.8	3.3	2.7	3.4
25–34 years	19.9	24.4	25.8	26.2	19.2	24.3	24.4	24.4	9.0	8.9	8.5	8.0	5.7	5.6	5.6	5.7
35–44 years	23.3	24.5	22.5	22.5	12.6	16.0	16.9	16.9	13.0	12.6	10.9	10.1	3.7	3.9	4.6	4.1
45–54 years	29.5	29.7	24.7	23.9	13.8	12.1	13.8	13.0	13.5	13.8	12.1	11.7	3.7	4.0	4.2	2.9
55–64 years	35.0	32.1	29.3	26.6	10.6	10.8	10.2	12.9	12.3	11.7	10.3	10.2	2.0	3.5	3.2	4.0
65 and over	41.1	39.4	40.8	39.2	6.7	11.3	11.7	12.9	8.5	8.5	7.9	7.3	2.6	2.3	2.3	2.5

*Includes other age groups not shown separately.
Source: U.S. National Center for Health Statistics, Vital Statistics of the United States, annual.

Part A. Reading the Outside of the Chart (the Literal *Level)*
1. In your own words, explain what subject this table is about.
2. What groups are represented?
3. What do the numbers represent?
4. What is the source of the information?

Part B. Making Meaning of the Chart (the Interpretive *Level)*
1. Who has the higher suicide rate—males or females?
2. Which group has the higher suicide rate blacks or whites?
3. Which age, sex, or racial group has the highest rate?

Part C. Going Beyond the Chart (the Applied *Level)*
1. Why do you think there is an increase in suicide rates for males in the teen years and a decrease in the thirties?
2. Why do you think females have much lower rates?
3. Why do you think that the suicide rates for males shoot up after age 65?
4. Have you ever known someone who committed suicide? If so, which categories (age, sex, race) did that person fit into? Why did that person commit suicide? Is there any way you could have helped the person?

Source: This lesson was developed by B. J. Schum, M.A.T., 1987, State University of New York, Binghamton, New York, and teacher in the Bainbridge-Guilford, New York, high school.

Locating Information. Students will find information in the same sources that teachers use. Middle school students should be quite familiar with almanacs, such as *The World Almanac, The Book of Facts,* both published annually, and *The Information Please Almanac.* Database software appropriate for middle school students is also available.

In addition, students can locate and gather information by using surveys or questionnaires as well as through participant observation and interviews. We discussed interviewing in Chapter 7; here we will examine surveys, questionnaires, and participant observation.

Political scientists often use questionnaires and surveys to gather information about voting behavior. Until the 1950s, however, assessing voting behavior was not a major concern for political scientists, who viewed the field as an academic area of studying government not empirically but primarily "through historical, philosophical, and the descriptive-institutional approaches" (Dahl, 1961, in Feldman & Seifman, 1969, p. 129). The move to adopt survey research brought political science into "closer affiliation with

Students must learn to locate, gather, and organize information.

the theories, methods, findings and outlooks in modern psychology, sociology, anthropology and economics" (Dahl, 1961, in Feldman & Seifman, 1969, p. 134).

But this change came slowly. One, if not the first, political science opinion poll was conducted in 1936 to predict the outcome of the presidential election. Alfred Landon clearly was a 15-point winner over Franklin Roosevelt, according to the poll. However, the sample of 2 million voters had been drawn from telephone directories and automobile registration lists, thus eliminating all who were too poor to afford telephones and cars—and a large number of poor people voted that year. By 1948 many other pollsters, including George Gallup, used a more accurate sampling technique (quota sampling) but still predicted Dewey over Truman (Best & Kahn, 1986, pp. 82–83). Had there not been so many undecided voters that year and had Gallup continued to poll as the election neared, his prediction might have been different.

But some political scientists and other social scientists saw the use of survey techniques as the wave of the future. The Social Science Research Council established a Committee of Political Behavior in 1945 and a new one in 1949. As survey methods became more scientific and therefore more credible, a burgeoning movement within the field of political science to adopt them emerged. This trend finally held sway, and, as we know, determining and analyzing voting behavior is now a chief concern of the discipline of political science (Dahl, 1961, in Feldman & Seifman, 1969).

Survey Research. The most common form of research in the social sciences is *survey research*, typically conducted through the use of surveys, questionnaires, and interviews (Williamson, Karp, Dalphin, & Gray, 1982, p. 125). These instruments are used to gather data from "a relatively large number of cases at a particular time" and "are not concerned with the characteristics of individuals as individuals . . . [but] with the generalized statistics that result when data are abstracted from a large number of individual cases" (Best & Kahn, 1986, pp. 80–81). The subjects surveyed usually represent a cross-section of a population but may focus on only a certain group at a given time, such as the number of women who work outside the home, the number of young, unmarried adults who live with their parents, or the reasons why individuals affiliate with a particular political party.

Survey research seeks not only factual information but attitudes, values, and preferences. Surveys seeking information on the last three items are usually referred to as *public opinion* surveys (see Figure 10.13). Such surveys are popular because the data gathered can permit predictions, change social policies or develop new ones, and solve problems. Most students are familiar with the national opinion polls of the Gallup Organization, Lou Harris, and Roper and can learn how to develop their own surveys on local, state, national, or international issues. For example, they could develop a survey to predict who will win a local election or determine whether the public supports the

FIGURE 10.13
Sample Lesson Using a Table

Public opinion polls conducted over a fifteen-year period reveal substantial changes in what people consider this country's most pressing concerns.

Americans' Perceptions of the Most Important
National Problems, 1965–1980

	1965 (%)	1970 (%)	1980 (%)	Change 1965–1980 (%)
Reducing crime	41	56	61	+20
Reducing unemployment	35	25	48	+13
Conquering "killer" diseases	37	29	41	+ 4
Improving public education	45	31	35	−10
Helping poor people	32	30	29	− 3
Reducing air and water pollution	17	53	24	+ 7
Improving housing and rundown neighborhoods	21	27	20	− 1
Reducing racial discrimination	29	25	13	−16
Improving highway safety	18	13	7	− 11
Beautifying America	3	5	5	+ 2

building of a new school. A state issue might be the location of a toxic waste dump or whether state aid to public schools should be increased.

Public opinion polls can be conducted over the telephone, in a face-to-face oral or written questioning session, or through the mail as a self-administered survey. With the use of computers so common in schools, some students will be able to use or even develop software to analyze their data and thus draw their conclusions quite quickly.

Questionnaires.   A *questionnaire* is another form of survey, usually much longer a than public opinion poll. It may focus on several areas rather than just one or two as polls do. Like polls, questionnaires need to have clearly defined objectives and be very clearly written.

Participant Observation.   You may also wish to introduce your students to *ethnographic* research, the type of research used by cultural anthropologists, and teach them how to engage in participant observation or merely observation. In *participant observation*, a skill used more by cultural anthropologists than by other social scientists, "social phenomena are observed firsthand in their natural setting" and the researcher "establishes continuing social relationships with the individuals being studied" (Williamson et al., 1982, p. 45).

Part A. Reading the Outside of the Table (the Literal *Level)*
1. Describe in your own words the subject of the table.
2. What is the source of the poll? Do you think that is a reliable source?

Part B. Making Meaning of the Table (the Interpretive *Level)*
1. In 1965, which national problem was considered the most pressing? Why do you think that was so?
2. In 1980, which national problem was considered the most pressing? Why do you think that was so?
3. Which problem showed the greatest change from 1965 to 1980?
4. Which problem showed the least amount of change? Why do you think that was?

Part C. Going Beyond the Table (the Applied *Level)*
1. Which problem did the Reagan administration attack most vehemently? Why do you think it chose that one?
2. How might the media (e.g., television, newspapers) have influenced the changes in public concern over the 15-year period in the table?
3. Might the drop in concern for reducing racial discrimination be a reflection of the apathy toward the problem on the part of the public? Or might it be an actual reflection of the reduction of tension between the races? What do you think the percentage is today?
4. Project what each percentage might be for 2000, and provide a reason for each figure. Assignment for the weekend: Each of you is to question 20 different people in your neighborhood on these same 10 problems and then add your percentages to the table. Be prepared in class Monday to discuss the changed or unchanged percentages and what influence the Reagan administration might have had.*

*This lesson was developed by Michael Piccirillo, M.A.T. candidate at the State University of New York at Binghamton and social studies teacher at the Pottersville Middle School, Pottersville, New York.
Source: Table from the Gallup Poll, *Americans' Perceptions of the Most Important National Problems, 1965–1980,* 1980, Princeton, NJ: Gallup Organization. Reprinted by permission of the Gallup Organization.

The purpose of research using participant observation skills is to "see the world as their subjects see it" (Williamson et al., 1982, p. 1982). For example, a student studying the problems of day care for working parents visits a day care center for several days at different times to observe and ask questions about what he or she observes. At the end of each visit, the student writes extensive field notes, trying to recall everything seen, asked, and heard. After several visits, the student may have enough information to develop some conclusions on the quality of day care at the particular center.

As another example, a student may be interested in determining who has the real power in his or her city. The student conducts the participant observation field work by observing several meetings of the city council, committees, chamber of commerce, Rotary Club, League of Women Voters, and the local political parties. After analyzing his or her field notes, the student may have an answer to the original question.

Archaeological Digs.   Archaeologists, who are closely related to cultural anthropologists, also use field notes. However, they obtain their information not necessarily from talking to people but by examining the material remains left behind by former societies. Often these remains, or relics, are buried deep within the ground and uncovered in a process known as a *dig*. Within the past 20 years or so, many teachers took their classes to a riverbank, an old dump, or other area purported to house societal remains to give students the experience of a real dig. However, because the classes usually were not accompanied by archaeologists, they often disrupted a real find that the experts had been unable to examine or misinterpreted items found. Thus, archaeologists now ask teachers not to take students on a field trip dig unless an archaeologist goes along to teach the class.

However, by enrolling in a basic archaeology field methods course, teachers can acquire some of the skills of a professional archaeologist. Armed with these skills, they can develop simulations of digs to help students learn how to learn from artifacts. One of the authors of this text has a collection of small Early American items. She simulates a dig by placing some of the less easily identifiable ones on the floor as though they had been found in different rooms or in different parts of a room in a colonial home. Students examine the artifacts and try to guess how the "family" who lived in "this house" earned a living, in what part of the colonies they lived, and what their recreational activities were. Some of these items have included a shuttle for making fishing nets, a fleam, a knife handle made of bone, and pieces of horned coral.

We encourage you to learn some of the basics of survey research so that you can teach them to your middle and high school students as they continue to learn how to locate and use information. However, because we do not have room in this book to teach you all there is to know about developing surveys, public opinion polls, and questionnaires, we suggest that you consult books on educational research. Three are cited in the references section in this chapter (Best & Kahn, 1986; Tuckman, 1988; Williamson, Karp, Dalphin, & Gray, 1982). For more information on archaeology, contact your local college or university anthropology department to see if a faculty member can meet with your class.

USING AVAILABLE PRINTED RESOURCES

Besides gathering information through actual research, high school students can delve into the many printed materials available, such as *Statistical Abstracts of the United States, Statistical Yearbook, Historical Statistics of the United States, Colonial Times to 1990*, and federal and state government census data, among other resources. Of course, students can also use almanacs and database software (we discussed teaching with computers in Chapter 6).

Organizing and Arranging Information

Students need either to be given a problem or question or—preferably—formulate a problem or question themselves and then find the data that will help answer it. Organizing the information in a meaningful way—that is, so as to make meaning of it—comes next. The final step is to arrange the data in a graph, chart, or table to share the answer, solution, or information with others. We suggest that you walk your students through the first data-gathering activity in preparation for making a visual.

For example, suppose your students are studying the countries of Southwest Asia and North Africa (SWANA). Because oil is the commodity that most people think of when they refer to those nations, your question to the students is "What are the oil reserves of the individual SWANA nations?" Next, you can ask them what sources they might check to find out. If this is an in-school assignment, students can use the school library, finding an almanac as a starter. If it is a homework assignment, students may use almanacs at home or in the neighborhood public library.

When checking the index of *The World Almanac and Book of Facts* for information on oil reserves, students are directed to look under "petroleum." There they find several entries, but the only one they can use to answer the question is under "World Production: (see individual nations)." Checking one nation that the students are certain is a SWANA nation. Egypt, they find, under the heading "Economy," "Crude Oil Reserves (1985): 4 bln. bbls." They figure out that the abbreviation means "billion barrels" and proceed to find a map in an atlas or their textbook that indicates all the SWANA nations. Next, they list the nations and their oil reserves as shown in Figure 10.14.

Next, students decide how to arrange their information. It could be a chart or a line or bar graph. A chart will be easier and quicker, however, because they will not have to figure out how many millions of barrels in each billion

FIGURE 10.14
Listing of Crude Oil Reserves in the SWANA Nations

Afghanistan	No oil reserves	Libya	22 bln. bbls.
Algeria	7 bln. bbls.	Morocco	100 mln bbls.
Bahrain	173 mln. bbls.	Oman	4.5 bln. bbls.
Cyprus	No oil reserves	Qatar	4.5 mln. bbls.
Egypt	4 bln. bbls.	Saudi Arabia	167 bln. bbls.
Iran	37 bln. bbls.	Syria	1.3 bln. bbls.
Iraq	38 bln. bbls.	Tunisia	1.8 bln. bbls.
Israel	1 mln bbls	Turkey	312 mln. bbls.
Jordan	No oil reserves	United Arab Emirates	36 bln. bbls.
Kuwait	82 bln. bbls.	North Yemen	370 mln. bbls.
Lebanon	No oil reserves	South Yemen	No oil reserves

Source: From *The World Almanac and Book of Facts*, 1986, New York: Pharas Books.

FIGURE 10.15
Ranking of Crude Oil Reserves of Southwest Asian and North African Nations

Saudia Arabia	167 bln. bbls.		North Yemen	370 mln. bbls.
Kuwait	82 bln. bbls.		Turkey	312 mln. bbls.
Iraq	38 bln. bbls.		Bahrain	173 mln. bbls.
Iran	37 bln. bbls.		Morocco	100 mln. bbls.
United Arab Emirates	36 bln. bbls.		Qatar	4.5 mln. bbls.
Libya	22 bln. bbls.		Israel	1 mln. bbls.
Algeria	7 bln. bbls.		Afghanistan	No oil reserves
Oman	4.5 bln. bbls.		Cyprus	No oil reserves
Egypt	4 bln. bbls.		Jordan	No oil reserves
Tunisia	1.8 bln. bbls.		Lebanon	No oil reserves
Syria	1.3 bln. bbls.		South Yemen	No oil reserves

Source: From *The World Almanac and Book of Facts, 1987,* 1986, New York: Pharas Books.

and multiply by the result to turn all the numbers into millions of barrels or, alternatively, turn millions into fractions (using decimals) of a billion. The chart in Figure 10.15 lists oil producers according to size of oil reserves, from largest to smallest.

Using the Information

How might you and your students use the acquired information in a class exercise? We will show you while simultaneously developing an inquiry lesson, which uses skills taught in social studies classes.

Recall that your original question to the students was "What are the oil reserves of the individual SWANA nations?" Once students have gathered the information, they divide into small groups and ask themselves the following questions, which you have given them:

What does this information say to me?

What questions do I have about it?

What else do I now need to know?

No doubt each group will come up with some of the same responses as well as some additional ones.

Discussion follows, and the class as a whole, led by you, develops hypotheses and tentative conclusions from the data. For example, one conclusion might be that "Saudi Arabia is now and will remain the economic and political leader of the SWANA nations because it has by far the largest oil reserves." But this statement immediately provokes this question: "Is Saudi Arabia the leading nation of SWANA now?" The students realize that they will have to find the answer to that question before they can go further with their hypothesis; therefore, the hypothesis is only a tentative one.

A second hypothesis might be: "If the nations bordering Saudi Arabia joined together in a political alliance, they could contest the power of Saudi Arabia, for their combined oil reserves would be over 160 billion barrels, or almost equal to Saudi Arabia's." But this hypothesis will generate more questions that need answers, such as

Why might they want, or not want, to join?

Is it feasible for them to join?

Do they have enough similarities—cultural and political—to want to work together in a close alliance?

What do they stand to lose if they merge?

Thus, the second hypothesis also is only tentative until the students find the answers to their questions.

Several other hypotheses might follow. The students, either individually or in groups (we prefer groups so that they can learn from one another), each take one of the tentative hypotheses and locate the additional information necessary to answer the questions generated by the hypotheses. In the next class period, all individual students or groups report their findings about the hypotheses they selected, and conclusions are reached.

Figure 10.16, based on a model developed by Barry Beyer, one of our colleagues (Beyer, 1971, p. 50), summarizes the inquiry process just described. See Chapter 4 for other inquiry models.

Now choose a classmate and match the steps we took in our discussion of the lesson on oil reserves with the Beyer model in Figure 10.16. Using the information from the charts on oil reserves (Figures 10.14 and 10.15) in an inquiry lesson is one way to use it. Suppose, however, that you, the teacher, have gathered the data and plan to develop it in a lesson. With a classmate (or alone, if you prefer), and using the data in the charts, develop a lesson using the three-stage format we developed earlier on Americans' perceptions of the most important national problems (see Figure 10.13).

TEACHING FROM PICTURES, PHOTOGRAPHS, ART, ARTIFACTS, AND OTHER REALIA

We can use the inquiry model in Figure 10.16 to teach other visual skills in social studies. Again the materials may be located or gathered by either the students or the teacher.

FIGURE 10.16
The Inquiry Process

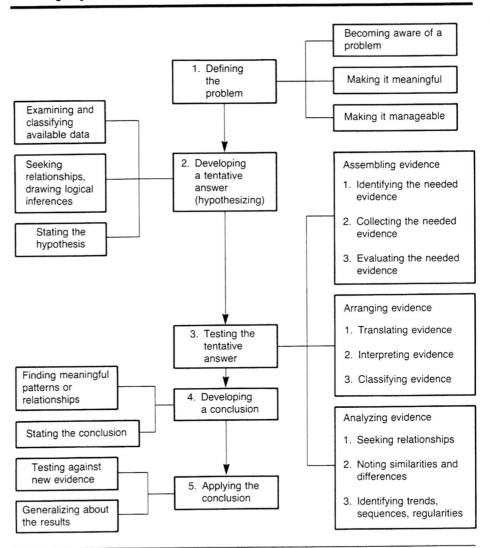

Source: From *Inquiry in the Social Studies Classroom* (p. 50) by B. Beyer, 1979, Columbus, OH: Merrill. Used with permission of the author.

We suggest that you start developing your own collection of materials: pictures from newspapers and magazines as well as old textbooks that schools toss out; photographs that you take on trips; realia from those trips, such as hotel and meal bills, menus, and magazines and newspapers from foreign countries; brochures from historical sites; and even small objects—a miniature oil rig purchased in Oklahoma, a model of St. Louis's Gateway Arch, a San Francisco trolley car, and so on. An excellent source for old posters, photos, and other realia is the Social Studies School Service in Culver City, California. Send for their catalog, or your methods instructor probably has one.

Pictures, Paintings, and Photographs

The old adage "a picture is worth a thousand words" is one we firmly adhere to, for we have seen the faces of middle school pupils light up when they looked at old photos of children their age playing in New York City in the 1890s. We also can recall the looks of astonishment when students saw pictures of the 300-pound president William H. Taft. A color poster-photo of the My Lai massacre in 1968 made the Vietnam War—and all wars—horribly real for students in modern U.S. history class, as did Mathew Brady's pictures of the Civil War era (Meredith, 1982; Horan, 1955). The murals painted by Mexican artists Diego Rivera, José Orozco, and David Siqueiros lend emotional depth and understanding to the lives of the Mexican people during their revolutions.

But we don't merely show students the photos, paintings, pictures, or posters. We incorporate these visuals into lessons, especially inquiry lessons. Pedro, whom you met at the beginning of the chapter, has adopted this approach:

ELISE: Hey, Pedro, watch it! I just got these papers all arranged for class, and you come charging in here as if we should play pick-up-sticks with them! What's going on?

PEDRO: Elise, I just had a great class, a great lesson! My kids were so tuned in to what we were doing—my plan worked like a charm! I just had to tell somebody, and you were the first one I bumped into. I didn't really mean to *bump* into you, though. I'm sorry.

ELISE: OK, OK, you're forgiven! I'm glad you had a great class, but I've got to run and try to do one myself. Tell me about yours later, though.

PEDRO: Sure. Over lunch?

ELISE: Great. You bring the peanut butter.

The subject of Pedro's most recent lesson was families.

Objectives. Pedro had two objectives for the lesson. The first objective was cognitive: to enable his students to discuss the concept of family. The second objective was affective: to get students to understand and appreciate the different types of families in the United States and West Africa.

Rationale. Before beginning a unit on West African culture in which students would study, among other concepts, African families, Pedro decided that his students needed to get rid of some of the ethnocentrism he had observed from working with them for three months. Although his students came from a variety of family types themselves (single-parent, foster home, blended, and "traditional"), they held the idealistic notion that the nuclear family of the storybooks and TV was the best one. Therefore, Pedro wanted to introduce them to the many different types of families within the United States before going into the variety of African family types, particularly polygamy, because it was especially alien to his students.

Inquiry Activity.   Pedro asked his students to brainstorm about what a family is. As they volunteered definitions or comments, he wrote them on several overhead transparencies, accepting their responses but asking the students to clarify them if he wasn't quite sure of what they meant. As he expected, the class came up with the typical responses or variations thereof: father, mother, and kids; people who live together harmoniously; all the relatives gathered at Thanksgiving; and so on.

Then Pedro posed the following questions:

Which one of these definitions can we agree on as the meaning of the word *family?* Are they all?

How is the word *family* defined in law?

Are families different now from what they once were?

What image comes to mind when you hear the word *family?*

Pedro split his students into groups of five and gave each group a packet of pictures of people engaged in different activities. Then he said to them, "In your group, decide which pictures are pictures of families and which are not. Be prepared to explain your answers to the rest of the class. Also, come up with a definition for the word *family.*"

After about 15 minutes, Pedro asked for a report from each group. One group decided that all the pictures could be families. Referring to the photos in Figure 10.17, the group had concluded that "the two white women [Figure 10.17(a)] could be sisters, or maybe mother and daughter; the three white women in the living room [Figure 10.17(b)] could be a family because the women could be either sisters or good friends who share an apartment; the white woman about 40 and the young black man [Figure 10.17(c)] could be mother and adopted son or stepson; the three men [Figure 10.17(d)]could also be a family—they could be a son and his father and grandfather or uncle." Other groups disagreed, saying that "you have to have a parent to have a family." But one student countered, "I live with my grandparents, and we think of ourselves as a family."

The discussion continued for nearly the entire remainder of the class period. Near the end, Pedro asked the students which questions they still needed answers to and how they proposed to find the answers. One student responded that they could check a dictionary, especially a law dictionary, for a legal definition. Another thought they could check with the county social services agency to see how their state defined *family* for purposes of public

FIGURE 10.17
Defining the Word *Family*

(a)

(b)

(c)

(d)

aid distribution. Each group chose one of the possible follow-up activities for the next class in an attempt to verify their hypotheses.

Using Beyer's model (Figure 10.16), let's see how the inquiry process played out:

1. *Defining the problem:* First, Pedro asked his students what a family is.
2. *Developing a tentative answer (hypothesizing):* In responding to Pedro, students were stating their hypotheses in a brainstorming session.
3. *Testing the tentative answer:* Pedro provided students with data (photos of two or more people), which they discussed and interpreted.

4. *Developing a conclusion:* In groups, students developed several new hypotheses (definitions of the concept *family*).

5. *Applying the conclusion:* In full class, students discussed the individual groups' hypotheses and applied them to their own groups' discussions. Pedro helped them realize that they needed to test their hypotheses against new evidence. Thus, their assignment for the next class was to seek additional resources and references.

Instead of teaching a concept using the inquiry approach, which takes considerable time, many teachers prefer to use the expository approach, that is, simply telling students what the concept means and giving them definitions from standard dictionaries, law dictionaries, bibles, and so on. This takes only about five minutes. As a student, which approach would you prefer? Why? As a teacher, which approach would you use? Why?

Teaching with Art, Artifacts, and Other Realia

ELISE: I agree, Pedro, that was a great class. I use the inquiry process in a similar way when I bring in objects from the colonial days in Latin America and have students figure out what life was like then by examining the tools, household objects, and other old things I have collected over the years from flea markets, antique shows, or wherever when I'm in Latin America. People even give them to me as birthday gifts. The kids have a good time "playing" archaeologists when I bring in the stuff.

PEDRO: Yasuko does something like that too when she goes to all the other classes when they are studying Japan. She also brings in a lot of realia—newspapers, birthday and holiday cards, clothing, tea sets, bamboo items, and whatnot.

ELISE: I know she does. She has her students, in groups, try to put together what life is like in Japan—the economy, the government, sports and recreation, and religion. Each group has a different set of items related to their topic.

PEDRO: And Brian brings in slides of paintings to illustrate how art depicts history. The ones he uses on the Reformation and on the Renaissance are borrowed from the art history collection at the local university. He has had courses in art history, so he can give a great slide lecture, but Kelly asks an art historian to come to her class when she does Greek and Roman architecture.

As you can see from the preceding examples, the same inquiry process model works well in helping students learn from studying artifacts and other realia. Remember that one of the main purposes in social studies teaching is to help students learn how to continue to learn on their own. Let's read that last statement again. Understand it? As social studies teachers, we have the opportunity to help students learn only about 45 minutes a day, 5 days a week, about 38 weeks a year. That doesn't mean that they never "think" social studies the rest of the time; they do. But how they think about it then is our responsibility, too. In order to learn when they're not with us, they need to have at their command the social studies skills we've discussed in this chapter and throughout the book. They need to be able to see a map in a weekly newsmagazine and be able to interpret it, make meaning of it, and ask questions of it. Likewise, they need to be able to see a chart or table and explain it to their parents or classmates, even to the point of recognizing that new information might change the meaning of the visual.

Political Cartoons

ELISE: Did you see Doonesbury this morning? Great cartoon—one of the best he's done in a long time. Want to have a look? You have five seconds, because I'm taking it to class. It'll fit in perfectly with my lesson on income taxes. Remember when Bush said "Read my lips: no more taxes" back in '88? Well, Trudeau is not going to let him forget it. I gotta go.

We are all familiar with political cartoons. In fact, some of us turn first to the editorial page of the newspaper just to see the day's cartoon. What is there about them that makes them so alluring? Is it just the humor? Many cartoons are funny, and the humor is easily and instantly picked up, whether it's the message or just the distortion of the features of the main subject. They are also inviting because the message is quick; we don't have to spend a lot of time with political cartoons, for there's little to read.

Students like political cartoons for the same reasons. Students who have difficulty reading text or are slow readers enjoy the chance to keep up with the rest of the class. So use political cartoons in your social studies classes. Their subject matter typically reflects social studies content anyway. Presidents are often the butt of cartoonists, as well as subjects such as economic policies, social problems, and world affairs.

Incorporating Political Cartoons into Class. We can teach students how to read and interpret political cartoons using the same three levels we examined in the sections on maps, tables, charts, and graphs. But there are some preinterpretive skills that students need to learn to fully understand cartoons. These skills include:

- Identifying symbols
- Recognizing caricature, distortion, and exaggeration
- Detecting bias and point of view
- Analyzing captions (Holub & Bennett, 1988, p. 214)

Symbols and Symbolism.   Perhaps the best way to teach symbolism is to talk about symbols that students see in their daily lives. Some symbols are local or national/international business and industry logos, such as IBM, 3M, and the apple with a bite taken out of it (Apple Computer): social agency logos, such as the red cross for the Red Cross; symbols of the U.S. government, such as the flag, the Statue of Liberty, the eagle, and Uncle Sam. There are also the "generic" symbols, such as the dollar sign ($), the peace sign, and the dove, to name just a few. No doubt you and your students can think of many more.

One activity is to have students make a list of as many symbols as they can think of. For longer lists, have them work in groups of about three. Allow them to explain a few of their symbols to the rest of the class. Explain some of the symbols frequently found in political cartoons, for example, the olive branch, the oil barrel, the hammer and sickle, the Star of David, and a Christian cross. Make a photocopy of several cartoons and then a transparency of them. That way, all students will be able to see the cartoon and symbols more clearly.

Recognizing Caricature, Distortion, and Exaggeration.   Caricature, distortion, and exaggeration help make cartoons funny. But students need to understand why these devices are used. One explanation is that these techniques make the subject of the cartoon easily identifiable. Abraham Lincoln's long, wiry build and beard turned him into an Ichabod Crane for cartoonists. The 300-pound frame of New York's Boss Tweed looked like 500 pounds in Thomas Nast's drawings of Tweed. More recently, Jimmy Carter's big, shiny teeth and Ronald Reagan's thick mop of dark hair standing on end made these subjects instantly recognizable. First Lady Barbara Bush's white hair and three strands of pearls have become standards for cartoonists. Show students several other cartoons, again on overhead transparencies, and have them identify the caricatures, distortions, or exaggerations. Then ask them to bring to class cartoons they have found in magazines and newspapers at home or ones that you have provided. Make a cartoon bulletin board, such as the one Elise has in her classroom.

Detecting Bias and Point of View.   Political cartoons contain as much bias and point of view as the print editorials—and you can detect these characteristics much sooner. Students need to learn how to recognize point of view and detect bias. For example, several cartoonists have poked fun at George and Barbara Bush's wholesomeness to the point of suggesting that 1600 Pennsylvania Avenue is really in "Mr. Rogers' Neighborhood." That example is one that students who have grown up with public television should readily relate to.

Analyzing Captions.   A one-line caption typically contains a very complex message. Try introducing the skill of analyzing captions by providing students with several familiar quotations or sayings: "A picture is worth a thousand words"; "It's not over till the fat lady sings"; "A penny saved is a penny earned"; "All the world's a stage." Have students write out the meanings

FIGURE 10.18
Sample Lesson Using a Political Cartoon

Directions: With two classmates, answer the following questions about the political cartoon shown above. After 20 minutes, be prepared to discuss each answer in full-group discussion.

Part A. Reading the Cartoon
1. Who is the main figure supposed to be?
2. What is the main figure carrying?
3. What are the elephants doing?
4. What do the elephants represent? Why?
5. What does the eagle represent?
6. What is the setting for this cartoon?

Part B. Making Meaning of the Cartoon
1. What does the Big Stick represent?
2. Where is Morocco? What are the people and elephants doing there? Why? (You may refer to your textbook.)
3. What is the message of the cartoonist? What is his point of view?

Part C. Going Beyond the Cartoon
1. How do you think people of that time reacted to this cartoon? Why?
2. If President Bush were carrying the Big Stick in this cartoon today, what might be the reaction of the American people?
3. Would you be surprised to see President Bush in this situation? Why or why not?
4. Do you agree with the message of the cartoon? Why or why not?

Source: Cartoon by W. A. Rogers, Library of Congress.

in as many sentences as they require and compare their interpretations with the few words in the original statements. Then they will see the importance of tight, carefully worded captions. Show them some easy political cartoons and have them, in groups of three, try to devise captions.

Figure 10.18 presents one of Elise's lessons using political cartoons.

Summary

We hope that from reading this chapter you will use many different types of activities in your social studies classes that will give students opportunities to learn the special social studies skills. Students need to learn how to continue learning on their own, and by providing them with the various graphic skills we have included in this chapter, you will be well on your way to satisfying that goal. Using maps, charts, graphs, political cartoons, realia, surveys, and questionnaires in addition to the standard print materials will enhance the learning of social studies. Students should learn not only how to use these various forms of visuals but how and where to locate them. They should even learn how to make their own visuals.

Decisions! Decisions!

1. Do you feel prepared to develop (and teach) lessons using several of the ideas from this chapter? Which ones are you most comfortable with? Why? Which ones are you least comfortable with? Why?

2. How would you assess your own geography skills? Are the five geography themes new to you? Select one theme and develop a lesson around it.

3. How many times a week do you think a teacher should incorporate visuals or artifacts/realia into a class? Justify your response.

4. Can you remember the use of artifacts or realia in your middle or senior high school social studies classes? Were they important to the lesson as far as you were concerned then? Now? Why or why not?

5. Other than the ones mentioned in this chapter, what free and readily available sources do you know of for acquiring graphs, charts, tables, political cartoons, and maps?

References

Anderson, C. C., & Winston, B. J. (1977). Acquiring information by asking questions, using maps and graphs, and making direct observations. In D. G. Kurfman (Ed.), *Developing decision-making skills* (47th Yearbook, pp. 71–106). Washington, DC: National Council for the Social Studies.

Best, J. W., & Kahn, J. V. (1986). *Research in education* (5th ed.). Englewood Cliffs, NJ: Prentice-Hall.

Beyer, B. (1971). *Inquiry in the social studies classroom.* Columbus, OH: Merrill.

Dahl, R. (1961). The behavioral approach in political science: Epitaph for a monument to a successful protest. *American Political Science Review, 55.* Also in M. Feldman & E. Seifman (Eds.). (1969). *The social studies: Structure, models, and strategies* (pp. 124–137). Englewood Cliffs, NJ: Prentice-Hall.

Garver, J. B., Jr. (1988). New perspective on the world. *National Geographic, 174*(6), 910–913.

Hawkins, M. L. (1980). Graphing: A stimulating way to process data. How To Do It, Notebook Series 2. Washington, DC: National Council for the Social Studies.

Holub, B., & Bennett, C. T. (1988). Using political cartoons to teach junior/middle school U.S. history. *The Social Studies 79*(5), 214–216.

Horan, J. D. (1955). *Mathew Brady: Historian with a camera.* New York: Crown.

Joint Committee on Geographic Education of the National Council for Geographic Education and the Association of American Geographers. (1984). *Guidelines for geographic education.* Washington, DC: Author.

McCune, G. H., & Pearson, N. (1964). Interpreting materials in graphic form. In H. M. Carpenter (Ed.), *Skill development in social studies* (33rd Yearbook, pp. 202–229). Washington, DC: National Council for the Social Studies.

Meredith, R. (1982). *Mathew Brady's portrait of an era.* New York: Norton.

Natoli, S. J. (Ed.). (1988). *Strengthening geography in the social studies* (Bulletin No. 81). Washington, DC: National Council for the Social Studies.

Robinson, A. H. (1987). Reflections on the Gall-Peters projection. *Social Education, 51*(4), 260–264.

Sabaroff, R. (1969). Improving the use of maps in the elementary school. In M. Feldman & E. Seifman (Eds.), *The social studies: Structure, models, and strategies* (pp. 330–336). Englewood Cliffs, NJ: Prentice-Hall.

Tuckman, B. (1988). *Conducting educational research* (3rd ed.). New York: Harcourt Brace Jovanovich.

Welton, D. A. (1988). Reassessing geographic literacy. *Educators' Forum,* 11–12.

Williamson, J. B., Karp, D. A., Dalphin, J. R., & Gray, P. S. (1982). *The research craft: An introduction to social research methods.* Boston: Little, Brown.

Chapter Eleven

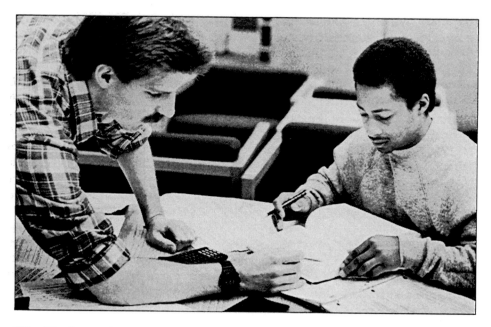

Evaluation, Measurement, and Reporting

Effective social studies teachers use various means to assess the attainment of goals and objectives of curriculum and instruction. These, in turn, reflect the diverse aptitudes and degrees of readiness of their students.

"Thanks for the gift," a 10th grader said to her teacher, who stood there feeling his neck begin to redden. While she said it appreciatively and she was a nice, serious student, he was irritated. Silently he vowed, "No more Mr. Nice Guy." Neither she nor any other students would receive a "gift" grade from him again.

The students had just received their report cards, and the teacher recalled the dilemma that had led to the "gift." Should this student receive a B– or a C+? He had based his decision primarily on a unit test, one of the few grades recorded in the grade book. How was he to decide? He had simply gone on the basis of his gut feeling that the girl was a serious student and deserved the higher mark. Next time, he would make sure she received the lower mark. He wasn't going to be known as a soft touch, for he wanted both his students and his colleagues to regard him as a "real" teacher, recalling the college faculty who had taught him and been hard with him.

Then his better judgment prevailed. It wouldn't be right simply to make it hard for students. Rather, he would have to develop a system to award grades based on achievement that would prove fair to his students and to his own standards for grading.

But what would that system entail? Vaguely he recalled the mumbo jumbo about bell curves, measures of central tendency, standard deviations, ad nauseam that he was supposed to have learned in "Tests and Measurements" in college. But what did that have to do with grading?

Also, he thought about how grading really seemed to be the worst part of the whole business of teaching. Why couldn't he simply teach? Grading made everyone uncomfortable, it seemed, except for those who didn't seem to care about school anyway.

WHY EVALUATE?

The teacher in the preceding vignette was stuck squarely on the horns of a dilemma. On the one hand, there are those who believe grades are an evil to which students are peculiarly subjected, interfere with genuine learning, and lead to a "wad-ja-get" mentality (Kirschenbaum, Napier, & Simon, 1971). On the other hand, the American public demands excellence from its schools, which in turn requires standards and some form of assessment to determine whether the standards are being reached.

Critics of the "wad-ja-get" mentality argue that schools—and therefore teachers—use tests and grades simply to distinguish the "bluebirds" from the "turtles." This is the sorting system that maintains the status quo and ensures "a properly disciplined work force for industrial America" (Selakovich, 1984, p. 36).

"Reformers," concerned that schools are being "eroded by a rising tide of mediocrity," want standards established and the degree of attainment of those standards documented (National Commission on Excellence in Education, 1983). But we have been through this before, *many* times, and it is hard to argue with the notion that schools are the common denominator: Schools are to serve all youth and to transmit the culture.

The fact remains that teachers cannot escape the responsibility for finding out whether their students have learned anything. *Evaluation,* the systematic collection of evidence to judge changes in learners and the amount and degree of change, "comes with the territory." If teachers are to avoid the frustration that often accompanies the awarding of grades, they must systematically collect evidence about students' learning: the degree of change in students' behaviors as a result of instruction. There must be some basis for making sound judgments about student achievement or lack thereof. Thus, teachers must refer to the goals and objectives for their curriculum (discussed in Chapter 5).

FORMS OF EVALUATION

Teachers have any number of ways to collect evidence. But first, they must determine what they intend to do with that evidence. Are they assessing the degree of learning of their students over an entire course or units within for the purpose of putting grades in a grade book? If so, they are opting for what is called *summative evaluation:* They are assessing the extent of learning of specific material and typically will assign scores and then translate them into grades. On the other hand, teachers could opt for *formative evaluation:* determining the degree of student mastery of some information during instruction to adjust the instruction or correct student deficiencies.

The mastery learning model that we examined in Chapter 4 uses both forms of evaluation, particularly the formative (Gronlund, 1981, pp. 500–503). Recall that in this model courses are divided into units (a set of activities, a chapter or learning unit), objectives are specified, criteria for mastery are set, and learning tasks are outlined. During and at the end of each learning activity or unit, *formative* tests are administered to determine student mastery of content and detect errors. Generally grades are not assigned at this point; rather, corrective measures are suggested to help students who have not mastered the content. When a more comprehensive evaluation is sought (at the end of a course or grading period or mid-semester), *summative* measures (tests) are administered. The purpose is to assign grades, send reports to parents, or assess instruction.

Figure 11.1 schematically illustrates the relationship among evaluation, instructional decisions, the learner, and learning outcomes. While it may appear unnecessarily complicated, the chart represents the three major components of the teaching-learning sequence and the vital role that evaluation plays for the teacher. We will refer to this sequence periodically in this chapter.

FIGURE 11.1
Relationship among Evaluation, Instructional Decisions, and the Analysis of Learners, Instruction, and Learning Outcomes

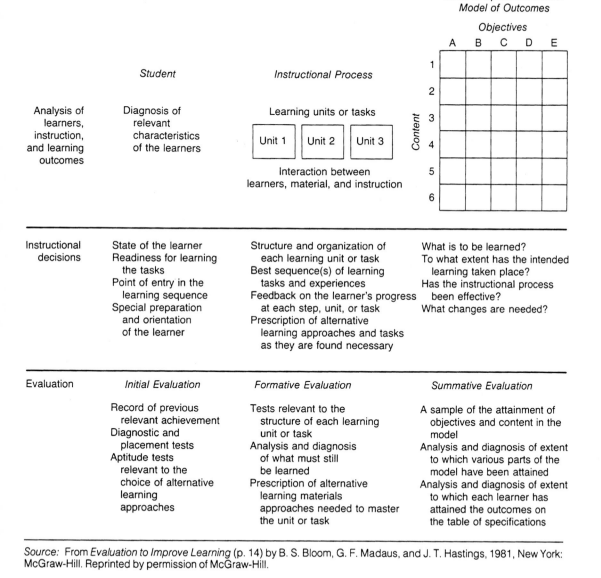

	Student	Instructional Process	
Analysis of learners, instruction, and learning outcomes	Diagnosis of relevant characteristics of the learners	Learning units or tasks Unit 1 Unit 2 Unit 3 Interaction between learners, material, and instruction	Table of Specifications for Model of Outcomes
Instructional decisions	State of the learner Readiness for learning the tasks Point of entry in the learning sequence Special preparation and orientation of the learner	Structure and organization of each learning unit or task Best sequence(s) of learning tasks and experiences Feedback on the learner's progress at each step, unit, or task Prescription of alternative learning approaches and tasks as they are found necessary	What is to be learned? To what extent has the intended learning taken place? Has the instructional process been effective? What changes are needed?
Evaluation	*Initial Evaluation* Record of previous relevant achievement Diagnostic and placement tests Aptitude tests relevant to the choice of alternative learning approaches	*Formative Evaluation* Tests relevant to the structure of each learning unit or task Analysis and diagnosis of what must still be learned Prescription of alternative learning materials approaches needed to master the unit or task	*Summative Evaluation* A sample of the attainment of objectives and content in the model Analysis and diagnosis of extent to which various parts of the model have been attained Analysis and diagnosis of extent to which each learner has attained the outcomes on the table of specifications

Source: From *Evaluation to Improve Learning* (p. 14) by B. S. Bloom, G. F. Madaus, and J. T. Hastings, 1981, New York: McGraw-Hill. Reprinted by permission of McGraw-Hill.

EVALUATION AND MEASUREMENT

It is important to distinguish between evaluation and measurement. Commonly teachers tend to concentrate only on *measurement,* collecting and sorting evidence to make a judgment, typically relying on tests. We want to make it clear at the outset, however, that tests are only one form of measurement from which we can make judgments. For example, student projects can reflect mastery of content, skills, and attitudes that tests may not measure accurately. And occasionally self-reporting is extraordinarily revealing. We recall one student who, when asked to evaluate herself, was particularly critical of her performance in class at one point. But after she gave her explanation, the teacher had to admit that the student knew better than anyone.

Observations of students by teachers also can be extremely valuable. Student behaviors reveal attitudes as well as demonstrate learning. Alert teachers can detect skills, work habits, participation, articulation, and other factors.

Basic Performance Measurements

Years ago, one of the authors coached high school gymnastics and annually faced the awful task of conducting tryouts for a limited number of spots on the team. To "cut" anyone was always a problem for the author-coach though worse for the individuals who did not make the team. It was most difficult in the case of ninth graders who had little or no gymnastics experience. What might they have become given the chance?

Criteria were established: strength, flexibility, agility, attitude, and other attributes. Attitude was especially difficult to assess. But with the help of some 12th graders on the team, evaluations were made. Note that *criteria* were used. Each student trying out was measured on these criteria and graded from 1 to 10. This form of measurement is called *criterion-referenced* measurement. The author-coach could require candidates to achieve, say, a 6, or 60% of what a successful gymnast would normally achieve. So the first obstacle was hurdled.

Later, once a team was selected, the task became to determine who would actually perform well in competition. A new form of measurement was needed. All the students wanting to perform on a particular apparatus competed, and the three with the highest scores, again 1 to 10, were selected to represent the team in the next meet. In other words, a *norm-referenced* measurement was used. Given all those who wanted to compete, the three who received the highest scores in face-to-face competition on a particular apparatus were chosen. This system prevailed in the meets throughout the season as well.

But day to day, it was also necessary to keep individual students improving. Yes, they knew the criteria against which all would be judged—the sequence of "tricks" (difficulty), form, and execution, with a 10 representing perfection. They knew the scores of gymnasts from other schools in the state against which they could judge their individual performances (norm-referenced). But they also had to be encouraged in the short run. Thus, the gymnasts were asked to compare their most recent performances against earlier ones, that is, against themselves—an example of a *self-referenced* measure. A state champion who was an 11th grader could always "coast," figuring on being a shoo-in to win again. It was necessary to measure today's performance against earlier performances as well as the norm, a perfect score, which might have seemed unattainable or too far in the future to worry about.

Ironically, the teacher-coach did not apply the same reasoning and different forms of measurement in the classroom. To have done so, however, would have produced a far more effective teacher. So what could, and should, have been done?

Criterion referencing would have been the easiest way to determine grades. If on a test a particular student achieved 9 out of 10 objectives, which represents 90%, that student could receive an A. This would have been similar to judging a gymnast on a 10-point scale or on the attributes of strength, flexibility, or agility against some magic formula of "perfection." Those who would rid American schools of "mediocrity" probably would prefer this form of measurement for assessing how well students, schools, and teachers are performing. The degree of excellence could be easily determined.

Norm referencing was another possibility: comparing a student's score on a test (summative) with those of all the other students who took that test. Did the student's score on the test fit into the top 1.5% (A), the top 15% (B), or the middle 67% (C) of all the students' test scores? "Curving a grade" often results from this scheme. For the "bluebirds," the students who have ability and can perform well on tests, this is quite satisfying given that they perform as expected. Some reformers prefer norm referencing, for example, "Are American schoolchildren doing as well as or better than students in Japan (or West Germany, or the U.S.S.R, or wherever they feel that "real" success is being achieved)?"

But what happens to the "turtles," who do poorly on every test and always receive low or failing grades? Couldn't they also be improving? Criterion referencing might well detect improvement. So could self-referencing, that is, how is a particular student doing now compared with his or her performance at the beginning of the year or unit? If the student was receiving primarily 40s (Fs) at the beginning of the year and now is getting a 59 (still an F), should this not be recognized?

But the same reasoning can apply to the academically talented. How is the "bluebird" encouraged to perform better than the minimal A he or she receives? Using criteria rather than measuring the student against others might well help the student to achieve his or her full potential.

In this chapter, we will address all of these issues.

ASIDE TO THE READER: Do you prefer norm-, criterion-, or self- referenced measurement? What has been your experience so far? Do you like to compete against others? Against some other standard? Against yourself?

Note that this is not a multiple-choice question. The three criterion forms are not mutually exclusive; in fact, a competent teacher employs all of them. What are some situations in which you might use more than one form? Would you want to compare students' performances on your tests with those on standardized tests? Would you want students to compare their earlier performances against their current ones?

How do you feel about grades? Do you think they accurately measure how well students are learning or have learned something? Have you ever been caught up in the "wad-ja-get" syndrome?

Did you panic when you took PSATs, SATs, or ACTs?

How would you most like to be evaluated?

REPORTING STUDENT PROGRESS

The reason for discussing evaluation, of course, is that we want to be able to make and report our judgments of student progress. But we need something to report, that is, the results of our evaluation, which we then put into a grade book (or on a computer spreadsheet, as in Figure 11.2). But how did we assign these grades, which look so neat and finite? How comfortable should we be with them? What does the very first grade we recorded, the most troubling one, represent? How did we derive it? What does an "88" really mean?

Typically we think of grade books and grade cards, but these are only two forms for reporting student progress. We need to consider the larger picture.

Are we evaluating to effect changes in our instruction or in the program itself? For example, did students generally do poorly on a particular content or concept that we were trying to teach? Are the materials we used inappropriate? Is our instruction tied to our objectives? These are only a few considerations.

Alternatively, are we using the results of our evaluation to rank students? Are we using the scores on tests and quizzes to alert parents, as well as students, to students' progress or lack thereof?

Gronlund (1981, p. 509) reminds us that we need to be clear on why we are summarizing student progress:

> Should the assigned mark represent level of achievement, gain in achievement, or some combination of the two? Should effort be included, or should high achievers be given good marks regardless of effort? Should pupils be marked in terms of their own potential learning ability or in relation to the achievement of their classmates?*

In other words, we need to return to earlier considerations about norm, self-, and criterion referencing.

---

*Reprinted with permission of Macmillan Publishing Company from *Measurement and Evaluation in Teaching* (4th ed.) by N. Gronlund. Copyright © 1981 by Macmillan Publishing Company.

FIGURE 11.2
Sample Grade Book

Second Period S.S. Class

NAME	QUIZ	QUIZ	AVG	COMP	COMP	AVG	HMWK	TEST	6 WKS' GR	STUD I.D.
Elizabeth	88	92	88.5	98	88	93	90	94	91.7	113548264
Heidi	75	82	83.5	82	85	83.5	87	69	80.2	124669518
Michele	85	85	83.5	82	82	82	80	66	76.8	385843150
Lada	75	78	81	88	82	85	84	67	78.7	128567069
Jay	78	78	76.5	70	73	71.5	76	79	75.8	79508690
Mary Lou	88	85	89.5	88	91	89.5	92	77	86.5	55567657
Thomas	85	82	82	85	88	86.5	86	69	80.4	125509790
Nathan	82	55	65	70	65	67.5	62	65	64.7	86604708
Lisa	88	85	86.5	92	85	88.5	87	80	85.2	120548671
Franklin	82	85	83.5	88	84	86	82	75	81.1	155488220
David	85	65	65	71	76	73.5	75	78	74.0	129641771
Jonathan	85	85	83.5		85	85	83	78	77.9	114562624
Tia	72	75	71.5	75	75	75		64	52.3	72621445
Marguerite	85	88	86	85	78	81.5	83	76	82.5	70689608
Daniel	85	80	80.5	72	77	74.5	75	81	75.7	77600942
Jesus	75	88	85	85	85	85	84	75	82.0	105403846
Carla	85	77	76	84	82	83	78	76	79.5	111587584
Raphael	82	62	77	82	85	83.5	90	80	81.6	123524771
Patricia	88	85	88.5	92	92	92	91	74	85.5	116584354
Melissa	85	85	83.5	88	82	85	86	73	84.5	67549077
Carolynn	85	75	73.5	75	72	73.5	76	83	73.5	81582587
Maria	75	82	83.5	85	86	85.5	88	71	83.7	129600680
Steven	85	82	80	85	88	86.5	84	78	84.0	89660334
Yang	88	74	78	66	68	67	75	72	72.8	120409671
Averages			80.5			81.8		74.8	78.6	
			x15%			x25%	x30%	x30%		

Keep in mind that teachers continually evaluate students' progress, whether praising or correcting responses in class or on written assignments. Nevertheless, grading is necessary and inevitable, and it is important to be fair in doing so, using methods that are appropriate and reasonable.

Methods of Grading

Commonly teachers use some scale—1 through 10, 1 through 100, or some derivation thereof, such as 42 correct out of a possible 50. Then they translate these raw scores into letter grades—A, B, C, D, and F (or E in many schools) with further gradations, such as pluses and minuses, or even into grade points, such as 4.0, 3.0, and so on. Conventionally, A equals 90–100, B equals 80–89, and F equals scores below 60.

However, as Bloom, Madaus, and Hastings (1981, p. 106) remind us, there are some problems with this type of scale. First, it is not necessarily either criterion referenced or norm referenced. Second, we don't know whether a 90 on a test reflects the range, mean, weighting, or percentile of a particular test or the ultimate grade to be assigned. For example, if a certain test were weighted as 20% of a grade for a grading period, a 90 might have a very different bearing than it would if it were weighted as only 5%. Third, a given score may not necessarily represent the importance of the attainment of the particular objective. Finally, a particular score may not reflect other students' scores. If most of the students in a class received a raw score of 90 and an individual student about whom we were concerned also received a 90, we would know only that this student had an average, or *mean*, score. We then might want to use some standardized test to see how this student (or any students) compared with a larger group of students studying the same material. This, of course, should be consistent with our objectives, such as to compare students' raw scores on our tests with the scores they would obtain on a statewide test (norm referencing).

If we were using norm referencing, we would be concerned with where particular scores fell on a *normal curve* (see Figure 11.3). Given a normal curve, we might compare our students' work with that of, say, other students at the same grade or age level. We could compare our students' scores in terms of reading "norms" for that age group or norms on aptitude tests (verbal, numerical, or abstract reasoning); that is, we might discover that our students, who averaged 90 on a test, compared favorably with others at their grade or age level. This finding would give us some confidence in our evaluation and measures.

Another advantage of using norms is that they can afford a way to assess "mastery" of some material (Bloom et al., 1981, p. 108). We could use norm referencing to determine criteria for acceptable levels of performance. For example, we may simply want to determine a "cut-off" score, which represents a "passing" or "satisfactory" performance. Students whose scores fell below that point would "fail" or be doing "unsatisfactory" work. We could say that a score of 60 or above is "passing." However, because the teacher may have set

FIGURE 11.3
Normal Curve

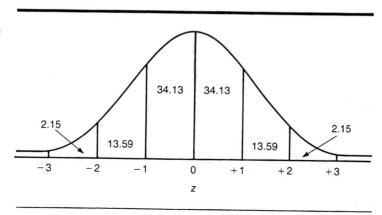

the cut-off score arbitrarily, we might refer to some norm, such as the average score on a summative test given earlier. We could set standards for current performance. A minimum passing score could be determined from past tests with previous classes or with some other norms. But because there are problems with using norms, we want to be especially careful to *choose norms with which we will work to judge current student performance.*

Also, we could use norms to assign grades. If we adhered strictly to a normal curve, only a tiny fraction of students would receive As or Fs, a larger fraction would get Bs and Ds, and a still larger fraction would receive Cs. However, we caution against such a practice. To award a percentage of As (or Fs) to students that would be lower (or higher) than common in other schools or with other measures might be unfair. If a B grade at our particular school represented an A grade at another school, we might well jeopardize our students' futures, including admission to colleges that demand a minimum high school average.

In contrast, we might use criterion referencing, whereby students are compared with some standard or set of criteria. Any student—indeed, all students—could receive As or Fs. For example, if there were 50 objectives for a unit, students who attained 45 or more would receive an A, those who attained 40 through 44 a B, those who achieved 35 through 39 a C, and so on. Or we might have a contract system at work, whereby students are given a set of objectives and agreements are negotiated between the students and the teachers as to what grade or percentage of objectives any student intends to attain. An A grade would represent satisfaction of all objectives, which in turn would reflect the conditions under which the objectives were to be attained and the degree or level of performance.

Another consideration is your school system's policies. If your school has tracking, or ability grouping, are grades of students in the lower tracks weighted differently from those in the higher tracks? Some schools give a heavier weighting to an A in the higher-track classes than to an A in the lower-track ones. If this were the case in your school, could you live with this system? Would you (or should you) have to? How easy is it for students to move from one track to another? What would you do with students who are able to handle work common to higher-track classes but refuse to go into those classes? How would you handle students who were pushed into higher-track classes by their parents but are unable or unwilling to do the work?

What about students who are working to ability (recalling that few of us probably live up to our potential)? Let's say a student is an "overachiever," one who, given scores or percentile rankings on various measures of ability, ranks in the lower percentile of students nationally but does fantastic work, puts out 1,000% on all the work he or she does. How will you reflect effort? What if a student's efforts produced nothing or only incorrect answers? Should a hard worker who received the same raw score as a lazier but more able student receive the same grade? How will you resolve these issues?

TYPES OF MEASUREMENT

Of course, before we can record any grades, we must have some ways to obtain grades. First, we need to know why and what we are measuring, what might be the best way to obtain that measurement, and what we will do with that measurement once we obtain it. We also need to keep in mind that the social studies may suffer problems that other fields do not. Recall that:

1. Social studies educators differ over goals for the social studies curriculum.
2. The social studies stand for different things—what we referred to as "alternative positions in the social studies" in Chapter 2.
3. Objectives for social studies lessons and units may not be stated behaviorally, nor, as some would argue, can they be.
4. The social studies is concerned as much with attitudes, "deep-seated and resistant to change" (Orlandi, 1971, p. 452), as with data.

We believe, however, that many of these concerns can be overcome if the teacher is an effective instructional decision maker.

Qualitative versus Quantitative Measures

Teachers evaluate learning in several distinct ways. One distinction is the extent to which they rely on qualitative or quantitative measures. *Qualitative* measures are more descriptive and typically involve value judgments, while *quantitative* measures suggest precision and expression of results in terms of numbers. Gronlund (1981, p. 135) asserts that there is no conflict between these two measurement types; rather, they serve different purposes.

Qualitative ("Softer") Measures. Teachers make judgments about students all the time, and often these are highly subjective. But there are some systematic ways to make these judgments that rely on observation and recording of observations. Qualitative instruments that we will examine include anecdotal records, rating scales, and checklists.

Anecdotal Records. A relatively unsophisticated and rough measure is the *anecdotal record*, wherein a teacher records his or her observations of a student ("doesn't live up to capacity," "is able to participate in classroom discussions," etc.). This instrument has obvious drawbacks. The most serious limitation is the degree of subjectivity. Time constraints also limit its utility. Another concern is that parents of underage students have access to such information under the Family Educational Rights and Privacy Act of 1974 (Buckley Amendment, U.S.C. Sec. 1232), and a teacher's comments could well become the subject of a libel suit.

As the term suggests, anecdotal records describe "meaningful incidents and events which the teacher has observed in the lives of his pupils" (Gronlund, 1981, p. 435). The chief advantage of anecdotal records is that they often yield data on students that would be unobtainable by other means. Still, it is important for the teacher to be as objective as possible, although personal interpretations are acceptable if used to supplement the objective descriptions.

Gronlund (1981, p. 436) suggests limiting observations to (1) areas that cannot be evaluated otherwise, (2) a few types of behavior of all pupils at a given time, and (3) a few students most in need of special attention. As a result, the use of anecdotal records will be limited to situations that preclude the use of more objective and practical methods.

Figure 11.4 illustrates an anecdotal record. Its significance is clear: The teacher observed something that could not be evaluated in the usual way. Ecurb's quiz score remains the same, but now the teacher has evidence about him that may well help in the future. Equally important, the teacher has become aware of Ecurb as a learner rather than as a body occupying a seat in class. The teacher can look for ways to help him retain his interest and perform better on future tests.

The disadvantages of anecdotal records are also evident. First, the teacher must take time to record observations. Second, the teacher must develop a system for maintaining these records. Third, the teacher must be consistent in recording events and behaviors. Fourth, it is difficult for the teacher to maintain objectivity. Finally, the teacher must ensure that there are sufficient samples to attain the necessary reliability.

Nevertheless, teachers make observations all the time, and efforts to observe students can be rewarding in themselves. Anecdotal records also offer a way to be systematic.

FIGURE 11.4
Illustrative Anecdotal Record

Name: Ecurb Dooham   Class: 6th period
Place: Classroom   Date: 4/12/90

Event
While reviewing weekly quiz, Ecurb hollered, "I've got it! I've got it!" when asked to correct an error made earlier. This was the first time any interest or understanding of the material has been shown.

My Interpretation
This is a breakthrough. Until now, I figured Ecurb *did not* want to do the work rather than *could not.*

Gronlund (1981, pp. 439–440) makes a number of suggestions for using anecdotal records that you may find useful:

- Anticipate what will be observed.
- Record enough to explain behaviors.
- Record behaviors soon after their occurrence.
- Limit anecdotes to specific situations.
- Separate descriptions and interpretations of situations.
- Note positive and negative incidents.
- Collect enough anecdotes before inferring.
- Practice writing up records.

Rating Scales. Rating scales offer a more systematic way to obtain information about students. Their purposes are similar to those of anecdotal records except that with rating scales the teacher specifies some degree or amount. This might require deciding whether the student's work was "excellent," "above average," "average," and so on or whether the student "never," "seldom," "occasionally," "frequently," or "always" performs in a certain way (Gronlund, 1981, pp. 441–449).

Rating scales require the teacher to judge some student qualities or characteristics, commonly on a 0–5 or 0–10 scale. Figure 11.5 presents two versions of a rating scale used to evaluate students' presentations of an oral report. We can see that the scale in the second example offers more detail than that in the first; it both specifies behaviors and suggests degrees of performance. Also, the second version tends to be more objective and accurate.

Basically the same comparison can be made between rating scales and anecdotal records. Although rating scales may offer no more detail than anecdotal records, they suggest degrees, are more encompassing, are more objective, and are easy to do.

However, there are limitations to rating scales, including the risk of bias. Bias can result from the way the teacher views the scale and/or because the

FIGURE 11.5
Illustrative Rating Scales

Example 1
Instructions: Circle the appropriate level for each part of the report.

$$1 = \text{unsatisfactory}$$
$$2 = \text{minimally acceptable}$$
$$3 = \text{average}$$
$$4 = \text{good}$$
$$5 = \text{excellent}$$

Oral reports:

Clarity of outline	1	2	3	4	5
Research	1	2	3	4	5
Introduction of topic	1	2	3	4	5
Development of topic	1	2	3	4	5
Concluding comments					
Response to questions					

Example 2
Instructions: Circle the number that best reflects the level of performance.

1	2	3	4	5
Presentation lacks coherence. Topic lacks focus		Generally logical flow; occasionally rambles		Clear, coherent, with relevant points raised

---

scale may not depict students as clearly as expected; that is, there may be a general tendency to rate pupils high or low. Also, Gronlund (1981, p. 447) suggests the possibility of a "halo effect," wherein the teacher's judgment is colored by personal feelings about the student being rated. For example, Mary always does her homework and is good in class, so 5s generally may seem more appropriate for her.

Gronlund (1981, pp. 449–450) suggests some guidelines for effective use of rating scales. Specifically, teachers should rate "educationally sound" characteristics, which are directly observable and clearly defined, using three and seven rating positions, omitting ratings when they feel unqualified to make them, and combining ratings from several teachers.

Checklists. If a teacher wants to award some credit for, say, participation in class, it is easy enough to put a check mark by a student's name each time that student answers a question. Or a teacher might want to monitor a student's progress in preparing a report (selecting a topic, handing in the draft or finished outline, etc.) or attaining certain skills ("distinguishes latitude from longitude, locates countries on a map," etc.). Such instruments are called *checklists* (Gronlund, 1981, pp. 449–452). Figure 11.6 presents an example.

FIGURE 11.6
Illustrative Checklist

　　　　　　　　　　　　　　　　　　Student's Name _____

　　　　　　　　　　　　　　　　　　Map Skills

	Yes	No
1. Marks cardinal directions	____	____
2. Places cities, objects at correct coordinates	____	____
3. Shows major streets	____	____
4. Marks major buildings with correct symbols	____	____
5. Accurately uses scale of miles	____	____

　　　　Checklists are probably the most objective of the qualitative measures, for they involve simply marking "yes" or "no," "present" or "absent," or "satisfactory" or "unsatisfactory." Also, checklists clearly define and specify performance or behaviors. Finally, checklists may be used to detect common problems or errors made by students and are relatively simple to grade.

　　　　A serious disadvantage of checklists is that they do not directly reflect any degree of performance and thus may fail to give credit for partial performance (although this criterion could be built into the checklist).

Quantitative ("Harder") Measurements.　　The quantitative measurement instrument teachers most commonly use is the written test ("Explain the causes of, participants in, and results of the Peloponnesian Wars"; "Which of the following factors led to the Fall of Rome?"). The "hardness" attributed to tests as opposed to rating scales, checklists, and anecdotal records stems from greater objectivity on the part of the teacher in marking. In other words, the teacher's feelings about a student usually do not enter into the determination of the degree of achievement of student learning. On a ranking from subjective to objective (or qualitative to quantitative), the essay test most closely approaches the former while short-answer items (e.g., multiple-choice, analogies, sequencing, completion, true-false, and matching) lean toward the latter.

　　　　Quantitative instruments provide more precise, numerical data on which to make judgments. However, there are some basic concerns for preparing tests that we need to identify before examining the specific tests.

Concerns about Test Construction

The three basic concerns for teachers in preparing tests are *validity, reliability,* and *usability:*

1.　Tests should measure student performance in terms of mastery of material relevant to a course or unit of study. *(validity)*

2. Tests should obtain consistent results when given to comparable groups or to the same group over a fixed (usually short) time period. *(reliability)*
3. Tests should be easy to construct and grade, but they should also measure different levels of thinking (see the Bloom taxonomy in Chapter 5). *(usability)*

These concerns are fairly obvious. Teachers are not expected to be experts in test construction, and they have a limited amount of time to prepare and grade tests. However, both teachers and students need to have some confidence that student learning is being evaluated as accurately as humanly possible. Teachers need not feel bad if a student says a test was "hard," but complaints that it was "unfair" should bother them.

Similarly, teachers should be concerned if it took them forever to write test items and then took even longer to grade the tests. Most teachers have learned the hard way and, unfortunately, may have learned to take the easy way out: give no tests or use only matching or true-false items (we will discuss the problems with these types of tests later).

Validity. We believe that the most troublesome complaint a student can raise is that a test is "unfair." Although a common (and sometimes inaccurate) criticism, it goes to the heart of evaluation. A test may be unfair for a number of reasons, but the most serious one is that it is invalid.

Validity means that the instrument used for evaluation (a test, for example) *measures what it purports to measure;* that is, it accurately assesses the degree of mastery of what students were supposed to learn. Validity can refer to either the content or the construction of the instrument. For our purposes, that instrument will be tests. Perhaps the simplest and most useful way to prepare a test that will be considered valid is to refer to one's unit goals and lesson objectives.

You may find it useful now to review the discussion of goals and objectives in Chapter 5, particularly the writing of objectives to reflect various levels of the Bloom taxonomy.

From this, the teacher can prepare what is variously called a *two-way chart, cross-axis grid,* or *table of specifications* (Gronlund, 1981, pp. 128–133). Figure 11.7 presents an example. The teacher simply prepares a matrix with rows running across that reflect the *content* of a unit of study. Down the page (in columns), the teacher records objectives in terms of levels of the Bloom taxonomy, that is, refers to the objectives and records them on the matrix. For each objective based on the content, the teacher looks across for the highest level of the Bloom taxonomy and puts a check mark for this and for all the objectives of the unit. Then the teacher simply sums the number of tallies in each row to determine how many objectives (or percentage of the total number of objectives) deal with a specific content. Similarly, the teacher sums the tallies at each level of the taxonomy and figures the percentages.

This suggests (but does not dictate) how you might begin to set up a test. In Figure 11.7, for example, you might later ask students to "write the words *India, Pakistan,* and *Bangladesh* in the appropriate place on the map [which shows only political boundaries]." Still later you could ask them to "distinguish the forms of government in the three countries in terms of the title of each country's leader, the form of authority this leader has, and the role of the elected officials who represent the people." The latter question clearly reflects analytical thinking; that is, recall, comprehension, and application are necessary before one can answer the question.

Figure 11.8 illustrates an alternative form. Here different types of performances ("behavior") are required, but the idea is the same as for the two-axis table in Figure 11.7.

Of course, there are other ways to prepare a valid test, including taking the test yourself after putting it aside for awhile. Another teacher could read over the test, especially one who is skilled in writing tests. Or you could try it out as a pretest, even administering it to a trustworthy student in a higher grade without clearly giving away the purpose.

We advise you not to rely too much on tests that come with teachers' editions of textbooks, for they may not represent *your* goals and objectives for instruction. However, old copies of any pertinent statewide tests might well serve as a basis for writing test items if they are consistent with your goals and objectives.

Other Ways to Validate Tests.   As we all know, students are quick to inform a teacher of any test items they consider defective, or "unfair," but we would want a somewhat more substantial measure. To this end, Gronlund (1981, 253–267) suggests other ways to determine test validity.

Possibly the most common means is the *item analysis* conducted after administering objective tests. This requires preparing three columns: (1) the number of the test item, (2) the number of students who correctly answered that item, and (3) the number of students who incorrectly answered it (see Figure 11.9). A rule of thumb is to consider an item valid, or potentially so, if 50% or more of the students answered it correctly. However, we would consider an item suspect if *all* the students answered it correctly. Either the question was too easy or somehow the answer was given away.

A related but more powerful way to achieve the same result—determine the validity of an objective test item—is to use *item discrimination analysis,* or *item analysis* for norm-referenced classroom tests (Gronlund, 1981, pp. 256–260). To do this, the teacher must first determine which students normally or on this test (if the teacher lacks a clear enough basis to make a determination) rank in the top and bottom quarter of the class. For a "small" class, say, 20 to 30, the teacher would take the top and bottom halves. Next comes a procedure that is similar to item analysis but requires five columns: (1) test item, (2) correct answers by the top quarter (or half), (3) incorrect

FIGURE 11.7
Two-Axis Table of Specifications

Content   Objectives

Content	Knowledge	Comprehension	Application	Analysis	Synthesis	Evaluation	Total	% of Total
India, Pakistan, Bangladesh								
Locate on map	1							
Label political boundaries	1							
Locate population centers	1							
Label physical features	1						4	24
Overlay U.S. and India maps		1						
Chart social and political differences		1						
Construct time chart		1						
Describe British forms of control		1					4	24
Identify laws common and imposed			1					
Specify political and social changes due to British			1					
List problems facing India today			1				3	17
Distinguish forms of government in three countries				1				
Compare political and geographical differences				1				
Contrast economic development of Bangladesh with Pakistan's				1			3	17
Summarize steps leading to civil war					1			
Predict Bangladesh future to relation with nations of the world					1		2	12
Appraise effect of Sheik Mujib importance to Bangladesh and India						1	1	6
Total	4	4	3	3	2	1	17	
% of total	24	24	17	17	12	6		

FIGURE 11.8
Table of Specifications
for a Government
Course

Behavior

Content	Facts	Concepts	Generalizations	Structures and Models	Location of Information	Identification of Central Issues and Underlying Assumptions	Evaluation of Evidence and Drawing of Warranted Conclusions	Formal Procedures	Awareness and Interest
	A	B	C	D	E	G	H	J	N
7.0 Governmental focus									
8.0 Process of government									
9.0 International relations									
10.0 Factors affecting politics									
11.0 Methods of inquiry									
11.1 Legal-institutional									
12.0 Major political issues									

Source: From *Evaluation to Improve Learning* (p. 468) by B. S. Bloom, G. F. Madaus, and J. T. Hastings, 1981, New York: McGraw-Hill. Reprinted by permission of McGraw-Hill.

answers by the top quarter (or half), (4) correct answers by the bottom quarter (or half), and (5) incorrect answers by the bottom quarter (or half). Figure 11.10 illustrates item discrimination analysis.

Again the teacher examines each item that does not "discriminate" the "better" students' ability to respond correctly from the "poorer" students'. For each item, a ranking of from 0 ("little or no discrimination") to 1.0 ("excellent discrimination") is made with gradations:

0– .3 Little or no discrimination
.4– .5 Fair
.6– .7 Good
.8–1.0 Excellent

A frequent objection to this procedure is that it labels and penalizes students who have done poorly. Such students may be permanently relegated to the "bottom" quarter or half.

FIGURE 11.9
Item Analysis of Objective Test

Item	Right	Wrong
1	19	3
2	15	7
3	20	2
4	22	0
5	17	5
6	10	12
7	16	6
8	6	16
9	17	5
10	16	6
11	3	19
12	10	12
13	14	8
14	21	1
15	19	3
16	13	9
17	16	6
18	21	1
19	19	3
20	11	11

What does the teacher do with "bad" items after performing an item analysis or item discrimination analysis? After all, grades must be determined from the test scores. The usual answer is to throw out the "bad" items, but this may result in a test that does not add up to a total of 100 (or 50 or 10) points. In that case, the teacher must exercise his or her judgment. One solution is to revise the percentages. Another is to examine a particular item to see which answer was most often (albeit "incorrectly") given and award points for that answer just as the teacher would do for the expected response. In future tests, however, the teacher should carefully review "bad" or suspect items if salvageable or eliminate them and write new ones.

The ultimate goal is to build a file of valid test items that you can use at different times or for alternative forms of the test. *But you need to be sure to remain true to your goals and objectives* so that you can be reasonably confident that the items will constitute a reliable measure.

Reliability. A second major concern regarding test construction is *reliability*, the consistency of the measurement; that is, are your test scores, or other means of measurement, giving you similar results over time with similar students or in like circumstances? If so, this also affords you confidence in the results obtained from measuring student achievement.

The stronger the relationship among sets of scores on tests, the greater the reliability and, ultimately, the validity. For example, we might have re-taken the SATs to raise our scores, but the test makers warned us that in a

FIGURE 11.10
Item Discrimination Analysis

Top 25%					Questions					
	1	2	3	4	5	6	7	8	9	10
Carole	r	r	r	r	r	r	r	r	r	r
Prak	r	r	r	r	r	r	r	r	r	r
Jim C.	r	r	r	r	r	r	r	r	r	r
Robin	r	r	r	r	r	r	r	r	r	r
Maria	r	r	r	r	r	r	r	r	w	r
TOTAL RIGHT	5	5	5	5	5	5	5	5	4	5

Bottom 25%					Questions					
Laurie B.	r	r	w	r	r	w	r	r	w	r
Laurie Br.	w	r	r	w	w	w	r	r	r	r
Norman	r	r	r	w	w	w	r	w	r	w
Sherman	r	w	w	w	w	r	r	r	w	r
Miguel	r	w	w	w	r	r	r	r	w	r
TOTAL RIGHT	4	3	2	1	2	2	5	4	2	4

Q 1 $\dfrac{5-4}{5} = \dfrac{1}{5} = .2$ Little discrimination

Q 2 $\dfrac{5-3}{5} = \dfrac{2}{5} = .4$ Fair discrimination

Q 3 $\dfrac{5-2}{5} = \dfrac{3}{5} = .6$ Good discrimination

Q 4 $\dfrac{5-1}{5} = \dfrac{4}{5} = .8$ Excellent discrimination

Q 5 $\dfrac{5-2}{5} = \dfrac{3}{5} = .6$ Good discrimination

Q 6 $\dfrac{5-2}{5} = \dfrac{3}{5} = .6$ Good discrimination

Q 7 $\dfrac{5-5}{5} = \dfrac{0}{5} = .0$ No discrimination

Q 8 $\dfrac{5-4}{5} = \dfrac{1}{5} = .2$ Little discrimination

Q 9 $\dfrac{4-2}{5} = \dfrac{2}{5} = .4$ Fair discrimination

Q 10 $\dfrac{5-4}{5} = \dfrac{1}{5} = .2$ Little discrimination retake our scores likely would differ by a maximum of 50 points, say, 650 on the verbal part the first time and possibly 700 on the retake, although the result could have been 600.

In the context of evaluation in schools, you want to ensure validity of your measurements, which in turn demands reliability. Note, however, that you can have reliability without validity but not the reverse.

Criteria for reliability are:

- *Stability:* Using the same instrument twice or more (test-retest)
- *Equivalency:* giving two forms of the test to the same group after a short (generally one-day) time lapse
- *Internal consistency:* using the same instrument once, but with only partial scores

In other words, you will be looking for consistency or a relationship among the particular measurements of learning.

Whichever measurement you choose, you will need two sets of scores. Let's say you have given two forms of the same test to your first-period social studies class to check on the test's reliability. In your grade book, you have recorded the scores in Figure 11.11. Given these scores, you can see that students achieved different results on the two versions of the test.

FIGURE 11.11
Test Scores for Period 1

Name	Form A	Form B
Frank A.	39	32
Mary A.	29	41
Ralph B.	30	42
Juan B.	26	35
Karen B.	29	37
Bob B.	34	38
Carol C.	30	46
Isaac C.	31	42
Juanita D.	35	43
Hector F.	42	33
Peter H.	25	32
Melissa L.	38	40
Patty L.	33	37
Maria M.	40	41
Bruce M.	44	48
Jesus O.	25	44
Lin-Chuh O.	20	33
Wang R.	46	38
Michelle S.	32	46
Harry W.	36	30

What do you make of this? Simply put, you check the reliability of the test. A "quick-and-dirty" way to determine the reliability (consistency) of a particular test for, say, stability or internal consistency is to use a *scattergram*. Recall that you are looking for a positive correlation—a direct linkage—between the two scores that will look like the solid line running diagonally from 0 to 50 in Figure 11.12. Note that this will be a perfect *positive* correlation, or +1.0. On the other hand, if the scores look like the dotted line that runs diagonally right to left from 50 to 0 in Figure 11.12, you will have a perfect *negative* correlation, or −1.0. A third possibility is that your scores will resemble the middle broken line in Figure 11.12, which represents a *zero* correlation. Of course, you are looking for a positive correlation, although it is unlikely to be a perfect one.

Taking these two sets of scores and plotting them on the matrix, we find that they result in virtually no correlation (see Figure 11.13). Thus, we would not consider this particular test reliable.

Rather than become unnecessarily technical here, we suggest that you refer to some of the sources listed at the end of the chapter for more accurate ways to determine the reliability of your measurement devices.

Summary

It is important to ensure that the means we use to measure student learning are well designed: that they measure what we intend to measure (are *valid*) and are dependable (*reliable*). In other words, we want to have confidence in

FIGURE 11.12
Structure of a
Scattergram

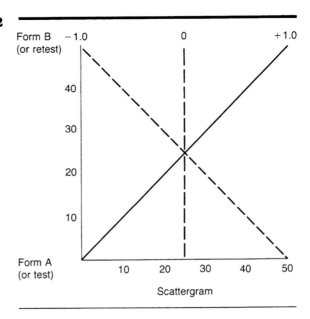

Scattergram

FIGURE 11.13
Completed Scattergram

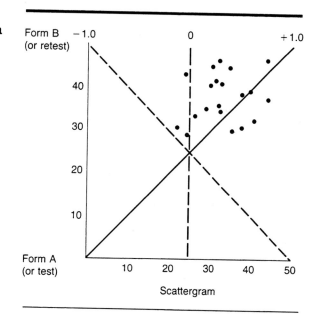

Scattergram

our measurements, and there are ways to achieve this. Few things are as frustrating as having students upset because they feel a particular test is "unfair." Trying to defend a test may be one of the most traumatic experiences we will encounter in a class in which the students are concerned about their grades. Worse would be our reliance on test grades that did not fairly measure our students' learning.

TYPES OF TESTS

As mentioned earlier, a third concern regarding test construction is *usability*. In this section, we will address this criterion with reference to the types of tests we can write and the benefits and liabilities of preparing and grading them.

Now let's look at the choices we have when preparing tests and the actual test construction. Recall earlier that we distinguished qualitative ("softer") from quantitative ("harder") measures. The classroom teacher typically relies on more objective measures for forming judgments about students' achievement, most commonly essay, multiple-choice, analogies, sequencing, completion, matching, and true-false (or alternative-response) questions. Which type of question to use depends on a variety of considerations, including the cognitive level to be assessed, ease of construction, and ease of grading. Figure 11.14 compares these measures with respect to these criteria. For a more definitive comparison, see Gronlund (1981, p. 139).

FIGURE 11.14
Comparison of Types of Objective Measures

	Cognitive Level of Assessment	Ease of Construction	Ease of Grading
Essay	High	Yes	No
Multiple choice	Moderate to high	No	Yes
Analogies	Moderate	No	Yes
Sequencing	Moderate	Yes	Yes
Completion	Low to moderate	Yes	No
Matching	Low	Yes	Yes
True-false	Low	Yes	Yes

Essay Questions

Essay questions generally can measure higher levels of achievement than can the other types of objective measures. They also are relatively easy to construct. However, they can cause headaches for the grader not only in terms of what a "model" student answer is but with respect to the ranking of individual

Recording grades is only a small part of evaluating students.

answers against that model or standard. Further, the essay test can be considered the most subjective of the measures in terms of grading. It is all too easy to give credit to an answer that corresponds to the rater's biases or expectations, thus penalizing a "creative" or offbeat thinker. Also, if one does not ensure anonymity of the test takers, the "halo effect" can operate ("She's a good student, so she must have intended to say . . . "). The teacher's mood also can play a role in the grading. For example, fatigue resulting from grading a large number of essay tests can affect how the teacher reads an answer. Also, as we all know from experience, articulate students can occasionally bluff a good mark on an essay test. Despite these drawbacks, however, the essay test can measure the highest levels of cognitive achievement and tends to be easier to prepare than other types of tests.

Recall that in Chapter 9 we linked writing and thinking and suggested that an essay is analytical or interpretive. You might want to return to that chapter and review the examples used there.

Gronlund (1981, p. 137) distinguishes between two types of essay questions: the *extended-response* and the *restricted-response*, using the following examples:

Extended-response type: Describe what you think should be the role of the federal government in maintaining a stable economy in the United States. Include specific policies and programs and give reasons for your proposals.

Restricted-response type: State two advantages and two disadvantages of maintaining high tariffs on goods from other countries.

The advantage of the extended-response type is that it allows students to organize a comprehensive answer, evaluate ideas, and express themselves. On the other hand, it makes grading for factual knowledge difficult and potentially less reliable. The restricted-response type makes it easier to grade for factual knowledge, but it measures students' ability to organize and integrate ideas less effectively. Thus, again the teacher must be a decision maker.

The essay question in Figure 11.15 combines the two types. First it asks for specific answers; then it has students build on those responses. The teacher is instructed to grant specific credits for answers and then assign a holistic grade. In other words, in Part A the teacher can give up to four credits depending on the accuracy of the answers and up to six credits in Part B according to the student's ability to use data, organize, and develop answers. Then the teacher assigns a holistic grade based on the criteria in Figure 11.16.

While the notion of holistic scoring has only recently gained popularity, teachers have used it informally (and possibly without a label) for years. Holistic scoring allows the teacher to give more credit for an essay answer

FIGURE 11.15
Extended- and Restricted-Response Essay Questions

Part A: Select *two* regions from the list below. For each region selected, identify *two* geographic characteristics that have encouraged economic growth and development.

Sub-Saharan Africa
Latin America
South Asia
East Asia
Middle East
Western Europe
Eastern Europe

Region	Characteristic #1	Characteristic #2
1 _____	_____ _____ (1)	_____ _____ (1)
2. _____	_____ _____ (1)	_____ _____ (1)

Part B: (Base your Part B answer on your Part A answer.) Write an essay explaining* how geographic characteristics in the regions you selected in part A have encouraged economic growth and development in those regions.

Explain means "to make plain or understandable; to give reasons for or causes of; to show the logical development or relationships of."

(e.g., on Part B in Figure 11.15) than would result directly from totaling specific credits granted. For example, the total credits for a student's paper might be 2 or 3, but the student has used data, demonstrated organization, and tried to develop ideas. Thus, a 2 or 3 would not accurately reflect the degree to which the student was developing what Gronlund calls an "extended response." Thus, an essay question might combine elements of both the extended-response and restricted-response types.

Figure 11.17 presents another sample essay question. Again the teacher could use holistic scoring after giving credit for responses to both parts of the question.

As with all types of tests, in preparing an essay test you should refer to your objectives for the material to be tested. (The cross- or two-axis table in Figure 11.7 should be useful in this regard.) Also, keep in mind the need for reliability, which you can obtain, as Gronlund (1981, 233–236) suggests, by

1. Preparing in advance an outline of expected answers
2. Using an appropriate scoring method

FIGURE 11.16
Criteria for Rating Student Responses to Part B in Figure 11.15

Category	6	5	4	3	2	1
Use of data	Always uses accurate and relevant data	Consistently uses accurate and relevant data	Uses mostly accurate and relevant data	Mixes accurate and inaccurate, relevant and irrelevant data	Uses mostly inaccurate and irrelevant data	Uses almost no accurate or relevant data
Plan of organization	Always demonstrates a logical and coherent plan of organization	Consistently demonstrates a logical and coherent plan of organization	Develops the assigned topics using a general plan of organization	Addresses the assigned topic but demonstrates weakness in organization and may include digression	Attempts to develop the assigned topic but demonstrates a profound weakness in organization and may include several digressions	Minimally addresses the assigned topic but lacks a plan of organization
Development of ideas	Always develops ideas fully and clearly, using appropriate examples, reasons, details, explanations, and/or generalizations	Consistently develops ideas fully, using appropriate examples, reasons, details, explanations, and/or generalizations	Demonstrates satisfactory development and expression of ideas through the adequate use of support materials	Demonstrates weakness in the development and expression of ideas with little use of support materials	Demonstrates profound weakness in the development and expression of ideas, with little use of support materials	Does not use support materials in the development or expression of ideas

Zero Paper

Uses no accurate or relevant data

Is totally unrelated to the topic

Is illegible, i.e., includes so many indecipherable words that no sense can be made of the response

Is a blank paper

345

3. Deciding how to handle irrelevant factors such as illegibility, spelling, punctuation, irrelevant information, and so on
4. Evaluating all the answers to one question before grading the next question (if more than one question)
5. Evaluating answers without looking at students' names
6. Obtaining two or more independent readings if especially important decisions are to be based on the results

To these suggestions, Armstrong and Savage (1983) add that the teacher might adjust the "scoring criteria in the light of content analysis" (p. 261); that is, the teacher should note specific information that students provide in their answers and subsequent references to that information, thereby drawing a profile of the class response to the essay item. The frequency of these responses will suggest whether the teacher should rethink the weight to be given to such answers.

Short-Answer Questions

Multiple-Choice Questions. The advantages of *multiple-choice*, or, as students often say, "multiple-guess," questions are that (1) they can assess learning at a variety of levels of the Bloom taxonomy, (2) they can test various subject matter mastery, and (3) they are relatively easy to score. However, they are the most difficult questions to prepare.

The basic format, as we know, is to present a problem, generally in a statement at the beginning of the question (the "stem") and a number of possible answers ("foils") from which students are to select the "best" answer.

FIGURE 11.17
Sample Essay Question

Position A: "To take a single step beyond the boundaries thus specially drawn around the powers of Congress [to incorporate a national bank], is to take possession of a boundless field of power [a power not] delegated to the United States by the Constitution."

Position B: " . . . The Constitution . . . shall be the *supreme law of the land*. . . . This general and indisputable principle puts at once an end to the *abstract* question, whether the United States have the power to erect a corporation. . . . It is unquestionably incident to *sovereign* power to erect corporations. . . . "

Directions: Given these two distinct views of the United States Constitution:
1. Label and interpret each (A or B).
2. Examine the consequences of holding either position by referring to a *current* constitutional issue.

While this is easier said than done, there are some general guidelines for writing multiple-choice questions:

1. Use either a direct question or an incomplete statement as the item stem, ensuring that the question is framed so that the problem is clearly presented.
2. Base each item on a single, central problem.
3. Avoid "window dressing": Tell students only as much as they need to know to understand the question; that is, use only relevant material.
4. Make the alternatives (foils) mutually exclusive so that one alternative does not include another.
5. Word each item such that there is only one correct answer.
6. Don't give students a clue by making the correct answer longer or more technical than the others.
7. Make sure that incorrect answers are plausible.
8. Avoid negative statements, leading to double negatives, and phrases like "of the following" and "none (or "all") of the above" as alternatives ("foils").
9. Be sure alternatives are grammatically parallel with one another and with the stem.
10. Arrange the alternatives in logical order, if one exists.
11. Keep the vocabulary as simple as possible, using simple words that have a precise meaning (unless that is what is being tested).
12. Make sure that grammar and punctuation are faultless.
13. Make drawings and maps as clear as possible.

Bloom et al. (1981, pp. 208–209) offer some useful suggestions for writing not only multiple-choice items but matching, true-false, completion, and essay questions. Figure 11.18 presents examples of knowledge, comprehension, application, and analytical questions that follow these guidelines.

Knowledge and *comprehension* questions simply test students' knowledge and understanding of facts, respectively. *Application* items ask students to address a problem that appears "novel" to them, which might include hypothesizing. *Analytical* questions have students break down information and distinguish among various factors. Figures 11.19 and 11.20 present some examples of *synthesis* questions, which require students to summarize or draw conclusions from information given or assumed. *Evaluation* questions, such as those in Figure 11.21, ask students to make judgments based on a summary of certain information.

As we mentioned earlier, multiple-choice questions can test students on a wide variety of material and at higher cognitive levels than can other types of questions, except for the essay. Also, they require students to demonstrate some critical thinking; students must know not only that the answer is correct but what *makes* it correct. Multiple-choice questions also tend to be free of the ambiguity often associated with other types of questions, especially completion. In addition, they offer greater reliability, for guessing is reduced. Finally, multiple-choice questions are relatively quick and easy to grade.

FIGURE 11.18
Sample Knowledge, Comprehension, Application, and Analytical Questions

Knowledge Questions
1. Recalling our study of designs for Korean houses, the "traditional" design typically was a(an):
   a. "U"-shaped house
   b. "L"-shaped house
   c. square-shaped house
   d. "A"-shaped house
2. Ming rulers modeled their government on an earlier form, specifically on the government of the:
   a. Yuan dynasty
   b. Kuomintang
   c. Ch'in dynasty
   d. T'ang and Sung governments

Comprehension Questions
1. In our study of the factors of production, we learned that capital goods are:
   a. made from capital resources
   b. used to produce other items
   c. distributed by the government
   d. not owned by individuals
2. Which of the following is an *opportunity cost* of choosing to attend college?
   a. increased education
   b. future higher earnings
   c. loss of current income
   d. higher socioeconomic status

Application Questions
1. Read the following paragraph; then answer the question below.

   Great Creator, who dwellest alone, listen now to the words of the people here gathered. The smoke of our offering arises to heaven. Give kind attention to our words. We thank thee for the return of the planting season. Give to us a good season, that our crops may be plentiful.

   What is probably true of the people who use this prayer?
   a. They believe in many Gods who dwell in various heavens above them.
   b. They believe in a God who controls their lives.
   c. They believe in offering thanks to a God at the end of each season.
   d. They believe in offering sacrifices to their God.

Analytical Questions
1. Franklin Roosevelt's foreign policy toward Latin American nations differed most from that of earlier administrations in that it stressed
   a. aggressive imperialism
   b. noninvolvement
   c. hemispheric cooperation
   d. economic domination
2. Which development was a result of the other three?
   a. The civil rights and voting acts of the 1960s were passed.
   b. Blacks were barred from voting in several states.
   c. State laws supported racial segregation.
   d. Sit-ins began, protests became violent, and civil rights movements were formed.

FIGURE 11.19
Sample Synthesis-Level Question (1)

DIRECTIONS: Base your answers to questions 1 through 3 below on the following graphs and reading.

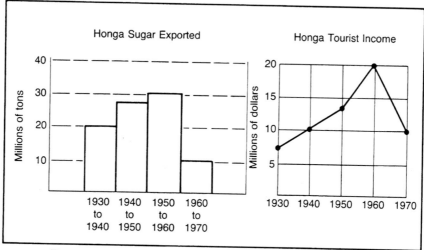

The imaginary nation of Honga was established in 1930. During the time period from 1930 to 1965 Honga and the much larger and more wealthy nation of Pensive enjoyed good diplomatic relations. From 1965 to 1970 Honga and Pensive were involved in a large military police action. In addition, Honga experienced severe drought conditions throughout the nation from 1963 to 1967. Honga and Pensive have now resolved their diplomatic problems and the drought is a distant memory.

Select the best conclusion from each of the three groups that follow:

1. 1. Honga is a tropical nation.
   2. Pensive is a large sugar consumer.
   3. Honga relies heavily on tourists from Pensive.
   4. Honga's sugar exports increased by 50% in 30 years.

2. 1. Honga and Pensive were on opposite sides during the police action of 1965 to 1970.
   2. The tourist income for Honga will increase now that they are reconciled with Pensive.
   3. All of Honga's increase in sugar exports and tourist income occurred within the period of good economic relations with Pensive.
   4. Honga enjoyed economic prosperity from 1930 to 1960.

3. 1. Honga experienced a depression from 1960 to 1970.
   2. From 1930 to 1960 tourism rose faster than sugar exports.
   3. Pensive experienced a sugar shortage from 1965 to 1970.
   4. Honga sugar exports since 1970 have probably risen.

**FIGURE 11.20
Sample Synthesis-Level Question (2)**

DIRECTIONS: Base your answers to questions 1 through 3 below on the following diagram.

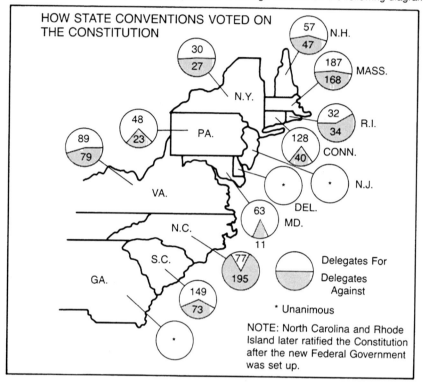

HOW STATE CONVENTIONS VOTED ON THE CONSTITUTION

1. Using the information provided in the diagram, we can conclude that all of the states ratified the Constitution before the new federal government was set up except:

   1. Ga. and S.C.
   2. N.C. and R.I.
   3. N.Y. and Va.
   4. N.J. and Del.

2. Unanimous ratification of the Constitution took place in how many states?

   1. two
   2. three
   3. nine
   4. thirteen

3. We can conclude from the diagram that

   1. The majority of delegates in two states were against ratification.
   2. The delegates from two states did not ratify the Constitution until after it went into effect.
   3. The majority of delegates from eight or more states were in favor of ratification.
   4. All of the above statements are true.

FIGURE 11.21
Illustrative Evaluation Questions

1. The most accurate statement concerning United States foreign policy generally is that the United States has:
   a. Acted according to national self-interest
   b. Reacted forcefully to imperialism around the world
   c. Formed alliances with countries in need
   d. Used military confrontation to solve disputes
2. The best evidence that third or minor political parties have had a significant influence on United States history is that frequently:
   a. Minor political parties have succeeded in dominating most state governments even though they could not control the federal government.
   b. The membership of Congress has been so divided among several political parties that Congress could take no action.
   c. Many of the proposals of minor parties have been passed into law.
   d. A minor party has replaced one of the major parties.

Multiple-choice questions have their disadvantages. First, good multiple-choice items are relatively difficult to prepare. Second, multiple-choice questions measure only verbal learning. Third, they generally are inappropriate for measuring students' ability to organize and integrate ideas. Finally, the foils require great care in preparation for students with limited reading abilities.

Analogy Questions. Next to multiple-choice questions, *analogy* questions are probably the most difficult to prepare. These items ask students to examine (or draw) analogies between two or more events or ideas, that is, to identify relationships that are unclear at the outset.

Figure 11.22 illustrates some analogy questions. In the first group, interpretation is necessary to answer the questions. In the second, questions use the true-false format (discussed later).

The primary advantage of questions that ask students to examine analogies is that they allow us to test higher-level thinking. They ask students to put their knowledge to use to examine relationships—to interpret. On the other hand, students must follow the logic of the item writer (the teacher) and have the necessary background. Also, analogy questions are relatively difficult to write.

Sequencing Questions. The notion behind asking students to sequence— to order or rank—answers is that it requires, at minimum, comprehension or, more likely, analysis of events or persons. *Sequencing* questions ask students to recognize events or persons, attach meaning, and sort variables. This can be particularly useful for measuring students' ability to interpret chronology or cause and effect. Figure 11.23 presents a sample sequencing question.

FIGURE 11.22
Illustrative Analogy Questions

Interpretive-Level Questions
1. Keynesian economics was to the New Deal as laissez-faire was to the economic policy of which other presidential administration in the early 20th century? _____
2. The notion of the "Imperial Presidency" was to the administration of President Nixon as the notion of "King Andrew" was to the presidency of. . . . _____
3. The critical term "Watergate" was to the Nixon presidency as the critical term _____ was to the Reagan presidency.

True-False Questions
T   F   1. The notion of "strict construction" of the U.S. Constitution is to President Hoover's administration as "loose construction" was to President Roosevelt's.
T   F   2. The confrontation known as the "Cuban missile crisis" was to U.S.-Soviet relations as the assassination at Sarajevo was to German-Russian relations.
T   F   3. The Mayaguez affair was to the Ford presidency as the Pueblo affair was to the Johnson presidency.

Sequencing questions allow testing of students' higher-level thinking and comprehension of cause and effect. Also, such test items are relatively easy to write and grade. Disadvantages include the need to ensure that items adhere to a common theme and are neither obscure nor obvious. Also, sequencing questions do not require students to supply events themselves, which essay

FIGURE 11.23
Sample Sequencing Question

Instructions: Referring to the events below, place a number to the left of each event corresponding to the occurrence of the event. For example, number 1 would be the Constitutional Convention.

___   Black Codes
_1_   Constitutional Convention
___   Gettysburg Address
___   Impeachment of Andrew Johnson
___   The Missouri Compromise
___   Lincoln-Douglas Debates
___   Bleeding Kansas
___   Thirteenth, Fourteenth, and Fifteenth Amendments
___   Emancipation Proclamation
___   Harper's Ferry and John Brown's Raid
___   *Dred Scott* v. *Sandford*

questions would, although in this respect sequencing questions share this disadvantage with the other forms of short-answer question.

Completion Questions.   *Completion* test items undoubtedly can measure a variety of "relatively simple learning outcomes" (Gronlund, 1981, p. 156). However, the extent to which they can require more complex thinking, including interpretation, may depend on the nature of the content. The important thing about completion items is that students must do more than simply place a mark on a paper; they may be required to do some problem solving, including interpreting data.

Figure 11.24 presents two examples of completion questions. The first requires interpretation using a lettered, contour map of China about which students are to supply some responses. The second asks students to select the correct term from a group of appropriate words.

Completion questions are considered one of the easier types of questions to write. Here are some guidelines:

1. Word items so that they require clear answers.
2. Use direct questions rather than incomplete statements as much as possible.
3. Make blanks to be filled in equal in length.
4. Limit the number of blanks to be filled in.
5. Avoid taking statements directly from textbooks, for the lack of context can confuse students. (Gronlund, 1981, pp. 159 162)

The strongest argument for writing completion questions is that they are "easy" to construct. Guessing is eliminated, and partial knowledge will not enable students to get the correct answers, which could occur with multiple-choice, matching, or true-false items.

On the other hand, completion questions typically measure less complex learning. Another limitation is the difficulty in grading answers if the question is not worded clearly and definitively. Students do not always follow the test maker's (teacher's) reasoning; the context for the items may be quite clear to the teacher but ambiguous to the students. Because of these disadvantages, *we recommend that completion questions, like matching and true-false, be relegated to use in quizzes or formative evaluations.*

Matching Questions.   *Matching* questions require students to link words, numbers, or symbols in one column with a phrase, word, or sentence in a parallel column. The key is association. But therein lies a limitation of matching questions: The terms in the first column, called the "premises," and those in the second column, called the "responses," must be homogeneous. In other words, the two columns must contain information that centers on a particular category, which might involve persons and achievements, dates and historical events, terms and definitions, symbols and concepts, objects and

FIGURE 11.24
Illustrative Completion Items

Example 1
Directions: Referring to the above map, write your answers in the spaces provided.

1. At the time of the Taiping Rebellion, in which of the regions identified would we most likely have found greater autonomy and less efficient government _____ ?
2. What type of economy would most likely be present in the province labeled A _____ ?
3. Which two types of crops, if any, are produced in the regions marked C _____ and F _____ ?

Example 2
Directions: In the blanks in the following passage, supply the correct term from those listed below. Include only terms from this list, and spell each term properly.

   A basic building block of sociology and anthropology is the concept of _____ **norms** _____ . Simply put, these are _____ **rules** _____ by which people live and range from "thou shalt not" to eating with a knife and fork. Those followed very closely for fear of severe punishment, called _____ **sanctions** _____ , are labeled _____ **mores** _____ by sociologists. Where the punishment is less severe and lip service is more likely applied to violation, the term _____ **folkways** _____ is applied.

enculturation	status
folkways	rules
sanctions	norms
socialization	roles
mores	institutions

---

names of objects, and so forth (Gronlund, 1981, p. 171). Figure 11.25 presents an example of a matching exercise.

   Gronlund (1981) makes the following suggestions for writing matching questions:

1. Stick to the same subject or content in a single matching exercise.
2. Use an *unequal* number of premises and responses, and tell students whether responses can be used more than once.
3. Make sure the lists of items are short, and place shorter responses on the right.
4. Develop a logical order to the list of responses.
5. Make sure that all items are on the same page.

   The most obvious advantage of matching questions is that they are relatively easy to write. Also, the learning of a fairly large amount of material can be tested in a relatively short time for purposes of formative evaluation. However, the use of matching questions can lead to memorization by students and may test only factual knowledge. In addition, extraneous material that requires greater knowledge on the students' part than should be expected

FIGURE 11.25
Illustrative Matching Exercise

On the line to the left, write in the *letter* from Column B, court cases, that best corresponds
to what is written in Column A, rulings by the courts. Each letter can be used only once.

	Column A	Column B
_g_	1. Held that states may make schooling compulsory	a. *Brown v. Bd. of Ed. of Topeka*
_a_	2. States may not enforce segregation in schools	b. *Pickering v. Bd. of Ed.*
_e_	3. Students enjoy constitutional rights in schools	c. *Wisconsin v. Yoder*
_b_	4. Teachers' rights to free speech may not be abridged	d. *Goss v. Lopez*
_d_	5. Schools must provide due process in student disciplinary cases	e. *Tinker v. Des Moines*
		f. *Mailloux v. Kiley*
		g. *Pierce v. Soc. of Sisters*

of them based on the teacher's objectives can creep into the questions. Finally,
as said earlier, they limit content to homogeneous material.

True-False ("Alternative-Response") Questions. "Well, I have a 50-50
chance on these questions, at least" is a typical student reaction when
confronting *true-false* items. However, the rewarding of correct answers
obtained by guessing can be eliminated with well-written questions that
employ the more generic format, "alternative-response" (Gronlund, 1981, pp.
162–170). That is, it is possible to include more than just two responses from
which to choose. Gronlund gives the following examples:

T(rue), F(alse), C(onverse of) T(rue), C(onverse of) F(alse)

or

T(rue), F(alse), O(pinion)

Another alternative to T(rue)-F(alse) is to use the dichotomy T(rue)-O(pinion).
Figure 11.26 shows an example of the latter.

If you plan to use true-false questions, you must take care that items are
neither obvious nor ambiguous. Also, there are limits to the particular material that you can test by means of true-false questions. This is especially true
in the social studies, wherein statements that appear to be generalizations
often must be qualified. The most obvious limitation, of course, is that

FIGURE 11.26
Sample True-False Exercise

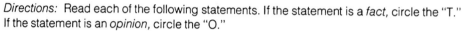

Directions: Read each of the following statements. If the statement is a *fact*, circle the "T."
If the statement is an *opinion*, circle the "O."

T   O   1. The Fourth Amendment to the U.S. Constitution protects individuals from
              unreasonable searches and seizures.

T   O   2. The Fourth Amendment should not be used to protect the privacy of
              individuals.

T   O   3. The Fourth Amendment is used by persons trying to hide something, often
              the results of a crime.

---

students can get by with guessing. Because of these limitations, Gronlund
(1981, 165–170) suggests using "alternative-response" items such as those
illustrated earlier.

Nevertheless, it is possible to write some good true-false questions appropriate to the social studies. A particularly good example is found in Armstrong
and Savage (1983, p. 270). There a chart is used to present data from which
true-false items are written. While the questions are limited to the comprehension level, they do represent a starting point for someone who wants to
write higher-level true-false questions.

SOME CAVEATS ABOUT EVALUATION
AND MEASUREMENT

Because as teachers we need to form judgments about students' achievement,
we require evidence with which to make them. This, in turn, requires us to
measure something. However, paper-and-pencil tests are not the only measures available to the teacher, nor are they necessarily the most appropriate.
In fact, the authors are concerned about the "quantimania" that grips a
public demanding accountability. For many teachers, the easy way out is to
make and give tests. In some schools, the latter third of the school year seems
to be devoted almost exclusively to the preparation and administration of
tests.

Perhaps the inclusion of this chapter implies that the authors too are
quantimaniacs. But we aren't! Rather, we are suggesting that if we are to
judge whether our students are learning (and we are teaching) anything, we
need to be skillful in measuring student performance. However, we caution
against relying exclusively on paper-and-pencil tests.

There are any number of alternatives for measuring learning, including
class discussions, student projects, oral and written reports, and even creative graffiti. An example of the last is a graffiti board on which students were
permitted—even encouraged—to write comments pertaining to the materials
being studied in class. One particular form resulted from the study of the U.S.

Constitution and the students' request ("demand") for more rights in the classroom. So every day the students put up some request-demand, to which the teacher typically responded by asking them to cite a provision of the Constitution that might justify it. Since this generally was an open "game," the teacher had a pretty good notion, even if a student did not sign his or her name, what kind of learning that student was demonstrating.

We mentioned projects in Chapters 4, 9, and 10. Often projects can take the form of analyzing some aspect of the subject matter current at the time: a position paper on how industry might be encouraged in the Amazon Valley without deforestation; an analysis of the historical struggle over Palestine; an examination of the causes of agricultural shortages in India. Using cooperative learning, classes could be broken into groups to prepare the papers and various means used to grade the projects.

Projects can also take more tangible forms, such as maps, scale buildings or sites, cartoons, and other artistic representations. One very bright college student recalled, long after the event, the building of an Iroquois longhouse in a seventh-grade social studies class. It was the highlight of all the social studies/social sciences courses the student had taken. The once popular project "People and Technology" required students to recreate artifacts of a whaling village.

Oral reports, however terrifying to some students, offer another way to measure learning. Grading could reflect how well students posed the problem to be examined, prepared an outline, used resources, organized the report, and expressed ideas. Thus, a poor speaker is not unduly penalized. Also, students could be involved in grading the actual presentation if all students are similarly peer graded. Obviously, checklists could be used for this grading.

Participation in class discussion is more difficult to grade, but again checklists can be used if criteria are clearly established, including quality of comments or ability to restate peers' comments.

Even given the most careful attention to evaluation standards applied to testing in general, we know that not all—in fact, maybe very little—student learning can be measured by paper-and-pencil tests. How can one measure the excitement a student feels when he or she comes up with an unexpected, innovative answer—albeit one that does not fit neatly on the answer sheet—or successfully demonstrates in the "real world" something learned inside the classroom? What if a student continually flunks tests but clearly shows progress in other ways?

We still recall the offbeat and clever oral presentation made by two students over a quarter-century ago. At the conclusion of the presentation, the other students spontaneously applauded. Would any letter grade have sufficed? Equally memorable is the student who had flunked the course twice before but prepared excellent syntheses of library materials for her group's project. No one was more startled than she by her success—and it came through her own effort. But on tests she continued to struggle and even occasionally fail.

The point is that we need to balance paper-and-pencil tests with other measurements. It is all too easy to forget that we are supposed to help students learn not only a body of knowledge but ways of thinking and acting that cannot always be readily measured. As social studies teachers we are asked to be decision makers, including deciding how to evaluate our students. This means making decisions—often difficult ones. But in so doing, we will hope-fully discourage the "wad-ja-get" mentality that can result from overreliance on testing.

Summary

Recall the statement that opens this chapter: "Effective social studies teach-ers use various means to assess the attainment of goals and objectives of curriculum and instruction. These in turn reflect the diverse aptitudes and degrees of readiness of their students." We really do know a teacher who was stung by a student's well-intentioned remark about a "gift" grade and vowed not to allow a recurrence of the situation that led to it. "Next time" that teacher would have some solid evidence on which to judge students' work; that is, he would systematically collect evidence to determine the amount and degree of changes in the students—what is termed *evaluation*. He vowed to use both *formative* and *summative* evaluation, both of which involve collecting and sorting evidence (*measurement*) with which to make evaluations. Evidence would be based on standards applying to others similarly situated (*norm-ref-erenced*), some established criteria (*criterion-referenced*), and self-compari-sons (*self- referenced*).

The next decision would be the particular types of measurements appro-priate to one's classes and objectives. Those types that rely primarily on teacher observations are *qualitative* or "softer" measures: anecdotal records, rating scales, and checklists. *Quantitative* or "harder" measures include essay, multiple-choice, analogies, sequencing, completion, matching, and true-false (or "alternative-response") questions.

Anecdotal records are simply descriptions of the teacher's observations of students. *Rating scales* require some judging of student characteristics or qualities. *Checklists* mark completion of clearly specific and defined tasks.

The particular tests to use depend on a variety of factors, including, of course, students' cognitive levels and general concerns such as validity, reliability, and usability. Tests should measure what we intend them to measure (*validity*), generate consistent results (*reliability*), and be adminis-tratively feasible (*usability*). The primary way to ensure validity is to construct some table of specifications reflecting the objectives, such as a cross- or two-axis table, coupled with the use of *item analyses* or *item discrimination analyses*. To ensure reliability, we would use the various formulas available.

The *essay* test is considered quantitative (though prone to subjectivity in grading), because it asks students to initiate, integrate, and express ideas, that is, employ higher-level thinking. *Multiple-choice* questions also can demand higher-level thinking, are freer from ambiguity than other measures, may be more reliable, and are easier to grade. If carefully written, *analogy, sequencing, completion, matching,* and *true-false* questions can test students' knowledge of a compact body of information and be written and graded relatively effortlessly. If posed carefully, they can offer alternative ways to measure student performance.

Decisions! Decisions!

1. How do you feel about grades? Have you ever felt caught up in the "wad-ja-get" syndrome? How should students be graded?

2. Would you prefer self-grading? Peer grading? Why or why not?

3. Do you like to be compared against others? Against some standard (criterion)? Against yourself? Which do you think is the fairest? Why?

4. What policies should schools have for evaluating students given a climate of accountability?

5. What makes a grade (on a quiz, test, project, report) fair? How can you ensure fairness in your evaluations?

6. What forms of measurement do you prefer? Essays? Multiple-choice questions? Analogies? Other? Why?

7. What school policies toward weighting grades differently for higher- or lower-track students would you write given the chance? Should effort be graded? If so, how would you grade it?

8. Should students grade one another's papers in class?

9. How do you feel grades should be reported? Should grades be posted? Should students be told their grades in front of others? What rights to privacy do students have? How far should that privacy extend?

References

Armstrong, D. G., & Savage, T. V. (1983). *Secondary education.* New York: Macmillan.

Bloom, B. S., Madaus, G. F., & Hastings, J. T. (1981). *Evaluation to improve learning.* New York: McGraw-Hill.

Gronlund, N. (1981). *Measurement and evaluation in teaching* (4th ed.). New York: Macmillan.

Kirschenbaum, H., Napier, R., & Simon, S. (1971). *Wadjaget? The grading game in American education.* New York: Hart.

National Commission on Excellence in Education. (1983). *A nation at risk: The imperative for educational reform.* Washington, DC: U.S. Government Printing Office.

Orlandi, L. R. (1971). Secondary school social studies. In B. S. Bloom, J. T. Hastings, & G. F. Madaus (Eds.), *Handbook on formative and summative evaluation of student learning* (pp. 447–498). New York: McGraw-Hill.

Selakovich, D. (1984). *Schooling in America.* New York: Longman.

Part Three

The Decision Makers

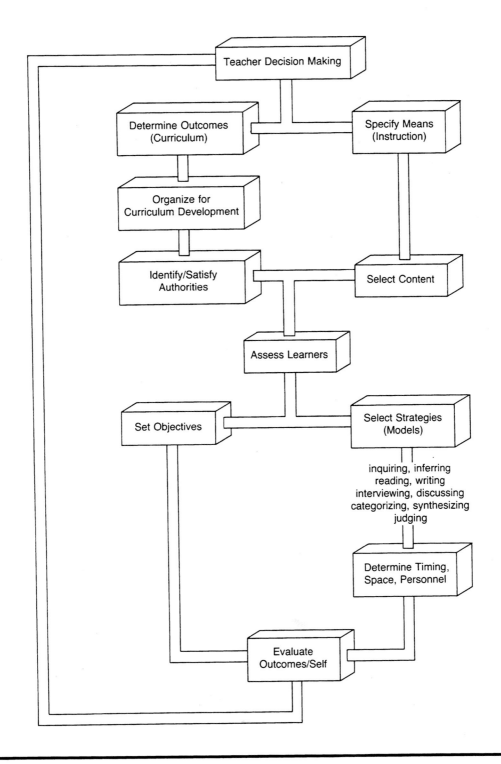

Chapter Twelve

Professionalization of Social Studies Teachers

The central theme of this book has been "teacher as decision maker." By this we mean that to be optimally effective, teachers must have a considerable amount of authority in deciding how best to serve their "clients." The degree of professional freedom for teachers should be limited only by the legitimate and demonstrated needs of individual learners and their society.

In this final chapter, we will explore the fascinating process of becoming a professional secondary teacher of social studies in our complex society. We will examine some demographic factors associated with the calling; how to obtain and retain a teaching job in America's organizational structure; the value of professional societies; the forms of assistance one may obtain from peers and support personnel; and the nature of contemporary reforms in teacher preparation and in the workplace.

But first we need to define *profession*. The literature abounds with definitions. Here are two sets of explanatory criteria that we find highly attractive.

First, Paul Woodring (1986) says,

> What distinguishes a profession from an occupation? High income is not the hallmark—some professionals take vows of poverty. A license does not identify a professional—physicians and lawyers are licensed, but priests and college professors are not. . . .
>
> Although the following criteria have not always been lived up to, they can be useful in identifying the professions.
>
> • A profession requires a deep commitment on the part of all of its members, going far beyond a desire for pecuniary gain.
> • A profession rests on an organized body of scholarly or scientific knowledge.
> • Members of a profession engage in work that improves the human condition.
> • Members of a profession meet rigorous standards of education and selection. *

Second, Richard Hall (1969) adds three vitally important characteristics that can be used to measure a particular occupation's degree of professionalism:

1. *Structural criteria:* The degree to which there is a formalized code of ethics and a prescribed and lengthy training process in certified training institutes or the like.
2. *Attitudinal attributes of members:* The degree to which the members believe in service to the public, self-regulation, autonomy, and similar professional values.

*From "Schoolteaching Cannot Be Considered a Profession as Long as Its Entrance Standards Remain So Low" by P. Woodring, November 12, 1986, *Chronicle of Higher Education, 6*, p. 6. Reprinted by permission of Paul Woodring.

3. *Societal recognition:* The degree to which society in general views the occupation as a profession.*

ASIDE TO THE READER: These lists seem to cry out for thought and discussion. We suggest you do just that. Are you about to enter a profession? Are there really degrees of professionalism? If so, should you strive to become more professional?

FROM SURVIVING TO THRIVING IN THE CLASSROOM

Sheri can still recall the days before teacher mentoring (a system in which a new teacher is assigned to work closely with a veteran). When she was hired, her department head volunteered, "If you have any questions, don't hesitate to ask. Helping teachers in my department is one of the things for which I get paid." Reassured, Sheri went about the business of getting acquainted with her students, the grade-level syllabuses, and the myriad details of the job she had taken with such enthusiasm.

Periodically Sheri took her department head's advice at face value and asked questions. So much was new (and, she felt, had not been covered in her college's education program). Things went well until midway through the semester, when Sheri received her first evaluation from the department head: "Can't handle responsibilities. Asks for help all the time."

However it was intended, Sheri was crushed by the evaluation—but not defeated. She had worked too hard at being a teacher to give up now. Shortly thereafter, Sheri began seeking the advice of others, circumventing the department head. From then on, her evaluations were uniformly good. In fact, her department head was quite impressed by Sheri's "new-found independence and initiative."

Kareem's excitement over his new job was dampened one day early in the first semester when he realized that he was sitting at lunch with a group of teachers who were "on the outs" with another, more influential group. Immediately he realized that he had to make a decision in the interests of survival. He resented that he had not been warned about factions in schools. In contrast, Yvonne's department head had tried to acclimate Yvonne even before she was officially on the job. He had helped her find housing, showed her the syllabuses, offered her some items for her bulletin board, and generally "mentored" her.

And recall from Chapter 5 how reassuring Beth's department head was to the novice teacher.

---

*From *Occupations and the Social Structure* by R. Hall, 1969, Englewood Cliffs, NJ: Prentice-Hall. Reprinted by permission of Prentice-Hall.

YOUR COLLEAGUES

If you find yourself in Sheri's or Kareem's situation, what will you do? Like Sheri and Kareem, you will have to size up the situation, including your more experienced colleagues.

Actually, you have met some of them in these pages. Remember Mary Ellen, the district social studies coordinator in Chapter 1? With an advanced degree, 20-plus years of teaching in various school districts, and some successful leadership skills, Mary Ellen had become an administrator. And there was Tom S., the intense, subject-centered teacher with his belief that history is the heart of social studies. Conrad C., despite his tendency to be pedantic, retained his enthusiasm for teaching after others in his age group had retired.

Then there was Maria Alvarez, the social-studies-turned-methods teacher, who introduced us to time management in Chapter 6. In Chapter 4 we met Beth, wrestling with all the problems a first-year teacher faces, and in Chapter 10 the more experienced Elise and Pedro. Finally, we just met Sheri and Kareem, who learned survival the hard way.

A Profile of Social Studies Teachers

A profile of your colleagues is fairly easy to draw relying on Metropolitan Life's (1986) survey of the American teacher and the research of James Leming (Leming, in press). Note, over the years secondary social studies has tended to be male dominated (between 60% and 75%), but that is changing.

Basically your colleagues are:

- Graying (approximately 42 years old)
- White (92%)
- Experienced (with between 10 and 24 years of teaching)
- Tenured
- Well educated (with approximately half holding at least a master's degree)
- Incommensurately paid (with most receiving between $20,000 and $25,000 a year)
- Married (roughly 75%)
- Concerned about lack of status (though less so than more novice teachers)
- Moderate in their political views (although they tend to be registered Democrats)
- Union members (almost 85%)
- Teaching in cities or suburbs (approximately 72%), but do not necessarily live in the districts in which they teach
- Working long hours (between 65% and 70% worked more than 46 hours per week)
- Supportive of mentor teaching programs (82%)
- Opposed to merit pay systems (a solid 71%)
- Lukewarm toward career ladder programs (46%)
- In favor of "teaching centers," teacher assistance programs, and more time to talk with and observe one another

- Demanding shared decision making (97% believe in a team approach to school management)
- Seeking better reasoning and analytical skills on the part of their students
- Rating other teachers well (93% gave fellow teachers an "excellent" or "good" rating)

However, many of your colleagues are also thinking about getting out of teaching. Fifty-five percent of the respondents in the Metropolitan Life survey said they have considered leaving teaching. But 75% to 80% of the social studies teachers surveyed reported that they are "very or somewhat contented."

These, then, are your colleagues.

What do you think of your colleagues (your classmates)? How do you compare? Would you be comfortable in secondary social studies, which traditionally has been a male-dominated occupation? How do you feel about some of the issues raised in the survey? What roles do you think teachers should play? How do you think you will get along with your future colleagues? How satisfied with teaching do you think you will be?

GETTING AND KEEPING A JOB

Getting the Job

Sheri survived the first step in her career by thinking like a social scientist; that is, she sized up the problem (getting help without going to her department head), asked the right questions (of whom she could safely turn for help when needed), collected and analyzed data (assessed her colleagues' relative strengths and weaknesses), posed a solution, and tested it—successfully. Actually, she had applied the same techniques to getting her job in the first place: She had sized up the market for social studies teachers, located names of school districts and administrators, talked to placement officers at her college, and began sending out cover letters and résumés.

The first thing Sheri had recognized is that demand for teachers generally is determined by student enrollments, which in turn are determined by live births. For example, in 1960 there were approximately 4.2 million live births. The rate dropped dramatically in 1975 (to 3.1 million), rose between 1975 and 1980, and has leveled off at approximately 3.7 million (Association for School, College and University Staffing, 1988). Generally, then, openings for teachers have declined, but there has been a slight increase in demand recently (although it probably will not attain the heights of the "baby-boom" period). Still, the good news is that the number of individuals certifying to teach halved between 1969 and 1987. Thus, the overall picture is encouraging.

Given this information, what about the demand for social studies teachers in particular, recognizing that the supply of social studies teachers always seems to somewhat exceed demand? The news at the time of this writing is not so good. On a 1 to 5 scale, with 1 representing a significant surplus, the national figure for social studies teachers is 1.98, meaning only moderate demand (Association for School, College and University Staffing, 1988, p. 5). In 1988, the greatest opportunities were in the Northeast, particularly Connecticut, Maine, Massachusetts, New Hampshire, and Vermont, followed by New York and Pennsylvania. The fewest were in Montana, Wyoming, Colorado, and New Mexico.

Keeping the Job

One thing that kept coming through in Sheri's social science courses throughout college was the fact that organizational life prevails in our society, including, of course, in schools. Most people are born in hospitals that demand assurance that bills will be paid before they leave. People routinely receive social security numbers to report income, identify themselves as students, and so on. Buying goods more often than not involves a credit card, as though cash were some strange, suspect medium.

But it is the normative consequences of living and working in, not just being a member of, an organization that are of real concern. Just as there are norms in the larger society, there are organizational norms in teaching to consider. Organizations shape "acceptable" behavior, and our perceptions of ourselves are influenced by reference to organizations. Our success is often measured by our degree of identification with and status in an organization. The more we internalize the goals of the organization, the greater the likelihood of our success in that organization.

The bureaucratic properties of organizations particularly stand out, for the primary model for 20th-century organizations is the bureaucratic one, wherein formal rules, a hierarchy of offices, spheres of competence, and reliance on written communication prevail. This appears to have been compounded by the accountability movement that characterized the 1970s and 1980s.

However, organizational patterns vary from open to closed, consistent with the degree of professionalization that exists at any one time. This is represented as a continuum in Figure 12.1. Organizations like those on the left are characterized as enjoying collegial relationships and typically include doctors, lawyers, college faculty, and other professionals. At the right is the organizational structure wherein autonomy declines markedly the lower one is within the organization. In between are organizations such as public schools, in which individuals enjoy less autonomy than "pure" professionals.

Dreeben (1973), however, notes that schools deviate from typical bureaucracies in various ways. This is particularly so in classrooms, in which a considerable degree of independence may prevail because goals tend to be vague and outcomes often "defy easy measurement" (pp. 452–453). A second

FIGURE 12.1
Individual Decision Making in Hierarchical Organizations

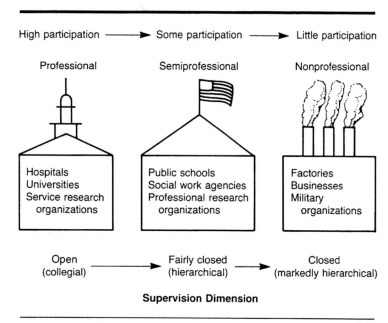

Source: From Robert G. Owens, ORGANIZATIONAL BEHAVIOR IN SCHOOLS, © 1970, p. 103. Adapted by permission of Prentice-Hall, Inc., Englewood Cliffs, New Jersey.

difference comes from many unpredictables within the classroom that require teacher judgment. The final difference is the degree of "quality control" that supervisors can exercise.

Still, it would be a mistake to consider teachers as being completely autonomous. Policies often are top-down, "jurisdictional lines separate teachers and administrators" (Dreeben, p. 453), and conflicts over working conditions influence the degree of freedom that teachers enjoy.

Selection-Socialization

Even more important in terms of fostering organizational goals is the "selection-socialization" process (Lortie, 1969, p. 19). Teachers tend to be recruited and selected based on qualities that precede their interest in teaching. As Feiman-Nemser and Floden (1986) state,

> Emphasis on the resistance of beginners to the effects of the workplace may underestimate the extent to which the teaching is transmitted from one generation of teachers to the next. Those entering teaching preparation have already had more interactions with experienced teachers than they may ever have again (p. 521).

Lortie (1975) calls this "apprenticeship by observation."

While we firmly believe that multicultural diversity among teachers is highly positive, a "middle-class" socialization seems to be a prerequisite. Although the image of the passive teacher easily molded by the workplace is being challenged, the fact remains that many beginning teachers tend to accept and exhibit certain behavioral standards: anxiety about how they appear to others, avoidance of aggressive behavior, and conflict camouflaging. Further, teacher education institutions and persons responsible for hiring teachers seem to reinforce such standards, whether implicitly or explicitly.

The case studies by Wise, Darling-Hammond, and Berry (1988, p. 83) are reminiscent of the hiring practices of administrators, despite attempts to improve the process. These researchers found administrators using screening devices that asked the "wrong" questions, tending toward "anti-intellectualism," and selecting candidates based on the peripheral needs of the vacancy, for example, hiring a football coach to teach social studies.

For the skeptical or unsuspecting, the following experience of a young graduate student in the beginning phase of his teacher education program is revealing. This student was required to observe classes at various schools. Having made an appointment, he arrived with another student anticipating at least some welcome, if not a cordial one. Instead, here is what he encountered, in his own words:

> When we arrived at the school, we were treated very cordially by the school secretary, who telephoned [the principal], who in turn led us to his office, checked teachers' schedules, and picked classes to be observed. Then he suddenly turned to me and said, "I don't know what we're going to do about you." I asked what he meant, and he said he did not like the way I was dressed. [The student noted that he had on a new shirt, his best pair of pants, and freshly polished shoes.] "Look, you don't have a tie and coat on. You're supposed to be a prospective teacher. I can't let you into any classes looking like that. . . ."
>
> I was, to say the least, stunned, but I controlled my anger and became almost timid. . . . I figured I had to conform for the good of my fellow students.
>
> After this fiasco, I was a little upset for a couple of weeks. . . . It was just another one of those things I could not figure out. I was well dressed, but I did not fit the principal's image of a teacher. I did not know that *to be a teacher one had to project a certain image* [Emphasis added].

While this is possibly an extreme case, the agony this young graduate student experienced is a part of the socialization-selection process. The process undoubtedly continues, at least in some respects, within the school, but the emphasis is necessarily reduced to the degree that the earlier socialization "took." As Feiman-Nemser and Floden (1986) note, "In many respects, descriptions of the cultures of teaching in Lortie (1975), Jackson (1968) and even Waller (1932) are still valid. . . ." (p. 522).

Thus, rules and standards, technical competence, hierarchical arrangements, and socialization all operate to ensure the functioning of the bureaucratic model on which our schools are patterned. But a built-in conflict erupts when teachers try to conform to the model while teaching individual students who have their own needs and may be attending school involuntarily. Despite teacher contracts, there remains a tendency to operate under norms preceding the contract, with teachers seeking the goodwill of principals to get desirable assignments and principals relying on the goodwill of teachers to carry out policies (Feiman-Nemser & Floden, 1986, p. 508).

Placement

The placement of staff contributes heavily to the degree of job satisfaction, but job satisfaction is also affected by the information flow and the organizational structure of the school. Adapting Abraham Maslow's classification of need satisfaction and comparing the formal organizational structure of six school districts, Carpenter (1969) found that teacher satisfaction was inversely related to the number of administrative levels in existence. In other words, controlling for length of experience and type of organization, Carpenter found that the "taller" the administrative levels (as opposed to "medium" or "flat" structures), the lower the perceived satisfaction of the classroom teacher. In part this reflected the information flow from the superintendent down to the teacher as well as the teacher's belief that he or she was being excluded from any decision making.

But satisfaction is also influenced by the degree of autonomy allowed or perceived by the teacher. Whether "tall" or "flat," the organization may be either democratic or autocratic. A tall organization (superintendent, principal, vice-principal, curriculum coordinator, team leader, etc.) may be democratic, while a flat organization (a superintendent and building principal only) can be ruled by fiat. Every decision comes from the person on top, with no sharing. Teacher satisfaction, then, is a multivariate notion.

Unfortunately, job placement too often tends to be accidental: the time of hiring, the administrator's perception of organizational needs, the teacher's assumed or real competence, and seniority or lack thereof. In larger districts, not only grade-level placement but school placement will be determined randomly, although generally by seniority. Typically new teachers are assigned what are considered the least desirable classes and periods and then forced to fend for themselves (Wise, Darling-Hammond, & Berry, 1988, p. 84), although teacher mentoring tries to counter this tendency.

Scheduling

As noted in Chapter 6, another aspect of the bureaucratization of schools is the determination of how to establish schedules for teachers and students. Again the basic decision tends to be how best to further the school organization—how to channel the greatest number of products in the most efficient manner. Whatever the particular pattern adopted by a school or school district, efficiency rather than pedagogical considerations may well prevail. In fact, it is not unusual to find scheduling interfering with instruction. This may be the case where the band or sports teams have brought whatever fame the school enjoys. Scheduling band practices, athletic assemblies, or athletic study halls has been a practice deplored by many a teacher who believes academics come first but soon learns that the priorities are reversed: The "hidden curriculum" takes precedence.

Consider the following. A young secondary social studies teacher working in a large city school district was concerned for the welfare of a Haitian immigrant student who was unable to speak English. The teacher asked his principal if he could shift his lunch period to the student's study hall period so he could help the student. The principal refused, because the teachers' contract required a half-hour lunch period in the middle of the day. Nor would the principal change the student's schedule to the teacher's lunch period. Thus, the principal not only effectively blocked the opportunity for a teacher to interact with a student; he barred the student from obtaining needed help. But the *organization* was preserved.

Sometimes administrative convenience dictates lunch periods that split classes into three parts. In more than one secondary school there will be a class period in the middle of the day in which students will report to class for roughly 20 minutes, go to lunch for another 20 minutes, and return to class for the final 20 minutes. This is healthy neither for learning nor for the digestive system.

Thus, scheduling, an often ignored aspect of working in a bureaucratic setting, can prove another obstacle to meeting the needs of students. (In fairness, however, scheduling is a major headache for administrators.

Decision Making

Throughout this book, we have referred to the teacher's role as decision maker and have encouraged you to consider how you will respond to the need to make decisions. Even seemingly minor decisions such as whether Johnny, Mary, and Carlos should work together (it seems that Mary and Carlos always get into fights about leading their groups) or whether to use mastery learning or concept attainment can, over time, tax one's patience. Yet such day-to-day and year-to-year decision making lies at the heart of teaching.

Sometimes it appears that decisions are made capriciously and osmotically. But teachers must cope. For example, Herndon (1971, pp. 101–102) asks why there are 38 students in a classroom is designed to accommodate 28:

> Who decided that thirty-eight kids in Room 3 ought to learn about Egypt in the seventh grade, from 10:05 to 10:50? Not the teachers. Who decided that there ought to be forty-five minutes for lunch and that there ought to be stewed tomatoes in those plastic containers? Not the teachers. Who decided about the curriculum and who decided about the textbooks? Not us. Not us!*

---

*From *How to Survive in Your Native Land* (pp. 101–102) by J. Herndon, 1971, New York: Simon & Schuster. Copyright © 1971 by James Herndon. Reprinted by permission of Simon & Schuster, Inc.

Decision making in schools can and should be shared.

It seems that everyone begs ignorance, but Herndon appears to have found the answer:

> Noman did it. Noman is responsible for them. The people responsible for the decisions about how schools ought to go are dead. Very few people are able to ask questions of dead men.*

Thus, everyone can claim it is not their fault, and often decisions in schools seem inexplicable, at best based on folk knowledge.

In fact, however, even in authoritarian schools teachers are asked to, and do, make decisions: about curricular and instructional matters, including topics to be taught; the particular instructional techniques; how much time to devote to a topic; and how to assess learning. Of course, this recognizes that "teachers will make stupid as well as wise" decisions, and administrators should not try to remove this authority because of its abuse by or incompe-

---

*Ibid.

tence of some teachers (Goodlad, 1971, p. 80). In other words, competence may develop out of teachers' need to examine what curriculum and instruction will be used and how they will be carried out. They may learn that conventional wisdom will not suffice and so will have to extend themselves—which is what we are asking you to do. But this means being prepared to make decisions and being willing to live with the consequences of one's decisions.

Risks of Decision Making. Charlie James, a social studies teacher and Quaker in a small, rural New York school, decided to wear a black armband to school to protest American involvement in Vietnam despite his principal's warning not to. He did not ask his students to follow suit, nor did he refer to the armband in his classes. Charlie James, father and provider of four children, was fired. But he felt he was wrongly fired, for he believed his actions were in no way harmful to his students or to the school and that he had an obligation to state, albeit without words, his position. In so doing, he felt he was practicing citizenship, exercising his rights under the First Amendment.*

In another case, a social studies teacher, in a class discussion during a unit on race relations, candidly answered a student's question to the effect that he did not oppose interracial marriages. Parental protest to that and other statements and readings led to his dismissal by the school board for "insubordination." The teacher argued on his own behalf that he was protected by the First and Fourteenth Amendments to teach controversial issues in the classroom.**

Along the same lines a Lawrence, Massachusetts, teacher introduced a lesson on taboos by writing a four-letter word on the chalkboard, asking the class to define the word, and then asking them to explain why the word was socially unacceptable. The teacher was suspended and then dismissed for "conduct unbecoming a teacher." The teacher challenged the action, arguing that 11th graders were sophisticated enough to treat the four-letter word from a serious educational viewpoint. Moreover, the teacher believed that other teachers would agree that what she had done was a reasonable teaching technique.***

Joan LaRocca, a 35-year-old teacher with nine years' teaching experience in her school district, was suspended and then dismissed after being found guilty of using school facilities to convert students to a religious sect known as the Julius Movement. LaRocca argued that her superintendent and prin-

---

***James v. Board of Education*, Cen. Distr. #1. 34 L.Ed. 2d 491 (1972). Another leading case in terms of free speech of employees was *Commick v. Meyers.*, 461 U.S. 138 (1983), wherein the dismissal of an assistant district attorney in New Orleans for preparing and distributing a questionnaire to fellow employees about office morale and policies was upheld by the Supreme Court. The Court cited *Pickering v. Board of Education*, 391 U.S. (1968), saying that because the speech in question was not a public concern, it was not protected by the First Amendment. However, *Commick* was cited in *Lewis v. Harrison School District No. 1*, 805 F 2d 310 (8th Cir., 1986) to protect a principal's speech that criticized his superintendent's treatment of the principal's wife, who was active in union affairs, because it was shown to be of public concern.

***Sterzing v. Ft. Bend Inc. School District*, Civil No. 69- H-319 (S.D. Tex., May 5, 1972).

****Mailloux v. Kiley*, 436 F.2d 359 (1st Cir., 1969).

cipal were violating her freedom of religion by warning her not to talk about "God, religion or the Bible in school."*

How would you decide these cases? How much freedom to teach should a social studies teacher have? Is one's right to speech limited because of one's role as a teacher? To what extent should a social studies teacher's decisions about content and teaching techniques be limited? What if either the particular content or methods offend parents or students? Are there certain standards to guide teachers in their decision-making? Who should set these standards? Should social studies teachers ever take the "safe" path and avoid controversial topics or state their opinions? Should social studies try to be "value free?"

The words of one court may be helpful:

A teacher's methods are not without limits. Teachers occupy a unique position of trust in our society, and they must handle such trust and the instruction of young people with great care. On the other hand, a teacher must not be manacled with rigid regulations, which preclude full adaptation of the course to the times in which we live. . . . A responsible teacher must have freedom to use the tools of his profession as he sees fit. If the teacher cannot be trusted to use them fairly, then the teacher should never have been engaged in the first place.**

Thus, we return to the role of the teacher in the school organization. In some ways, the teacher is a "semiprofessional" who will be subject to "selection" and "socialization" by school districts. Yet the teacher is charged with fostering the welfare of a group of students, which means making decisions of all kinds, often on the spur of the moment, but presumably also in the best interests of the organization he or she serves. Still, these decisions may run counter to the opinions and feelings of parents, administrators, boards of education, other teachers, and, occasionally, students. The teacher, then, is caught among personal, professional, social, and organizational goals. If any individuals should be able to survive such conflicting goals, they are social studies teachers, who have the benefit of their education in the social sciences and who aspire to be professionals.

Let's now turn to a consideration of professional associations. How can they help you become effective and even more professional?

---

*In the Matter of Joan LaRocca v. Board of Education of the Rye City School District, 63 App. Div. 2nd 1019 (New York, 1978); The New York Times, October 21, 1976. Similarly, in May v. Evansville-Vanderburgh School Corp., 787 F. 2d 1105 (7th Cir., 1986), the court denied the claim of seven elementary teachers to the protection of free speech to hold prayer meetings in school before classes on Tuesday mornings. Despite the fact that no students participated and the meetings were not disruptive, the court held that the school had the right to avoid controversy by prohibiting non-work-related meetings.

**Sterzing v. Ft. Bend Inc. School District, pp. 12–13, 15–16.

PROFESSIONAL ASSOCIATIONS

JASON: I'm afraid I'll never be as good a teacher as you are, Elise. I'm just not very creative. You have all these neat ideas for presenting material, and you always seem to be on top of what my professors on campus say are the newest teaching strategies. What we read about in methods class is what you are doing.

ELISE: Well, I was doubtful about myself when I was a student teacher, too. I still have doubts. Really, I'm not all that creative. But, I do try to be constantly on the lookout for good ideas that I can adapt to my goals and my students.

JASON: But where do you look for these ideas? I realize that some of you teachers in the building share ideas, and I've also recognized some of the lessons from my methods class that you have used, changing them a little from what Professor Malliacki presented.

ELISE: Well, your professor and I read the same social studies education journals, I guess. And I did pick up a lot of my ideas when I studied for my master's with Malliacki.

Social Studies Organizations

Like more than 22,000 other social studies teachers in the nation, Elise is a member of the National Council for the Social Studies (NCSS), the largest national organization for social studies teachers. With membership comes the journal *Social Education,* which NCSS publishes seven times a year. Referred to casually as "Social Ed," the journal tries to keep its membership informed about a variety of matters aimed at improving social studies teaching. Each issue tends to have a particular theme, with both substantive (that is, curriculum and content) and process (teaching strategies) articles. Elise faithfully reads hers to pick up instructional ideas and to keep abreast of current curricular issues and other controversies in the field. As one example, each issue has a "Document of the Month" section that is easily reproducible and can provide a fine springboard for instruction.

In addition to *Social Education,* NCSS publishes a journal especially for elementary school educators, *Social Studies and the Young Learner.* Elise has borrowed copies of it from her sister-in-law, a fourth-grade teacher, and modified some ideas to use with her slower-reading eighth graders. Most college libraries subscribe to these two journals, so if you have not been introduced to them in your social studies methods class, peruse them in the library. Better yet, become a member of NCSS yourself (there is a reduced student rate), and you will receive *Social Education* regularly.

With membership, you will also find in your mailbox *The Social Studies Professional (TSSP),* the newsletter of NCSS. It contains all sorts of current news in the field as well as lists of professional opportunities for summer travel, workshops and institutes, and curricular ideas. In addition, the newsletter will help you become more familiar with the workings of NCSS.

Nearly all states have a state council for the social studies, and there are many local social studies councils within states. These organizations tend to provide the same types of information and materials but are likely to be directed toward more localized needs.

In addition, NCSS and many state councils provide books and curricular materials at a reasonable cost. Also, social studies councils tend to hold at least one meeting a year. The NCSS annual meeting is usually about four days, state and regional conferences may be one to three days, and local conferences typically are a half-day or a full day. At these meetings, exemplary classroom teachers and other educators, including social studies supervisors and college professors, demonstrate the latest teaching techniques, report on results of action research, provide academic content updates, and discuss curricular issues. There is always time for substantive debate and socializing, both of which are important.

At most conferences, exhibits of new books and other print materials, software and hardware, multimedia packages, and even realia are available for perusal. Examining these state-of-the- art materials will inform you about the future of social studies teaching.

Being a professional teacher is more than meeting four or five classes a day, five days a week, and planning, preparing, and evaluating student work every night, weekends, and "vacations." One needs to be aware of all the ongoing changes in one's profession, and the journals and other materials provided by the social studies councils and the conferences and workshops they offer help the busy teacher stay up to date and informed.

In Chapter 1, you read that the field of social studies has to justify itself more than other fields, partly because of its depth and breadth. As a teacher, you will be called upon to do that with students, parents, school board members, and others—even friends—who want to know why you're a social studies teacher. The journals and other materials and professional opportunities offered to members of the social studies councils will help you strengthen your commitment to the field. The scope and sequence, curriculum guidelines, and ethical standards of NCSS are three such sources and will lend national support to your personal arguments justifying the social studies. You're not out there alone—you have colleagues and a national and state association supporting you!

Yes, we believe you should be an active participant in NCSS and its affiliates. But, for reasons that are not entirely clear to us, social studies teachers are less active than they should be. For example, the premier organizations serving English, science, mathematics, vocational education, fine arts, special education, and foreign language teachers are all larger than the social studies group. Perhaps the reason is that NCSS has been less effective than it should be. If this is the case, it will only improve if potential members are actively engaged.

In addition to the social studies councils, there are many other professional societies and sources of information that are particularly valuable for teachers of the social studies. Here are a few of the most important:

- The College and University Faculty Association (CUFA), which is part of NCSS, publishes a valuable, research-oriented journal, *Theory and Research in Social Education*.
- *Social Studies* is a useful monthly that offers articles on curriculum and instruction in social studies education.
- *The History Teacher* and *The Senior Economist* contain analyses of both content and pedagogy in history and economics, respectively. There are specialized journals for other fields as well.
- Educational Resources Information Center/Clearinghouse for Social Studies/Social Science Education (ERIC/ChESS) is one of 16 subject-specialized clearinghouses that provide ready access to social studies curriculum guides, teaching units, descriptions of innovative programs, bibliographies, articles, and research reports. Its free newsletter, *Keeping Up*, will keep you informed about the remarkable variety of available products and services. By all means, get on the mailing list. All you have to do is write to them at Indiana University, 2805 East 10th St., Bloomington, Indiana 47405
- The Social Science Education Consortium (SSEC) is a not-for-profit corporation that produces a wide range of workshops and institutes, publications, and other services for social studies professionals. It is supported by its invitational members and by grants and contracts from state governments and private foundations. Write to SSEC for information (3300 Mitchell Lane, Boulder Colorado, 80301). They will be happy to add you to their mailing list.
- Most states and large school districts have departments or bureaus of social studies education to serve teachers. All you need to do is write or telephone them with questions and/or requests.
- Most of the disciplines that form the base for the social studies are eager to assist secondary school social studies teachers. Figure 12.2 lists the most appropriate of these organizations. Consult the *Encyclopedia of Associations* for the addresses and publications of these organizations. Any well-stocked college library will have most of their journals.

Other Professional Associations and Sources

In addition to the major professional social science/history societies and sources, there are several helpful general professional organizations and their publications. Here are a few of the most useful:

- *Teacher unions.* As soon as you get a job, most of you will join or at least pay dues to one of the two major teachers unions: the American Federation of Teachers with its state and local affiliates or the National Education

Association and its subgroups. Both provide numerous services for teachers and publish extensively, including *American Teacher* (AFT) and *NEA Today* (NEA).

- *American Education Research Association (AERA).* AERA is the leading research organization in education. Among its numerous publications are *Educational Researcher* (nine issues per year), *American Educational Research Journal* (quarterly), *Review of Educational Research* (quarterly), and *Review of Research in Education* (annual).
- *Association for Supervision and Curriculum Development (ASCD).* ASCD produces a host of monographs and other publications on curriculum and instruction, including the monthly *Educational Leadership* and the quarterly *Journal of Curriculum Supervision.*

You may be wondering when you will find time to read more than the national and state social studies journals, let alone all these other ones. It is tough, we agree. Most of us sometimes let our journals get stacked up for weeks before we get around to reading them. You may just have to schedule them in, setting aside an hour or two on Sunday, during your lunch period every day, or as your nighttime reading. But keeping up with professional associations is an essential part of your job.

WORKING TOGETHER

Membership in a professional social studies association, a subscription to an academic or generic pedagogical journal, or attendance at the annual confer-

FIGURE 12.2
Professional Associations Representing Social Science Disciplines

- American Academy of Political and Social Science
- American Anthropological Association
- American Association for State and Local History
- American Association of Museums
- American Economic Association
- American Geographical Society
- American Historical Association
- American Political Science Association
- American Psychological Association
- American Sociological Association
- American Studies Association
- Association for the Study of Negro Life and History
- Association of American Geographers
- Organization of American Historians

ence of a social studies organization will help you maintain your status as a professional. Your role as a professional, however, expands beyond that of classroom social studies teacher. There are many other individuals in your school district or building who will also view you as a professional, assuming that you live up to their expectations of the professional teacher. Who are these other individuals?

First, there are your peers—other social studies teachers. Your school district likely will provide you with a mentor, an experienced teacher who will assist you during your first teaching year. In some schools, each of you will teach only four classes instead of the usual five, so that you and your mentor will have time to observe each other teach, plan together, and learn from each other in a nonthreatening manner. You should feel free to call on other teachers for their advice and counsel as well. Many districts also have a social studies supervisor, coordinator, or department chair available to assist you. Do call on your colleagues for the benefit of their experience. Remember, they were once first-year teachers too.

We realize that beginning teachers often just need to talk to one another. And why not? It's a good idea. You will learn that you're not the only one who is unsure about evaluating essay papers or handling students who turn in papers late. Why not be the one to organize this "talk time"—perhaps a Friday afternoon session in your classroom, your apartment, or a local watering hole? You will find the sharing therapeutic.

Because many students with handicapping conditions are now mainstreamed in regular classes for part of their school day and few social studies teachers have had extensive preparation in special education, another support person to connect with in your school is a special education teacher. Many special education teachers at the middle and high school levels have only a minimal background in "regular" education—working with non-handicapped students—so the two of you can really help each other.

In Chapter 6, we underscored the need for you to develop a working relationship with the librarian/media specialist/computer coordinator. In some schools, that is one person; in others, it's two or more. These specialists, like the special education teacher, will rely on you for content expertise, so you need to collaborate with them to gain as much technical assistance as you need. They want to help! We know of no librarians who feel overworked because of teacher demands. They are usually stretched to the limit because teachers have not notified them in advance of materials needed for class activities and assignments.

There is another large group of school personnel who often feel that teachers do not view them as significant. They tend not to have college degrees; in fact, some may not have high school diplomas. However, they are the people who help the school run smoothly. We're talking about the teacher aides, the secretarial and clerical people, the custodians, security personnel, and the cafeteria workers. Some of these people actually know the students better than some teachers do.

We often tell our student teachers to get to know these people right from the start. They can be of great help if, for example, you want to plan an ethnic dinner. They will help you build a guillotine as a class project studying the French Revolution. They will track down a parent for a conference or even come to your rescue during third period when the copying machine has jammed and your quiz for fourth period was a late decision. It's nice to remember them at holiday times and even birthdays.

We have not as yet mentioned the guidance counselor, school psychologist, dean, or social worker. These highly significant people are usually introduced to you during orientation for beginning teachers. Do get to know and consult with them. They can provide much valuable information about students, the community, and the school organization.

Finally, there are the general administrators: principals, headmasters, head teachers, house administrators, and their assistants. As we promote the professionalization of social studies teachers and hence their increased empowerment, we still recognize the vital importance of the building leader. In a compelling anthropological analysis of "good" high schools, Sara Lawrence Lightfoot (1983) describes the attributes of six of these leaders in fascinating detail. In her final chapter, she says, "An essential ingredient of good schools is strong, consistent and inspired leadership" (p. 323). She's right! The leader can make or break a school. Likewise, your relations with this person can make or break your effectiveness as a teacher.

In truth, all of the support personnel we have mentioned are as key to the school and its students as you are. Collectively and cooperatively, all must help make each student's schooling an optimally beneficial learning and growing experience.

JASON: Whew! I guess I never stood back to look at all of the people in this school who work together to help kids. I get so concerned about what I'm doing tomorrow in my class that I tend to forget that I'm only a small part of this whole operation called "school."

ELISE: But don't forget you're a *key* part of it. Each of us brings to school every day a particular expertise, skill, or understanding attitude that helps kids get through each day feeling good about themselves. It's a great challenge, but it's worth it. I wouldn't consider any other career.

REFORMS IN TEACHER PREPARATION

As we have noted repeatedly, the 1980s became known as a decade of educational reform at least equal to that of the 1960s. The earlier movement was spurred by the Russian launch of Sputnik, the first spacecraft, in 1957. The Toyota became the "Sputnik of the 80s" as American industry found itself no longer number one and blamed the schools for its decline. The federal government supported industry's claim as it issued its scathing indictment of American education, *A Nation At Risk*, in April 1983. That report was followed by several others concurring that American students' test scores were too low, their content background was too weak, and their lack of basic literacy and numeracy skills was abominable.

The first wave of reform was aimed at correcting the perceived sad state of American elementary and, particularly, secondary school education by increasing the academic course requirements, the amount of homework assigned, and the length of the school day. But soon critics felt that the administrators and students alone could not be blamed for the apparent weaknesses in American education. The real problem, they argued, was the teachers, whose preparation had been inadequate. Charges and counter-charges filled education journals, newspapers, and electronic news media. And there was truth on all sides.

Indeed, some teachers came from the lowest quarter of their college graduating class, but others came from the top. Some teachers had extremely weak academic backgrounds, but others had the equivalent of a full slate of doctoral course work. "How were individuals with weak academic back-grounds ever allowed into teaching anyway?" you may ask. The answer is that each state decides on the requirements for teacher licensure in that state. As you might imagine, some states require much more academic and pedagogic preparation than others. Also, alternate routes and emergency licenses often are available to those who have not completed an approved college program of teacher preparation. These shortcut licenses typically are awarded in areas of teacher shortage, such as special education, Spanish, physics, and chemistry.

College-registered programs in social studies teacher education, for example, such as the one most of you are completing, typically concentrate on history and the social sciences, preteaching field experiences and coursework in education—both pedagogy and foundations of education—and a culminating experience known as "student teaching."

A study that one of the authors completed at his campus indicates that students preparing to be social studies teachers in the 1980s indeed had a much stronger academic background than their counterparts in previous decades (Mahood, 1988). For example, practicing social studies teachers in 1988 had, on average, 16 more content hours in history and the social sciences than did 1968 graduates. The 1988 graduates averaged 58 credits, while their 1968 counterparts averaged only 42.

Typically colleges now require more academic and pedagogic preparation of their students who wish to teach social studies than they did 20 years ago. One program demands that students have not only a major in history or the social sciences but an additional 22 credit hours in related social science areas, and student teaching has increased to a full semester. One of the authors teaches exclusively in a graduate program. Students entering the Master of Arts in Teaching program to acquire initial licensure must present a minimum of a major in history or one of the social sciences and a minimum of 30 additional credit hours in related fields. Those students then complete an additional 20 graduate credits in history and/or the social sciences. Thus, as beginning teachers they have at least 80 semester hours in the content area of teaching social studies.

So where do those who report on the low academic preparation of teachers get their information? Well, there are many teachers out there who did not receive licensure through a college or university program—they merely met a state's minimum criteria for licensure—or they graduated from a very weak program, typically one that fulfilled only these minimum standards. That's not to say that those people cannot become good teachers and acquire the background they are lacking when they begin to teach. But we wouldn't want them practicing on our children until they do.

Tests for Teachers

To ensure that teacher education students from colleges whose programs are considered weak do not become licensed, several states now require passing an examination in one or more of the following: the subject area they will teach, general fields of knowledge, communication skills, or pedagogy. Because these tests have little to do with how one actually performs in the classroom, they have come under fire during the past few years. As a result, the Educational Testing Service, the largest publisher of such examinations, is in the process of developing a replacement for the National Teachers Examination that will include a performance assessment. Interactive video will be used.

Several states, believing that they do not need a nationally normed exam and that their own needs differ from those of the nation as a whole, have developed their own teacher tests. California, for example, has its own test of basic skills for teachers.

Does the Test Really Make a Difference? Historically students have rated social studies lower than their other subjects. As early as 1949, a study by Jersild and Tasch informed us that students feel social studies topics are of high interest in general but are a poor classroom subject. John Goodlad's 1984 report, *A Place Called School*, reaffirmed the 1949 study: "[S]omething strange seems to have happened to [social studies topics] on the way to the classroom" (p. 212).

Goodlad puts part of the blame on how social studies is taught. Studies in the mid-1980s by Lee Shulman of Stanford emphasized that to teach content effectively, a teacher needs a broad and deep knowledge to draw on to develop comparisons, analogies, and metaphors, for teaching is "an intellectual and imaginative process" (Shulman, 1987, p. 41). Shulman continued by reminding us that teachers need to understand both the substantive and syntactic structures of the discipline they will be teaching (Shulman, 1987, 9).

Thus, teachers need not only the content preparation but adequate pedagogical training to enable them to transfer knowledge into usable form to be learned by students. Once they accomplish this, perhaps social studies teaching will be more exciting and students will give it a higher ranking.

By the early 1990s, most colleges will have modified their social studies teacher preparation programs so that all prospective teachers have both more depth and more breadth in their history/social science background as well as education course work that will better help them meet the needs of all of their students. Study in multicultural education, mainstreaming and special education, and children at risk of failure will be required components of most programs.

Continuous Professional Development

Many school districts and teacher organizations are finally aware that good teaching is a lifelong learning process. As a result, they have instituted inservice experiences for teachers to keep them continually updated in both academic content and the teaching process. Several of the topics we included in this text are the subject of continuing professional development workshops or institutes for practicing teachers, such as teaching reading and writing across the curriculum, cooperative learning, and computers in the classroom.

The National Endowment for the Humanities often sponsors summer institutes in history. Teachers spend five weeks immersed in study at a college or university. Many state and local social studies councils and college education or history/social science departments also offer summer institutes on pedagogy or academic content. Also, teacher-managed centers for professional development are growing rapidly.

As a new teacher, you will soon realize that inservice workshops or conferences will be an excellent resource for acquiring new teaching ideas as well as updated content information.

Professional Certification

If you choose to be considered for the forthcoming professional certification by either the National Council for the Social Studies or the National Board for Professional Teaching Standards, attendance at conferences and workshops will be important. Here we need to distinguish between *licensure* and *certification*, two terms that tend to be used synonymously but are actually very different. Licensure is required by state education departments to teach in a public school; certification is offered to experienced teachers by professional associations. For example, after seven years of teaching, you may choose to become an NCSS-certified teacher and/or a National Board–certified teacher.

Schools may decide that only NCSS- or Board-certified teachers can mentor a student teacher or first-year teacher; only certified teachers may be allowed to interview applicants for teacher, coordinator, or principal positions; or perhaps only certified teachers will be given release time to work on a curriculum development project for the district. Such teachers may even be eligible for higher salaries than noncertified teachers.

We think you should strive to become a professionally certified teacher and to assume new roles within your district. We believe that the schools you teach in will allow teachers more autonomy than in the past. Research tells us that many teachers will remain in the field only if opportunities for professional growth become available (Bredeson, Fruth, & Kasten, 1983; Chapman & Hutcheson, 1982; Frataccia & Hennington, 1982).

REFORMS IN THE WORKPLACE

The assumption behind having increased power for teachers is that teachers know their craft better than anyone else and their expertise is wasted in a top-down, routine-dominated, factorylike setting. Throughout this book, we have mentioned many of the current attempts to improve the lot of school personnel. At this point, we will highlight some of the contemporary changes that are directly associated with the professionalization of teachers in their workplace. We will center on one urban school district, Rochester, New York, which is widely reputed in the popular and professional media to be a leader in school reformation (see Buckley, 1988; Graham, 1989). However, we should note that the ideas being tried in Rochester are being implemented in a less concentrated fashion across the country.

Rochester is a snow-belt (or rust-belt) Great Lakes city with the all too common problems of the urban Northeast. Surrounded by more affluent suburbs, the city school district has approximately 32,000 students, a shocking 40% percent of whom live below the poverty level.

Numerous local citizens and their organizations have repeatedly warned this community about the social pathology that exists in the city and its schools. Many Rochesterians, including the teachers, have come to realize that the schools are failing to serve large numbers of their youth.

Two vigorous professionals (both former social studies teachers), Superintendent Peter McWalters and teachers' union President Adam Urbanski, formed an alliance to promote positive change. Negotiations between them culminated in a three-year contract that was signed in October 1987. There are intriguing stories connected with the making of this contract, but suffice it to say here that McWalters calls it "the soul of this whole experiment" (Buckley, p. 64).

The agreement led to a handsome increase in teachers' compensation, making Rochester one of the best-paying districts in the country. Increased salaries were absolutely necessary, for although teachers never had been well paid, the situation dramatically worsened in the 1970s. But, according to Urbanski (1988),

> Most important is the spirit of the contract: that collective bargaining can build a genuine profession for teachers; that unionism and professionalism are comple-

mentary, not mutually exclusive; that the contract ought to serve as the floor, not the ceiling, for what teachers are willing to do for students; and that there can be no accountability without empowerment nor empowerment without accountability. (p. 50)

The details of the reforms are still being created, but the contract was intended to provide a framework for achieving the needed improvements in a cooperative rather than adversarial climate. At least five key developments have emerged:

1. *Peer assistance and review:* A system controlled by teachers who work in cooperation with many others to improve instruction through study, experimentation, evaluation, internships, intervention/remediation, and mentoring.
2. *Career in teaching plan:* A program that creates a four-tiered profession: intern teachers, resident teachers, professional teachers, and lead teachers. The plan is aimed at preparing, recruiting, retaining, and developing master urban teachers who don't need to leave the profession to get rewarded and recognized. The effort is managed by a panel on which a majority are classroom teachers.
3. *Home base guidance:* A program in which each secondary school teacher is responsible for supervising the cognitive and affective development of approximately 20 youngsters over a sustained period of time. Each student is to have a responsible, committed advocate who works closely with his or her parents, other teachers, administrators, and anyone else who might help in securing that child's well-being. Daily interactions are conducted, and home visits are common.
4. *School-based planning:* A shared-governance model in which all of the major actors—parents, students (in secondary schools), administrators, support personnel, and teachers—serve on a team to make consensual, school-level decisions, including those on curriculum, instruction, budget, personnel, and student behavior. A mechanism for obtaining waivers is available if the team makes a determination that conflicts with district or union policies. Teachers are in the majority in these building-level teams.
5. *Teacher center:* While not a part of the 1987 contract but significantly strengthened at the same time, Rochester has a very active teacher center in which teachers are responsible for their own growth and development. In an important sense, the teacher center is playing a facilitating role in achieving the other four reforms.

It is too soon to tell whether the initiatives in Rochester are going to work, but there is certainly a feeling of excitement and promise. Traditional roles are changing. Sacred cows of both management and trade unionism are becoming hamburger.

For two valuable national analyses of this subject, we recommend *The Empowerment of Teachers: Overcoming the Crisis of Confidence* by Gene Maeroff (Maeroff, 1988) and *Building a Professional Culture in Schools*, edited by Anne Lieberman (Lieberman, 1988).

Summary

As we have said repeatedly in these pages, these are exciting times to be entering teaching. In this portion of the book, we examined the ferment that surrounds the movement to professionalize social studies teachers. We defined *professional* and demonstrated some of the difficulties in becoming one.

The complex organizational structure of schools has, we hope, been realistically, albeit briefly, presented. We described the current members of the social studies teaching corps and the processes of finding and keeping a job. We indicated the nature of the assistance you may obtain from peers, other colleagues, professional societies, and publications. We discussed the changing process in which many of you are currently participating—teacher preparation. Finally, we identified some phenomena directed toward greater empowerment of teachers.

The essence of all this is that to serve your students and society properly, you must have a large measure of control over your working conditions.

Decisions! Decisions!

1. Do you have the "right stuff?" That is, do you have the necessary commitment to

- The improvement of the human condition?
- Your work with each and every one of your students?
- The continuing search for wisdom?
- Ethical, self-regulated behavior?
- Colleagueship?
- Active participation in professional affairs?

2. Are you willing to pay the price to become a professional?

3. Will you be a survivor or a thriver? If your answers to these questions were positive, we suggest that you draw up a list of "New Career Resolutions." Indicate all the steps you will take to ensure that you become a true professional. Discuss the list with your colleagues. Put it in a safe place. Reflect on it at the beginning of each term. Revise it as necessary. Most of all, try to live by it.

References

Association for School, College and University Staffing. (1988). *Teacher supply and demand in the United States: A look ahead.* ASCUS Research Report.

Bredeson, P. V., Fruth, M. J., & Kasten, K. L. (1983). Organizational incentives and secondary school teaching. *Journal of Research and Development in Education, 16,* 52–58.

Buckley, J. (1988, January 18). The Rochester experience—A blueprint for better schools. *U.S. News and World Report,* 60–65.

Carpenter, H. H. (1969). *The relationship between certain organizational structure factors and perceived needs satisfaction of classroom teachers.* Unpublished doctoral dissertation, University of Houston.

Chapman, D. W., & Hutcheson, S. M. (1982, Spring). Attrition from teaching careers: A discriminant analysis. *American Educational Research Journal, 19,* 93–105.

Dreeben, R. (1973). The school as a workplace. In R. M. W. Travers (Ed.), *Second handbook of research on teaching.* Chicago: Rand McNally.

Feiman-Nemser, S., & Floden, R. E. (1986). The cultures of teaching. In M. C. Wittrock (Ed.), *Handbook of research on teaching* (pp. 505–526). New York: Macmillan.

Frattacia, E. V., & Hennington, I. (1982). *Satisfaction of hygiene and motivation needs of teachers who resigned from teaching.* Paper presented at the annual meeting of the Southwest Educational Research Association, Austin, TX.

Goodlad, J. (1971). What educational decisions by whom? *The Science Teacher, 38,* 16–19, 80, 81.

Goodlad, J. (1984). *A place called school.* New York: McGraw-Hill.

Graham, E. (1989, March 31). Starting from scratch—Rochester wipes the slate clean, gives teachers new responsibilities. *The Wall Street Journal,* R1, R2, R5.

Hall, R. (1969). *Occupations and the social structure.* Englewood Cliffs, NJ: Prentice-Hall.

Herndon, J. (1971). *How to survive in your native land.* New York: Simon & Schuster.

Jackson, P. W. (1968). *Life in classrooms.* Chicago: University of Chicago Press.

Jersild, A., & Tasch, R. (1949). *Children's interests and what they suggest for education.* New York: Bureau of Publications, Teachers College, Columbia University.

Leming, J. (in press). Teacher characteristics and social studies education. In J. Shaver, (Ed.), *Handbook of research on teaching social studies.*

Lieberman, A. (Ed.). (1988). *Building a professional culture in schools.* New York: Teachers College Press.

Lightfoot, S. L. (1983). *The good high school.* New York: Basic Books.

Lortie, D. (1969). *The semi-professions and their organization.* New York: Free Press.

Lortie, D. (1975). *School-teacher: A sociological study.* Chicago: University of Chicago Press.

Maeroff, G. I. (1988). *The empowerment of teachers: Overcoming the crisis of confidence.* New York: Teachers College Press.

Mahood, W. (1988, March 19). *The preparation of new colleagues: A profile and a paradox.* Speech delivered at the annual meeting of the New York State Council for the Social Studies, Albany, NY.

Metropolitan Life. (1986). *The American teacher, 1986.* New York: Author.

Owens, R. G. (1970). *Organizational behavior in schools.* Englewood Cliffs, NJ: Prentice-Hall.

Shulman, L. (1987, September). Assessment for teaching: An initiative for the profession. *Phi Delta Kappan, 69,* 38–44.

Urbanski, A. (1988, November). The Rochester contract: A status report. *Educational Leadership,* 48–55.

Wise, A. E., Darling-Hammond, L., & Berry, B. (1988, February). Selecting teachers: The best, the known and the persistent. *Educational Leadership,* 82–85.

Woodring, P. (1986, November 12). Schoolteaching cannot be considered a profession as long as its entrance standards remain so low. *Chronicle of Higher Education,* 6.

Appendix A

Preparing a Unit of Study

Topic: The Great Plains and the American Destiny

Focus Generalization: The Great Plains have bent and molded Anglo-American life, have destroyed traditions, and have influenced institutions in a most singular way. (Webb, *The Great Plains*, p. 8)

Major and Subordinate Concepts:

Major:	institutions	habitat	scarcity	social change	culture
Subordinate:	consensual government	adaptation	economic fluctuations	causation	territorial expansion
Data:	government regulation	climate	land values	conflict	political parties
	slavery	98th Meridian	trade	equality	frontier justice
	public policy	mountains	barter	radicalism	Cattle Kingdom
	community	aridity	industry	innovation	literature and art
	traditions	vegetation	transport	survival	
		minerals	markets	revolution	

Goals: Students will become aware of social, political, and economic consequences of territorial expansion beyond the 98th Meridian.

Objectives:

1. (institutions) The students will state and describe institutional changes necessitated by geography.

2. (habitat) The students will list and compare major climatic conditions east and west of the 98th Meridian.

3. (scarcity) The students will interpret economic fluctuations in terms of effects on various occupations, including farmers, particularly from 1875–1890.

4. (social change) The students will list, describe, and state some consequences of various innovations, e.g., barbed wire, Colt revolver, cattle drives.

5. (culture) The students will name some authors and titles of books and describe themes that best characterize the Great Plains, such as H. Garland, O. Rolvaag, O. Wister, F. Remington.

Key Questions:

1. What kinds of institutions did easterners try to transport to the Great Plains? What success did they have with these institutions? What kinds of changes did they make? What were the consequences of these changes?

2. Exactly where is the 98th Meridian located? What territories (and states) did the Meridian cross? What kinds of climatic conditions (precipitation, wind) and geographic features prevailed?

3. What kinds of activities were best suited to the climatic and geographic conditions? What problems were encountered in farming? What happened to land values upon settlement?

4. What specific innovations were prompted by the special conditions settlers found beyond the 98th Meridian? What effects did these innovations have on politics, economics, and social life? What new "industries" were created by these innovations, and with what effects?

5. How did adaptation to the Great Plains affect family life? What relationship did these settlers have with the Great Plains Indians? What cultural patterns were created by these adaptations and this relationship?

Index

About the Authors

Professor of Education at State University College at Geneseo, New York, **Wayne Mahood** received his B.A., M.A., and Ph.D. from Hamilton College, the University of Illinois, and Syracuse University, respectively. He has taught social studies in his native Illinois, chaired the Department of Elementary and Secondary Education at SUNY–Geneseo, and served as president of the New York State Council for the Social Studies. Dr. Mahood's publications include *Government USA, The Market Place, The Human Dynamo,* and *The Plymouth Pilgrims* (a Civil War regimental history). He has also written articles in a variety of journals, including *Social Education, The Social Studies, The Clearing House, Kappa Delta Pi Record, Theory and Research in Social Education,* and *Civil War Times Illustrated.* Recognitions include the SUNY Chancellor's Award for Excellence in Teaching in 1976 and Distinguished Social Studies Educator from the New York State Council for the Social Studies in 1984.

Linda Biemer is Dean of the School of Professional Studies at State University College at Binghamton, New York. Prior to this appointment, Dr. Biemer had served as Interim Dean and Associate Professor of Social Studies, SUNY–Binghamton, and as a member of the Board of Directors of the National Council for the Social Studies and the New York State Council for the Social Studies. She has chaired numerous state and national committees, including the NCSS Task Force on Advanced Certification. She has also taught junior high social studies. An Elmira College graduate, she received her M.S. from State University College at Cortland, New York, and her Ph.D. from Syracuse University. Her numerous publications include *New York: Our Communities, New York and Its Western Hemispheric Neighbors, Women and Property in Colonial New York,* and *New York City: Our Community.* She has also written articles in *Law Studies, Social Science Record, New York History,* and the

Journal of Long Island History. Recognitions include the Distinguished Social Studies Educator award from the New York State Council for the Social Studies in 1986.

Bill Lowe grew up in the Midwest and received his B.A. and M.S. degrees from the University of Cincinnati and his Ed.D. from the University of Illinois. He has taught and supervised social studies in city schools. His teaching and research experience also has been at Cornell University and the University of Rochester, at which he chaired the Department of Curriculum and Teaching and served as acting dean of the School of Education and Human Development. Among Dr. Lowe's publications are *Structure and the Social Studies* and *Urban Life* and articles in a wide variety of journals, including *Social Education, The Social Studies, Theory & Research in Social Education, Teachers College Record,* and *Journal of Educational Research.* Recently retired, he is a volunteer in urban secondary schools and consultant to community organizations, for which he has been recognized, including University of Rochester chapter of Phi Delta Kappa Educator of the Year. Lowe, whose real joys are teaching and family, has been married for 37 years and has three grown children who have presented him with six delightful grandchildren.